MIRROR
OF THE PAST

A History
of Secret Diplomacy

MIRROR
OF THE PAST

A History
of Secret Diplomacy

By

K. ZILLIACUS, M.P.

With an Introduction by
Max Lerner

New York
Current Books, Inc.
A. A. WYN, Publisher
1946

D
511
.256
1946

Designed by Jerome Mulcahy

Printed in the United States of America
American Book–Stratford Press, Inc., New York

69413

Introduction

HISTORY, as the eighteenth-century French thinkers used to put it, is "philosophy teaching by example." That is the best possible description of the essay in history contained in the pages that follow. Mr. Zilliacus has not gone back to the history of World War I and the decade that followed it in a spirit of idle inquiry. He is an impassioned British Labourite: a genus which in its best embodiment spells the socialist, the democrat, the internationalist, the humanist. Like others of the middle generation, he has lived through two catastrophic world wars. He is determined that there shall not be another. He goes back to World War I and its aftermath in order to find what went wrong in the peace, so that, having marked out the fatal road, we can flee it for the future as we would flee pestilence and death. Or, to use the words of the book's title, here is the "mirror of the past." This is historical writing at its best. It was William Blake who wrote: "The tigers of wrath are wiser than the horses of instruction." If we cannot use history for instruction, then we may as well dig in for the days of wrath to come.

Americans have had in the past few years at least one example of the value of this kind of inquiry. When the United Nations Charter was being prepared for submission to the United States Senate, our historians and biographers and publicists went back to the tragic episode of the defeat by the Senate of Woodrow Wilson's Treaty and the Covenant of the League of Nations. By retelling the story of Wilson and Henry Cabot Lodge, of the "gentleman from Massachusetts" and of the "little group of wilful men" whom he led in a phony crusade against the League Covenant, they were able to warn the American people against a repetition of that heartbreaking chapter of our history. I will not say the almost unanimous acceptance of the United Nations Charter by the Senate happened only because of the retelling of the Wilson episode. It came about also because of events and especially the blow which World War II had given to America's traditional and obsessive isolationism. But the historians helped to interpret the events and to shape a meaning out of them for the future. It was a case of ideas being used as weapons for life and not for death.

But while we have hurdled that danger, we now find an even more ominous one in our path. The United Nations is functioning and America is part of it, but it is functioning badly, and the One World for which the people have striven is not one world, but is being split sharply into two worlds. As I write this in the summer of 1946, a year after the end of World War II, the world seems drifting as by a fatality toward World War III. The basic premise on which not only General Staffs, but also Chancelleries and Foreign Offices are operating in every capital in the world, is that another war is coming and the whole duty of military and political leadership is to prepare for it. Men know, or ought to know, that war in an atomic age will mean the annihilation of man; that no nation can emerge the victor from it; that a war between the Anglo-American and the Russian empires would be both senseless and criminal. Yet, like a chicken fascinated by a snake, the generals and diplomats and statesmen seem unable to rouse themselves from their obsession.

The dramatic importance of this book is not only that it tells us in detail that we have been over this road before, after World War I, and that it led us to World War II. That sort of "deadly parallel" warning has by now become familiar. But it is not in itself adequate to guide our steps. The transcending merit of the book is that it carefully unravels the various historical strands of the deadly parallel and isolates with a clinical exactness the strands of death. From the vantage ground of a quarter century

we can see clearly what the fatal ideas and fatal actions of the
1920's were and how they could have been avoided.

What I have called above the "strands of death" were the transformation of the machinery of peace into a machinery for guard-
ing the world against Russian revolutionary ideas and hemming
in the Soviet power. The impulses behind this transformation
were the property fears which the movers and shakers in the capitalist nations felt in the face of a rapidly changing world. I put it
with a baldness and nakedness of statement which does little justice to the rich embroidery and the ample documentation of Mr.
Zilliacus's book. The story is far more tangled than a single sentence makes it out to be. But the crux of it is nevertheless there.

The great failure of the 1920's was only partly the clumsiness
of the League machinery and the weakness of its sanctions; only
partly the failure of America to adhere to the League. Much more
centrally, the great failure lay in the diversion of the energies of
the western world from the making of peace to the building of a
cordon sanitaire. The ominous fact about Versailles was not even
its economic consequences which John Maynard Keynes so dramatically pointed to at the time; it was rather the specter of the
Russian Revolution which hung over the deliberations of the
men of the West. A League born out of such fears could not hope
to function except by a heroic collective effort to dispel the fears.
But instead of making the effort, men allowed fear to redouble
fear until it became a massive weapon for splitting the world into
two. This split between a capitalist West haunted by the nightmare of Bolshevism and a socialist Russia neurotically driven first
to world-revolutionary adventurism and finally, after a last desperate effort at collective security, to isolationism—this was the
split that gave the Nazis the green light for their career of world
aggression and that resulted in World War II.

This is not an unsupported hypothesis. It flows directly, as Mr.
Zilliacus narrates the story, from the succession of world conferences, the speeches of the statesmen at Geneva, their diaries
and correspondence, the whole diplomatic and military and intellectual and moral history of the period. I don't see how anyone
can tell the full story of the closing year of World War I and the

decade that followed it without being driven to give the emphasis that Mr. Zilliacus gives his book. And the ghastly thing about it is that as we read it we recognize in it ourselves and our own time. It is the same story that is being unfolded now, only a year after the end of World War II. It is a story not only about men, many of whom are now only names in history books, but in the deepest sense about ourselves.

Historical parallels have their danger, of course, as all seductive things have. This one must not be pressed too far. What repeats itself in history is not the same event, or sequence of events, in the same context, but the same kinds of forces functioning in a new but parallel context and on a more developed level. This it is which makes the art of history, as philosophy teaching by example, so difficult and dangerous. The differences between the two situations blur the essential pattern, so that the onlooker gets lost in a forest of trees and is tempted to discard all the lessons of experience. On the other hand, the similarity invites the mechanical mind to a mechanical approach and makes fresh and creative thinking a heroic exertion.

Russia in 1946 is a very different Russia from that of 1917, or even of 1926. It is no longer the world's pariah. The Revolution has proved a success, at least in terms of national power and national stability. The economic blueprints have been translated into a going concern, and the national cohesiveness has been subjected to as fiery a test as any in history and not found wanting. To use the classic Marxian terms, the "conditions of production" which have been borrowed from the West have been built into a new set of "relations of production," so that modern industrial technology now finds itself operating successfully under state socialism. The old dream of a classless and stateless society has given way to the realities of a new ruling-power group, a highly concentrated state power, a one-party dictatorship, a highly perfected apparatus for repressing political opposition. The slogan of "world revolution" has been followed by the slogan of "socialism in one country," and that in turn by an intensive nationalism and by a dynamic socialist expansion into surrounding areas which is at present writing unmistakably a form of socialist imperialism that the rest of the world must reckon with. The energies that formerly went into organizing a new socialist society are now turned outward in an effort to achieve security by expansion.

I do not mean to saddle Mr. Zilliacus with this appraisal, for which I must alone take the responsibility. He has written a history of the past, not an analysis of the present; and besides he finished his book during the closing phase of World War II, before the members of the Allied coalition had begun to quarrel about who would organize the power vacuum left by the defeat of Germany and Japan. But if we are to make use of the mirror of the past, we must make allowances for the changes in the present.

In fact, there are those who are so obsessed with the new phase of Russia's power that they point to a quite different deadly parallel from the one I have outlined above in the first section of this introduction. The parallel they seek to draw is between Russia today as an expanding imperialism and Germany in the 1930's, from which they derive the moral *Ecrasez l'infame.* I cannot go along with them. The dynamism of Russia in the 1940's will prove far different from the dynamism of Germany in the 1930's. The Nazis thought that they alone were the master race. The Russians don't. The Nazis had a mad philosophy of world conquest. The Russians don't. The Nazis made a cult of military power and military virtues. The Russians don't. The Nazis had an unstable economy which had to expand or die. The Russians don't. The point of similarity lies only in the dynamism of two radically different totalitarianisms. It is not a historical parallel, but rather a literary metaphor where two dissimilar symbols touch at only one point.

But it is exactly the seductiveness of this metaphor to British socialists and American liberals which constitutes the great danger of our time and gives added point to Mr. Zilliacus's study. No one would expect that our fear of the Russians in the 1940's would derive from exactly the same sources as our fear of them in the 1920's. The old fear was that of the Russian Revolution, the new fear is that of Russian expansion. To the contemporaries of Lloyd George and Clemenceau, of Woodrow Wilson and Sir

Edward Grey, the old fear had as much immediacy as the new one does to the contemporaries of Mr. Byrnes and Mr. Bevin. Time has proved that the fear of the Russian Revolution was hysterical and neurotic and that the strategy of turning a fascist power into a bastion against Russia led inevitably to war. The same strategy today of tolerating Franco's Spain and of cherishing the residues of German economic strength as a bastion against Russia is bound to have the same results.

This does not mean that Russia is blameless in the present struggles for power, any more than it was wholly blameless in the 1920's. But it is futile to try to organize the future by apportioning blame for the present. In fact, it is exactly because the Russians have thrown their weight around a good deal that they have awakened very real fears. But the fact that these fears have a foundation is what gives them the driving emotional force to split our world into two worlds. And the tragedy of our time, like the tragedy of the 1920's, lies in the split. When a house is on fire, it is less important to argue about whose sins of omission or commission caused the blaze than to recognize that the flames are gaining and to put them out. The house of peace is on fire.

If Russia's role in world affairs has changed drastically in the twenty years since the close of Mr. Zilliacus's historical study, so also has Britain's role. Britain is no longer a capitalist government presiding over a strong capitalist economy within a relatively stable empire. It is now a Socialist government presiding over a declining capitalism, seeking to transform it into a socialist economy, and doing so within the difficult frame of an empire in retreat. The outlook of a British Labourite and internationalist is of necessity a heartbreaking one. The larger number of Mr. Zilliacus's colleagues in the Labour Party find themselves in a position vis-à-vis Russia that runs counter to the whole historical orientation of British labor. It was the strike of the British dock workers against the loading of ships to be used in the Russian Civil War in 1919 which first took the heart out of Allied intervention in that civil war. It was the British Labour Party people who, throughout the decade before the outbreak of World War

II, were the most bitter opponents of the Baldwin-Chamberlain policy of appeasing the fascists, and who were the most vigorous champions of Spain and Czechoslovakia and the Jews and other victims of fascism. Yet today Britain finds itself supporting a policy toward Spain and Eastern Europe and Palestine which is to no substantial degree a break from the policies of the Tory governments.

This presents a problem with which the reader of Mr. Zilliacus's book must grapple. For the basic analysis that Zilliacus offers is that the obsessive fear of Russia through the 20's came from the structure of capitalist power. It is, in essence, a sharp class analysis. If one follows it out logically, one would expect that a socialist government like that of Britain would no longer be caught in these fears. Actually the conflict between Britain and Russia has been sharpened by the Socialist-Communist rivalry for the leadership of the popular forces throughout Europe, and especially in Western Europe. Thus a class analysis that runs wholly in terms of Russia's threat to the propertied groups is no longer adequate and John A. Hobson's theory of imperialism, on which Mr. Zilliacus so heavily draws, must be supplemented by other factors. The truth is that the struggle of power politics goes deeper than the class struggle and is not resolved when two different types of socialist organization are involved, as they are in the case of Russia and Britain. What we have today is an amalgam of national and imperial rivalries on the one hand and of capitalist and collectivist struggle on the other. We can no longer say with assurance, as was said in the 1920's, that the first set flows from the second. They strengthen and feed on each other. And we must add to both the specific malady of our age: the atomizing of the human conscience and the corrosion of the human heart which are the heritage we owe to the age of fascist terrorism, and which make it possible to talk of a war in an age of atomic energy.

A word about the author. Mr. Zilliacus is now a Labour member of Parliament, having been elected in 1945 when the Labour Party was swept into power in the overturn of the Churchill Government. But it is to his credit that he is not, at present writing, in sympathy with the foreign policy which his Government pursues. Like a good thinker, he sticks to his basic insights, despite the changing winds of doctrine in the world around him. He is acting to avert now, in his practical political life, the policies which, as his book shows, wrecked the peace after World War I. He is fighting against the prevalent impulse, now as in the 1920's, to let the fear of social revolution turn us from the tasks of building a structure of world order.

Perhaps one reason for his tenacious devotion to internationalism is that its strands have been woven into his whole life. His father was Swedish-Finnish. His mother came from Brooklyn, New York. He himself was born in Japan, and he received his schooling at Yale University. He fought in World War I and (as he tells the story in his foreword to his little book *Between Two Wars?*) he was, during the years 1918–19, an intelligence officer in General Knox's military mission in Siberia, where he "saw intervention in Russia from start to finish, and from the inside." He left Siberia "in a state of seething indignation and revolt and with a queer, indescribable, desolate feeling that it was impossible to trust the judgment or humanity of those responsible for the conduct of public affairs." But his belief in the ruling groups of a capitalist society and anarchic world was not strengthened by the ten years (1920–30) which he spent on the staff of the League of Nations at Geneva, where at best he saw the friends of peace defending it ineffectually, and its enemies betraying it. Out of the rich material of his experience with the League, he wrote a series of fighting pamphlets under the pen name of Vigilantes and became the Cassandra of the cause of collective security. But, as in Cassandra's case, his warnings went unheeded. I trust that will not happen with the present book which, although a history rather than a polemic, nevertheless carries a sharp moral.

For the American reader of an English book, there remains the question of the role that America has played and will play in the struggle to create a world order. In Mr. Zilliacus's early chapters, dealing with the formulation of war aims and the Versailles Con-

ference, the role of Woodrow Wilson's America was an enormous
one. In his later chapters, dealing with the League's travail in a
series of international conflicts, America's role was that of abstention and default. What will our role be in the international
travail of the next decade?

Twenty years have made an enormous difference in America's
world position, as they have in Russia's and Britain's. We are now
easily the dominant world power in economic and financial
strength, in productive power, in our command of the newest
military technology. America has moved beyond the isolationism
which kept it out of the League. It is, for better or worse, im-
mersed in commitments in every corner of the globe and it
carries the major share of the United Nations burden.

Some American readers of this book may seek to distort its
moral. They may reason that if the League of Nations went so
wrong in the 1920's, then it would be wise for America to stay
clear of any replica of it, like the United Nations. Others may
reason, as do some of the proponents of immediate world government, that no league of national states can possibly maintain the
peace, and that the United Nations idea must be smashed in
order to give way to the idea of a genuine world government in
which the lines of national sovereignty have been wiped out.

I cannot go with them any more than I can go with those who
call for a showdown with Russia as the method of building the
peace. One of the deep convictions that emerges from the reading
of Mr. Zilliacus's book is how superficial the purely legal approach
to world peace is. The imperfections of the League did not lie in
the document of the Covenant: they flowed from the failure of
will to enforce the available sanctions and to make the available
machinery work. Today, also, the imperfections of the United
Nations do not lie in the document, or in the machinery. They lie
in the failure of the collective international will. Those who
would scrap the existing United Nations in the hope of achieving
a world government are indulging in a pathetic fallacy which
ascribes to blueprints and machinery the vitality that lives only
in the will of people.

The key to the collective international will must be found in the relation of America and Russia. Between them, they represent the polar points of future growth in world order. If they can resolve their tensions, then the world's future is assured. If they cannot, then chaos will be king.

The beginning of wisdom for Americans is to recognize that while Russian diplomacy presents real problems for American diplomacy, they are soluble problems; that the functions of the United Nations machinery will be smoothed exactly to the extent that America and Russia resolve their crisis of confidence; and that the real stumbling block of peace is the bitterness and blindness of those who use the symbol of Russia as the screen for their fear of social change in the world at large.

For those whose primary concern is world stability and the avoidance of war, it is important to see that these cannot be achieved by an organized effort to arrest the forces of social change. To bottle up those changes, whether in India or in China, in Yugoslavia or in France, in Palestine or in Iran, means to store up explosive energies which will ignite an atomic-bomb war. For those, on the other hand, whose primary concern is the achievement of a new social order, it is important to see that the big issue today is not whether the socialist changes will win out in the world, but whether there will be a world for them to win out in.

Mankind has three roads ahead of it. One is world conquest by a single people, which is unthinkable from any humanist standpoint. The second is world chaos. The third is world order. The merit of this book is that it underscores the need for that reconciliation of the socialist and capitalist orders which is the essential of any hope for world order.

MAX LERNER

New York
August, 1946

Contents

Preface

STUDYING THE past is chiefly of interest as an aid to understanding the present. To-day it has become literally vital to understand what is happening in the present in order to know what we must do in the near future to prevent a third world war.

That is why it is important to set at naught the gloomy saying that history teaches us only that men never learn from history, by considering how civilization drifted into the catastrophe of World War I, why the great Western democracies made the first attempt at establishing a system of world government, how they conceived that enterprise, and why it failed.

Therefore this book begins with a full-length study of international anarchy, imperialism, and power politics. The nature of international anarchy is demonstrated from standard text-books on international law. What imperialism means is illustrated by an account of the scramble for colonies in the last century. Power politics in action is the story of how we stumbled into World War I. The connection is traced between these things and the development of the capitalist economic system.

After that comes an account of the clash between reaction, reform, and revolution in the closing years of the war and the first years of the peace.

After some thought, I have narrated events roughly in their chronological sequence rather than arrange them according to subjects. The Allied governments and public opinion did, after all, have to face all these issues simultaneously, and were not able to tackle them one at a time. The account given does not lose in clarity of exposition and gains in realism by following the natural order of events.

Chapters IV, V, and VI, on the birth of the League, the assumptions of the Covenant, and the first decade of the League, show the relation between the Peace Conference clash, the social motive that underlay pre-war politics, and the attempt to found a system of world government. These chapters also show how concern for the preservation of the old social order weakened the new system of world government from the outset, and led to the fatally successful endeavour to revert to imperialism and power politics within its framework.

Now that our thoughts are already turning to the peace conferences at the end of this war, it is instructive to study in some detail what happened at the last peace conference and after.

The narrative ends on the eve of the great slump, which was a watershed in history quite as towering as World War I and World War II, although, being bloodless, its importance was less easy to perceive. It marked the end of the post-war and the beginning of the new pre-war period in world history.

In a book already three-quarters written, the mirror of the past is lengthened to include the period between World War I and World War II. After that there is a section applying the lessons of the past to the task of peacemaking that lies before us.

These two books, although independent of each other and complete in themselves, are both derived from the fourth revision of the big book I wrote and rewrote during my last ten years as a member of the Information Section of the League of Nations Secretariat at Geneva. That book was based on my nineteen years' experience as a League official and on the resources of the Secretariat library.

I kept interrupting the work on it to cope with emergencies as best I could, in a series of pamphlets and books with gloomy titles, such as The Dying Peace; Inquest on Peace; The Road to War; Why the League Has Failed; Why We Are Losing the Peace; Between Two Wars? Then I would go back to the big book and try to rewrite it in accordance with the development of

the situation and my own changing views. Finally the war I had
so long dreaded came, and I put the book aside, as I thought for
good.

But now most of it may serve to draw the lessons of the past
and apply them to the problems of the future. For the situation
developing to-day presents remarkable resemblances to what happened in the closing stages of the last war. So far as Great Britain
is concerned, the same political party, often even the same statesmen, that dominated the last peace settlement and the years between the wars, was in power until recently. They were backed
by the same vested interests and inspired, with rare exceptions,
by an unabated faith in international anarchy, power politics, and
"what-we-have-we-hold" imperialism. Even their technique for
securing public assent to their policy did not vary substantially.
Above all, they were as fanatically bent as ever on preserving the
capitalist social order, and seeking the most dubious political
bedfellows on the Continent for the purpose, all under the guise
of "military expediency" and "getting on with the war," just as
they did in and around revolutionary Russia from 1917 to 1921.

There are, of course, important differences, too, between this
war and the last, of which the greatest is the fact that the Soviet
Union was an ally of the Western powers this time. Another is the
fact that whereas in the last war it was the military victory of
the Allies that prevented revolutions in Europe, and a negotiated
peace was the policy favoured by the Left, in this war the Left
is determined to smash the fascist war machines in order to help
their peoples to overthrow the fascist régimes. If an attempt is
made to negotiate with fascists, quislings, and reactionaries, it
will come from the Right. But it may not come at all.

I thought it would be useful to give a full and faithful account
of what happened last time, because of the bearing of past events
on the shape of things to come. I have deliberately loaded my account with quotations from unimpeachable sources—mostly official documents or reputable eyewitness reports.

I did so because the world of power politics and imperialism is
so unfamilar to the democracy of Great Britain and so wholly
alien to British concepts of civilization that the story would seem

incredible if it were not supported at every point by overwhelming and irrefutable evidence. This book claims to have supplied that evidence, and to draw no conclusion that goes beyond what it warrants.

I hope that the effect of this introduction to the morals and methods of the jungle world of international affairs will be that democracy will at last conquer the realms of foreign and colonial policy and defence, and that Anglo-American policy in all three fields will change from top to bottom and conform to the standards and serve the needs of international co-operation. If so, we may win the peace this time. If not, we shall lose it again as surely as we did last time.

K. ZILLIACUS

MIRROR OF THE PAST

*A History
of Secret Diplomacy*

CHAPTER I

International Anarchy and Imperialism

INTERNATIONAL ANARCHY

IT HAS BECOME a truism to say that war is ultimately due to international anarchy. "International anarchy" means that each state is a law unto itself. In the community of states each government is judge in its own cause, and every government considers that it is the trustee for its own national interests and bound to consider that those interests are supreme. That means that national egotism is the highest moral duty of governments. International law and treaties are merely customary and conventional rules that governments habitually observe for the sake of convenience, but which it is not only their right but their duty to break whenever they appear to the governments concerned to conflict with vital national interests.

In the international law based on the premises of international anarchy the right of every sovereign state to existence and self-preservation is the first of all rights and duties.

Thus Wheaton, in *Elements of International Law,* one of the classic books on the subject, declares that:

> Of the absolute international rights of States, one of the most essential and important, and that which lies at the foundation of all the rest, is the right of self-preservation. It is not only a right with respect to other States, but a duty with respect to its own members, and the most solemn and important duty which the State owes to them.[1]

[1] Numbered notes are at the end of the text.

Hall's *International Law* says:

Even with individuals living in well-ordered communities, the right of self-preservation is vital in the last resort. A *fortiori* it is so with States, which have in all cases to protect themselves. . . . But the right in this form is rather a governing condition, subject to which all rights and duties exist, than a source of specific rules. . . . It works by suspending the obligation to act in obedience to other principles.[2]

What this means is stated with uncompromising lucidity by an equally famous French classic on international law—namely, Rivier's *Principes du droit des gens:*

When a conflict arises between the right of self-preservation of a State and the duty of that State to respect the right of another, the right of self-preservation overrides the duty. *Primum vivere.* A man may be free to sacrifice himself. It is never permitted to a Government to sacrifice the State of which the destinies are confided to it. The Government is then authorised, and even in certain circumstances bound, to violate the right of another country for the safety (*salut*) of its own. This is an excuse of necessity, an application of the reason of State. It is a legitimate excuse.[3]

A German writer, Haller, draws the same logical conclusion from the universally accepted premises of international anarchy:

It may be the duty of any State to break a treaty when its vital interests demand it, and the statesman or ruler who is faced with this question will have to calculate whether the moral loss, in reputation and confidence, which results from such a breach is not greater than the immediate practical gain. This question has been answered in different ways at different times. But those who live in glass houses should not throw stones.[4]

The same writer adds:

No State has ever yet entered into a treaty for any other reason than self-interest. A statesman who had any other motive would deserve to be hanged.[5]

It follows from each state's being a law unto itself and each government's having the duty of absolute egotism that, in Lord Birkenhead's words:

The maxim *"Nemo potest judex esse in re sua"* has no place in the law of nations, and the interested nation itself decides on the extent of provocation and imminence of peril.[6]

In other words, in international anarchy each government is also judge in its own cause. It has not only the right but the duty to decide for itself what action it should take in "self-preservation," and how far it considers it necessary to violate the rights of other states for this purpose. It follows, says Fenwick, that "while the right of existence is possessed in principle equally by all States, its actual enjoyment is largely conditioned by the physical power of the individual State."[7]

In short, in the conditions of international anarchy international law rests on the principle that might is right, and observes "the good old rule, the simple plan, that he should take who has the power, and he should keep who can."

That being the case, according to Lord Birkenhead,

the principles of international law . . . are not infrequently violated, and breaches may be consecrated by adding successful violence to the original offence. . . . As between Nation A and Nation B international law declares A bound to do a certain act. A refuses: it has broken the law. War follows, in which A is victorious. So far as international law is concerned, the nation is now justified in its refusal.[8]

In fact, to quote Bryce:

Although in civilised countries every individual man is now under law and not in a State of Nature towards his fellow-men, every political community, whatever its form, be it republican or monarchical, is in a State of Nature towards every other community; that is to say, an independent community stands quite outside law, each community owning no control but its own, recognising no legal rights to other communities and owing to them no legal duties. An independent community is, in fact, in that very condition in which savage men were before they were gathered together into communities legally organised.[9]

Force, and not justice, is the final arbiter between states living in international anarchy. Success or failure in using force is the ultimate criterion of right or wrong.

The reign of law ultimately implies publicity and at least the moral virtue of honesty. The reign of force necessitates secrecy and fraud, for they are part of the technique of using force successfully.

In international anarchy affairs are concluded by bargaining between states. If the bargaining is between the parties only, it is called "diplomatic negotiation." If the good offices of third parties are resorted to, the bargaining is called "conciliation" or "mediation." Sometimes the bargaining may include an agreement to refer certain issues (generally of minor importance) to arbitration—i.e., to a verdict based on law. But behind the bargainers lurks always the final argument of force. Each government keeps armaments in order to be able to uphold its view of its interests against rival views. The kind of compromise reached in the bargaining is of course influenced by the skill of the bargainers—i.e., the diplomats and statesmen. But it also reflects the relative armed strengths of the parties to the bargain.

In these circumstances war, as Clausewitz said in his famous definition, is "policy continued by other means." Or, to use a more modern formula, defence means "the use of war as an instrument of national policy." In diplomacy the maximum of fraud is legitimate in the endeavour to get the best of a bargain, and the threat of using unlimited force lurks in the background as the final argument.* The use of fraud and the threat of force both depend for their efficacy on secrecy. Moreover, the threat of force would soon lose its potency if it were a mere bluff. A government might yield once or twice. But sooner or later it would have to make a stand at the risk of war rather than accept diplomatic defeat, or it would lose prestige and never be able to stand up for its view of its rights in disputes with other powers.

* Louis XIV carved *Ultima ratio regum* on his cannon.

Why the institution of war is part of the statecraft of international anarchy has been clearly explained by Mr. R. G. Hawtrey in *Economic Aspects of Sovereignty*:

If war is an interruption between two periods of peace, it is equally true that peace is an interval between two wars. That is not a mere verbal epigram. It is significant in a very real sense. War means the imposition of the will of the stronger on the weaker by force. But if their relative strength is already known, a trial of strength is unnecessary; the weaker will yield to the stronger without going through the torments of conflict to arrive at a conclusion foreknown from the beginning. The reputation for strength is what we call *prestige*. A country gains prestige from the possession of economic and military power. These are matters partly of fact and partly of opinion. Were they exactly ascertainable and measurable, conflicts of prestige could always take the place of conflicts of force. But it is not possible to measure exactly either the wealth of a country or the degree of its mobility, and even if the military force that could be maintained were precisely known, there are imponderables to take account of, the military qualities of the men, the proficiency of the leaders, the efficiency of the administration, and, last but not least, pure luck. The result is that there is a wide margin of error. Prestige is not entirely a matter of calculation, but partly of indirect inference. In a diplomatic conflict the country which yields is likely to suffer in prestige, because the fact of yielding is taken by the rest of the world to be evidence of conscious weakness. The visible components of power do not tell the whole story, and no one can judge better of the invisible components than the authorities governing the country itself. If they show want of confidence, people infer that there is some hidden source of weakness.

If the country's prestige is thus diminished, it is weakened in any future diplomatic conflict. And if a diplomatic conflict is about anything substantial, the failure is likely to mean a diminution of material strength.

A decline of prestige is therefore an injury to be dreaded. But in the last resort prestige means reputation for strength in war, and doubts on the subject can only be set at rest by war itself. A country will fight when it believes that its prestige in diplomacy is not equivalent to its real strength. Trial by battle is an exceptional incident, but the conflict of national force is continuous. That is inherent in the international anarchy.[10]

As a natural corollary of this state of affairs governments try to be stronger than possible rivals by increasing their armaments and concluding alliances, so as to have the advantage in the continuous clashes of prestige that may at any moment result in ordeal by battle.

Thus the balance of power, maintained through rival alliances and an arms race, as well as secrecy, fraud, and the constant fear and threat of war, are the direct and inevitable results of international anarchy. Any statesman, however honourable and peace-loving he may be personally, is bound to be secretive and dishonest, to prepare for war, to use the threat of war, and ultimately to act on his threat, in his dealings with other countries so long as he is responsible for conducting foreign affairs in the conditions of international anarchy.

International anarchy is a vicious system that makes vicious conduct necessary and ultimately makes war inevitable, however good may be the intentions of the statesmen who are trying to make the anarchy work. It is important to grasp this fact, for it applies to British policy as much as to the policy of other countries, and to British policy today as much as to British policy before 1914.

INTERNATIONAL ANARCHY AND CAPITALISM

It is also important to realize that international anarchy is a comparatively recent development in our civilization. It is part of the price Europe paid for the transition from feudalism to capitalism. "The Holy Roman Empire," as its name implied, was mediaeval Europe's attempt to borrow from the old Roman Empire the immemorially ancient idea of uniting civilized mankind. The attempt failed for many reasons, of which the rivalry between Pope and Emperor was not the least. The very idea expired in the struggle between feudalism and the new middle class of merchants, manufacturers, and bankers. That struggle underlay the Reformation and religious wars that broke up the unity of Europe. The need of the middle class for new forms of order and unity was satisfied by the emergence of the sovereign state based on undivided temporal power.

The formal beginning of the state system we now call international anarchy is usually dated as from the Peace of Westphalia that closed the Thirty Years' War in 1648. At this peace the equal right was recognized of all states, whether Protestant or Catholic, great or small, to existence and independence. The practice was inaugurated of states' keeping permanent envoys (ministers or ambassadors) in each other's capitals. Later Russia, Denmark, and Sweden joined the community of nations acknowledging the new state system. The United States and the Latin American republics on their foundation became members. Finally states such as Turkey, Persia, China, and Japan were also recognized as belonging to the community of sovereign states, although with restrictions of which the exterritorial privileges for the "treaty powers" in China, formally abrogated during World War II, were the last surviving remnant.

The struggle between feudalism and capitalism reduced Europe to a chaos that put back civilization for generations and threatened a return to utter barbarism. It was as a revolt against the threatened relapse that Grotius published his famous *De Jure Belli ac Pacis* in 1625, nearly a quarter of a century before the Peace of Westphalia. Grotius was still imbued with the ancient tradition of the unity of civilization. He attempted to find the basis for a new unity based on a new concept—that of international law—to replace the old idea of unity that had disappeared. But he built the new structure out of old materials. He derived the law that he argued should bind princes (*i.e.*, the sovereigns who rule states) in their conduct to each other from (1) the law of nature—what we should now call social and ethical impulses and reason, (2) Christian theology, (3) the old Roman *jus gentium*, which was regarded as "written reason."

As the logical result of the concept that there was some body of laws that could or should bind states in their mutual relations, Grotius and his eighteenth-century followers devoted much thought to the difference between "just" and "unjust" wars, the former being allowed, the latter forbidden, to princes. They further taught that it was the duty of all other states to do nothing to assist a prince engaged in an unjust war, and that neutrality was permissible only when it was impossible to ascertain which side's cause was just. Christian Wolff, in his *Jus Gentium,* published in 1749, not only declared that the right to remain neutral was limited to those cases where the justice of a war was doubtful, and that no state should assist a belligerent whose cause was unjust; he also argued that all states were bound to assist a country whose war was just.

These views showed how the old tradition of the unity of civilization lingered amidst the new conditions of international anarchy. Another indication of the survival of this tradition was the number of schemes for re-creating unity by some sort of federation or league of nations. So much was this the case that the Phillimore Committee, set up in Britain during the war of 1914–18 to consider how to give effect to the idea of a League of Nations, began its report on the subject as follows:

> We have held nine meetings, in which our attention has been directed mainly to the various proposals for a League of Nations which were formulated in the sixteenth and seventeenth centuries and to those which have been put forward since the recent revival of the movement.

By the nineteenth century the old idea of universality had well-nigh faded out of men's minds. The selfishness of rulers and the subtlety of jurists had worked out the uttermost implications of the international anarchy with which capitalist civilization had replaced the mediaeval European order. What an Italian politician called "sacred egotism" became the moral foundation of statecraft. It was not even tempered by the belief, on which capitalist social morality was based, that the good of the community would follow from each individual's pursuing only his private gain. For in the community of nations no common good or international interest even theoretically transcending national interests was recognized. The right to make war was unlimited. The threat to use war to back their claims was the supreme argument of sovereigns (*ultima ratio regum*) in bargains between states (power politics).

Neutrality was based on the same principle of "sacred egotism." It came to be mere inverted power politics, mostly the power politics of those who had little power. Its moral foundation was the same as that of its brutal big brother; namely, total indifference to issues of international right and wrong and to the weal or woe of civilization, and exclusive concern with one's own national interests.

Laissez-Faire and World Peace

But by the middle of the nineteenth century it looked as though civilization were laying the foundations for some new form of world unity and order. There had been a tremendous advance in man's powers over nature. Within states this formed the material basis for a new civilization, based on law, democracy, and reason, capable of yielding a continually rising standard of living. Between states it led to swift and easy international communications and to the growth of international trade, until the peoples of the earth multiplied and became interdependent as never before. With the development of a world market peace became the greatest common interest of the civilized nations. Was it unreasonable to hope, as many did, that in these new conditions reason might find some way to make law and democracy operate through a form of world organization that would banish war?

There were two facts that greatly strengthened the case for believing that some such development was not only desirable, but necessary. The first was the growing discrepancy between the modern reality of economically and culturally interdependent nations and the statecraft of international anarchy, based on the fiction that states were sovereign entities recognizing no international duty or interest greater than their "right" to be judge in their own cause and to use war as an instrument of national policy. Pound says:

> The seventeenth- and eighteenth-century theory of international law grew out of and was an interpretation of the facts, whereas the nineteenth- and twentieth-century applications of that theory to the facts of the political world since the middle of the nineteenth century do not interpret and grow out of the facts, but give the facts a juristic or metaphysical cast to make them fit the theory.[11]

The second fact was that the advance of man's powers over nature made it possible to mobilize the whole population and resources of a nation for war and vastly increased the destructive power of the weapons used.

The combined effect of these two facts was that the objects for which states formed rival alliances, tried to outarm each other, and threatened war became more and more trivial in relation to the real interests of the vast mass of their populations, whereas the threatened wars promised to be a greater and greater calamity. International anarchy meant that statesmen were accumulating ever vaster potentialities of death and disaster in order to outwit and outbluff each other over issues that grew ever smaller and more sordid when compared with the material needs and moral standards of the world civilization they were jeopardizing. The methods of power politics applied to the modern world increasingly resembled chasing black-beetles with tanks or destroying ant-hills in a crowd by air-bombing.

Why, then, were the high hopes belied that were so generally cherished in the first two-thirds of the last century, that the new capitalist civilization would find some way of applying law and democracy to the relations between states? Why, instead of advancing towards some form of organized internationalism, did the great powers indulge in an orgy of imperialism? Why did they go on playing power politics and preparing for war?

To understand this it is necessary to look more closely at the development of capitalist civilization in the nineteenth century, and at the social and political consequences of that development.

Great Britain had such a long start in the Industrial Revolution as to give her a position of unchallengeable leadership. Through most of the last century British goods were first in the world's markets, the City was the world's banking centre, and the British Navy was two or three times stronger than the next largest in the world. British economic methods and political thought enjoyed unrivalled prestige. The evolution of Great Britain therefore gives the key to what happened in the rest of the world.

The hopes, so strong in that country in the first two-thirds of the last century, that international trade and investment were going to give the world peace, were based on the "ideology" of the philosophical radicals. The philosophical radicals were uncompromisingly rationalist, so far as conscious thinking could carry them. But their thinking was deeply influenced, without their knowing it, by the traditions and needs of the middle class to which they belonged.

The middle class was dominated during the first half of the last century by small independent traders and manufacturers. Competition was still the basis of economic life. The middle class was still fighting the landed aristocracy for social equality and political power. It looked upon the workers as its ally in this struggle, which was severe. The Reform Bill of 1832 and the repeal of the Corn Laws, for instance, were measures passed only after grave disorders and under the threat of revolutionary action by the masses.

The middle class, then, was warmly on the side of revolutionary movements on the Continent, for they were middle-class revolutions against semi-feudal landowning aristocracies, for ends which were the same as those of the British middle class. The mid-Victorian middle class was uncompromisingly rationalist and materialist in its politics, because it was fighting the appeals made to prejudice, authority, mysticism, and idealism by the aristocracy. Its attitude was summed up in John Stuart Mill's remark that when an abuse became too evil to defend on rational grounds its defenders fell back on religion. It was for free trade because, owing to Great Britain's long industrial start, free trade was altogether in its favour. It was against state interference in economic life because the power of the state was still largely in the hands of the landowning class it was fighting.

The ideas of the philosophical radicals, although believed by them to be of universal validity, were part and parcel of the hopes and needs of the middle class at that time—although in their turn they influenced the thinking, and so the subsequent evolution, of the middle class.

The central idea was laissez-faire. The state should maintain law and order, but not interfere in economic or social questions. In the economic field it should hold the ring for private enterprise. But within the ring private enterprise could do what it liked. For if every member of the community were free to pursue his self-interest, the maximum benefit for the whole community would result. From this central tenet and the belief in reason followed hostility to imperialism and war, and belief in the free market as the basis of peace and human brotherhood.

WHERE THE PHILOSOPHICAL RADICALS WENT WRONG

There was much truth in the views of the philosophical radicals. The nineteenth century was the age of the epoch-making changes and rapid increase in human welfare referred to above. But there were social, psychological, and economic flaws in the reasoning of the believers in laissez-faire that explain why their hopes of peace through the working of capitalism were doomed to failure.

The philosophical radicals assumed—and this was their social mistake—that their doctrine of laissez-faire for private enterprise would benefit all men equally. In practice it proved of advantage primarily to those who owned the means of production and distribution—i.e., to the middle class, the merchants and manufacturers, those who lived by rent, interest, and profit. Indirectly and in the long run it also helped the workers—that is, those who had only their labour to sell, the proletariat. But it did so chiefly by exploiting them so hideously that they were compelled to organize, agitate, and to use their trade-unions and political rights to fight for tolerable conditions of life and a tiny share of the vast increases in wealth and comfort. In this long, bitter struggle, lasting over generations and still continuing, the bulk of the owners of capital most of the time fought the workers doggedly and unscrupulously.

The philosophical radicals unconsciously identified themselves so wholly with the middle class that they failed to perceive that its interests were not necessarily the same as those of the whole of society. Since they identified the middle class with the community, they could not see its campaign against the landowning aristocracy as the end of one class struggle, nor the claims of the proletariat as the beginning of another.

The psychological failure of the philosophical radicals lay in over-estimating the capacity of the human animal—at least when economic survival depends on competition and placing self-interest first—to take long views. When they preached the duty of making self-interest the sole guide in economic life, they meant "enlightened self-interest." They did not realize how short-sighted most men are and their almost unlimited capacity for deceiving themselves by making their wishes the fathers of their thoughts. Or perhaps it would be fairer to say that, being unconscious of the class bias that coloured their own views, they did not see that preaching the pursuit of self-interest as the way to secure the maximum benefit for the whole community would in practice work out as identifying the class interest of the owners of capital with the vital interests of the nation. Nor did they have any idea of how unscrupulous, cruel, and generally predatory men could be in pursuit of profit.

Finally, in the economic field, to quote Bertrand Russell:

> the principle of free competition, as advocated by the Manchester School, was one which failed to take account of certain laws of social dynamics. In the first place, competition tends to issue in somebody's victory, with the result that it ceases and is replaced by monopoly. . . . In the second place, there is a tendency for the competition between individuals to be replaced by competition between groups, since a number of individuals can increase their chances of victory by combination.[12]

This inherent tendency in capitalism to move from competition to combination was due to technical developments and the economic advantages of large-scale enterprise over small. Giant trusts and concerns of every kind began to dominate economic life. They in their turn began to be dominated by a few huge banks, which supplied the capital necessary for their operations.

It was these three facts—social, psychological, and economic—overlooked by the philosophical radicals, that largely accounted for the growing discrepancy between their hopes and what actually happened.

The middle class, once it was securely in power, began to develop an upper layer of very rich bankers and business men who fused, socially and economically, with the remains of the landowning aristocracy into a powerful plutocracy that dominated economic life, the principal parties, and most of the press. Its members and hangers-on also manned the higher ranks in the pulpit, the judiciary, the army and navy, diplomacy, education, and the civil service.

So long as the state was in the hands of the landowning aristocracy the middle class was radical, allied itself with the workers, and was against government interference in economic life. But once securely in power, the plutocracy, which had grown out of and now dominated the middle class turned conservative, was hostile to the workers' demands, and used its political influence actively to promote its own interests, which it identified with "national" interests.

How this change took place, and its connection with the growth of large-scale, monopolistic private enterprise—so-called "finance capital"—is described as follows by Mr. Leonard Woolf in *Empire & Commerce in Africa:*

> There was no difference between Cobden and his opponents over the ends of political action, there was only a disagreement as to the right means for attaining those ends. The policies of free trade, non-interference, anti-imperialism, and peace, were recommended to the British people as the surest means of attaining material, *i.e.*, industrial and commercial, prosperity. To the mid-Victorian radical and demo-

crat the "Real and Substantial" national interests were "Commercial interests," and since commercial interests could be best attained by the operation of enlightened self-interest, the whole duty of the State was to keep the ring, nationally and internationally, and allow competition and enlightened self-interest to perform their beneficent work of money-making, whether in Manchester or Birmingham, Paris or Berlin, the opium trade in China or the gin-traffic in West Africa.

And now look again from the desires and beliefs of the Manchester school to those of the political schools which succeeded them in the latter part of the nineteenth century. The outstanding feature of that period is the intensive growth of industrial and commercial organization. The big factory, the Trust and Kartel and Syndicate, the multiple shop, are all symptoms of this development. Vast and complicated organizations were considered to be necessary for industrial and commercial efficiency. But men who believed this and were themselves manufacturers and traders could not overlook the possibility of using the power and organization of the State for economic ends. If trade and industry were the ultimate goals of national policy, the golden goal might surely be attained more effectively by an active and aggressive use of the national power and organization than by a policy of passivism and pacifism.[13]

THE GROWTH OF IMPERIALISM

What were the ways in which "national power and organisation" were put to "active and aggressive use" in aid of the plutocracy's pursuit of profit? The answer is to be found in the colonial scramble in the last third of the last century, because of which "more than half of the world's land surface, and more than a thousand million human beings, are included in the colonies and 'backward countries' dominated by a few imperialistic nations." Professor Parker Moon, who begins his book on *Imperialism and World Politics* with this statement, adds, "Little as the general public may realize the fact, imperialism is the most impressive achievement and the most momentous world-problem of our age."[14]

Imperialism, in the form of trading-stations and the colonization of empty territories, is as old as history. But there were new features in the imperialism that broke out in the last third of the last century. The speed with which the great powers proceeded to annex territories in Africa and elsewhere was as unprecedented as it was startling. The intensive exploitation of these territories in order to convert them into markets and fields of investment was a new development of imperialism.

The driving force behind the new imperialism was the new plutocracy, the great monopolistic business and banking combines that had begun to dominate economic life and to exert a decisive influence on political parties and governments. It is necessary to understand clearly why this was so and how the process worked.

In the first place it must be remembered that, as the *Manchester Guardian* once pointed out, "the capitalist system . . . has depended and depends for its prosperity upon the constant opening of new markets." This remark was made in the course of an editorial (June 23, 1934) commenting on an article by Sir Arthur Salter in which he wrote:

> As we survey in retrospect the rapid rise and decline of our competitive capitalist system we cannot fail to be struck with the fact that its earlier period of prosperity was largely due to the constant opening of new markets. Without such new outlets the system becomes congested.

In *World Trade and Its Future* (first published in 1937) Sir Arthur develops this point, observing that:

> In the great era of expansion the foreign trade of the world depended to a very great extent upon a continuous stream of new capital from countries which had reached a relatively advanced stage of industrial development, like Great Britain, to rapidly developing countries like the Argentine, Australia, and Canada, which in effect bought British manufactures partly with the proceeds of their exports and partly with capital lent from Great Britain. . . .
> The opportunity of external expansion in markets where

the general standard of living was lower, and a demand was therefore constantly becoming effective for just those classes of articles which were in danger of reaching saturation point at home, was of inestimable assistance to the whole capitalist system at its point of greatest weakness.[15]

In the last third of the nineteenth century capital and productive capacity were accumulating at a faster rate than trade could be expanded and investments absorbed by the British home market, the Dominions, the United States, and Latin America. The British business and banking world began to feel the growing competition of Germany and the United States on the world market. Profits became smaller and harder to get. Rates of interest dropped. In 1866 there was a big slump, followed by a decade of semi-depression.

In these circumstances the business and banking world began to look around for new markets and fields for investment, and to use their influence on governments to secure them. The incentive was great—quick, easy, and big profits, and rates of interest several times higher than at home.

The cotton and iron industries were perhaps the most important factor in what might be called the "dynamics of imperialism."

As an example of the working of this factor we may recall how the explorer Stanley, in a speech to the Manchester Chamber of Commerce (mostly composed of cotton merchants), drew an alluring picture of the rich rewards that would result if the naked Negroes of the Congo could be taught by civilization and Christianity to wear decent cotton clothes, at least on Sundays. One Sunday dress for each native, he estimated, would mean "320,000,000 yards of Manchester cotton cloth." (Cheers from the audience.) In time, when the natives had been educated up to dressing on week-days as well as Sundays, he thought they could absorb £26,000,000 worth of cotton cloth per annum. Stanley wound up with the following peroration:

> There are forty millions of people beyond the gateway of the Congo, and the cotton-spinners of Manchester are waiting to clothe them. Birmingham foundries are glowing with

the red metal that will presently be made into ironwork for
them and the trinkets that shall adorn those dusky bosoms,
and the ministers of Christ are zealous to bring them, the
poor benighted heathen, into the Christian fold.

The Manchester Chamber of Commerce published this speech
as a pamphlet in 1884. But in this case it was King Leopold of
Belgium who was first in the field—with results to the natives of
the Congo that soon reduced their numbers to 8,500,000. *

Next to iron and cotton as factors in the dynamics of imperialism, says Professor Parker Moon, from whom the above quotation is taken, come the import interests.

The British merchants who import tea from India, the
Belgians who import rubber and palm nuts from Congo, the
Frenchmen who import wines from Algeria are vital factors
in imperialism. The development of such business enterprises
on a large scale requires at least a degree of orderly government sufficient to protect investments in plantations, ware-
houses and railways; often it demands expensive public
works, such as dams, irrigation systems, roads, and railways,
which a backward native government cannot or will not undertake; occasionally, also, governmental authority is considered necessary to compel natives to work. In short, imperial control by a progressive nation is demanded. And the
importers, together with planters and other allied interests,
usually desire that the imperial control shall be wielded by
their own nation, because from it they may hope to receive
privileged treatment. There is only one reason why 197 million francs' worth of rubber, palm nuts and palm oil, copal,
and copper from the Congo are exported to Belgium and handled by Belgian merchants, whereas only 13 millions go to
England, 17 millions to all America, and only two-fifths of a
million to France. The reason is that Belgium owns Congo.
And the Belgian importers are aware of this fact, as are their
competitors in other imperialist countries.

Of late years this group of import interests has been enor-

---

* But Stanley's figure of 40,000,000 was a gross over-estimate—16,000,000
to 20,000,000 was nearer the mark before King Leopold got to work.

mously strengthened by the demand of giant industries for colonial raw materials—rubber, petroleum, iron and coal, cotton, cocoa. The oil trusts of England and the United States have enlisted the aid of naval and diplomatic officials in their world-wide rivalry. . . .

Shipping magnates form a third powerful business group. The annals of empire-building bristle with the names of shipowners. It is no accident that the greatest shipping nation has the greatest of empires. Shipowners demand coaling stations for their vessels, and naval bases for protection; they desire development of colonial trade and of emigration. . . .

To these interested groups may be added the makers of armaments and of uniforms, the producers of telegraph and railway material, and other supplies used by the government in its colonies. These have been aptly styled the "parasites of imperialism." They do not directly cause imperialism, but thrive on it.

Finally, the most influential of all business groups, the bankers, may be said not only to have a direct interest in imperialism, through colonial investments, but to represent indirectly all the above-mentioned interests, for banks have financial fingers in every industrial pie. The many billions of francs, pounds, and dollars invested in colonies have been invested through banks, for the most part. Banks underwrite the loans of colonies and backward countries, the capital issues of railways and steamship lines; they extend credit to colonial plantation-owners, to importers, to manufacturers and distributors. . . .

All these business interests taken together may be much less important than the interests which have no direct concern in imperialism, since nothing like half the world's commerce, shipping, production and finance is accounted for by colonies. But the imperialist business interests are powerful, well-organized, and active. Through lobbies and campaign funds they influence political parties. . . .

Moreover, the imperialist business interests have influential allies. Military and naval officers are often predisposed in favor of imperialism. . . . Quite similar is the interest of diplomatists, colonial officials and their families. . . . To this motley company of business men, fighting men, and "younger sons" must be added another incongruous element—the missionary.

How did these vested interests in imperialism go to work on the governments in order to make them do their bidding? Mr. Leonard Woolf, in *Empire & Commerce in Africa,* sums up the process as follows:

> Policy, particularly foreign and colonial policy, is determined by the beliefs and desires of a comparatively small number of men. The interference of the French, Italian, German, and British States in Tunis, Tripoli, Ethiopian Africa, and East Africa, was accomplished long before any one outside an extremely small circle in the various countries was aware that any action was even contemplated. The policy of interference is finally determined by an agent or two of the Governments in Africa—a M. Roustan or a Signor Pinna or a Sir Charles Euan-Smith—a few high officials in the Foreign and Colonial Offices, and a politician, a Secretary or Minister of State. These men are only the last levers which put in motion the power of the State; they are themselves set in motion by another small group of persons, the financiers, traders, and capitalists, who are seeking particular economic ends in Africa. . . .
>
> What happens is that the governing group is subjected to a persistent and powerful pressure from the small and influential profit-seeking group, and even when, as not infrequently happens, it is actually opposed to the immediate aims of the financial and capitalist interests, it yields to the pressure. . . .
>
> The relations between the British Foreign Office and the British East Africa Company are most instructive from this point of view. The Government of Great Britain and its governing classes are certainly far less open to *direct* influence of groups of financiers and capitalists than are those of France and Italy. There is clear evidence that our Foreign Office was not eager to support all Sir William Mackinnon's schemes and interests as fully as he himself considered that they deserved—"in the national interests." Yet our policy, whether under Lord Salisbury or Lord Rosebery or Lord Kimberley, was indisputably shaped by Sir William Mackinnon and his

co-directors [of the British East Africa Company]. This was possible because at need the Company could exert pressure from so many different sides upon the Government and the governing classes. Public opinion, as expressed in *The Times* leading articles, was consistently behind Sir William Mackinnon. Wires, only waiting to be pulled, ran between the board room of the Company and the Archbishop of Canterbury and the Church of Scotland, wires which were as invisible to Lord Salisbury as they were to the Archbishop and the "Moderators and other dignitaries." The invisibility of wires, when pulled at crucial moments, adds to their effectiveness. Again, at crucial moments Sir William Mackinnon could walk round to the Foreign Office or the Treasury with the son-in-law of Queen Victoria as a certificate of his Company's character, a symbol of philanthropic patriotism, or an expert on finance. When we find *The Times*, the Archbishop, and the Marquis of Lorne uniting to support the policy of a group of "prominent British capitalists," it is hardly necessary to look farther for the reason why the policy of prominent capitalists is translated into the policy of British Governments.[16]

In addition to these specific influences it should not be forgotten that the British plutocracy finances the capitalist parties and is connected to their leaders and members of Parliament by ties of business and family, nor that imperialism, in John Stuart Mill's famous phrase, is "a vast system of outdoor relief for the younger sons of the upper classes," as officials and army officers.

Both Professor Moon and Mr. Woolf give details of the major imperialist enterprises of those days, showing what were the companies and adventurers that reaped vast profits, how they manipulated the governments, the frauds and cruelties practised on the natives, the hideous exploitation of the latter, including their enslavement through forced labour and torture and murder if they rebelled, and the way the whole beastly business was surrounded with an aura of patriotic and religious motives and cant about the "white man's burden." Latter-day imperialism has purged itself of many of the evils of its full-blooded youth, and developed some incidental good qualities. But it is still essentially a system

of exploitation of natives by white men, miscalled more or less
honestly by the latter "trusteeship."

The profit-making motive was dominant in the imperialist
scramble. But there was also a social motive. W. T. Stead records
the following remark made to him by Cecil Rhodes in 1895:

> I was in the East End of London yesterday and attended a
> meeting of unemployed. I listened to the wild speeches,
> which were just a cry for bread, bread, bread, and on my
> way home I pondered over the scene and became more than
> ever convinced of the importance of imperialism. . . . My
> cherished idea is a solution for the social problem, *i.e.* in
> order to save the forty million inhabitants of the United
> Kingdom from a bloody civil war, we colonial statesmen
> must acquire new lands for settling the surplus population,
> to provide new markets for the goods produced in the fac-
> tories and mines. The Empire, as I have said, is a question of
> the stomach. If you do not want civil war, you must become
> imperialists.

This statement reveals the truth of Mr. J. A. Hobson's remark
that imperialism is partly

> the endeavour to divert the peril of internal economic and
> political strife, conducted by strikes and lock-outs, wage-
> conflicts, tax burdens, subsidies to favoured trades, into the
> wider field of international struggles for closed markets,
> forcibly seized areas of development and settlement, and
> other outlets for improperty at home. If the wider struggle
> can be substituted for the narrower by diverting the surplus
> national product into external markets and by engaging the
> national emotions of pride and pugnacity in the interests of
> this imperial game, capitalism and property not merely secure
> themselves against a class-war but maintain that formal or
> informal domination which has hitherto made popular gov-
> ernment impotent for all the serious tasks of economic
> democracy.[17]

What has been said makes it fairly clear that the pressure of
the plutocracy on governments was the main cause of the world's
plunge into imperialism and gives some idea of the mixture of

social—or more accurately class—and self-regarding motives that inspired the plutocracy. It is important, however, to realize that these motives were "rationalized" in the minds of the persons concerned into patriotic and religious beliefs which, so far as conscious thinking went, were perfectly sincere. There was more humbug than hypocrisy about the imperial idealism of the plutocracy, more of what Plato calls "the lie in the soul" than the "lie in the mind."

IMPERIALISM AND POWER POLITICS

Mr. R. G. Hawtrey's *Economic Aspects of Sovereignty* (first published in 1930) gives an invaluable insight into why imperialism aggravated all the evils of international anarchy and ultimately precipitated World War I. This is a book written by a man who is not only a distinguished economist, but a high official of the British Treasury. It is therefore not only technically competent but is based on personal experience from the inside, of just how relations between governments and capitalist vested interests work in practice, and how and why they result in war. "The principal cause of war is war itself," says Mr. Hawtrey, and adds:

When I say that the principal cause of war is war itself, I mean that the aim for which war is judged worth while is most often something which itself affects military power. Just as in military operations each side aims at getting anything which will give it a military advantage, so in diplomacy each side aims at getting anything which will enhance its power. Diplomacy is potential war. It is permeated by the struggle for power, and when potential breaks out into actual war, that is usually because irreconcilable claims have been made to some element of power, and neither side can claim such preponderance as to compel the other to give way by a mere threat.[18]

At the same time Mr. Hawtrey tells us that the causes of war "are partly and perhaps predominantly economic." [19]

The apparent contradiction between this and the previous statement disappears in the light of the fact that war is an industry, and preparation for war one of the chief activities of states, because:

> Under the international anarchy peace is potential war. The successful exercise of force is the paramount end in peace as well as in war. Any human activity which conflicts with the furtherance of the country's strength for the purposes of war stands condemned.[20]

Beyond a certain point the immediate evils of preparing for war may seem as great as the hypothetical evil of submitting to the will of a conqueror. In particular:

> Opposition to militarism will be directed against an excessive burden of armaments in peace time, against compulsory service or against excessive naval and military appropriations. But there are other and more insidious applications of the policy, which are neither so burdensome nor so obviously bellicose. It seems entirely legitimate and laudable to aim at economic power, and all the more so that the measures which increase economic power so often also promote the welfare of the community.
>
> Economic power is the foundation of prestige, and from time immemorial Governments have held it to be their duty to do whatever may lie in their power to enhance every component of economic power.[21]

Economic nationalism is one way of enhancing economic power. Imperialism—*i.e.*, making new and/or retaining and exploiting old colonial conquests—is another way. Direct war preparations, such as rearmament, is a third.

Mr. Hawtrey shows how largely capitalist vested interests are responsible both for economic nationalism and imperialism.

"Sovereignty," he points out, "is not property, but it carries with it important economic rights which are closely related to the rights of property."

The newer and more undeveloped and "politically vacant" a territory is, the more closely the position of the conquering state approaches to that of a landowner over his estate (that is, the freer it feels to dispose of the land and labour of the native inhabitants by confiscation and compulsion). Generally:

plans for new development require the intervention of the Government and the legislature. Town planning, public utilities, roads, railways and bridges, harbours and docks, irrigation, drainage and land reclamation, the opening up of mines, all these are likely to involve the acquisition of land or of rights or wayleaves from the owners of land.[22]

In so far as the State disposes of the rights of an owner, who are the beneficiaries? [Chiefly] the promoters and traders who undertake the actual business of development. . . . To the profit-maker the biggest business is the most attractive, and a new country, or a country calling for new developments, is likely to afford special opportunities for the creation of a big business out of nothing.[23]

In a chapter on "Sovereignty and Economic Development" Mr. Hawtrey explains in some detail why the exploitation of "new" countries brings higher rates of interest and bigger profits than business in old markets. In the latter there is more direct competition and less chance of getting the advantage of a privileged position.

In a new country the positions of the leaders of trade and industry are vacant. Those who get concessions from the sovereign authority are enabled to fill the positions, and to receive the profits which are their reward.[24]

Moreover, the pioneers who thus secure control of some potentially productive land or development project stand to gain indirectly as well as directly. They give the initial impulse to an ever-growing volume of profit-making activities:

Every operation incidental to development will be a source of profit to those to whom it is entrusted. Contractors will come on the scene to build railways, to make roads and to carry out various works of construction and improvement. Trade will spring up, and passenger traffic. There will be a tendency for all these opportunities of profit to go to the countrymen of the concessionaires.[25]

In short, when a government is administering a new country:

the most important beneficiaries of the rights which it exercises are the profit-makers who obtain concessions and privileges enabling them to pursue the work of development.[26]

This being so:

The profit-seekers will ask, not only how will the State discharge its various functions in relation to the openings for development, but how will it choose the favoured recipients of concessions? The concessions may be regarded as a highly lucrative piece of patronage. The profit-seekers will ask on what principle the patronage is to be exercised. By what rules, by what accidents, or by what prejudices or propensities will the authorities be guided?

This is a question of policy and therefore of politics. It is a question which tends to be thrust into the background. Neither those who grant nor those who receive concessions are anxious to court publicity or to invite criticism. That does not mean that there is necessarily or even usually anything sinister about the transaction, still less anything corrupt. But where an enterprise has to be undertaken by a corporation or syndicate in control of large capital, the matter is likely to be settled by direct bargaining between the Government and the concessionaire, and the public will know little beyond the terms of the resulting agreement. . . .

The principles on which applicants are favoured may never be publicly formulated at all. It may be a matter of tacit understandings. But the tendency almost invariably is to follow a nationalist policy. The Government favours applicants from among its own people, and lays its plans to suit their interests.

This nationalist policy has far-reaching effects, in that it makes sovereignty over new or under-developed countries an object of cupidity. The profit-seekers are usually in a position to exercise influence over their own Governments, and Governments regard the support of their profit-seekers' activities in every part of the world as a highly important aim of public policy.

Each Government possesses in virtue of its sovereignty

over its various territories rights which are really rights of property. It has the power to delegate out of these rights concessions and similar privileges to private people. In this process of concession granting there may be clash of interests. . . .

If it has constantly been an aim of public policy to use the authority of the State to favour the activities of those who undertake economic development, even to the extent of acquiring undeveloped territory as a field for their activities, and possibly risking war in the process, that is because this policy has been believed to further the power of the State. . . .

So long [concludes Mr. Hawtrey] as international relations are based on force, power will be a leading object of national ambition. There results a vicious circle. When a political leader says that war is necessary in his country's vital interests, what he usually means is that war is necessary to acquire or to avoid losing some factor of national strength. The interest is only vital in the sense that it is vital to success in war. The only end vital enough to justify war is something arising out of the prospect of war itself.[27]

These quotations make perfectly clear how, as from the last third of the last century, the vested interests of the plutocracy, issuing in economic nationalism and imperialism, increasingly supplied the content of the conflicts of power politics out of which wars and war preparations arose. Finance capital was not responsible for international anarchy—although it is a historical fact that state sovereignty and nationalism have been part and parcel of capitalist civilization since the collapse of feudalism. But finance capital was the main factor in making international anarchy and power politics so unmanageable as to end in the monstrosity of World War I and to repeat the performance a quarter of a century later.

CAPITALISM AND THE ARMS RACE

Similarly, finance capital was not responsible for national armaments. But, with a kind of vicious irresponsibility, it injected a stimulus into the arms race that made the latter in itself a cause

of war. It did this in two ways: first, by creating the need for
ever greater and more rapid rearming for imperialist adventures
and for the conflicts of power politics and dangers of war that
were the result of these adventures. Second, by the activities of
the arms manufacturers, who became a powerful vested interest
in war and war preparations.

How the arms manufacturers stimulate the arms race and increase their profits by bribing officials, spreading war scares in
the press, forming international rings to raise prices, etc., is beginning to be dimly realized by public opinion. Mr. P. J. Noel
Baker's *The Private Manufacture of Armaments* contains a formidable accumulation of evidence on these points.

But two facts should never be forgotten in connection with the
arms industry. The first fact, amply documented in Mr. Noel
Baker's book, was referred to as follows by Miss Dorothy Detzer,
the originator and moving spirit in the American Senate's comprehensive enquiry into the arms traffic:

> You cannot just enquire into the munitions industry itself.
> You cannot separate it from other branches of industry and
> finance. Tied up with the munitions business are all that deal
> in raw materials; the banks also are concerned, the struggle
> for markets is involved, and so are the navies. It has been an
> investigation into big business and into American imperialism.

The arms industry in all countries is part and parcel of big
business and banking as a whole. No one was more eloquent in
stressing this fact than the Chamberlain National government,
which drew from it the conclusion that therefore the arms manufacturers must be left a free hand, for interfering with them
would ultimately mean public ownership and control over a large
section of economic life.

The second fact was the point made by Senator Bone, of the
United States Arms Enquiry Committee, in the *News Chronicle*
of September 13, 1934:

> They [the arms manufacturers] nearly all have admitted
> to me privately that the mad race for armaments will bank-
> rupt every country now engaged in it, and yet they say if
> they don't do this business somebody else will. They admit

the world is heading for disaster, but they justify their conduct by business ethics.

Lord Halifax, in the House of Lords in March 1935, made the same point in even broader terms:

I do not profess to any professional knowledge, but having perhaps some little knowledge of human nature, I do not suppose myself that people who trade in armaments are very much better or very much worse than any other ordinary business men, and I do not suppose that business men are very much better or very much worse than many politicians.

In other words, it is the system, and not the shortcomings of individuals, that is at fault. "Finance" or "monopoly" capital does in fact use its power in sovereign states in such ways as to engender economic nationalism, imperialism, war preparations, and ultimately war.

Before World War I the clashes of imperialist interests about which world politics revolved centred principally on three areas: (1) Equatorial Africa, which was being seized and "developed" at a great rate. (2) The remains of the Ottoman Empire. As the latter decayed and fell to pieces, adventurers and exploiters representing big business and banking interests swarmed in and were backed by their respective governments. The areas involved were North Africa (Morocco, Algeria, Tunis, Libya, Egypt), the Near and Middle East (what are now Syria, Palestine, Iraq, and Persia), and the Balkans. (3) China, where all the great powers except the United States were scrambling for concessions and "zones of influence."

In the Balkans the situation was complicated by the national irredentism of Serbia, which, however, was fostered by the imperialist rivalries of the great powers. In Western Europe, the national irredentism of France for her two lost provinces, Alsace and Lorraine, was a factor making for war. But these provinces had been taken after the Franco-Prussian War largely because German big business coveted their rich iron-ore deposits and used the argument of "economic power" to justify their annexation. In France the nationalist grievance was kept open chiefly by the parties of the Right under the influence of the French metallurgical and coal interests who wanted the Lorraine iron ore back.

It is therefore fair to say that the pressure of capitalist vested interests, expressed in imperialist and trade rivalries and the arms race, was the factor chiefly responsible for the war—not out of malice prepense by the interests concerned, but because they were irresponsible; that is, incapable of tempering their scramble for profits by any sense of political or social responsibility.

The relation between capitalism and war may be illustrated by a rough analogy: Let us compare states to motor-buses, their governments to the drivers, international anarchy to the absence of rules of the road, and power politics to the practice of each driver's claiming the right of way and threatening the other drivers with collisions if they did not turn aside.

Naturally each driver would in those circumstances want a bigger and stronger bus than the others, so as to over-awe them by his mere threat of a collision and to come out best if it did end in a crash.

So far, so bad. One would have to be sanguine indeed to believe in any long-continued immunity from accidents under such traffic conditions.

But suppose in addition each driver had beside him a person who was a monomaniac on the subject of the speedometer (of profits)—someone who said he was not interested in the position or direction of the bus, for that was the driver's job, not his, but was determined to keep the speedometer registering as high as possible. For this purpose he would keep stamping on the driver's foot to make him "step on the gas."

That analogy comes close to the workings of international anarchy under the gentle ministrations of finance capital. Naturally it all culminated in the appalling crash of 1914–18. Unfortunately the lesson was not learned the first time.

TENDENCIES TOWARDS INTERNATIONAL CO-OPERATION

But reality is complex. There were also other tendencies at work before World War I, which if they had had more time to develop might possibly have grown strong enough to avert the calamity.

For one thing, governments, while being pushed into imperialism by their vested interests, were also beginning to feel the need of international co-operation, because of the growing interdependence of their peoples. From about 1840 the number of international conferences roughly doubled in every decade.

As from the latter part of last century governments began to feel the need of putting an end to international anarchy on various technical issues where their common interest in order and organization had become obvious. Not without considerable difficulties and overcoming objections based on "sovereignty," the International Telegraphic Union was established and followed by the Universal Postal Union. These were the forerunners of a considerable number of what came to be known as "public international unions," such as the Public International Health Office at Paris, the International Institute of Agriculture in Rome, the International Association for Labour Legislation at Berne, etc. But these were scattered, sporadic beginnings, the germs of a new order perhaps, but unable to arrest the fell disease that was killing the old.

After the Napoleonic Wars the custom was established of co-operation between the great powers to avert threats to peace. This custom was at the outset partly an attempt to revive the old "universalist" and semi-feudal tradition of the Holy Roman Empire. But the need for co-operation made it linger on through the nineteenth century in the form of the "concert of Europe" or "concert of the great powers," to which Lord Salisbury once referred as "the rudimentary legislature of Europe." But the concert was never more than self-constituted meetings of great powers to haggle about their own selfish ends. It began to fade away so soon as the great powers began to line up into two great rival alliances.

The most direct efforts to tackle international anarchy and the arms race were made at the Hague Peace Conferences of 1899 and 1907. The first was summoned by the Czar of Russia; the intiative for the second was taken by the United States.

G. Lowes Dickinson, in *The International Anarchy*, shows how at both conferences Germany was the bluntest and most emphatic in rejecting either limitation of armaments or compulsory arbitration, but how the other governments, although more discreet, adopted substantially the same attitude. They did so because they believed that each state was sole judge of what it should do to protect its own interests, and could not therefore accept a limitation of its means of action (*i.e.*, armaments) or any obligation to submit to third-party judgment (*i.e.*, arbitration) on what were its rights.

An attempt was made, it is true, to draw up a list of subjects that could not possibly affect "honour and vital interests," and so might safely be settled by arbitration—for it was universally agreed that war was the only final way of settling questions of "honour and vital interests." Of this attempt Mr. Leonard Woolf writes:

> One imagines that there must have been someone at the Conference possessed of a cultivated sense of irony and cynicism to choose as subjects for obligatory arbitration the interests of indigent sick persons, of the working classes, of dead sailors, of writers and artists. We shall be too near the millennium to need any but a Celestial Authority when the Foreign Offices of the world think sufficiently about the interests of such persons for the Third Secretary of an Embassy even to remember that they exist. Meanwhile it is hardly necessary to take steps to prevent our rulers mobilizing fleets and armies on their behalf. If the interests had been those of capitalists and financiers, syndicates and concessionaires, our conclusion might have been different, but the diplomatists at The Hague were silent as regards such persons.[28]

The silence to which Mr. Woolf refers was of course due to the fact that the governments and their diplomats were unanimous in believing that the interests of "capitalists and financiers, syndicates and concessionaires" were precisely those questions of "honour and vital interest" that must be left to the arbitrament of war. Lowes Dickinson writes:

But it was not possible, under the circumstances, to do more than pass a pious resolution recognising the "principle" of compulsory arbitration, declaring that certain topics are suitable for settlement in that way, and announcing that there had "disengaged itself from the discussion a highly elevated sentiment of the good of mankind." This "highly elevated sentiment" presently translated itself into the Tripoli war, the Balkan wars and the Great War.

(It should be added that the Second Hague Conference did set up some machinery and rules for arbitration and conciliation that were available for any states that chose to resort to them.)

Mr. Dickinson concludes from his survey that

There was not any chance that The Hague Conferences, under any circumstances, would have done anything to prevent the approaching catastrophe. Public opinion was either indifferent or unorganised throughout the world, and the diplomats and Governments had the game in their own hands. The object, as they saw it, was to fend off a tiresome, incipient, but fortunately dispersed and feeble agitation. They did this by fine words and phrases, while taking care that nothing more substantial should be adopted. They thus kept what rhetoricians call their "swords" bright, and were able, when the time came, to enter into the war for Right, unhampered by rules which it might otherwise have been necessary to break.[29]

One of the greatest contrasts between the pre-World-War I era and the world today is in the attitude of public opinion to foreign affairs. It seems almost incredible, for instance, that there were only two debates on foreign policy in the British House of Commons in the three years preceding World War I. Or that the majority of the British Cabinet, let alone the House of Commons, did not know the commitments into which Britain had entered—had, indeed, been assured they did not exist—until they were revealed by Sir Edward Grey on the eve of war.

Secret diplomacy and secret treaties were part and parcel of the system of international anarchy. So was untruthfulness. France and Great Britain were just as autocratically and disin-

genuously governed when it came to foreign affairs as Czarist
Russia or Imperial Germany.

Public opinion, in so far as it was concerned about peace at all,
was sentimentally pacifist and isolationist, much like American
opinion between the two wars. But above all it was incredulous
—people simply could not take seriously the suggestion that their
governments would one day really let loose the horrors of a world
war. They looked upon the recurring diplomatic crises as much
ado about nothing, as spectacles that had their entertaining side
but were not connected with their daily lives.

A few saw farther. Perhaps the most considerable intellectual
revolt against the drift to war was Norman Angell's *The Great
Illusion,* that appeared in 1910. It supplied the pacifist movement
with formidable intellectual weapons. But it suffered from two
defects. The first was that it was negative. It shattered for all
time, with brilliant, remorseless logic, the claims of imperialists to
be acting in the interests of their respective peoples. But it contained no positive program for anything like a League of Nations,
international mandates, etc., as a substitute for international
anarchy and imperialism. The second defect was that its reasoning made the same assumptions as the philosophical radicals—
and applied them to a world which even by 1910 had developed
a plutocracy, and was rent by a class struggle between them and
the proletariat that partly falsified those assumptions.

The nearest thing to a popular revolt against the drift to war
appeared in the labour movement. There is no space here to trace
how the latter grew during the last century, took shape through
trade-unions and co-operatives and later in political groupings,
and gradually detached itself from liberalism. The important
point is that the labour and socialist movement was international
from the outset. Allen Hutt's *This Final Crisis* gives interesting
evidence of the internationalism of the Chartist movement. On
the Continent Marx and Engels founded the First International,
under the name of the International Association of Workers, in
1864. It broke up ten years later as a result of the Franco-Prussian War and the quarrel between Marx and the anarchist
Bakunin. In 1889 the Second or Labour and Socialist Interna-

tional was formed, and included the chief Socialist parties of the world. It held conferences of its constituent parties every two or three years.

As the danger of war increased, these conferences came to concern themselves more and more with the idea of a joint working-class refusal to work or fight in a capitalist and imperialist war. The idea was that the "horizontal" international class loyalty of the proletariat could be made strong enough to override the "vertical" national loyalties binding together workers and capitalists in the several countries. In this way the working-class was to preserve peace by direct action.

This policy was discussed and adopted unanimously at the International Socialist Congresses of Stuttgart (1907), Copenhagen (1910), and Basel (1912). The gist of the resolutions adopted was that the working-class parties and their affiliated trade-unions should, by joint action in all the countries concerned, including a general strike, (1) prevent war breaking out, (2) if it did nevertheless break out, oppose it, (3) utilize the war situation to overthrow their capitalist governments.

But when the war came it showed that the class solidarity of the workers was too weak, their confidence in their own power too small, and their credulity towards their governments too great, to enable them to offer any effective opposition to the vast calamity.

Conclusion

This chapter has briefly sketched the condition of the world before World War I. It has shown international anarchy, imperialism, and the arms race as the factors making for war, and "finance" or "monopoly" capital as informing and aggravating all three. It has indicated the rudimentary beginnings, in the increase of conferences, the public international unions, the concert of Europe, and the Hague panel of arbiters, of international order and organization. It has pointed to the first stirrings of protest, both sentimental and intellectual, against the drift to war, in a public opinion that was heedless because it was kept ignorant.

Lastly, it has described how the gathering revolt of the working-class against the whole existing order of society also included a pledge of international revolutionary opposition to imperialist war.

The next chapter will trace, against this general background, how British foreign policy, working in the conditions of international anarchy and under the pressure of British imperialist plutocracy and irresponsible arms manufacturers, committed its full share of crimes and betrayals and helped to plunge the world into World War I, in spite of all the personal good intentions of the statesmen.

CHAPTER II

How World War I Started

GREAT BRITAIN's foreign policy played a decisive part in the power politics that ended in World War I. British were some of the chief strands in the tangled web of destiny woven by the great powers within the framework of international anarchy and under the impulse of imperialism. Moreover, British policy is the factor in the situation that concerns the author most directly. Therefore the description of events in this and the following chapter takes British policy as its central feature.

"SPLENDID ISOLATION" AND THE BALANCE OF POWER

For centuries the traditional British policy had been to maintain the balance of power—that is, to prevent any power from becoming so strong on the Continent that it could attack the British Empire. That meant Britain joined with the next strongest power on the Continent to hold the strongest in check and if necessary to defeat it in war. It also meant that Britain wanted the Low Countries (Holland and Belgium) and the north coast of France to be in the hands of a power that was weak and if possible friendly to the British.

During the greater part of the nineteenth century the long start of Britain in the Industrial Revolution enabled that country to maintain the balance of power in "splendid isolation." That is, the British kept free of commitments on the Continent, took sides in international crises as their interests at the moment dictated, and took the lead in the scramble for colonies and concessions, behind the secure shelter of a two-power naval standard (*i.e.,* a navy twice as big as the next biggest in Europe).

As the nineteenth century wore on, the unification of Germany and Italy created two new great powers; Germany and Austria-Hungary became allied, and Italy was somewhat precariously attached to this new grouping; France and Russia concluded an alliance; and France joined vigorously in the colonial scramble. Later Germany and Italy did the same.

These developments were reflected in the changing attitude adopted by Great Britain to the treaties guaranteeing the neutrality of Belgium.

"Splendid Isolation" and Belgian Neutrality

The truth about this matter is so important that it must be considered in some detail. The Vienna Peace Congress, after the Napoleonic War, had joined Belgium and Holland together under the Dutch king.

In 1831 Belgium seceded from this union and set up as an independent state. Article 7 of a treaty between Belgium and the Netherlands regulating the position declared that "Belgium will form . . . an independent and perpetually neutral state. She will be bound to observe this same neutrality towards other states."

In 1839 Austria, France, Great Britain, Prussia, and Russia concluded a treaty with the Netherlands. Article 2 of that treaty declares that the articles of the 1831 Belgian-Netherlands treaty "are considered as having the same force and value as if they were textually inserted in the present Act, and that they were thus placed under the guarantee of Their Majesties." (The 1839 treaty was concluded as between the sovereigns of the countries concerned.)

In 1870, when faced by the war between France and Prussia, the British Government took the view that its chief interest was to prevent either France or Prussia from violating the neutrality of Belgium. To effect this end it concluded identical treaties with France and Prussia, of which the operative clause, *mutatis mutandis,* read:

Her Majesty the Queen of the United Kingdom of Great Britain and Ireland declares that if during the said hostilities the armies of France [or Prussia] should violate the neutrality of Belgium, she will be prepared to co-operate with his Prussian Majesty [or the Emperor of the French] for the defence of the same in such manner as may be mutually agreed upon, employing for that purpose her naval and military forces to ensure its observance.

The 1870 treaties further provided that they were to lapse after one year, and that the situation would thereupon revert to what it was under the 1839 treaty.

In taking these steps the British Government was careful to make clear that it was acting not because it felt bound by the 1839 treaty to take this course, but on broader grounds. Mr. Gladstone told the House of Commons on August 10, 1870:

> There is, I admit, the obligation of the Treaty. It is not necessary, nor would time permit me, to enter into the complicated question of the nature of the obligations of that Treaty; but I am not able to subscribe to the doctrine of those who have held in this House what plainly amounts to an assertion, that the simple fact of the existence of a guarantee is binding on every party to it, irrespectively altogether of the particular position in which it may find itself at the time when the occasion for acting on the guarantee arises. The great authorities on foreign policy to whom I have been accustomed to listen, such as Lord Aberdeen and Lord Palmerston, never to my knowledge took that rigid and, if I may venture to say so, that impracticable view of the guarantee. The circumstance that there is already an existing guarantee in force is of necessity an important fact, and a weighty element in the case to which we are bound to give full and ample consideration. There is also this further consideration, the force of which we must feel most deeply, and that is, the common interest against the unmeasured aggrandisement of any Power whatever.

In 1887 there was grave tension between France and Germany. The British Government believed war might result and that the contending armies might violate Belgium's neutrality. But at that time France was regarded as the rival of Britain because of her active policy of colonial expansion, and Germany as Britain's friend because of Bismarck's "moderation" in such matters.

Accordingly the *Standard* of February 4, 1887, published a letter signed "Diplomaticus" and a leading article, which was regarded as semi-official.

"Diplomaticus" pointed out that owing to the fortification of the French frontier with Germany, Belgium was the only gap in French defences through which the Germany Army could invade France. He recalled the European guarantee of Belgium's neutrality and England's position as one of the guarantors, and continued:

> In 1870 Earl Granville, then at the head of the British Foreign Office, alive to this danger, promptly and wisely bound England to side with France if Prussia violated Belgian territory, and side with Prussia if France did so.
>
> Would Lord Salisbury act prudently to take upon himself a similar engagement, in the event of a fresh conflict between those two countries? It is for Englishmen * to answer the question. But it seems to me, as one not indifferent to the interests and greatness of England, that such a course at the present moment would be unwise to the last degree. However much England might regret the invasion of Belgian territory by either party to the struggle, she could not take part with France against Germany (even if Germany were to seek to turn the French flank by pouring its armies through the Belgian Ardennes), without utterly vitiating and destroying the main purposes of English policy all over the world.
>
> But it will be asked, must not England honour its signature and be faithful to its public pledges? I reply that your † Foreign Minister ought to be equal to the task of meeting this objection without committing England to war. The temporary use of a right of way is something different from a permanent and wrongful possession of territory; and surely England would easily be able to obtain from Prince Bismarck ample and adequate guarantees that at the close of the conflict, the territory of Belgium should remain intact as before?

* This suggests that "Diplomaticus" was a German diplomat.
† This again suggests that "Diplomaticus" was a German diplomat.

The *Standard's* leading article endorsed the conclusion of "Diplomaticus." It pointed out that owing to the fortification of the Franco-German frontier there was a far greater danger now than in 1870 that a Franco-German war would mean the invasion of Belgium.

Our readers will at once perceive that the situation is absolutely different from the one that existed in 1870, when Earl Granville quickly and cheerfully imposed on England the obligation to take part against either combatant that violated Belgian soil. Neither combatant was so much tempted to do so; and thus the engagement assumed by England—a very proper one at the time—was not very serious or onerous, and saved appearances rather than created responsibility. Now the position is entirely changed. If England, with a view to obtaining respect for Belgian territory, were to bind itself, as in 1870, to throw its weight into the balance against either France or Germany, should either France or Germany violate Belgian ground, we might, and probably should, find ourselves involved in a war of giants on our own account.

We think that "Diplomaticus" understands the English people when he hints his suspicions that such a result would be utterly alien alike to their wishes and to their interests. For, over and above the fact that, as we have seen, the temptation to violate Belgian territory by either side is much greater than it was in 1870, the relations of England with the European Powers have necessarily and naturally undergone considerable modification during that period. We concur with our correspondent in the opinion he expresses that for England and Germany to quarrel, it matters not upon what subject, would be highly injurious to the interests of both. Indeed, he is right when he says that the main outlines of our policy would be blurred and its main purposes embarrassed, if not defeated, were we suddenly to find ourselves in a state of hostility to Germany, instead of one of friendliness and sympathy.

No doubt if Germany were to outrage the honour, or to disregard the interests of England, we should be ready enough to accept the challenge thrown down to us. But would the violation of Belgian territory, whether by Germany or France, be such an injury to our interests? It might be so in certain circumstances; and it would assuredly be so if it involved a permanent violation of the independence of Belgium. But, as "Diplomaticus" ingeniously suggests, there is all the difference in the world between the momentary use of a "right of way," even if the use of the right be, in a sense, wrongful, and the appropriation of the ground covered by the right of way. We trust that both Germany and France would refrain even from this minor trespass. But if they did not? If one or the other were to say to England, "All the military approaches to France and Germany have been closed; and only neutral approaches lie open to us. This state of things is not only detrimental, but fatal to our military success, and it has arisen since the Treaty guaranteed the sacredness of the only· road of which we can now avail ourselves. We will, as a fact, respect the independence of Belgium and we will give you the most solemn and binding guarantees that, at the end of the conflict, Belgium shall be as free and independent as before." If Germany—and, of course, our hypothesis applies also to France—were to use this language—though we trust there will be no occasion for it—we cannot doubt what would be the wise and proper course for England to pursue, and what would be the answer of the English Government. England does not wish to shirk responsibilities. But it would be madness for us to incur or assume responsibilities unnecessarily, when to do so would manifestly involve our participation in a tremendous war.

The same afternoon the *Pall Mall Gazette*, then a Liberal paper, commented on the subject as follows:

The *Standard* this morning gives special prominence to a letter signed "Diplomaticus," on the neutrality of Belgium. It also devotes its first leading article to the subject. The gist of these utterances may be summed up in two propositions: (1) England is under a treaty of obligation to defend the neutrality of Belgium; (2) but circumstances have altered since the contraction of the said obligation, and as against Germany, at any rate, England must pocket its pledges, and allow France to be invaded through Belgium without protesting or interfering.

Considerable importance is likely to be attached to these conclusions abroad owing to its being understood that the *Standard* is at present the Governmental and Salisburian organ. Each of the propositions laid down by our contemporary is, it will be seen, likely to be taken hold of. Germany might read the second as an invitation to invade France through Belgium; France might read the first as an admission of our obligation to prevent, or rather to punish, such an infringement of neutral territory, *if we dared*.

It becomes important, therefore, to point out that the *Standard's* argument rests on a false assumption. We do not for the present argue whether in the contingencies contemplated it would be England's *interest* to intervene by declaring war against whichever belligerent might violate the neutrality of Belgium; we confine ourselves to the preliminary statement—essential for clearing up the case—that it is not England's *obligation* to do so.

The *Pall Mall Gazette* then analyzes the 1831 and 1839 treaties, and comes to the conclusion:

> There is, therefore, no English guarantee to Belgium. It is possible, perhaps, to "construct" such a guarantee; but the case may be summed up as follows: (1) England is under no guarantee whatever except such as is common to Austria, France, Russia, and Germany; (2) that guarantee is not specifically of the neutrality of Belgium at all; and (3) is given not to Belgium but to the Netherlands.

The next day the *Spectator* also argued that the British guarantee for Belgium "is not a solitary one, and would not bind us to fight alone."

Great Britain guaranteed the neutrality of Belgium because it was traditionally the British interest to keep the Low Countries in the hands of weak and friendly powers.

In 1870 and 1887 Britain was still strong enough to indulge in "splendid isolation"—that is, to protect her interests while remaining uncommitted to any great power.

In 1870 it did not much matter to Britain whether France beat Prussia or *vice versa*, and so she concentrated on the traditional

British interest of maintaining the neutrality of Belgium. Hence Granville's prompt action to preserve that neutrality inviolate. In 1887 the British Government was, on grounds of imperial interest, friendly to Germany and hostile to France. It therefore took the view that it need not do anything in particular if Belgium were invaded, except to extract an assurance from the invader—which it was assumed would be her then friend Germany —that she would restore the *status quo ante* after the war.

The interesting point about these events is that treaty obligations were throughout regarded as valid only in so far as they subserved national interests. The Conservative *Standard* was almost candid about that view. The Liberal *Pall Mall Gazette* deplored the immorality of the *Standard's* argument, but arrived at the same conclusion by proving to its own satisfaction that the treaty guarantee which happened to be contrary to its view of the national interest also happened, by a strange but happy coincidence, not to be a binding treaty obligation at all. This was a typical example of the kind of moralistic wishful thinking summed up in the famous saying that if Mr. Gladstone had been found with an ace up his sleeve, he would have solemnly declared that God put it there.

Take as an apposite instance the following statement by Mr. Gladstone, quoted by Sir Edward Grey in his eve-of-war speech:

> We have an interest in the independence of Belgium which is wider than that which we may have in the literal operation of the guarantee. It is found in the answer to the question whether under the circumstances of the case, this country, endowed as it is with influence and power, would quietly stand by and witness the perpetration of the direst crime that ever stained the pages of history, and thus become participators in the sin.[1]

Participation in the sin, it will be observed, is not ruled out categorically and forever, but only "under the circumstances of the case." And in 1887 the circumstances were different from 1870.

In 1914 circumstances had changed again. The resulting

change in the British view of their treaty obligations will appear in the rest of this chapter, and was summed up in 1908, when the Casablanca crisis brought Europe within sight of war. Grey asked Sir Eyre Crowe (then a high Foreign Office official, later the Permanent Under-Secretary) for a memorandum on Belgian neutrality. The memorandum took a strict view of the British obligations, on the ground that Belgian neutrality had been guaranteed not only because it was a Belgian interest, but also because it was a British interest. To this memorandum Sir Charles Hardinge, Permanent Under-Secretary of State for Foreign Affairs, appended the following comment:

> The liability undoubtedly exists as stated above. But whether we should be called upon to carry out our obligation and to vindicate the neutrality of Belgium in opposing its violation must necessarily depend on our policy and the circumstances of the moment. Supposing that France violated the neutrality of Belgium in a war against Germany, it is, under present circumstances, doubtful whether England or Russia would move a finger to maintain Belgian neutrality, while if the neutrality of Belgium were violated by Germany the converse would be the case.

INTERNATIONAL ANARCHY, IMPERIALISM, AND THE BALANCE OF POWER

G. Lowes Dickinson, in *The International Anarchy*, surveys the whole complex of treaties and agreements that grew up in the forty years before World War I as a result of the continually shifting balance of power and the manoeuvrings and intrigues of those international anarchs, the great powers, driven by the seven devils of imperialism. It is an amazing story. The treaties are so numerous, so short-lived, so ambiguous, often contradictory,* generally secret, and always cynically disregarded the moment they run counter to the self-interest of their signatories.

* *E.g.*, the Russo-German "Reinsurance" treaty, which cut across Franco-Russian and Germano-Austrian treaties; the Franco-Italian treaty of 1902, which was incompatible with Italy's obligations to Germany and Austria, etc.

This careful, scrupulously fair account, supported by a wealth of evidence, makes it plain beyond any possibility of doubt that no government, the British included, ever dreamed of observing treaty obligations or international law at the expense of what they regarded as vital interests, or hesitated to deceive each other of their own public opinion when deception seemed expedient. "International morality" and "international law" are practically contradictions in terms in the conditions of international anarchy.

But there was a difference of technique between British and Continental methods. Continental diplomats were cynical (or candid) about resorting to fraud. British statesmen were generally more scrupulous (or devious) about the form of doing the thing. Thus in 1887 Great Britain concluded treaties with Austria and Italy providing for mutual approval of Britain's previous seizure of Egypt (1882) and Italy's future seizure of Tripoli (which took place twenty years later), and contemplating war against Russia or France in certain circumstances. Mr. Dickinson says:

> The treaties were secret, which meant, in this case, that though known to and favoured by Germany, they were not to be known either to Russia or to France, or to the Parliament or people of England. In this latter connexion attention must be drawn to the form of the agreement. This is peculiar, consisting of separate notes by the several parties, instead of the usual single document signed by all. The reason for this is given in a despatch by the German Ambassador in London. In Lord Salisbury's view, he writes, it was necessary to clothe the agreement in such a form as would allow the Government, in case of a question in the House, to deny the existence of an "alliance." Such denial was, in fact, more than once made in Parliament. Thus when Sir Charles Dilke, in 1902, referred to the arrangement as a "virtual alliance," he was corrected by Lord Cranborne, who even went so far as to say that "there was never a treaty or agreement with Italy" (Hansard, July 3, 1902, cx, p. 733). Lord Lansdowne, a few days later, referred to it as an "exchange of views" (ib., cxi, p. 660). More important, however, than the name of the thing were its actual commitments. In 1888 Sir John Fergu-

son said, in answer to a question, that England "was not under any obligation to use military or naval action" (*ib.*, February 22, 1888, cccxxii, p. 1184). As England was bound, in certain contingencies, to proceed to the "provisional occupation" of points in Ottoman territory, this seems to be rather a questionable statement. Perhaps one may fairly assume that the British Government felt obliged to give some satisfaction to Italy, while at the same time they were unwilling to admit to the House of Commons that they were bound, in certain contingencies, to go to war.[2]

It is impossible even to summarize the evidence accumulated by Lowes Dickinson as to why international anarchy makes war inevitable. All that can be done in this chapter is to touch on the main international crises that led up to World War I. Each of these crises emerged from and was linked up with a vast network of complicated intrigues and the clash of imperialist vested interests.

Towards the end of the last century it became clear that the British were losing their industrial start and no longer had the strength to indulge in the luxury of "splendid isolation." Mr. Joseph Chamberlain, the Secretary for the Colonies, therefore approached Germany in February 1898 with a proposal for an Anglo-German alliance. The German Government declined the offer, on the double ground that it did not believe the British Parliament would approve the agreement, and that it would therefore be unstable, and because it was afraid of being dragged by England into a war against Russia.

Soon after, the Boer War broke out. This was an imperialist adventure of the "new" type undertaken at the instigation of "finance" or "monopoly" capital. In British home affairs it showed, as Mr. J. A. Hobson pointed out in his classic book *Imperialism* (published in 1903), that the plutocracy which was now the social and financial backbone of both the Conservative and Liberal parties had heavily infected the Liberals too with imperialism.

In international affairs the Boer War revealed the grave danger of a Continental combination against Great Britain. For a couple of years after that war Great Britain wavered between continuing "splendid isolation," coming down on the side of her traditional friend Germany against her traditional enemies France and Russia, or joining the latter powers against Germany.

German trade rivalry, colonial ambitions, and naval program cast the die in favour of France and Russia.* Then it was rapidly discovered that the "conflicts of vital interests" which had frequently brought Britain to the verge of war against France and/or Russia were matters that could be easily settled.

EGYPT

France had deeply resented the British occupation of Egypt in 1882—another typical bit of "finance capital" imperialism,† and the British failure to withdraw, in spite of no less than sixty-six pledges to do so "shortly." France and England began a race for the occupation of the Sudan which ended in a French and a British detachment meeting at Fashoda in 1898. The French gave way. The defeat made them realize the need for agreement between British and French imperialism in face of the common danger from German imperialism. Hence the new policy of an Anglo-French "entente" or understanding.

* But only after Mr. Chamberlain and the Duke of Devonshire had regretted "the sacrifices they would have to make in Morocco, Persia and China"—*i.e.*, the aggressions they would have to refrain from committing in deference to Britain's new Allies.

† It was preceded as from the sixties by the "development" under pressure of Egypt. Between 1864 and 1873 four loans totalling £52,500,000 and bearing a high rate of interest were thrust upon the Khedive. Only £35,-400,000 of this sum was received by Egypt, the rest going into the pockets of London bankers as commission and expenses. The money was then spent by the Egyptian Government in payments to British contractors. The harbour works of Alexandria, for instance, cost the Egyptian Government £2,-500,000, of which £1,100,000 went in profits to contractors. By 1876 Egypt owed £80,000,000 and had to pay interest to the tune of £6,000,000—out of a total State revenue of £10,000,000. After the occupation Sir Evelyn Baring of Baring Bros., Bankers, became the virtual dictator of Egypt, under the title of Lord Cromer.

MOROCCO

To cement the Entente, France and Great Britain settled all outstanding issues in 1904 and concluded two treaties, one public and one secret. By the public treaty France recognized Britain's position in Egypt, and Britain recognized that it "appertains to France" to "preserve order" in Morocco and "to provide assistance for the purpose of all administrative, financial and military reforms which it may require." The treaty pledged the contracting parties to preserve the sovereignty and integrity of Morocco.

In the secret Anglo-French treaty, reinforced by a secret Franco-Spanish treaty, the subjugation and partition of Morocco were provided for in some detail, with France getting the lion's share and Spain the strip of coast opposite Gibraltar (*i.e.*, Tangier, because Britain did not want a strong power to command the Straits).

The whole transaction was another typical example of imperialism, undertaken at the instigation of capitalist vested interests and with an admixture of power-politics motives. In modern parlance France and Great Britain decided to make Morocco a victim of aggression, and decided beforehand how the victim was to be carved up. The quality of the whole transaction, judged by ordinary standards of morality, is neatly summed up as follows by Bertrand Russell, in *The Policy of the Entente, 1904–14: A Reply to Professor Gilbert Murray* (who had written an elaborate *apologia* for the foreign policy of Sir Edward Grey, with the assistance of the Foreign Office. In charity to Professor Murray it should be mentioned that his was a war-time publication):

> To those who are unaccustomed to diplomatic methods, there is something repellent in the contradictory character of the public declaration and the secret understandings of England, France, and Spain in the matter of Morocco. Publicly, they stated that they "remained firmly attached" to the integrity of Morocco. Secretly, they arranged how the booty was to be divided in case this attachment should become less firm. If two men were to declare publicly that they had no intention of stealing their neighbour's goods, and were at the

same time to draw up and sign a careful secret contract as to how his goods were to be shared in case they came into possession of them, they would not be believed if they declared, on being caught, that at the time they sincerely hoped they would remain honest. France and Spain had no right to Morocco except that of contiguity—the very same right which the King had to Naboth's Vineyard. The Moorish Empire was independent, and its international status was regulated by the Madrid Convention of 1880.* If misgovernment were to produce a genuine need for European intervention, the obviously right course was to make the intervention international, as in the case of the Boxers in China. But this was not the course adopted by England, France, and Spain. While publicly declaring that they hoped the integrity of Morocco could be preserved, they secretly arranged who was to have what in case Moroccan independence came to an end. And this contingency was considered sufficiently probable for France to be willing, on account of it, to withdraw its long-standing opposition to our occupation of Egypt. The analogy is exact with our illustration of the two burglars, with the addition of a third who is paid to stand out of a job at the very moment when the two are publicly protesting their wish to remain honest.

Professor Murray's explanation [of the secrecy which was preserved as to the terms of partition] is that the political status of Morocco would have been more difficult to maintain if it had become known that England and France contemplated the possibility of having to change it; and so anxious were the two Powers to do nothing to hasten the downfall of Morocco, that, like benevolent bedside doctors, they concealed the danger from the patient and from his friends. This was very kind, certainly. But the kindness did not end here. One of the doctors, who had expectations from the patient's demise, paid the other to leave him in sole charge, and subsequently administered many small doses of poison. Finally the patient died, and the doctor came into his

* Which provided (*inter alia*) that all the signatories (among whom Germany was included) should enjoy most-favoured-nation treatment in Morocco. (Russell's note)

inheritance. Those who can believe, with Professor Murray, that he grieved sincerely for the sick man's death, are to be congratulated on their charitable disposition.[3]

That was the situation. But it must be clearly understood that ordinary moral standards are inapplicable to power politics, where might is the only right. The Moroccan transaction was part and parcel of an innumerable series of similar transactions, all conducted by the same methods and inspired by the same motives. This was the stuff of which international relations were made in the eyes of the governments. These were the objects with which diplomats were concerned. The great powers were almost continually occupied in bargaining or quarrelling about how to divide between themselves the possessions of third parties, to be acquired by a judicious mixture of force and fraud. And it was generally the activities of their financial and industrial interests that determined the issues about which they haggled, disputed, and fought. Territory, trade, and prestige were what was meant by "honour and vital interests," in the pursuit of which—*i.e.*, in the defence of which, for there was no difference between the two—any amount of duplicity and violence must if necessary be used. And of course the whole business was always conducted in the most high-flown language, and public appeals were always made to the loftiest and vaguest of rights, principles, and ideals.

This does not mean that Foreign Ministers and diplomats were any less honourable than other public servants. But it does mean that in order to perform their public duty they had to do dishonourable things. International anarchy was a vicious system, and power politics—that is, bad faith and war—were bound up with that system. It is of the first importance to grasp this fact.

The French Government lost no time in carrying out the program of the secret treaties. As a French author quoted by Lowes Dickinson puts it: "After receiving the blessing of Great Britain on her work in Morocco, France turned to the task of reform with new zeal." A loan guaranteed on the customs, a French military mission to train the police, a state bank, and a program of building roads and telegraphs (of course by French *entrepreneurs*) were among the reforms pressed on the protesting Sultan. As Lowes Dickinson observes:

> The situation was typical. It was the story of Tunis, of Egypt, and, later, of Tripoli. The Great Powers proceed, in such cases, by measures that are well understood. They complain of disorder, and introduce military control; they lend money to a frivolous ruler, foreclose upon his finances, and thus assume, by steps more or less gradual, according to circumstances, the control of the Government and of the economic resources of the country.[4]

TANGIER

Everything seemed to be going according to plan when on March 21, 1905, the German Kaiser landed at Tangier from a German warship and formally took the Sultan of Morocco under his protection. He insisted on the latter's independence and on his own determination to do all in his power to safeguard German interests in Morocco. He expressed the hope that under the Sultan's sovereignty "a free Morocco will remain open to the peaceful competition of all nations, on a footing of absolute equality."

The German Government had got wind of the existence of the secret treaties and suspected their contents. It was determined, in the classical tradition of power politics and imperialism, to claim its share if the Moroccan oyster were going to be pried open by the bayonets of the great powers. For it was a logical, although peculiarly unsavoury, development of the doctrine of the balance of power that if one great power lopped a piece off a victim of aggression, the other great powers demanded equivalent pounds of flesh—either from the same or some other victim. This was called "compensation."

"Compensation" was what Germany was demanding, and backing her demand with the usual threat of force, although in a particularly crude and provocative manner. But what she asked for was not, according to modern standards, unjust. She pointed out that an international treaty—that of 1880—guaranteed the sig-

natories "most-favoured-nation" treatment in Morocco, and proposed, therefore, that the future of the country should be settled
at an international conference on the basis of the "open door" and
respect for the sovereignty of the Sultan and the territorial integrity of his country. This, of course, did not mean that Germany
cared any more for these principles or for treaty obligations than
any other great power, but simply that it suited her interests at
the time to take that line.

The German Government's view was expressed by the Kaiser
when he told President (Theodore) Roosevelt that France's object was to absorb Morocco and surround it with a ring-fence of
high tariffs, and that:

> For thirty-five years Germany has been obliged to keep an
> armed defensive against France. As soon as France discovers
> that Germany meekly submits to her bullying, we feel sure
> that she will become more aggressive in other quarters, and
> we do not consider a demand for a revision of the Treaty of
> Frankfort to be far off.[5]

This referred to the failure of Germany since 1870 to induce
France to accept the loss of Alsace-Lorraine and abandon the
idea of "revanche." The interesting point is that from the German point of view it was a choice between bullying or being
bullied—there was no third alternative. That was also how the
matter looked to France and Great Britain, but with the rôles
reversed. Both sides, on the assumptions of power politics, were
right.

M. Delcassé, the French Foreign Minister, who was violently
anti-British before 1904, violently anti-German after 1904, and a
jingo and imperialist all the time, wanted to resist the German
demand by war if necessary. The British Foreign Secretary, Lord
Lansdowne, assured France of full British support in case of war.
When the Conservative government went out of office at the end
of 1905, the assurance was renewed by Sir Edward Grey. It is
true the Liberal Foreign Secretary was careful to couch his assurance in terms that gave it a democratic flavour. On being asked

by the French Ambassador whether in case of war Great Britain would support France, he replied:

> I could promise nothing to any foreign Power unless it was subsequently to receive the whole-hearted support of public opinion here if the occasion arose. I said, in my opinion, if war was forced upon France then, on the question of Morocco—a question which had just been the subject of agreement between this country and France, an agreement exceedingly popular on both sides—that if, out of that agreement, war was forced on France at that time, in my view public opinion would have rallied to the material support of France. I gave no promise, but I expressed that opinion during the crisis, as far as I remember, almost in the same words to the French Ambassador and the German Ambassador.

But Sir Edward Grey's as compared with Lord Lansdowne's assurance was essentially a distinction without a difference. For, as Lowes Dickinson observes:

> In such matters the Foreign Secretary, the Cabinet, and the Press have the power to determine opinion. It would have been easy to represent the French as a peaceable, innocent people and the Germans as hectoring bullies, for no one then knew anything about the secret treaties. Moreover, the fate of Gibraltar and of the entrance to the Mediterranean was likely to appeal much more to the British than the quarrel between Serbia and Austria did in 1914. So that it is at least questionable whether the then House of Commons would have overthrown the Government rather than sanction war.[6]

French pacifist and radical opinion compelled the French Government to get rid of the fire-eating M. Delcassé, even though this could be represented as yielding to German pressure, and in spite of the fulminations of the Right in both France and Great Britain. After coming within an ace of war, the Entente powers agreed to Germany's demand for a conference, which was held at Algeciras.

At first sight it seems shocking that the British Government—and a Liberal government at that—should have been willing to

plunge that country into war for the sake of resisting Germany's
demand for an international conference and the "open door" in
Morocco, and in order to support France in acting on the iniqui-
tous, secret Anglo-French "deal," which was contrary to the public
treaty obligations of the two powers, for the subjugation and partition of Morocco. But there are several facts to remember.

By 1906 the British plutocracy—that is, "finance capital"—dominated both the Conservative and Liberal parties. The leaders of
the two parties were for the most part so much in agreement on
fundamentals, and so closely united by family, social, and economic ties, as to give some colour to Mr. Hilaire Belloc's political
satires. The bulk of the Liberal party supported the purely imperialist Boer War. After victory, Campbell-Bannerman's personal stand on what he believed was a question of right swung
the Cabinet in favour of giving autonomy to the Union of South
Africa. This was a great thing, a bold application of the principle
of nationality which was always a Liberal tradition, and a further
development of the tradition, painfully implanted in our ruling
class by the American Revolution and early troubles in Canada,
that British possessions ruled by whites should have self-govern-
ment.

But after the war British finance capital was in any case in control of South African investment opportunities, and so the City
did not much object to political and even tariff autonomy. In
other words, the Liberal government's South African policy was
an enlightened and up-to-date form of imperialism. But it did not
challenge the main driving force—finance capital—behind modern
imperialism.

The Liberal government believed just as implicitly as its Conservative predecessors in the fundamental assumptions of capitalism and their international application—imperialism. Indeed, it
was not conscious that these things were "assumptions" at all. To
the Liberal imperialists who were in charge of the government's
foreign policy they seemed part of the order of nature. They had
inherited the British Empire as a going concern, as the greatest
of the great powers, functioning in a world of international
anarchy and imperialism. They were trustees, and their job was

to keep their end up in the balance of power, to do their best to preserve peace so far as "honour and vital interests" allowed, and to prepare as effectively as they could for war against the day when this should no longer prove possible.

Given this unquestioning acceptance of the fundamentals of the social and imperial order, the Liberal government naturally felt constrained to continue the foreign policy of its Conservative predecessors. It felt it must back France, whatever the merits of the issue between France and Germany, or risk the break-up of the Entente and the success of Germany's attempts to bring France and Russia into a Continental combine that would isolate Britain, destroy the balance of power, and peg out claims in Africa and China highly distasteful to British imperial ambitions. These were the "reasons of state" that alone counted, for they were grounded in the necessities of self-preservation.

For the same reason, and in view of the acute danger of war, Sir Edward Grey agreed to the French request that there should be conversations—secret, of course—between the two general staffs. Later there were naval conversations as well.

The theory was that these conversations would result in agreements as to just how British and French forces could co-operate in case the British Government decided to support France in a war, but would leave Britain free to decide her political course of action in the light of the circumstances at the time. How this policy worked out in practice will be made clear subsequently in this survey of the events that led to World War I.[7]

THE ANGLO-RUSSIAN ENTENTE AND PERSIA

An Anglo-Russian understanding was the necessary corollary to the Western Entente. The negotiations were complicated by the fact that Russia and Japan were at war, and that Japan was at the time Britain's ally.* The end of the war removed this difficulty. But only to raise a greater.

* The Far Eastern situation was one section of the general scramble of the Great Powers for colonies, concessions, "spheres of influence," etc. As it does not directly constitute one of the stages to World War I, it is not mentioned in this chapter.

Defeat at the hands of Japan had led to the outbreak of the first Russian Revolution. The Czarist Government's need of support was becoming desperate. The disorders throughout the country grew worse and worse. On October 31, 1905, the Czar was forced to grant a constitution. The army and navy were in a mutinous condition and money was urgently required to put things right.

But the Duma (*i.e.*, parliament) under the constitution had nominal control of taxation, and would not relieve the Government of its financial embarrassments until it had agreed to reforms.

The Kaiser would gladly have helped his Russian cousin, but had no money to spare. France, which had hitherto been Russia's financier, began to feel that the security was shaky. French public opinion thought that support of the Czarist bureaucracy was unworthy of the French Republic.

M. Clemenceau, in the *Aurore*, warned his countrymen against floating any Russian loans until the state of the country had improved:

After having furnished the Czar with the financial resources which were destined to lead to his defeat abroad, it now remains for us to supply him with the financial resources destined to assure his victory over his own subjects.[8]

According to *Gil Blas*, the representatives of Parisian finance in January 1906 drew up conditions for any fresh loan to Russia, including the granting of full control over finance to the Duma.

All liberal opinion in Russia was against the conclusion of a loan while the status and powers of the Duma remained in doubt. On April 9, 1906, the *Times* correspondent at St. Petersburg reported:

The Opposition organs continue their campaign against the conclusion of a foreign loan before the Duma meets. A host of arguments is adduced in support of their contention, but all amount to this, that they are afraid that the Government, having secured a large sum of money, will try to terrorise the Duma just as it terrorised the elections. The Russian press has, unfortunately, too deep and too lasting a mistrust of its Government.

A few days later an Anglo-French loan to Russia of £90,000,-000 was concluded.* The initiative was taken in this matter by Great Britain, and the Foreign Office exerted its influence on the City in raising the loan. The first Duma was opened by the Czar on May 9, and dissolved on July 22. After that the counter-revolution began with a vengeance. The day after the dissolution of the Duma the *Times* wrote:

> The Government's arbitrary step, indeed, justifies only too completely those Russian reformers who besought the friends of constitutional liberty in the West not to lend more money to the autocracy.... The Russian Government obtained their loan by what now looks uncommonly like false pretences, but they cannot live on it for ever ... how can they hope to hold down for ever an exasperated people?

But, observes Bertrand Russell, from whose pamphlet *The Policy of the Entente, 1904–14*, most of these facts were taken:

> The hopes of the *Times* were vain, and its penitence was brief. Step by step, the Tsar recovered his power. The more venal of his opponents were bought, the rest were dispersed to the scaffold, the gaols, and the convict settlements of Siberia. Finland was punished for its moment of freedom, Poland for the hundredth time tasted the bitterness of bondage, the army was reorganized, and soon the Tsar was at liberty to extend the blessings of his rule by the suppression of freedom in Persia. If the loan had been postponed for a few months, none of these results could have been achieved. Russia's gratitude is only to be secured by signal services, but fortunately for our Foreign Office the moment was one at which a signal service was possible. A Liberal

---

* The purchasing power of the pound in those days being two to three times what it is today, and government budgets being only a fraction of their present dimensions.

Russia, which would have meant a new Europe and a new
Asia, was prevented by our timely intervention.

There can be no reasonable doubt that it was the English
and French command of capital that inclined Russia to reject
the offered friendship of Germany. The experience of the
Western Powers during the first Moroccan crisis, in 1905, had
shown them the dangers of a policy of conquest while Russia
was weak: deliberately and patiently they set to work to
make Russia seem strong through suppression of liberty.[9]

Sir Henry Campbell-Bannerman, it will be remembered, deplored the dissolution of the first Duma in a great speech which
ended with the famous cry "The Duma is dead! Long live the
Duma!" But he omitted to mention that the Duma had been
killed with the help of the money lent to the Czar through the
good offices of his government.

At first sight this contrast between words and deeds seems
shocking. But in the first place it is not certain how far Sir
Edward Grey had informed his Prime Minister of the transaction,
nor even how far the Foreign Secretary himself knew what his
officials had done to persuade the City to raise the loan. Moreover, as usual, all concerned had what may be described as a
moral alibi—their trust in the good intentions of the Czar and
their refusal to believe that he really intended to break his
promises and suppress the Duma. One-way credulity, wilful ignorance, and wishful thinking based on class bias are a psychological phenomenon that is met with again and again in studying
British foreign policy.

Quite apart from what could be done in the way of class-
biassed self-deception there was always the straight realist argument that Russia should be kept strong and not allowed "to fall
into disorder." In power politics a state is always treated as a
unit, and strength is measured in terms of physical force. It was
clean against all the traditions of power politics to calculate that
if the revolution were successful in Russia it might have effects
inside Germany that would liberalize that country as well. Then,
as now, there were powerful elements in the City and in the Liberal as well as the Conservative party that, although friends of

democracy in the abstract, distrusted any revolutionary movement in the concrete, even in a country so reactionary as Czarist
Russia.

Finally, on August 31, 1907, Russia and Great Britain concluded their outstanding differences in an agreement by which
Tibet was to be left alone as a sort of buffer state under Chinese
suzerainty; Afghanistan was recognized by Russia as being under
British suzerainty; in Persia a Russian sphere of influence was established in the northern half of the country and a British sphere
was established in the southern half of the remainder, with the
intermediate territory as a neutral zone. Both parties recognized
the independence and integrity of Persia, and each recognized
the other's "special rights" in their respective spheres. Afghanistan and Persia, which were nominally sovereign states, and Tibet,
which was nominally a part of China, were, needless to say, not
consulted in making these arrangements.

The Anglo-Russian agreement over Persia was part of the
drawing together of those two countries against Germany, and
was a further step in "peaceful penetration" of the usual type in
Persia. Germany was pressing her Baghdad railway project,
which would have brought her into the Middle East, and the
Anglo-Persian agreement was the usual combination of power-
politics and finance-capital motives to keep her out of Persia and
to get ready to fight her if she tried too hard to push herself into
the Persian market.

The Russians had gone to work by lending large sums to the
corrupt and frivolous Shah, with control over Persian revenues as
security. British financial interests concentrated on buying up
concessions. In one transaction a monopoly was given to a British
firm for the production, sale, and export of all the tobacco of
Persia. The capital was £650,000 and the annual net profit was
estimated at £371,000! The concession was given by the Shah
and was regarded by him as his personal property. But the
Persians boycotted the tobacco, because they refused to smoke
what had been soiled by the hands of infidels. Thereupon the
company demanded half-a-million-pounds' compensation for the
cancelling of its concession, and this was raised by a loan from a

British bank at 6 per cent. The Persian people stood the racket in the form of taxes. And of course British gunboats and Russian troops were in the background to see that their respective country's financiers were given a warm welcome and handsome treatment by the Shah.

As far back as 1900 a French resident wrote that "from concession to concession Persia will soon be entirely in the hands of foreigners."

What Persian patriots thought about it is picturesquely expressed in the following passage from the writings of Sayyid Jamal ud Din:

> Verily the King's purpose wavereth, his character is vitiated, his perceptions are failing and his heart is corrupt. . . . He hath sold to the foes of our faith the greater part of the Persian lands and the profits accruing therefrom, to wit, the mines, the ways leading thereunto, the roads connecting them with the frontier of the country, the inns about to be built by the side of these extensive arteries of communication, which will ramify through all parts of the kingdom, and the gardens and fields surrounding them. Also the tobacco with the chief centres of its cultivation, the lands on which it is grown, and the dwellings of the custodians, carriers, and sellers wherever these are to be found. He has similarly disposed of the grapes used for making wine, and the shops, factories, and wine-presses appertaining to this trade throughout the whole of Persia; and so likewise soap, candles, and sugar, and the factories connected therewith. Lastly there is the bank. And what shall cause thee to understand what is the bank? It means the complete handing over of the reins of government to the enemy of Islam, the enslaving of the people to that enemy, the surrendering of them and of all dominions and authority into the hands of the foreign foe. In short, this criminal has offered the province of the Persian land to auction amongst the Powers, and is selling the realms of Islam and the abodes of Muhammad and his household (to whom be greeting and salutation) to foreigners. But by reason of the vileness of his nature and meanness of his understanding he sells them for a paltry sum, and at a wretched

price. (Yea, thus it is when meanness and avarice are mingled with treason and folly!)[10]

There was, in fact, a strong patriotic movement in Persia demanding the modernization of the country and a parliament and constitution. This movement compelled the Shah in August 1906 to grant their request. The new-born parliament met in October of that year and immediately took in hand the balancing of the budget by cutting down expenditure, including the Shah's civil list.

The conclusion of the Anglo-Russian agreement in August 1907 alarmed all progressive opinion in Persia. Thereupon the British Minister in Teheran, with the knowledge and co-operation of the Russian Legation, issued an explanatory commentary to the Persian Government on the Anglo-Russian agreement.

> Information has reached me [says the commentary] that the report is rife in Persia that the result of the Agreement concluded between England and Russia will be the intervention of these two Powers in Persia, and the partition of Persia between them.[11]

The negotiations between England and Russia, the commentary goes on, are of a wholly different character. Sir Edward Grey and the Russian Foreign Minister are completely in accord on two fundamental points:

> Firstly, neither of the two Powers will interfere in the affairs of Persia unless injury is inflicted on the persons or property of their subjects.
> Secondly, negotiations arising out of the Anglo-Russian Agreement must not violate the integrity and independence of Persia.
> Sir Edward Grey also observes that hitherto antagonism has existed between England and Russia, each of whom has endeavoured to prevent the continuance of the other in Persia, and had this antagonism been prolonged in the present uncertain state of Persia, one or both of these Powers might have been tempted to interfere in the internal affairs of Persia, so as not to allow the other to profit by the existing

state of things, or to profit by it to the detriment of others. The object of the present negotiations between England and Russia is to prevent such difficulties from arising between them. . . .

Both Ministers are entirely in accord as to the policy of non-intervention in Persia, and have left no possible ground for doubt in the matter. . . .

As to the reported partition of Persia between Russia and England, concerning which it is asserted that the two Powers above-mentioned wish to define spheres of influence for themselves, Sir Edward Grey and M. Isvolsky have explicitly declared that these reports have no foundation. What the two Powers desire is to come to an agreement which will prevent future difficulties from arising, by guaranteeing that neither Power will aim at acquiring influence in those parts of Persia which are adjacent to the frontier of the other. . . .

From the above statements you will see how baseless and · unfounded are the rumours which have lately prevailed in Persia concerning the political ambitions of England and Russia in this country. The object of the two Powers in making this Agreement is not in any way to attack, but rather to assure for ever the independence of Persia. Not only do they not wish to have at hand any excuse for intervention, but their object in these friendly negotiations *was not to allow one another to intervene* on the pretext of safeguarding their interests. The two Powers hope that in the future Persia will be for ever delivered from the fear of foreign intervention, and will thus be perfectly free to manage her own affairs in her own way, whereby advantage will accrue both to herself and to the whole world.

One curious fact about this declaration is that when asked about it a few years later (December 14, 1911) Sir Edward Grey had no knowledge of its existence. Similar ignorance had been expressed by his Under-Secretary, Mr. Acland, on December 5, 1911.

Another curious fact is that these questions were asked because by December 1911 more than half of Persia had been absorbed by Russia and was under Russian military occupation, and more than half of the remainder had been absorbed by Great Britain.

The third curious fact is that in the process of achieving the extinction of Persian independence the liberal patriotic movement had been crushed by Russia and Great Britain, the corrupt and reactionary Shah had been supported, and fearful atrocities had been committed. Incidentally, an American adviser—Mr. Shuster—who was fearless, honest, and devoted to the cause of the government he served and who had been appointed by the Persians, was dismissed in reply to a Russian ultimatum to which Sir Edward Grey assented.

The dirty work was done by the Russian Czarist Government and its agents in Persia, with the local British officials and Sir Edward Grey in the background being dragged along from one outrage to another as unhappy accomplices and accessories after the fact.

However, it would be an error to suppose that the Foreign Office and British diplomats on the spot had any particular sympathy for the Persian national liberation movement. Their attitude was summed up in a despatch from Sir Arthur Nicholson, then British Ambassador at Petrograd and later Permanent Under-Secretary for Foreign Affairs. The despatch pointed out that if, as was proposed and as subsequently happened, Russian troops intervened at Tabriz, where foreign consuls were said to be in danger, the result would incidentally help the nationalists besieged in that town by troops of the Shah.

> But I submit that the chief object to be kept in view is the safety of the Consuls, even at the risk of the measures which circumstances have rendered necessary proving of benefit to the popular movement at Tabriz.[12]

The Foreign Office naturally could not feel much sympathy for attempts by Orientals to make themselves independent and run their own finances, for this was setting a very bad example from the point of view of the imperialist powers.

When the Russians did get into Tabriz, they established a reign of terror and carried out the most appalling atrocities, both directly and by giving a free hand to one Samad Khan Shuja-ud-Dowleh, a henchman of the Shah. This man became *de facto*

Governor of Tabriz with the approval of the Russians and of the British consul.

The Russians had begun, after a good deal of indiscriminate work with the bayonet, by hanging eight of the leading nationalists, including the Moslem equivalent of the Archbishop of Canterbury, the Sikat-ul-Islam, described by a British officer who knew him as "a man of very unusual ability, great personal charm and singularly broad-minded. He was on excellent terms not only with his co-religionists, but with the Christians of the city." He had previously been refused the right to seek refuge in the British consulate. Shuja-ud-Dowleh then began tortures and executions, not sparing even children of twelve. Men were beaten to death in water ponds; the mouths of some of those who had spoken in favour of the constitution were sewn up; horseshoes were nailed to men's feet and they were driven through the bazaar; an orator had his tongue cut out before execution; other men were blinded, etc.

The British consul sent no report of these events to the Foreign Office in order to make it quite clear that officially he knew nothing about them and had no responsibility.

However, the British Government did join with the Russians in urging the Persian Government to confirm the appointment of Shuja-ud-Dowleh as governor. But the Persians refused.

Prodigies were done by the Foreign Office in the hushing up at home of what was happening in Persia. But even so some of the news leaked through. As Russian and British encroachments on Persian independence grew, British public opinion began to display an inconvenient curiosity.

Sir Edward Grey was in a painful dilemma. On the one hand, it was essential for the sake of the balance of power and British imperialism to maintain the entente with Czarist Russia and the British grip on Southern Persia, which was important both as a source of oil and for strategic reasons. The Russians exploited this fact. Sazonov, the Russian Foreign Minister, wrote in 1910:

The English, pursuing as they do vital aims in Europe, will if necessary sacrifice certain interests in Asia in order to

68

maintain the Convention with us. These circumstances we can naturally turn to our advantage, for instance in our Persian policy.

Moreover, the Russians were blackmailing Great Britain with the possibility of turning to Germany if Britain did not do what they wanted.

On the other hand, the situation in Persia was so unsavoury that the repercussions on public opinion might upset Sir Edward Grey's whole foreign policy. Dickinson gives instance after instance of Grey's warnings to the Russians of the possible reaction on the Anglo-Russian agreement of what they were doing in Persia. A few examples will suffice:

. . . should the unity of our action in Persia come to an end, this would necessarily mean the disruption of the Entente. It would result—in a far shorter period than is generally believed—in a new orientation of English politics.[13]

This was in the course of regretting a Russian ultimatum and the advance of a Russian division towards the Persian capital. The Russian demands, suggested Sir Edward Grey, should have been more moderate and presented in a milder form.

But the Persians accepted the Russian ultimatum. Whereupon the Russians presented three new ultimata demanding (1) the payment by Persia of the costs of their military expedition; (2) the dismissal of the American adviser; (3) the assurance that henceforward the Persian Government would appoint no foreigner without the approval of the Russian and British Ministers at Teheran. Sir Edward Grey deprecated the first of these three demands, but did not object to the other two. He urged that Russian troops should occupy the Persian capital "only in case of extreme necessity."

I fear that the St. Petersburg Cabinet does not sufficiently take into account how unexpectedly the Persian question, if it be not properly handled, may bring about a discussion of foreign policy as a whole. If demands be made which we cannot declare to be covered by the Anglo-Russian Convention, then the Persian question would be lost sight of, and the question of foreign policy in general, Russia's as well as England's, would take its place. This would be regrettable, and I am in the greatest anxiety.

Sir Edward Grey then went on to suggest that if with Russian connivance he could overcome the present difficulties:

> We could perhaps form a Persian Government which would recognise the necessity of taking Russia's interest into account, instead of continually setting up opposition.[14]

"Non-intervention" in Persia, it will be observed, was going from strength to strength.

The Russians refused Sir Edward Grey's modest requests and timid suggestions, and the Persian parliament refused the three Russian ultimata because, as one member said:

> It may be the will of Allah that our liberty and our sovereignty should be taken from us by force, but let us not sign them away with our own hands.[15]

The final tragedy, the bloody finish, has already been described. This record of events may be left to speak for itself. But in justice to those responsible for it it must be emphasized that it appeared in their eyes as the price to be paid for the Anglo-Russian Entente, which they regarded as a necessity. How strong that argument seemed to the generation that was called upon to estimate those needs may be gathered from the fact that Professor Gilbert Murray, in the pamphlet already referred to, says of Sir Edward Grey's policy in Persia that "as a Liberal and a reasonable man I cannot condemn it, though I admit that it failed to achieve its full object." He adds that so far as he can see Liberals have no right "to attack and denounce Sir Edward Grey for his policy in Persia."

This is the argument of "reasons of state," which rests upon accepting the social foundations of power politics and imperialism as something beyond the control of man, at least in the day and age of the Asquith-Grey government.

THE ANNEXATION OF BOSNIA-HERZEGOVINA

The scene now shifts from Morocco and Persia to the Balkans, from the westernmost and easternmost to the northernmost extremity of what used to be the Turkish Empire. The Austro-Hungarian and Ottoman empires, which met in the Balkans, were both survivals of an older political tradition. Each was multinational in structure and each grew more ramshackle and precarious as the ideas of liberalism, democracy, and nationality, released by the French Revolution, advanced eastwards in Europe during the nineteenth century. Among the welter of nationalities kept together and held down by the Ottoman Empire in the Balkans, the Serbs, Bulgars, Rumanians, and Greeks emerged as independent states in the last century, but each with unsatisfied territorial and ethnic claims. In the case of all four powers these claims were directed against what remained of the Ottoman Empire in Europe—namely, Macedonia and Albania. In the case of Serbia and Rumania there were also irredentist claims to be satisfied at the expense of the Austro-Hungarian Empire. But these claims were allowed to lie dormant, in the case of Rumania until the great war and in the case of Serbia until near the end of the last century. Rumania was an ally of Austria until she was bought over by the Entente in 1915, and Serbia was in the Austrian camp until induced to accept Russian protection.

At the Berlin Conference in 1878 Austria received the assent of the powers to occupy the nominally Turkish provinces of Bosnia and Herzegovina, inhabited by Croats, a people closely allied to the Serbs and speaking the same language (although Roman Catholic instead of Greek Orthodox in religion, and using the Latin instead of the Cyrillic alphabet). The occupation was, of course, preceded by negotiations with the other great powers. The Italians objected to the Austrian occupation.

I expressed [says Crispi, the Italian Foreign Minister at the time, in his *Memoirs*] the opinion of the Italian Government, to Lord Derby and Bismarck, who both replied "Take Albania," with a simultaneousness that struck me as astonishing. I naturally demanded: "But what would I do with it?" Whereupon Derby said: "After all it is something," and Bismarck added: "If you don't like Albania, take some other Turkish territory on the Adriatic."

The conversation is interesting as casting light on the methods and morals of power politics, for all the three great powers concerned had given solemn and repeated pledges to maintain the territorial integrity of the Turkish Empire (so had Austria-Hungary, for that matter).

At the time Austria-Hungary contented herself with reserving "the right to annex these provinces at whatever moment she deemed opportune," although occupying them immediately. She chose to exercise this "right" in 1908, for reasons into which it is needless to enter.

By that time Germany was doubly interested in the Balkan Peninsula, first as an ally of Austria, and secondly because the German Government was supporting the ambitious project of German bankers, big business men, and power politicians for a railway to Baghdad. Russia was interested as the "protector" of the small Slav states, Bulgaria and Serbia, which meant that she wanted to use them to stop the increase of Austro-German influence in the Balkans because of Czarist Russia's own ambition to seize Constantinople and the Straits. The success of Germany's Baghdad railway project and the accompanying increase of German influence in Turkey would have made it impossible to realize this ambition. Italy had her eye on bits of the Adriatic coast, which were also coveted by Serbia. France and Great Britain were interested in the situation through their allies and on general balance-of-power grounds.

In the case of Austria, Balkan affairs were in the literal sense of the term a "vital interest," because Serbian nationalism could not be satisfied except by the disruption of the Austro-Hungarian Empire. The interest of all the other powers concerned was essentially a question of imperialism and the balance of power.

The Austrian annexation of Bosnia-Herzegovina, although it merely legalized the *de facto* situation that had existed for half a century, caused fury in Serbia. One Serbian newspaper called for "immediate mobilization and war to life and death against the monarchy," with the interesting addition that "only in that case will other powers support Serbia." The Serbian statesman Milo-vanovich reports Protitch as saying: "Between us and Austria-Hungary there can only be peace and good neighbourly relations if Austria renounces her position as a Great Power, if she makes up her mind to assume the *rôle* of an eastern Switzerland."

But Russia was still suffering so severely from the effects of her defeat at the hands of Japan that she could not support Serbia. France and Great Britain were unwilling to risk war on this issue. On the other hand, the German Government demonstratively took its stand by the side of Austria and proclaimed its readiness to back that country, even at the cost of war. The German Chancellor adopted this attitude because, as reported by Von Schön of the German Foreign Office:

> He was not averse to letting things take their course to a climax and to a trial of strength between the Central Powers bloc and the Triple Entente, which was not yet firmly established, as he was convinced that none of the Powers would draw the sword, and that, when it came to a question of bending or breaking, Russia would climb down from her high horse and would also call her vassal Serbia to order.

In short, the Austro-German combination had successfully asserted their will in the game of power politics against the Triple Entente and by the usual means of threatening war. The consequences, in the words of a Serbian diplomat, Bogishević, were that:

> From this time forward all the political activities of Russia were directed, in the most intense manner, toward the creation of as large a combination of Powers as possible against Austria-Hungary and Germany, with the clearly recognisable purpose to compel a decision by force of arms at a chosen moment favourable to Russia.

Mr. Churchill, in *The World Crisis*, confirms this view of the consequence of this particular piece of power politics:

The Teutonic triumph was complete. But it was a victory gained at a perilous cost. France, after her treatment in 1905, had begun a thorough military reorganisation. Now Russia, 1910, made an enormous increase in her already vast army; and both Russia and France, smarting under similar experiences, closed their ranks, cemented their alliance, and set to work to construct, with Russian labour and French money, the new strategic railway systems of which Russia's western frontier stood in need.[16]

AGADIR

The road to World War I now doubles back to Morocco. At the Algeciras Conference, France, with the help of Great Britain and Spain and by her own skilful diplomacy, had succeeded in getting the practical arrangements as regards the police forces and similar matters in Morocco settled on lines that gave her the freedom of action she wanted. Germany, on the other hand, had got in the Algeciras treaty the statement that the introduction of reforms into Morocco should be based upon the "threefold principle of the sovereignty and independence of His Majesty the Sultan, the integrity of his dominions, and economic liberty without any inequality," and that the provisions of the Act of Algeciras should prevail over the terms of any treaties, conventions, or other arrangements that contradicted those provisions.

Nominally, therefore, the Act of Algeciras set aside the secret treaties providing for the subjugation and partition of Morocco. But the British, French, and Spanish governments continued to base their policy on the secret treaties and paid only lip service to the Act of Algeciras (to which they were, of course, parties).

Left opinion in France, led by the Socialists, put up a really gallant and long-drawn fight to base French policy on the Act of Algeciras. Mr. E. D. Morel, in *Ten Years of Secret Diplomacy*, enumerates no less than nine resolutions between 1908 and 1911 passed by the French Chamber by large majorities expressing its determination to observe the Algeciras Act and disclaiming intervention in the internal affairs of Morocco. He also gives startling details of how the French Foreign Office, colonial officials, military authorities, and financial interests, using French politicians as their cat's-paws, set at naught the will of the parliament and pushed the country farther and farther along the road to the conquest of Morocco.

All the classic methods of imperialism were used. Trivial incidents were seized upon as excuses for large-scale military occupations for which the Moorish Government was then called upon to pay. There was more than a suspicion that these incidents had in some cases been encouraged to provide the necessary excuse for military intervention. M. Delcassé, the French Foreign Minister, practically forced the Sultan to contract a £2,500,000 French loan at 5 per cent, which was floated by the French banks in such a way that they kept £500,000 as a profit and actually paid Morocco only £1,920,000. Sixty per cent of the customs was pledged as revenue for this loan.

In 1908 a further big consolidated loan was floated on the remaining 40 per cent of the customs. This was an international loan with French banks taking up to 40 per cent, German 20 per cent, British 15 per cent, and Spanish 15 per cent. The bonds, of a nominal value of 500 francs, were taken up by the banks at 435, issued to the public at 485, were several times over-subscribed, and went up to 507 on the afternoon of the day of issue. This consolidated loan amounted to over £4,000,000. The Sultan had to be compelled by a French ultimatum to accept it!

An attempted agreement providing for Franco-German economic co-operation broke down owing to the greed of the vested interests concerned.

Finally, after extensive violations of every provision of the Act of Algeciras, the time was ripe for abandoning it altogether.

In the spring of 1911 the French agent at Fez, the capital of Morocco, sent alarming reports as to the safety of the Europeans in that city. The French Government launched a military expedition to rescue them. There was no danger to the Europeans when the expedition arrived. Mr. Morel, in *Ten Years of Secret Diplomacy*, quotes a mass of contemporary evidence to show that there never was any real danger and that the whole thing was a "ramp" by the imperialist interests grouped in the Comité du Marog, to bring about the military occupation.

Meanwhile, Spain had also occupied the strip assigned to her under the secret treaty, on a similar pretext of "maintaining order."

It became clear that the Act of Algeciras had ceased to exist, and that French military occupation was the end of even the pretence of respect for Morocco's independence and territorial integrity.

The German Government had for some years been watching the progress of events in Morocco without many illusions as to how the whole thing would end, but with the intention of seeking "compensation" so soon as it became clear that the French were out for the annexation of Morocco. On July 1, 1911, the German Government judged the time was ripe to demand "compensation" and sent a gunboat to the Moroccan port of Agadir, by way of filing notice that it proposed to press its claim.

This was a clumsy and provocative act even according to the non-moral standards of power politics. But the abundant evidence that has since been published makes it possible to state categorically that all Germany wanted was to ask for compensation in Africa (to wit, the Congo) in exchange for withdrawing objections to the French seizure of Morocco, and that the German Government did not want war.

But at the time the British Government believed that Germany's object was to seize a naval station on the Atlantic coast of Morocco. Some years before, when Germany was the friend and France the enemy, there had been a tentative British proposal offering Germany her choice of Moroccan Atlantic ports. During the heyday of appeasement in the thirties British policy again veered towards this position. But in 1911 the prospect was regarded as an intolerable threat to British honour and vital interests. Moreover, the British Government was chagrined at Germany's failure to include Great Britain in the conversations which she began with France.

The British position was rather difficult. For while Sir Edward Grey was threatening the Germans with war if they took Agadir, he was prepared to hand over the whole territory to France. He was not able, therefore, to make any reply when the German Ambassador asked him to apply to France for explanations if he attached so much importance to the inviolability of Moroccan territory.

But Sir Edward Grey was very emphatic to the German Ambassador on the point that Great Britain approved of the French occupation and that even if it were prolonged "England in any case and under all circumstances would fulfil her obligations to France." Upon the German Ambassador's then asking what the consequences would be if the Moroccan Government came under French influence and the Algeciras Act were violated, Sir Edward Grey replied "that in the event of entanglements all British obligations would become operative."

Nevertheless, the French Prime Minister, M. Caillaux, still had doubts of the British position because, as he put it:

> I know, like all who have studied closely the history of the British people, the considerable influence exercised on the Government of this great country by the higher administrative officials; but I know also that the men who at this moment represent the majority in power in the House of Commons, entertain very different sentiments. Sir Francis Bertie [the British Ambassador at Paris] does not conceal this fact, and what he said to me on this subject is not reassuring. There is, so it seems to me, an uncertainty in the mentality of the rulers of Great Britain.[17]

In reply to French *démarches*, Sir Edward said that if Germany took possession of Agadir he would consult his colleagues in the Cabinet, and that the concession of a protectorate to France would justify territorial concessions by her to Germany in the Congo. If the negotiations broke down, the only way out would be to propose the summoning of a conference.

This makes it clear that the British attitude was to take a strong line with Germany in order to discourage that country from pushing things too far while at the same time exerting a moderating influence on France.

Franco-German negotiations accordingly began on the basis of Germany's leaving France a free hand in Morocco and France's giving compensation in the Congo. These negotiations proved dangerous and difficult. Mr. Dickinson tells us:

Seven different proposals were put forward to secure agreement; and all this time it was hanging in the balance whether millions of Europeans should perish because the Governments of two States could not agree as to how they would divide between them a piece of equatorial Africa to which neither had any right except that of theft by arms. The Governments, it is true, on both sides were egged on by "public" opinion, which meant, in this case, as it usually does, "jingo" opinion; and it is some satisfaction to know that in both countries there was disappointment at the result finally reached. Once more Europe had escaped, by the skin of the teeth, from the Great War.[18]

How near Britain came to war few people realized at the time. Mr. Lloyd George's famous speech to the bankers at the Mansion House on July 21 strained Anglo-German relations almost to breaking point. This was the operative passage of that speech:

I believe it is essential in the highest interests, not merely of this country, but of the world, that Britain should at all hazards maintain her place and her prestige amongst the Great Powers of the world. Her potent influence has many a time been in the past, and may be in the future, invaluable to the cause of human liberty. It has more than once in the past redeemed continental nations, who are sometimes too apt to forget that service, from overwhelming disaster, and even from international extinction. I would make great sacrifices to preserve peace. I conceive that nothing would justify a disturbance of international good will except questions of the gravest national moment. But if a situation were to be forced upon us in which peace could only be preserved by the surrender of the great and beneficent position Great Britain has won by centuries of heroism and achievement, by allowing Britain to be treated where her interests were vitally affected as if she were of no account in the Cabinet of Nations, then I say emphatically that peace at that price

would be humiliation intolerable for a great country like ours
to endure. National honour is no party question.

The transition here [observes Lowes Dickinson] from interest to honour might be called classical. It reveals the
whole position. Honour will only be defended by arms if,
and when, it is believed to coincide with interest. It is, in
fact, a word without content, employed to excite or to sus-
tain emotions. Interest, on the other hand, has a content,
though it may be questionable whether it has one worth fighting for.

This speech, he adds,

. . . is an admirable specimen of the way in which the devotion of the blind and ignorant masses is exploited for dubious
policies. What was really at stake was the simple point, who
is to steal Morocco? The rest was the rivalry of States, due
to their ambitions and their armaments. But few of those
who read Mr. Lloyd George's speech could be aware of this.
He asked, in effect, for men to come and die; and that they
are always ready to do, if they are told the cause is their
country's. It is enough that certain phrases should be used,
certain passions stimulated; and the more noble and heroic
such passions may be judged to be, the more tragic is the
irony of their abuse.[19]

So tense were Anglo-German relations that the British Navy was
warned against the danger of sudden attack from Germany, as
Mr. Churchill, who ought to know, for he was the man who gave
the orders, tells us in his book *The World Crisis.*

In August Sir Edward Grey asked the Russian Ambassador in
London what Russia would do in case of complications, and was
told that without any doubt "the terms of the treaty would be
strictly carried out." Upon this Sir Edward said:

I will tell you why I believe we must know this. In the
event of war between Germany and France, England would
have to participate. If this war should involve Russia, Austria
would be dragged in too, for although she has not the slightest
desire to interfere in this matter, she will be compelled by

force of circumstances to do so. . . . Consequently it would
no longer be a duel between France and Germany—it would
be general war.[20]

Isvolski, the Russian Ambassador in Paris, states that the British
Government was prepared to move against Germany not only the
fleet but the Expeditionary Force.

A Belgian general—Jungbluth—reports a conversation just
after the Agadir crisis with the British military attaché in Brussels, Colonel Bridges, in which the latter told him:

The British Government, at the time of the recent events,
would have immediately landed troops on our territory, even
if we had not asked for help.

The Belgian general protested that his Government's consent
would be necessary for this. The military attaché observed that
he knew that, but that "as we were not in a position to prevent
the Germans passing through our territory, Great Britain would
have landed her troops in any event."

Wilfrid Blunt, in his *Diaries,* mentions that he was told by
George Wyndham that orders had been given for the landing of
the Expeditionary Force in France in case of hostilities arising
over the recent crisis in Agadir.

In his *War Memoirs,* Mr. Lloyd George states that at a meeting of the Committee of Imperial Defence during the Agadir
crisis Sir Henry Wilson (the chief of staff)

with the aid of a pointer and a big map, explained to us the
whole of the arrangements entered into with the French Foreign Office: they were contingent upon a German attack
upon Belgium and the march of German divisions through
that country to attack France. In that contingency our Expeditionary Force was to be taken to the Belgian frontier
along the French railways, for the purpose of giving every
support to the army which was to resist the invader in that
quarter.[21]

From this Mr. Lloyd George draws the conclusion: "There was
no definite commitment to give military support to France in her

quarrels with Germany," except in case the neutrality of Belgium was violated.

But a few pages earlier in his *War Memoirs,* Mr. Lloyd George says, referring to his Mansion House speech:

> My intervention was due largely to the fear that if things were allowed to drift, we might find ourselves drawn into a great European War on a question in which we were inextricably involved. For the French position in Morocco was part of the Lansdowne Treaty [the 1904 Anglo-French "deal" over Morocco and Egypt], and Sir Edward Grey, in his book, *Twenty-five Years,* makes it clear that he regarded a dispute on anything which constituted a challenge to that settlement as something which we were bound to put in a different category from any dispute which might arise between France and Germany outside the four corners of that arrangement.[22]

In short, the Liberal government was clearly prepared to risk a world war rather than to let Germany assert her claim that the Act of Algeciras should be respected, or that, if it were not, France should pay "compensation" for being allowed by Germany to annex Morocco in defiance of that Act. It is equally clear that the violation of Belgian neutrality was by that time regarded by both sides as a "military truism" and an automatic consequence of the outbreak of a European war, whatever the issue out of which the war arose.

At first glance it seems shocking that in 1911 the British Liberal government should have been prepared to risk a world war to help France carry out a treaty-breaking conquest of Morocco. The explanation given by Mr. Lloyd George is that whereas Germany thought the French Government was weak and might have yielded if threatened with war, she was not prepared to fight both France and Great Britain "to make good this gamble." Germany was not prepared to call the British bluff; "it was in truth by no means bluff," concludes Mr. Lloyd George. Therefore she climbed down.

Professor Gilbert Murray, in his semi-official pamphlet, carries the explanation a stage farther. He says:

Germany might try the policy of detaching France from Great Britain. We had ourselves had the experience of her attempt to detach us from France. She might now be trying to persuade France privately to promise neutrality in Germany's next war, as she tried in the previous year to persuade us. There was naturally a party in France which was somewhat shy of commitments to Great Britain and might be glad to obtain temporary security at the price of dissolving the Entente. This danger would become greater if Great Britain took no step to show that she would stand by France in the present difficulty. So from this point of view, also, we were bound to show our interest in France.

The reference in this passage was to Germany's proposal, of which more is said below, in the course of the Anglo-German negotiations in 1909, that "in the event of either Power being attacked by a third Power or group of Powers, the Power not attacked should remain neutral."

These explanations, it will be noted, did not even attempt to put up a moral or legal case. They approach the matter wholly from the standpoint of power politics. And on that basis they make a perfectly good case.

For Germany's gunboat or "mailed-fist" diplomacy was undoubtedly what the Germans call a *Kraftprobe*—that is, a test or trial of strength. We now know that whereas the German Chancellor was threatening war, the Kaiser had made up his mind not to risk war, and that the whole thing was bluff and blackmail for getting "compensation" in the Congo. It also happened that Germany's legal case was better than that of France or Great Britain.

But if weakness had been shown, it is very probable that the Entente might have broken up, or that Germany would have been encouraged to go farther and do worse next time.

In power politics there is unfortunately no middle course between bullying and being bullied. The general moral to be drawn is pointed out at the end of this chapter. At this point we are merely concerned to warn against the danger of judging the policy of the Liberal Government of Asquith and Grey too harshly by forgetting to judge it in its historical context.

That war did not come in 1911 appears to have been due to the fact that not a single one of the great powers really wanted to risk war at that moment. That is now quite clear from the information that has since come to light. One of the lessons of the Agadir crisis is that even when none of the parties concerned wants war, the practice of power politics may very well precipitate a war, just as the story of the outbreak of World War I makes it clear that in power politics a world war may be the result of even one great power's wanting a little war.

But the "humiliation" suffered by Germany in having to climb down gave a great stimulus to German jingoism, just as the "humiliation" suffered by France and Russia in previous crises had had the worst effect in those countries.

The French military attaché in Berlin, writing in 1912 of the effect in Germany of the Agadir crisis, says:

> We discover every day how deep and lasting are the sentiments of wounded rancour against us provoked by the events of last year. . . .
> The resentment felt in every part of the country is the same. . . . The Emperor and the Government yielded; public opinion has neither forgiven them nor us. Public opinion does not intend that such a thing shall occur again.

The effect in Russia is made clear by Isvolski's conclusion in December 1911, that peace had been saved this time by "the resolute attitude of the three Entente Powers," but that:

> After the crisis just experienced the political situation in Europe is less secure than ever. Beyond all doubt any local collision between the Powers is bound to lead to a general European conflict, in which Russia, like every other European State, will have to participate. With God's help, the conflict may be postponed for a while, but that it may come at any moment we must bear in mind, hour by hour, and we must arm against it hour by hour.[23]

In December 1911 the Serbian Minister in London reported a conversation with the French Ambassador, M. Cambon, which he sums up as follows:

France is conscious that in any case the war will be forced upon her. But France together with her allies is of the opinion that the war must be postponed to a more distant period, *i.e.*, 1914–15, even at the cost of greater sacrifice. The necessity of this postponement is not dictated so much by the material military preparation of France, which is excellent, as by the reorganisation of the supreme command, which is not yet carried out. This delay is also necessary for Russia. England alone will have no advantage from it, as each year brings a decrease of the supremacy of the fleet over the German; but nevertheless England, in view of the preparations of its allies, advises France to come to an agreement with Germany for the present.* [24]

M. Tardieu, a prominent politician of the French Right, drew the following moral in his book on Agadir:

The country deserves, by the wakening of its moral forces, to be better protected against bad shepherds. It has too long admitted as a valid excuse the idealism which the Socialists invoked. It discerns today the utilitarianism that lurks beneath these, and resists the dissociation of its living forces. It understands what it owes to its Army. It escapes from the pacifist dream. It regains the sense of realities. In 1911 it affirmed its resolution. It would be found ready in the same circumstances to affirm it again. The Governments of yesterday could believe that regard for life counseled weakness. This same regard will counsel energy to the Governments of to-morrow. [25]

Possibly M. Tardieu's remark about the Socialists was a reference to the fact that at the height of the Agadir crisis French and German Socialists arranged big peace demonstrations in Berlin and Paris. But, if so, that is the only evidence that those demonstrations made any impression whatsoever on the governments

---

* Marshal Joffre tells in his *Memoirs* how in one of the recurrent crises he was, as chief of the general staff, asked by the Prime Minister whether the French Army had a 70 per cent chance of beating Germany. He said "No." "Very well," said the Prime Minister, "then we will negotiate." That is power politics.

absorbed in the great game of power politics in defence of imperialist interests.

The next milestone on the road to Armageddon was Italy's war on Turkey for the conquest of Tripoli. Italy became an independent state at a time when finance capital was beginning to develop and imperialism was getting into its stride. As a result Italian democracy was almost from the outset so afflicted by corrupt political "bosses" who were the tools of banking and big-business interests that it was a sham democracy. The Italian people had, if possible, even less to say about their country's foreign policy than the peoples of France and Great Britain about theirs (and the Western democracies were little, if any, better off in this respect than Germany, Austria-Hungary, and Russia).

The ruling capitalist interests, power politicians, and diplomats of Italy plunged into the imperialist scramble with a bland unscrupulousness remarkable even in power politics. Italy was like an all-in wrestler who attracts attention even among his professional brethren for fighting foul. There was hardly any time during the period under review when Italy was not bound by at least two sets of incompatible secret treaties to both the Entente and the central powers. In all the major crises between the rival groups her position was more complicated than that of any other state, generally because of her endeavours to double-cross both sides. This was not due to a double dose of original sin in Italians, but to the simple fact that Italy had to try to compensate by an overdose of fraud for her lack of force in the great game of power politics, which is compounded of both.

But with all the strenuous efforts of Italian diplomacy, Italy had neither the economic nor the military power to hold her own in the imperialist scramble. In 1896 her attempt to acquire Abyssinia ended with a defeat. Italy had to sign a treaty promising to respect Abyssinia's independence. Neither she nor any other great power paid any attention to that treaty, and in 1906 France, Great Britain, and Italy signed an agreement on what might be called the standard lines. That is, it began by guaranteeing the independence and integrity of Abyssinia and went on to lay down in some detail how the three powers would divide up the country at an unspecified future date.

But Italy was unable to begin acting on this treaty. She had to suffer the chagrin of seeing France take Tunis under her nose. She had to wait a long time before embarking on the conquest of Tripoli.

Italian agreements with other powers "squaring" them in return for a free hand in Tripoli stretched back for decades before the event. The Italians recognized France's "right" to Morocco, Great Britain's occupation of Egypt, and Russia's claims to the Straits and Constantinople, in return for these powers' promising their good will for Italy's conquest of Tripoli. It is almost needless to observe that all these powers had over and over again pledged themselves to respect the sovereignty and territorial integrity of the Ottoman Empire, of which Tripoli was a part.

The long-prepared war was started by an Italian ultimatum to Turkey in the autumn of 1911. Signor Giolitti, the Italian Premier, boasted in his memoirs of how patiently and skilfully he had made the necessary diplomatic and military preparations for this war of conquest.

As early as the end of July, he records, Sir Edward Grey promised that England would give her "sympathetic support," which, however, would be only of "a moral nature." But he added:

. . . in a friendly and personal manner, that it was indispensable that any eventual action on our part should be justified by a flagrant violation of our rights, or by the evident demonstration of Turkey's intention to put us in an inferior position in Tripoli with respect to other nations.

In particular he desired that we should "avoid any appearance that our action was determined by any desire on our part to obtain an economic position based on particular interests granted us by Turkey," as that would make it difficult for him to maintain in Parliament the "sympathy and moral support" he intended to display . . .

Sir Edward thus laid down from the beginning the two conditions which would make it easy for him to support Italy before British opinion: first, the show of a good moral cause; secondly, consideration for British trading interests.[26]

The Entente powers proved more complaisant towards Italy's projected war than Italy's nominal allies, Germany and Austria-Hungary. But the Italian Government solved this problem by keeping the matter secret until it was too late for them to prevent her going to war.

The reasons for going to war, according to Signor Giolitti, were: (1) That Tripoli was the only part of the Turkish Empire on the African littoral not occupied by a great power and was therefore an "anachronism." (2) The requirements of Italy's dignity and prestige. (3) The existence of slavery. (4) The need to protect the interests of the Banco di Roma.

The war was exceptionally cruel and full of atrocities, even for a colonial war. The Italians carried out a policy of exterminating whole villages, men, women, and children. The Italian Socialist party protested vigorously but vainly. Particularly vehement were the flaming protests of a young Socialist leader who denounced imperialism and demanded strikes, refusal to bear arms, and other forms of strong action. The name of this bitter enemy of imperialism and colonial warfare was Benito Mussolini.

The horrors of the war created considerable excitement in British public opinion, which, says Dickinson, "in its simple way was indignant at an outrage which it did not know to have been sanctioned by its own Government." It is interesting to speculate on how the Nonconformist conscience in the Liberal party would have reacted if it had known that the Foreign Secretary had given his blessing and promise of "moral support" beforehand to this particular orgy of theft, rape, arson, and murder, on condition that the City came in for a fair share of the booty.

But it must be remembered that these were the exigencies of power politics. The Entente powers favoured Italy's war of aggression because they hoped thereby to detach Italy from the central powers (the German-Austrian "axis") and so to shift the balance of power in their favour.

THE BALKAN WARS

Italy's war against Turkey for Tripoli helped to precipitate the war of the Balkan States against Turkey for Macedonia.

Since the crisis over the annexation of Bosnia-Herzegovina, Russia had on the one hand concluded an agreement with Austria and Germany to maintain the *status quo* in the Balkans and had on the other hand secretly engineered a Serbo-Bulgarian alliance, with a program of making war against Turkey and eventually against Austria.

In the First Balkan War, Bulgaria, Serbia, and Greece jointly defeated Turkey. The acute danger to peace arose out of the question of how they were to divide the territory conquered from Turkey.

A European war was avoided by the new procedure of holding a conference of the powers in London to discuss and decide upon the terms of the peace settlement. Austria would not allow Serbia or her diminutive ally Montenegro to take any territory on the Adriatic coast. Russia, on the other hand, would not allow Austria to use force to prevent Serbia or Montenegro from acquiring territory. The most dangerous point was reached when the Montenegrins besieged the Albanian town of Skutari and refused to withdraw when asked to do so by the powers. The Austrians at last threatened to act alone if the powers could not jointly compel Montenegro to withdraw. This might have led to Russian intervention, and so to world war.

Finally, the Montenegrins were induced, after taking the town, to withdraw, so that World War I did not break out that time. The moral is drawn by the Serbian diplomat Bogishević:

> Owing to their mutual feelings of mistrust the Great Powers had come to such a miserable and shameful pass that their very existence or non-existence, the weal or woe of England, France, Germany, might depend upon the favor and ambition of a few politicians and fanatics, the representatives of small States which are less advanced in civilization.[27]

By setting up an independent Albania, and so cutting Serbia off from the sea, the great powers were indirectly responsible for making the Serbians revoke their agreement with Bulgaria about the division of Macedonia. This precipitated the Second Balkan War, in which the former allies fought each other. Bulgaria was defeated and lost territory to both Serbia and Rumania. The Serbians, flushed with victory, thereupon occupied Albania, and were induced to remove themselves only by an Austrian ultimatum. At one time the tension was so great that there were troop movements and preliminaries to mobilization in both Austria and Russia. Once more we escaped world war by a hair's breadth.

‾The reasons World War I was not precipitated immediately by the Balkan Wars of 1912–13 were: First, the fact that all the great powers were in conference and therefore in constant touch with each other. Secondly, the British and German governments were working closely together for peace throughout this conference. Thirdly, the German Government exercised a restraining influence on Austria and was aided in doing so by Italy. In the fourth place, the French President, M. Poincaré, who had first suggested the summoning of the London Conference, took the view that French opinion would not understand the necessity for a war about the Balkans. Finally, the Russians, although they would have fought if Austria had annexed any territory, were not ready for war. The Russian Ambassador in Sofia, M. Nekludov, tells how, when he was received by the Czar before proceeding to his post in 1911, Nicolas II said to him:

After an intentional pause, stepping backward and fixing me with a penetrating stare: "Listen to me, Nekludov; do not for one instant lose sight of the fact that we cannot go to war. I do not wish for war; as a rule I shall do all in my power to preserve for my people the benefits of peace. But at this moment, of all moments, everything which might lead to war must be avoided. It would be out of the question for us to face a war for five or six years—in fact till 1917. . . . Though, if the most vital interests and the honour of Russia were at stake, we might, if it were absolutely necessary, accept a challenge in 1915; but not a moment sooner—in any circumstances or under any pretext whatsoever."

Sir Edward Grey, who was chairman of the London Conference, was largely responsible for its success. His policy, as on previous occasions, was to intimate to the Germans that in case of war they could not count on British neutrality, while informing the Russians and the French that they could not count on England's assistance.

But the Permanent Under-Secretary, Sir A. Nicolson, told the French Ambassador, M. Cambon, that he thought England would take part in the war if the Triple Alliance were fighting against the Entente. The Russian Ambassador, who records this observation, adds:

Monsieur Cambon seems to be persuaded, and I believe in this respect he is right, that England would certainly rather let war break out than let the power of France be endangered. This is one reason which would force arms into her hands. The second would be an ultimatum or a brutal attack on the part of Germany, whether against France or against Russia.[28]

On the other hand, the Russian Foreign Minister, M. Sazonov, writes:

It will be difficult for public opinion in England to understand that . . . a Serbian harbor on the Adriatic or the size of Albanian territory . . . might step by step lead up to the war.[29]

After the Second Balkan War Serbia was aggrandized, but left with a grievance. She was therefore more dangerous to Austria than ever before. But she needed a breathing space to recover from the past war and prepare for what the future had in store. What that would be is made clear in the following passage of a despatch from the Serbian Minister in Bucharest to his Foreign Secretary:

The Ministers of Russia and France advise, as friends of Serbia, that we should declare ourselves satisfied with a guarantee of an unconditional free use of an Adriatic port; and the time will come when we shall be able to retain some such port as our own. It would be better that Serbia, which would be at least twice as large as formerly, should strengthen herself and gather herself together, in order to await with as great a degree of preparedness as possible the important events which must make their appearance among the Great Powers. Otherwise, if a European war started, Europe will make Serbia responsible for the catastrophe.[30]

The veteran Serbian statesman M. Pašic told Bogišhević in 1913, after the conclusion of the Second Balkan War:

For the sake of acquiring Bosnia and Herzegovina likewise, I might have caused a general European war to break loose, already at the time of the first Balkan war; but I feared that in that case we should find ourselves compelled to make greater concessions to Bulgaria in Macedonia. I desired, above all, to secure possession of Macedonia for Serbia, in order that, when that was secure, we might then move forward to the acquisition of Bosnia and Herzegovina.[31]

Later Pašić told the Greek Minister, M. Politis, at the Bucharest conference which closed the Second Balkan War:

The first game is won; now we must prepare for the second, against Austria.

Hartwig, the Russian Minister at Belgrade, made the same point:

Turkey's business is finished; now it is Austria's turn.[32]

At the same time the Russian Government was most anxious that when world war did come it should do so in a way that put the responsibility on the other side. Thus the Russian Ambassador in London wrote his Foreign Minister in December 1912, during the session of the conference:

If, in spite of the moderation of our demands with regard to the solution of current questions, Austria nevertheless decided for some active step, the whole world will have seen that the war is due not to Russia or to any unreasonable demands by Serbia, but to the attempt of Austria and Germany to establish their hegemony in the Balkans. The French Government ought to be grateful to us for this way of putting the question, which is the more necessary in that it is only in these conditions that we can count upon England.[33]

There were, it will be observed, fairly substantial reasons on this occasion for Sir Edward Grey's policy of attempting to exert pressure on the Russians by leaving them in doubt as to whether or not Great Britain would support them.

Once again the reader must be warned against applying ordinary moral standards to the facts related. The Serbians wanted union with their brothers in Austria-Hungary, and believed that the Dual Monarchy was bound in any case to disappear sooner or later and give rise to more modern state structures based on the principle of nationality. These beliefs were no more immoral or unjustified than the opposite belief of the Austrians that they should defend their existence as a great power. Behind and around this purely national conflict were the conflicts of rival imperialist and power-politics interests, none of which had any relation to morality or law.

Before describing the final crisis which precipitated the long-prepared world war we shall now touch upon certain further factors that throw light on the situation—namely, the relation between Belgian neutrality and the rival alliances; the causes and consequences of the naval and military conversations that bound England to the Entente powers; the Anglo-German conversations; and the arms race.

BELGIAN NEUTRALITY AND THE RIVAL ALLIANCES

The great powers guaranteed Belgian neutrality because each was jealous of the disturbance that would have resulted to the balance of power from any great power's annexing that country. So long as Great Britain was strong enough for "splendid isolation" she was not committed to any combination of Continental states, but could intervene in any crisis in whatever way seemed to suit her interests best at the time. This was a period in which there were no stable alliances, and wars between the great powers could still be fought out without involving the whole of Europe (e.g., the Franco-Prussian War).

During this period Belgian neutrality was threatened only in case of war in Western Europe and was unaffected by disturbances in Central, Southern, or Eastern Europe. When war did occur or was threatened in Western Europe, Belgian neutrality was safe if Great Britain was not on the side of either belligerent, as happened in 1870, but was practically sure to be violated if, as in 1887, Great Britain was friendly to Germany and hostile to France.

By 1911 the situation had been fundamentally changed by the lining-up of Europe into two rival coalitions and by the fact that Great Britain had been compelled to join one of those coalitions in order to maintain the balance of power against the other. As Mr. Lloyd George's statement, quoted above in connection with the Agadir crisis, makes perfectly clear, Belgian neutrality was not only threatened but sure to be violated in case of war starting anywhere in Europe, North Africa, or the Near East, for any such war would, if it involved a great power, be well-nigh certain to spread all over Europe.

In such a war Germany would be fighting on two fronts, and her whole strategy was governed by that fact, as well as by the further fact that France was a highly organized but relatively small country that could mobilize quickly, whereas Russia was a country of vast distances and resources but slow and badly organized. This meant that Germany would be compelled, as a matter of military necessity, to strike her first blow at France with the object of paralyzing that country and then turning on Russia. But the French frontier was heavily fortified. Therefore the only way of carrying out the German strategic plan was by attacking France through Belgium.

That the so-called Schlieffen plan did so provide was known in every Chancellery and War Office in Europe for many years before World War I. Germany's building of strategic railways and roads to the Belgian frontier, the installation of huge sidings at frontier stations, etc., made the situation obvious to all military experts.

The Allies in their turn concerted their military plans with each other and with the Belgian military authorities for meeting this invasion. That also was known to the War Offices and Chancelleries of every European power for years before the war. In other words, both the great rival coalitions were preparing to fight each other for years, and both treated the invasion of Belgium by Germany as an automatic military consequence of the general war for which they were preparing, regardless of where and for what reason the war originated. Both sides were thinking exclusively in terms of the balance of power and of their imperialist interests. Neither dreamed of considering the moral or legal aspects of the violation of Belgian territory.

This does not mean that the Allies were not sincere in wanting to defend Belgium. But it does mean that their reason for wanting it was not the "sacredness of treaty obligations," but their own view of their interests.

It must never be forgotten that international law and international morality are concepts irrelevant to power politics except for propaganda purposes.

THE MILITARY AND NAVAL CONVERSATIONS

It has been mentioned that after the 1905 crisis Sir Edward Grey authorized conversations between the British and French general staffs, with the object of arranging in detail how the two countries should co-operate in case of war. These conversations were kept secret even from the Cabinet until the Agadir crisis of 1911, and were not revealed to Parliament until Sir Edward Grey's eve-of-the-war speech on August 3, 1914.

In this speech Sir Edward explained that he had told the French that in his view public opinion would have supported the British Government in standing by France in case of war over Morocco in 1905. Thereupon the French Government had suggested conversations between naval and military experts, so as to make it possible for Great Britain to act on her intention if, on an emergency arising, she did decide to give France the armed support which she could not promise in advance.

Sir Edward authorized these conversations:

> On the distinct understanding that nothing which passed between military or naval experts should bind either Government or restrict in any way their freedom to make a decision as to whether or not they would give that support when the time arose.[34]

There was a general election in prospect, so that there was no opportunity, Sir Edward Grey explained, for bringing the matter before the Cabinet. But Sir Henry Campbell-Bannerman, the Prime Minister, Lord Haldane, who was then Secretary of State for War, and Mr. Asquith, then Chancellor of the Exchequer, were consulted. They authorized the conversations on the distinct understanding that they "left the hands of the Government free whenever the crisis arose."

In 1912, after the Agadir crisis, the matter was discussed in the Cabinet, which decided that there should be a definite understanding in writing that these conversations "were not binding upon the freedom of either Government."

Accordingly on November 22, 1912, Sir Edward Grey wrote a letter to the French Ambassador, and received a reply in similar terms, in order to make clear that:

> Whatever took place between military and naval experts, they were not binding engagements upon the Government.

Sir Edward then read the letter to the House of Commons:

> My dear Ambassador, From time to time in recent years the French and British naval and military experts have consulted together. It has always been understood that such consultation does not restrict the freedom of either Government to decide at any future time whether or not to assist the other by armed force. We have agreed that consultation between experts is not and ought not to be regarded as an engagement that commits either Government to action in a contingency that has not arisen and may never arise. The

disposition, for instance, of the French and British Fleets respectively at the present moment is not based upon an engagement to co-operate in war.

You have, however, pointed out that, if either Government had grave reason to expect an unprovoked attack by a third Power, it might become essential to know whether it could in that event depend upon the armed assistance of the other.

I agree that, if either Government had grave reason to expect an unprovoked attack by a third Power, or something that threatened the general peace, it should immediately discuss with the other whether both Governments should act together to prevent aggression and to preserve peace, and, if so, what measures they would be prepared to take in common.[35]

It will be observed that in Sir Edward Grey's mind these "conversations" left Great Britain entirely free and uncommitted. Mr. Asquith takes an even more robustly "non-committal" view, and in his *Genesis of the War* asserts that "there were neither military nor naval compacts." [36]

That, however, was not the view of most of the Cabinet. Mr. Lloyd George complains in his *War Memoirs* that "there was in the Cabinet an air of 'hush-hush' about allusions to our relations with France, Russia and Germany." All information, he says, was carefully filtered and much essential information was "deliberately withheld." It was delicately conveyed to the Cabinet that foreign affairs were too august a subject altogether for common discussion.

There is no more conspicuous example of this kind of suppression of vital information than the way in which the military arrangements we entered into with France were kept from the Cabinet for six years. . . . When in 1912 (six years after they had been entered into) Sir Edward Grey communicated these negotiations and arrangements to the Cabinet the majority of its Members were aghast. Hostility barely represents the strength of the sentiment which the revelation aroused: it was more akin to consternation.

Grey and Asquith "allayed the apprehension" of their colleagues "to some extent" by "emphatic assurances that these military arrangements left us quite free, in the event of war, to decide whether we should or should not participate in the conflict."
On the other hand:

There is abundant evidence that both the French and the Russians regarded these military arrangements as practically tantamount to a commitment on our part to come to the aid of France in the event of her being attacked by Germany. When the British Government was hesitating at the end of July, 1914, as to whether it would support France in the event of a German attack, French statesmen almost reverted to the "Perfidious Albion" mood, and even the meek M. Paul Cambon * said that the only question was whether the word "honour" was to be expunged from the British dictionary. On the whole, the view summarised in that pungent comment is the one I heard expressed by most supporters and opponents of our intervention in the Great War; and yet the Cabinet were never informed of these vital arrangements until we were so deeply involved in the details of military and naval plans that it was too late to repudiate the inference.[37]

The Franco-Russian view was shared by Sir Henry Campbell-Bannerman and Mr. Churchill. When the conversations were initiated Campbell-Bannerman put it on record that:

I do not like the stress laid on joint preparations. It comes very close to an honourable undertaking, and it will be known on both sides of the Rhine. But let us hope for the best.

Mr. Churchill took the same view:

This was a step of profound significance and of far-reaching reactions. Henceforward the relations of the two staffs became increasingly intimate and confidential. The minds of our military men were definitely turned into a particular channel. Mutual trust grew continually in one set of military relationships, mutual precautions in the other. However ex-
* French Ambassador to the Court of St. James's.

plicitly the two Governments might agree and affirm to each other that no national or political engagement was involved in these technical discussions, the fact remained that they constituted an exceedingly potent tie.[38]

To judge of the truth of Mr. Churchill's remark, it should be realized that "conversations" between general staffs mean that the mobilization and strategical plans of the countries concerned are co-ordinated and worked into a single plan. All general staffs must always be making plans against the contingency of war—that is part of their job—and the "conversations" meant that the British and French military authorities were drafting joint plans against the contingency of war with Germany. This meant very real commitments and pledges. For instance, Lord Haldane observes in *Before the War* that upon becoming War Minister he completely revolutionized the organization of the British Army, with the result that after three years' work it became

practicable quickly to mobilise not only 100,000 but 160,000 men; to transport them, with the aid of the Navy, to a place of concentration which had been settled between the Staffs of France and Britain; and to have them at their appointed place within twelve days, an interval based on what the German Army required, on its side, for a corresponding concentration.[39]

Lord Esher records a conversation with Mr. Asquith in October 1911:

I reminded him that the mere fact of the War Office plan having been worked out in detail with the French General Staff (which is the case) has certainly committed us to fight, whether the Cabinet likes it or not. . . . It is certainly an extraordinary thing that our officers should have been permitted to arrange all the details, trains, landing, concentration, etc., when the Cabinet have never been consulted.[40]

The naval conversations resulted in an agreement by which the British Navy was concentrated in the North Sea and the French in the Mediterranean. On this Mr. Churchill comments:

Consider how tremendous would be the weapon which France would possess to compel our intervention if she could say, "On the advice of and by arrangement with your naval authorities we have left our northern coasts defenceless. We cannot possibly come back in time." Indeed it would probably be decisive, whatever is written down now. Everybody must feel, who knows the facts, that we have the obligations of an alliance without its advantages, and above all without its precise definition.[41]

Mr. J. L. Hammond, in an article in the *Manchester Guardian* of May 6, 1938, on Vol. X, Part II of Gooch and Temperley's *British Documents on the Origin of the War*, says that the documents on the discussion of Anglo-French relations after the conclusion of the naval convention

show how serious were the difficulties of the British Government, obliged to refuse to commit Parliament and yet compelled to recognise that the re-distribution of the fleets involved large political consequences. So far as England and France were concerned the problem was resolved by the exchange of the Notes that were read to the House of Commons by Grey on the eve of the war, Notes that satisfied the French that they would not be left in the lurch and satisfied the British Cabinet that its hands were free.

These facts show the truth of Isvolski's remark:

The Anglo-French military convention has a character as complete and finished as the Franco-Russian convention.

But the latter had been framed to implement the Franco-Russian alliance. The former, in fact, implied that the Entente was the equivalent of an alliance.

The French and the Russians had a naval convention, as had the British and the French. The Russians from the autumn of 1912 began to press for a similar naval convention with Great Britain. Sir Edward Grey agreed when approached by the French Government, but said it would be difficult to get members of the government party and certain members of the Cabinet to agree, owing to their prejudice against Czarist Russia. The first step was

to communicate the text of the arrangements already entered into
with France, together with the 1912 letter referred to above, formally reserving liberty of action for the British Government. The
Russians were asked whether they would like to enter into a similar arrangement, and said yes. "Conversations" began between
the two Admiralties. They were not reported by Sir Edward
Grey to the Cabinet.

The Russians from the outset regarded the naval convention as
"an important step towards bringing England into closer union
with the Franco-Russian alliance" and as "possessing great political significance." These were the phrases by Sazonov, the Russian Foreign Minister, in a despatch to his Minister in London.
The latter (Benckendorff) in writing to his Government observed:

> After the results which have just been described [the
> naval agreement] shall have been achieved, we, as I believe,
> shall have attained the main object in view, namely, to sub-
> stitute for the hitherto far too theoretical and pacific basic
> idea of the Entente something more tangible.

He goes on to say that he is convinced that a formal alliance is
impossible; but "I doubt whether a more powerful guarantee for
common military operations could be found, in the event of war,
than this spirit of the Entente, as it reveals itself at present, reinforced by the existent military conventions." [42]

In power politics there is no clear dividing line between "defence" and "foreign policy," for defence means war or the threat
of war to back the aims pursued or claims asserted in one's foreign policy. For this reason it was impossible to conclude military
and naval arrangements of this sort without repercussions on the
political relations of the states involved. It meant that Britain was
committed, for the sake of the balance of power, to backing
France and Russia in their dealings with the central powers
whatever the merits of the dispute and without any corresponding control over their foreign policy.

This becomes clear in the discussion below on the final crisis.
What is interesting at this point is to see how the British Govern-

ment dealt with Parliament and public opinion on the matter of these agreements.

In the House of Commons on March 10, 1913, Lord Hugh Cecil, in the debate on the Address, said:

> The Right Hon. gentlemen and his colleagues are generally believed—I speak with the utmost diffidence in regard to allegations which may not be well founded—to have entered into an arrangement, or, to speak more accurately, to have given assurances, which in the contingency of a great European war would involve heavy military obligations on this country. . . .
>
> There is a very general belief that this country is under an obligation, not a treaty obligation, but an obligation arising owing to an assurance given by the Ministry in the course of diplomatic negotiations, to send a very large armed force out of this country to operate in Europe. This is the general belief. It would be very presumptuous of anyone who has not access to all the facts in the possession of the Government . . .
>
> The Prime Minister: I ought to say that it is not true.
>
> Lord H. Cecil: I am very glad to have elicited that explanation.[43]

On March 24, 1913, Sir William Byles asked the Prime Minister:

> **Whether he will say if this country is under any,** and, if so, what obligation to France to send an armed force in certain contingencies to operate in Europe; and if so, what are the limits of our agreements, whether by assurance or treaty, with the French nation.

On the same day Mr. King asked the Prime Minister:

> (1) Whether the foreign policy of this country is at the present time unhampered by any treaties, agreements, or obligations under which British military forces would, in certain eventualities, be called upon to be landed on the Continent and join there in military operations; and (2) whether, in 1905, 1908, or 1911, this country spontaneously offered to France the assistance of the British army, to be landed on the Continent to support France in the event of European hostilities?

The Prime Minister:

As has been repeatedly stated, this country is not under any obligation not public and known to Parliament which compels it to take part in any war. In other words, if war arises between European Powers there are no unpublished agreements which will restrict or hamper the freedom of the Government or of Parliament to decide whether or not Great Britain should participate in a war.

On April 28, 1914, Mr. King asked the Secretary of State for Foreign Affairs:

. . . whether the policy of this country still remains one of freedom from all obligations to engage in military operations on the Continent?

Sir Edward Grey said the position remained the same as stated by the Prime Minister on March 24, 1913.

On June 11, 1914, Mr. King asked the Secretary of State for Foreign Affairs:

. . . whether any naval agreement had been recently entered into between Russia and Great Britain; and whether any negotiations with a view to a naval agreement have recently taken place or are now taking place between Russia and Great Britain?

Sir William Byles asked the Secretary of State for Foreign Affairs:

. . . whether he can make any statement with regard to an alleged naval agreement between Great Britain and Russia; how far such an agreement would affect our relations with Germany; and will he lay the papers?

Sir Edward Grey:

The hon. member for North Somerset asked a similar question last year with regard to military forces, and the hon. member for North Salford asked a similar question also on the same day, as he has done again today. The Prime Minister then replied that, if war arose between European Powers,

there were no unpublished agreements which would restrict
or hamper the freedom of the Government or of Parliament
to decide whether or not Great Britain should participate in
a war. The answer covers both the questions on the Paper.
It remains as true today as it was a year ago. No negotiations
have since been concluded with any Power that would
make the statement less true. No such negotiations are in
progress, and none are likely to be entered upon so far as I
can judge.

If Mr. Asquith and Sir Edward Grey had been witnesses in a
court, giving testimony under oath, they would both have been
liable to prosecution for perjury for replying as they did to these
questions.

At the same time that public opinion was being deliberately
misled Sir Edward Grey was being pressed by the Germans to
state whether or not he was negotiating a naval convention with
Russia.

After Sir Edward's denial in the House, quoted above, the
German Chancellor wrote to his Ambassador in London that the
British Minister's "denial of a naval convention is very gratify-
ing," for had the rumours been true, the result would have been
disastrous encouragement to Russian and French and therefore
German chauvinism.

Thereupon the German Ambassador, Lichnowsky, visited Sir
Edward Grey and thanked him "for the frank and honest statement he had made in the Lower House disavowing the rumours
of an alleged Anglo-Russian convention."

Sir Edward, the German Ambassador reported, took cognizance
of these remarks with "visible pleasure" and assured him "that
there existed no agreement between Great Britain and her Entente
companions that had not been made public."

Unfortunately, however, at that time Siebert, a gentleman employed in the Russian Embassy in London, was a spy in the pay
of the German Government and was sending copies of all despatches to Berlin. Therefore the Germans knew of the Anglo-
Russian naval conversations. Consequently the German Foreign
Secretary wrote to Herr Ballin, a big shipowner with friends in

England, to say that after looking into the matter he had come to the conclusion, "to my most intense regret," that there was probably more behind the report of a naval agreement than "the good Lichnowski is willing to believe."

There is actually in negotiation between London and Petersburg a naval convention by which . . . on the part of Russia very broad military and naval co-operation is being sought.

The convention was not yet concluded, and in fact Grey had "become a little dilatory." The Russians, on the other hand, are urgent. Grey will probably not oppose the conclusion of the compact in the end, if he does not meet with opposition from his own party or the Cabinet.

Like a Pilate, he may be able to persuade himself that the transactions are not really being conducted between the two Cabinets, but between the naval authorities. I will admit that it is an open question whether the English will not act with their unique casuistry and conclude the agreement with a mental reservation not to intervene at the critical moment if it should not suit them to do so, as a *casus foederis* is intentionally not provided in the convention. But even if the convention should hang indecisively in the air, it would nevertheless have the result of materially encouraging Russia's aggressive tendencies.[44]

Ballin then proceeded to London and "sounded" Lord Haldane and Sir Edward Grey at a dinner. He asked whether there was any truth in the rumours of an Anglo-Russian naval negotiation, and was told by Sir Edward Grey that no naval convention existed and "it was not England's intention to agree to any such convention."

Technically, no doubt, the result of the conversations between the British and Russian Admiralties was embodied in an agreement that did not have the diplomatic status of a convention. But it is doubtful whether Sir Edward would have escaped conviction for perjury if this matter had come before a court of law, and the incident was naturally not calculated to promote confidence between the British and German governments.

But it is hardly necessary to point out that the standard of truthfulness was no higher in German diplomacy than in the British. Both diplomacies employed the methods of power politics and were not so much immoral as "non-moral."

ANGLO-GERMAN RELATIONS

After each crisis there were spasmodic attempts to negotiate an Anglo-German agreement. Under the growing pressure of finance and monopoly capital the German Government was becoming more and more insistent upon a "place in the sun"—that is, on colonies, markets, and fields for investment. Germany was generally thwarted by one or other of the powers of the Entente, but had by the most obstinate tenacity succeeded in acquiring some pieces of territory in both East and West Africa, generally after quarrels that involved threats of war.

In 1913–14 negotiations with the British Government resulted in two agreements. The first was a revival of an old project going back to 1898 for a partition of Portugal's colonies between Germany and Great Britain. Portugal, it should be remembered, is Great Britain's "oldest ally," and the British Government had guaranteed Portugal's territory. The Anglo-German agreement therefore provided that the British guarantee to Portugal should not be operative if the colonies should separate from the mother country, and contained an understanding that if Portugal's misgovernment should lead to the intervention of another power, Great Britain would not interfere.

The stage was therefore set for engineering an "independence" movement in Portugal's colonies or for complaining on humanitarian grounds of the ill-treatment of the natives, or both, in order to give Germany a pretext to take over the colonies. Portugal, needless to say, was not consulted when these arrangements were made and would presumably have been disagreeably surprised at such treatment from her old ally and protector.*

* Indeed, the arrangement seems to have caused twinges of conscience even in its authors. Mr. J. L. Hammond, in an article in the *Manchester Guardian* of May 6, 1938, reviewing Vol. X, Part II of Gooch and Temper-

The second agreement gave British assent to Germany's Baghdad railway project, which had been hanging fire for many years owing to the stubborn opposition of British, French, and Russian vested interests and power politicians.

Thus Anglo-German imperialist rivalry was on the way to settlement at the expense of third parties. But there was still a trade rivalry, for although the British and German peoples were each other's best customers, the chief capitalist interests of the two countries were competitors.

The Austro-Serbian antagonism and behind that the imperialist rivalry between Russia and Germany in the Balkans were still left, as was the tension between France and Germany because of Alsace-Lorraine and French apprehensions about German colonial

---

ley's *British Documents on the Origin of the War,* describes this episode as follows: "In 1898 Salisbury's Government had signed a secret treaty with Germany about the Portuguese colonies. Portugal was in great financial difficulty, and it was believed that she might borrow from France and thereby incur obligations to her. Germany suggested to England that the two countries should agree that they would only lend money to Portugal jointly and that the colonies should be pledged as security. They also divided up the colonies into spheres of influence between England and Germany. The whole scheme depended on Portugal's financial collapse. Salisbury disliked the treaty and was persuaded by Soveral, the Portuguese Ambassador, to reassure Portugal by renewing the old guarantee against attack. Thus England was at once pledged to Portugal to protect Portuguese territory and to Germany to act with her if Portugal needed financial help. It was an ambiguous position, and it is not surprising that Salisbury was uncomfortable about it—the agreement, which was mainly the work of Chamberlain, was concluded and signed in his absence—or that when the Germans wanted to revert to it in 1912 Grey found himself in an embarrassing position."

Grey tried to get out of it by insisting that the agreements when concluded should be published. To this Germany at first demurred, and then agreed to publication in the autumn of 1914.

Mr. Laski, reviewing the same book in the *New Statesman and Nation* of May 21, 1938, puts the whole thing less blandly and more pithily than Mr. Hammond: "Out of an entirely dishonourable secret treaty for which the Salisbury Government in 1898 was responsible, we find Grey struggling to dispose of property that is not his, while he keeps to the strict letter of the Anglo-Portuguese alliance. It was not, of course, a possible adventure; and the picture that emerges of the double-dealer trying to maintain all the habits of a gentleman deserves description from the pen of a Swift."

ambitions. As Great Britain belonged to the same camp as France and Russia on balance-of-power grounds, a partial Anglo-German settlement could only slightly relieve the situation.

Finally, there was the friction arising out of the arms race, which in the end became the greatest single cause of the war.

The negotiations between Great Britain and Germany in 1909 and 1912 were directed to securing a naval agreement regulating the relative sizes and pace of building of the two fleets. At the same time, there was an attempt to reach a political agreement. The German Government's view was that the latter should come first, whereas the British Government wished to begin with the naval question.

The Germans had their way over putting the political agreement first, and both in 1909 and 1912 suggested a formula by which if they were involved in war Great Britain would undertake to be neutral.

The British Government proposed a formula undertaking not to make any "unprovoked attack" on Germany. As a concession Germany proposed to qualify the undertaking to be neutral by saying it should apply to a war in which the other party to the agreement "cannot be said to be the aggressor."

All these formulae were almost meaningless. For each of the contracting parties was to be sole judge of what was meant by "unprovoked attack" or "aggression," and there was not even a definition of what these terms implied. Nevertheless, agreement could not be reached, for each distrusted the intentions of the other. Britain thought the German Government was reserving a free hand to fight France or Russia while binding the British to be neutral, whereas in the German view the British formula meant Britain might join the Entente in making war upon Germany. As "defence" in the conditions of international anarchy means using war as an instrument of national policy, it is as a rule impossible to distinguish it from aggression.* Therefore both sides were justified in entertaining the suspicions they did.

* The rule applies primarily to war between great powers, not to war between a strong and a weak state.

THE ARMS MANUFACTURERS AND THE DYING PEACE

What finally broke up the negotiations was the victory of Admiral von Tirpitz over the German Chancellor. As a result of the humiliation suffered by Germany in 1911 over Agadir, Von Tirpitz brought in a new naval law. This was also the outcome of the nation-wide propaganda carried out by various colonial societies, navy leagues, etc., in the pay of the German arms industry and big business generally.

Mr. Noel Baker produces conclusive evidence, in his book *The Private Manufacture of Armaments*, for the view that the propaganda of the arms interests in Germany and in Great Britain (the Mulliner scandal) created an atmosphere which ensured the failure of the attempts to negotiate a naval holiday. He quotes Mr. Churchill's statement that a naval holiday might have changed the history of the world—that is, might have prevented World War I—and his prophetic remark at the time of the breakdown of the naval negotiations in 1912 that the continuation of the arms race would lead "to war within the next two years." The German Emperor, too, became resigned to war. Bishop Boyd Carpenter, after visiting him in 1913, wrote: "He was quite cordial but he spoke with a note which was new to me. He seemed apprehensive. . . . I felt that he was under the influence of a great fear." The same year the French Ambassador in Berlin wrote that the Emperor had "ceased to be a friend of peace because he had come to think the war with France was inevitable" and was "becoming accustomed to an order of ideas which were formerly repugnant to him." These were the effects of the arms race.

The table on page 108, prepared by Mr. P. Jacobson, formerly of the Financial Section of the League of Nations Secretariat, later of the British Information Service, for the *Economist* in 1929, shows the character and intensity of the pre-war competition in armaments.

This table shows that the great powers were spending five times as much on armaments in 1913 as they did in 1858 (and, it may be added, about six times as much in 1938 as they did in 1913). During the five years before World War I the rate of in-

crease accelerated and the armaments expenditure of Europe rose
by more than 50 per cent. About five-sixths of this expenditure
was incurred by the great powers.

DEFENCE EXPENDITURE IN £'S (MILLIONS) *

	1858	1883	1908	1913
Great Britain	23	28	59	77
France	19	31	44	82
Germany	5	20	59	100
Italy	2	12	18	29
Austria-Hungary . . .	11	13	21	24
Russia	19	36	60	92
Total, great powers . . .	79	140	261	404
Total, other states . . .	16	23	38	82
Grand total	95	163	299	486
Average price level (1913 = 100) .	110	95	90	100
European population in millions .	278	335	436	452

* *Economist*, Armaments Supplement, October 19, 1929

Between 1909 and World War I the cost of British armaments
increased by more than 30 per cent; of Russian armaments by
53 per cent; of German by 69 per cent; and of French armaments
by 86 per cent.

The money for these armaments was found in France, Great
Britain, and Germany through taxation, in Austria-Hungary
partly by loans, and in Russia chiefly by foreign loans. Dr. Paul
Einzig's *The Economics of Rearmament* shows what an important part the arms industry and the financing of the arms race
played in the economic life of the great powers before World
War I (and since the great slump of 1929–33).

By 1913 Germany was feeling the strain so much that she had
to raise a fifty-million-pound capital levy, while Russia was
drawing on a special war fund. The number of men under arms
was increased rapidly. Between 1899 and 1914 the combined
standing armies of France and Russia rose from 1,470,000 to
2,239,000. The corresponding increase for Germany and Austria-
Hungary was from 950,000 to 1,239,000.

In the last twelve months before the war the pace grew hotter. Germany increased her standing army by 170,000 men; Russia increased her annual contingent of recruits by 135,000 and lengthened the period of service by six months; France restored the three years' military service law.

The Russian Ambassador in Berlin, writing in March 1913 of the latest measures for increasing the arms of France, Germany, and Russia, comments:

> The question arises what will be the position of Europe, armed from head to foot in an armour of steel and groaning under the unsupportable burden of military taxation? The tension, it would appear, will become such that at length war will become inevitable.

Mr. Noel Baker, in Part III of Vol. I of his book *The Private Manufacture of Armaments*, entitled "Private Manufacture as a Factor in the Historical Process from Which War Results," gives abundant and really horrifying evidence of the baneful influence of the arms industry in poisoning the international atmosphere and thwarting all attempts at an Anglo-German naval agreement.

The German historian Dr. Eckert Kehr has made a careful study of the growth of "navalism" in Germany before the last war. The American historian Mr. Charles Beard has summarized this work, and is quoted by Mr. Noel Baker:

> Dr. Kehr opens with an introduction on the evolution of opinion respecting naval imperialism from 1867 to 1894, tracing the intimate relationship between the two aspects of the same thing—navy and imperialism. Then he gives a minute survey of the rise and development of the conflict in Germany over big navalism—a survey sketched in meticulous detail, with data on profit-makers, prices of steel and ship-yard stocks, intrigues, newspapers, journalists, officials, millionaires, propagandists and politicians, all set down with frosty precision. This is followed by a calm analysis of the "opinions" of parties, classes and orders of state on imperialism and the sea power.[45]

The interested classes were "aligned," in Mr. Beard's phrase, as follows:

> It was not difficult, of course, to enrol powder manufacturers, coalowners, armour-plate makers and shipbuilders. For them patriotism was clearly a paying proposition. If any of them had any doubts on the point, they were quickly reassured when they saw the stocks of pertinent industries shoot upward in a bull market as soon as the first great grant of money to the navy had been voted. And after the building had begun and plants had been extended to meet additional requirements, gentlemen of this order thought the navy should be still bigger. Otherwise their enlarged establishments would be partly idle, and, as they pitifully urged, their working men would be unemployed.[46]

But other capitalists had to be brought in by judicious propaganda by the Navy League and the Colonial Society:

> If a big industrialist helped to finance a Navy League intellectual for a speaking tour before local chambers of commerce, it looked better and gave an air of disinterestedness to the operations of a patriotism founded on *Rentabilität*. Capitalists gathered under the auspices of the Navy League did not seem to be so capitalistic. For example, when the League gave a great naval dinner in Hamburg and assembled a goodly company containing twenty millionaires, it spread the mantle of idealism over an enterprise that served the country, God and the Kaiser (and the profit-makers).[47]

Further details are given of the growth and activities of the German Navy League, the subsidizing of part of the press by German heavy industry for imperialist and naval propaganda, etc. These were the forces that gave Admiral von Tirpitz his power to wreck the sincere attempts of the German Chancellor to reach agreement with England for a naval holiday.

As for Great Britain, Mr. Noel Baker devotes several chapters to proving in minute detail how:

> . . . a British Private Manufacturer of Arms, Mr. Mulliner, the Managing Director of the Coventry Ordnance Works,

succeeded in starting a colossal anti-German campaign. This campaign was carried on over a long period of months; it was sponsored by the official [Conservative] Opposition in Parliament itself; it was venomously fomented by important papers. The campaign was accompanied by "scare" tactics of every kind—plays in London theatres, novels and stories in magazines—all on the theme of Germany's plans for a sudden murderous invasion of the British Isles. This campaign was conducted in a spirit of suspicion and hostility, which not even the German agitators could excel. It was all founded on certain "information" which the Private Manufacturers claimed to have found out about German Dreadnought building—information which in itself was at least inadequate, if not wholly false, and on which were built interpretations so fantastic that in the light of history they seemed utterly grotesque.[48]

The indirect importance must not be underestimated of the arms race and war propaganda in staving off unemployment and creating a temper in the masses conducive to the perpetuation of the rule of the plutocracy. In the words of Wingfield-Stratford:

If the war peril from Germany delayed much longer to materialise, it seemed quite on the cards that it might be forestalled by revolution. As the Edwardian passes into the Georgian age . . . class rises against class . . . faction against faction—it is a question whether international will not be anticipated by civil war.[49]

The growth in armaments had two direct effects. One was to increase the pressure on the governments at every crisis. The more elaborate the preparations for war, the greater the weight of the vast military apparatus in every international negotiation.

For instance, the minutes of the meetings of the French and Russian military staffs between 1911 and 1913 show that the military chiefs neither anticipated defeat nor feared a conflict; that they made elaborate plans for immediate and simultaneous mobilization in both countries in case of a mobilization of the German Army; that mobilization in their view was tantamount to war because it compelled similar measures on both sides; that their strategical plans were for an offensive military campaign; that in the case of war "in twelve days the French Army will be ready to take the offensive against Germany with the British Army on its left wing"; and finally that Russia would not be able to wage war against Germany "with the certainty of success" before two years—*i.e.*, before 1913–15.

Lowes Dickinson shows in his book how the Austrian Chief of Staff, Conrad, urged war in every one of the international crises in the Balkans, and how Von Moltke, the German Chief of Staff, became convinced that war was inevitable in the near future, and how this belief influenced his action in the final crisis of 1914.

Mr. Lloyd George writes in his *War Memoirs* that the Germans believed their Army was invincible.

> The French Army, on the other hand, were equally con- fident of their powers. . . . There never was a time since 1870 when the French Army had less fear of its great rival. The Russians had improved their Army in equipment and or- ganisation since their defeat in Manchuria. They felt infinitely superior to the Austrian Army, and deemed themselves quite a match for what was left of the German Army, after the better half of it had marched to the West. Generals in this frame of mind hungered for war and had no difficulty in manoeuvring statesmen who did not know their own minds into positions where war became inevitable. Thus great armaments made war.[50]

The second direct effect of the arms race was to create a mood of fatalism in the peoples and governments. They felt themselves in the grip of vast blind forces beyond their control, hurrying them towards a catastrophe they could not avert. The govern- ments were like men struggling helplessly in a nightmare.

In 1912 Sir Edward Grey made a speech that contained a solemn warning:

> If this tremendous expenditure on armaments goes on it must, in the long run, break down civilisation. You are hav- ing this great burden of force piled up in times of peace, and if it goes on increasing by leaps and bounds as it has done in

the last generation, in time it will become intolerable. There are those who think it will lead to war, precisely because it is becoming intolerable. I think it is much more likely the burden will be dissipated by internal revolution—not by nations fighting against each other, but by the revolt of masses of men against taxation. . . . The great nations of the world are in bondage to their armies and navies at the present moment—increasing bondage.

After the war Sir Edward Grey drew the moral in his book *Twenty-five Years,* in the following terms:

> The moral is obvious; it is that great armaments lead inevitably to war. If there are armaments on one side, there must be armaments on the other sides. . . .
> The increase of armaments, that is intended in each nation to produce consciousness of strength, and a sense of security, does not produce these effects. On the contrary, it produces a consciousness of the strength of other nations and a sense of fear. Fear begets suspicion and distrust and evil imaginings of all sorts. . . . The enormous growth of armaments in Europe, the sense of insecurity and fear caused by them—it was these that made war inevitable. This, it seems to me, is the truest reading of history, and the lesson that the present should be learning from the past in the interests of future peace, the warning to be handed on to those who come after us.[51]

THE FINAL CRISIS

During the year 1913–14 Russian diplomacy was active in the Balkans, binding Serbia, Greece, and Rumania into a new alliance hostile to Austria.

Lowes Dickinson quotes an interesting conversation in February 1914 between the Serbian Minister Pašić and the Czar of Russia, in which both spoke with the utmost frankness of the necessity for military and political preparations for the "solution of the Serbo-Croatian question"—that is, for the break-up of the Austrian Empire.

The Austrians were aware of what was going on. In a memorandum addressed to the German Kaiser in the summer of 1914 the Austrian Government drew a picture of the situation which tallied closely with the Serbo-Russian account, but from the opposite point of view. It urged Germany to realize that Russian policy and military preparations were as inimical to German interests as they were to those of Austria.

By a dramatic coincidence this memorandum had just been completed when on June 28 the Austrian heir to the throne, the Archduke Ferdinand, was murdered at Sarajevo. The assassins were Austrian subjects, but Serbs.

A postscript to the memorandum concludes thus:

> The above memorial had just been finished, when the awful deed of Serajevo occurred. The entire possible consequences of this foul murder cannot at present be estimated. It serves, however, to prove the impossibility of bridging over the opposition between the Monarchy and Serbia, as well as the danger and intensity of the greater Serbian movement, a movement that will stop at nothing. Austria-Hungary has never been lacking in good will and accommodating spirit in order to bring about endurable relations to Serbia. But it has been proved by recent events that all these efforts have been in vain, and that the Monarchy, in the future as in the past, will have to reckon with the obdurate, uncompromising, aggressive antagonism of Serbia. All the more is the Monarchy faced with the imperious necessity to break with a strong hand the threads that her foes are trying to weave into a net about her head.

In a personal letter accompanying the memorandum the aged Emperor Francis Joseph told the Kaiser:

> The outrage upon my nephew is the direct consequence of the agitation carried on by the Russian and Serbian pan-Slavists, whose only aim is the weakening of the Triple Alliance and the breaking up of my Empire. According to all inquiries hitherto made the Serajevo murder was not the bloody deed of a single individual, but a well organized plot, the threads of which can be traced to Belgrade; and even if, as seems likely, it should be impossible to prove the com-

plicity of the Serbian Government, there yet can be no doubt
that its policy, aiming at a union of all the South Slavs under
the Serbian flag, encourages such crimes as these, and that
the continuation of this state of affairs forms a lasting danger
to my dynasty and my countries.[52]

The Austrian Cabinet decided to send Serbia an ultimatum
couched in terms which would certainly be unacceptable, with
the object of thereupon declaring a punitive war. It further decided that the object of that war should be to diminish Serbian
territory, not by annexation, but by distributing it to Serbia's
neighbours. Count von Berchtold (the Austrian Prime Minister),
says a Hungarian Minister (Sándorz Hoyos),

was not an unconditional supporter of immediate war
against Serbia, any more than was the Emperor Francis
Joseph. What he wanted to avoid was new tension in the
international situation caused by a threat on our part, as had
happened in 1908 and 1912, which, nevertheless, should not
result in a final settlement of the Serbian question. We could
not endure any longer the continual unrest caused by our
Serbian neighbor. The repeated mobilizations of our reserves
threatened to undermine discipline in the Army, trade and
industry stood still, and it seemed to all parties, at that moment, that war was preferable to preparedness for another
six years.[53]

The Austrian Government knew that this policy would involve
a grave risk of war by Russia, but felt that the provocation was
so severe and the menace to Austria's very existence as a great
power so urgent that it must take that risk.

It appealed for German support in "localizing" the conflict—
that is, in threatening Russia with war if she did not let Austria
have her way with Serbia.

So long as she believed that Great Britain would stay out,
Germany encouraged Austria to go ahead. Later, when she
found Great Britain would fight, the German Government turned
round and put pressure on Austria to be conciliatory. But by that
time the Austrians had gone too far and mobilization cut short

the efforts of the diplomats. It is instructive to follow in some
detail just how the nations, in Mr. Lloyd George's phrase, "glided
or rather staggered and stumbled into the war."

Germany's motives in giving Austria a free hand were set forth
in a long despatch from the German Foreign Secretary to his
Ambassador in London, from which the following passages may
be quoted:

> Austria, which has forfeited more and more prestige as
> the result of her lack of vigor, hardly counts any longer a
> really Great Power. The Balkan crisis weakened her posi-
> tion still further. Our group of allies has also been weakened
> by this retrogression of Austria's position as a Power.
>
> Austria no longer intends to tolerate the sapping activities
> of the Serbians, and just as little does she intend to tolerate
> longer the continuously provocative attitude of the small
> neighbor at Belgrade. . . . Austria is now going to come to a
> reckoning with Serbia, and had told us so.[54]

Germany had not urged Austria to take this course, but neither
could she attempt to stay Austria's hand:

> If we should do that, Austria would have the right to
> reproach us (and we ourselves) with having deprived her
> of her last chance of political rehabilitation. And then the
> process of her wasting away and of her internal decay would
> be still further accelerated. Her standing in the Balkans
> would be gone forever. You will undoubtedly agree with
> me that the absolute establishment of Russian hegemony in
> the Balkans is, indirectly, not permissible, even for us. The
> maintenance of Austria, and, in fact, of the most powerful
> Austria possible, is a necessity for us both for internal and
> external reasons. That she cannot be maintained forever, I
> willingly admit. But in the meantime we may perhaps be
> able to arrange other combinations.
>
> We must attempt to localize the conflict between Austria
> and Serbia. Whether we shall succeed in this will depend
> first on Russia, and secondly on the moderating influence of
> Russia's allies. The more determined Austria shows herself,
> the more energetically we support her, so much the more

quiet will Russia remain. To be sure, there will be some agitation in Petersburg, but, on the whole, Russia is not ready to strike at present. Nor will France or England be anxious for war at the present time. According to all competent observation, Russia will be prepared to fight in a few years. Then she will crush us by the number of her soldiers; then she will have built her Baltic Sea fleet and her strategic railroads. Our group, in the meantime, will have become weaker right along. In Russia this is well known, and they are therefore determined to have peace for a few years yet. . . .

If we cannot attain localization [of the conflict] and Russia attacks Austria, a casus foederis will then arise; we could not throw Austria over then. We stand in the midst of an isolation that can scarcely be called "proud." I desire no preventive war, but if war should come we cannot hide behind the fence.

I still hope and believe, even today, that the conflict can be localized. In this matter the attitude of England will prove of great significance. . . .

Sir [Edward] Grey is always talking of the balance of power represented by the two groups of Powers. It should, therefore, be perfectly obvious to him that this balance of power . . . would be made to totter considerably by a world conflagration. Therefore, if he is honorable and logical, he must stand by us in attempting to localize the conflict.[55]

The Russians accepted the various proposals made by France and Great Britain for a peaceful settlement and made one or two on their own account. They put strong pressure on the Serbs to return a very conciliatory reply to the Austrian ultimatum. At the same time they made it clear that they would back Serbia if she were attacked by Austria.

M. Poincaré, the French President, had made two remarks in the beginning of 1914 which are quoted by Dickinson:

In two years the war will take place. All my efforts will be devoted to preparing for it.

Whatever be the issue, small or great, which may arise in the future between Russia and Germany, it will not pass by like the last. It will be war.[56]

The Austrians had carefully timed their ultimatum, so that the news reached St. Petersburg and Paris when M. Poincaré was on a French cruiser half-way between Russia and France. One of the first things he did on his return was to propose an international inquiry into Austrian grievances against Serbia. A similar proposal had been made by the Russian Foreign Minister. In general, French policy was to make it perfectly clear that in case of war France would stand by Russia but would support all British attempts to find a peaceful solution.

Sir Edward Grey was at first inclined to take an optimistic view. The German Ambassador records a conversation on July 6, when he spoke of Russian hostility to Germany. Sir Edward said he had no knowledge of any such feeling and also denied the existence of a naval agreement between Great Britain and Russia. He said he had been trying to persuade the Russians to be peaceful and conciliatory towards Austria and that much depended on the Austrians' not taking measures that would arouse Slav sentiment. In general, says the German Ambassador, Sir Edward Grey:

> . . . was in a thoroughly confident mood, and declared, in cheerful tones, that he saw no reason for taking a pessimistic view of the situation.

The moment the Austrian ultimatum on July 23 made it clear that the situation was desperately serious, Sir Edward Grey strained every nerve to prevent war. He tried plan after plan to keep the peace of Europe. He supported the Russian proposal for an extension of the two days' time-limit laid down in the ultimatum. He proposed a conference of the powers, and failing that, joint Anglo-German mediation between Austria and Russia. He besought Germany to put pressure on Austria. He proposed after the Austrians had actually gone to war that they should stop after occupying Belgrade and accept mediation by the powers. He supported a final Russian formula and secured its amendment to make it more acceptable to Austria.

But there was one fatal flaw in the British Government's policy. While exhausting the resources of conciliation, it failed to make clear what it would do if conciliation broke down and war began. As late as July 31, when Russia, Austria-Hungary, and Germany had already begun full mobilization, which, as we have seen, all the general staffs regarded as tantamount to beginning war, and barely twenty-four hours before Germany invaded Belgium, Mr. Asquith defined British policy as follows:

> All turns on what England may do, and the object of our Foreign Office at present is to keep Europe in suspense on that point. So long as Europe does not know what England is likely to do, there is a great steadying influence upon both France and Russia, for they both feel that Germany might be difficult to tackle unless the other Powers had us supporting them. Germany in the meantime shrinks from aggressive action—e.g., through Belgium—because it does not know whether we should vehemently oppose; and, if we did, their task would be doubled in difficulty. Hence the expediency of our not saying at present what we shall or will not do.[57]

History records few instances of more tragic fatuity than this remark. The more the details of how Europe slid into World War I are studied, the clearer it becomes that the shilly-shallying of the Liberal government during those fatal three weeks bears a crushing responsibility for the vast calamity. For each side interpreted that ambiguity in a sense favourable to its own wishes.

Mr. Lloyd George is undoubtedly right when he states in his *War Memoirs* that a clear and emphatic pronouncement of where Great Britain stood, delivered at the outset of the crisis, would probably have prevented war.

This lesson is so important, and still so badly needs to be learned, that it is worth seeing just how the war began.

The Austrian Government kept its ultimatum a profound secret until it was delivered. The German Government knew of its contents a few days beforehand. The German Foreign Secretary told direct lies in response to questions by the Entente Ambassadors, alleging at the very moment he possessed the text that he did not know what the Austrians were going to say to Serbia.

The Russian proposal for an extension of the time-limit of the ultimatum, which was supported by Great Britain and was made

120 MIRROR OF THE PAST

to Berlin, was deliberately sabotaged by the German Government, which delayed transmission (while falsely stating that it had passed on the request at once) until it was too late. The day after the ultimatum expired—*i.e.*, on the twenty-sixth—Sir Edward Grey proposed a conference between France, Germany, Great Britain, and Russia on the analogy of the London Conference during the Balkan Wars.

Lichnowsky, the German Ambassador in London, who throughout was out of sympathy with his Government's policy, reported in transmitting this proposal to Berlin that in the opinion of the British Foreign Office this conference was "the only possibility of avoiding a general war," but that it could not succeed unless military activities ceased because:

> Once the Serbian border was crossed, everything would be at an end, as no Russian Government would be able to tolerate this, and would be forced to move to the attack of Austria, unless she wanted to see her status among the Balkan nations lost for ever.

This proposal was rejected by the German Government, and the Kaiser expressed his disapproval of Lichnowsky's point of view. The latter, however, returned to the charge in a despatch stating that "the impression is constantly gaining ground here [*i.e.*, in London] that the whole Serbian question has developed into a test of strength between the Triple Alliance and the Triple Entente."

On this the German Under-Secretary of State commented: "Where will the balance of power be if Austria gives in?"

Germany stuck to her policy of trying to "localize" the war. Meantime, on the morning of the twenty-seventh, Sir Edward Grey had seen the text of the Serbian reply, which accepted all the drastic demands in the Austrian ultimatum except that which called for the participation of delegates of the Austro-Hungarian Government in the investigations against accessories to the Sarajevo murder on Serbian territory.

Thereupon Sir Edward Grey made a fresh proposal; namely,

that Germany and Great Britain should intervene respectively with Austria and Russia to bring about a peaceful settlement. This time the German Government did transmit the proposals to Vienna. But at the same time the German Foreign Secretary assured the Austrian Ambassador in Berlin that his Government was directly opposed to these proposals and forwarded them only:

> In order to take account of the British request. The reason for doing so is that it is of the utmost importance at the present moment, to prevent England from making common cause with Russia and France, and that is what might happen if Germany refused to forward British proposals.

At 11 A.M. on the twenty-eighth Austria declared war on Serbia "chiefly to frustrate any attempt at intervention," as the German Ambassador in Vienna reported. This, of course, meant partial mobilization.

Thereupon the Russian Government, which had been begging Germany to co-operate in persuading Austria to modify her demands so as to give "Serbia her deserved lesson while sparing her sovereign rights," decided to begin mobilizing in the military conscriptions of Odessa, Kiev, Moscow, and Kazan as from July 29.

By this time it began to dawn on the German Government that in spite of the British Government's reserve and of the Ulster rebellion, Great Britain might come in if there were war. (The Conservative party's readiness to support the Ulster rebels had encouraged Germany's belief that Great Britain would be so busy at home that she would stay neutral.)

The crucial factor in the German attitude was the question of whether or not Germany could count on British neutrality. On this point German opinion fluctuated. Lichnowsky was sure England would come in. The German Under-Secretary of State, according to the Bavarian Ambassador in Berlin, took a similar view:

> A war between the Dual Alliance and the Triple Alliance would be unwelcome in England at the present time, if only

in consideration of the situation in Ireland. Should it, however, come to that, according to all opinion here, we should find our English cousins on the side of our enemies, inasmuch as England fears that France, in the event of a new defeat, would sink to the level of a Power of the second class, and that the "balance of power," the maintenance of which England considers to be necessary for her own interests, would be upset thereby.

On the other hand, Austrian diplomatic documents report the German Government's belief that Great Britain would not take part in a war arising out of the Balkan question, even if Russia and France should be involved.

On the morning of July 28, an hour before the Austrian declaration of war was presented, the Kaiser wrote to his Secretary of State saying that the Serbian reply had given Austria practically everything she wanted and that it would suffice therefore if the Austrian Government occupied Belgrade until its demands had actually been complied with. On that basis, said the Emperor, Germany would be ready to mediate for peace.

These views were embodied in a note to the Austrian Government which, after ciphering and deciphering, was presented only at 4:30 A.M. on the twenty-ninth, being despatched at 10:15 the preceding evening from Berlin.

The arguments for inducing the Austrian Government to accept this view were stated as follows:

> According to the statements of the Austrian General Staff, an active military movement against Serbia will not be possible before the twelfth of August. As a result, the Imperial Government is placed in the extraordinarily difficult position of being exposed in the meantime to the mediation and conference proposals of the other Cabinets, and if it continues to maintain its previous aloofness in the face of such proposals, it will incur the odium of having been responsible for a world war, even, finally, among the German people themselves. A successful war on three fronts cannot be commenced and carried on on such a basis. It is imperative that the responsibility for the eventual extension of the war

among those nations not originally immediately concerned should, under all circumstances, fall on Russia.

The Russians no longer, continued the note, appeared so unconditionally opposed to the Austrian point of view as they were earlier. They might come round still more if the Vienna Cabinet repeated at St. Petersburg its distinct declaration that it would make no territorial acquisitions in Serbia and would be content with a temporary occupation of Belgrade and certain other localities on Serbian territory pending the complete fulfilment of its demands and guarantees for future good behaviour.

As soon as the Austrian demands should be complied with, evacuation would follow. Should the Russian Government fail to recognize the justice of this point of view, it would have against it the public opinion of all Europe, which is now in the process of turning away from Austria. As a further result, the general diplomatic, and probably the military, situations would undergo material alteration in favour of Austria-Hungary and her allies.[58]

The British Government was informed of the German attempts to restrain Austria and expressed its gratification.

But at this point military preparations began to exert overwhelming pressure on the efforts of the diplomats.

Austria had, of course, carried out a partial mobilization for her war against Serbia. This had led to the Russian announcement on the twenty-eighth of partial mobilization against Austria to begin the next day.

Whereupon the Austrian Prime Minister telegraphed to Berlin pressing the German Government to declare that Russian partial mobilization would be followed by total mobilization in Germany. Preliminary measures also began to be taken in France, and the British fleet was put in a state of readiness.

The German Government was in a dilemma, which is summed up by the Bavarian Minister in Berlin as follows:

Germany's procedure was rendered very difficult by the fact that no one knew whether the measures taken in Russia and France were meant as a bluff or were serious.

The German general staff stated the dilemma in a memorandum on the twenty-ninth with uncompromising lucidity:

Russia has announced that she will mobilize against Austria if Austria invades Serbia. Austria will therefore have to mobilize against Russia. The collision between the two States will then have become inevitable. But that, for Germany, is the casus foederis. She therefore must mobilize too. Russia will then mobilize the rest of her forces. She will say: "I am being attacked by Germany." Thus the Franco-Russian alliance, so often held up to praise as a purely defensive compact, created only to meet the aggressive plans of Germany, will become active, and the mutual butchery of the civilized nations of Europe will begin. . . . After this fashion things must and will develop, unless, one might say, a miracle happens to prevent at the last moment a war which will annihilate for decades the civilization of almost all Europe.

The chief of the German general staff, Commander-in-Chief von Moltke, was absolutely convinced that

a war of aggression against Germany was planned and prepared for between Russia, France, and England for the year 1917. Moltke considers Russia to be the head of the conspiracy.[59]

Therefore he considered it fortunate that the Sarajevo assassination had exploded the mine before Russia was ready and while the French Army was in a state of transition. In other words, the chief of the German general staff thought the opportunity, although unwelcome, was favourable for a "preventive" war.

At 11 A.M. the same day (twenty-ninth) the German Ambassador at St. Petersburg, in an interview with the Russian Foreign Minister, mentioned Germany's attempts to restrain Austria and protested strongly against the partial Russian mobilization.

The Russian Foreign Minister said the Austrians had made no move to begin conversations, and that Russian mobilization was much slower than mobilization by other great powers and did not, as in their case, mean war (which, however, was contrary to the agreement of the Russian and French general staffs mentioned above; but presumably the agreement did not apply to partial mobilization).

The German Ambassador pointed out:

> The General Staffs of the possible opponents of Russia would not be willing to sacrifice the advantage of getting a start over Russia in the matter of mobilization, and would press for counter measures. I earnestly begged him to consider this peril.[60]

After this interview and a further talk in the evening, the Russian Foreign Minister knew for a certainty that Germany would back Austria in case of war, but was not sure whether Germany was really trying to put pressure on Vienna or merely attempting to postpone Russian mobilization in order to gain time for her own preparations.

The net result was that the partial mobilization was put in hand at once, after a struggle between the Czar and the general staff, which had decided on general mobilization on "technical" grounds.

At first the Czar yielded to this decision, particularly after the news had come in of the bombardment of Belgrade, which led to the breakdown of discussions between the Austrian Ambassador and Sazonov. But then the Czar received a telegram from the Kaiser speaking of his mediation at Vienna, and adding:

> Of course, military measures on the part of Russia, which would be looked on by Austria as threatening, would precipitate a calamity which we both wish to avoid, and jeopardise my position as a mediator, which I readily accepted on your appeal to my friendship and help.[61]

The Czar thereupon countermanded the general mobilization, for which the orders were being prepared at 9:30 P.M. These orders were withdrawn about midnight and partial mobilization substituted. The information about the original orders and the change made in them was communicated to London and Paris. The French War Minister urged the Russians to be as secret and

as little provocative in their preparations as possible, so as not
to make the situation more difficult.

A further despatch from Berlin sent at 4:10 A.M. on the thirtieth
and received at 6 A.M. urged the Austrian Government that

> in order to prevent a general catastrophe, or at least to put
> Russia in the wrong, Vienna should inaugurate and continue
> the conferences proposed by Germany.[62]

The German Government also forwarded to Vienna copies of
despatches from Lichnowsky in London recording two interviews
with Sir Edward Grey on the twenty-ninth, in which the latter left
him with the conviction that:

> Unless Austria is willing to enter upon a discussion of the
> Serbian question, a world war is inevitable. Mediation
> seemed to him now to be urgently necessary if a European
> catastrophe were not to result. While England could stand
> aside so long as the conflict was confined to Austria and
> Russia, yet, if Germany and France should be involved, the
> British Government would, under the circumstances, find
> itself forced to make up its mind quickly.

The German Chancellor appended to these despatches the following note:

> We stand, in case Austria refuses all mediation, before a
> conflagration in which England will be against us; Italy and
> Rumania, to all appearances, will not go with us, and we two
> shall be opposed to four great Powers. On Germany, thanks
> to England's opposition, the principal burden of the fight
> would fall. Austria's political prestige, the honor of her arms,
> as well as her just claims against Serbia, could all be satis-
> fied by the occupation of Belgrade or of other places. She
> would be strengthening her status in the Balkans, as well as
> in relation to Russia, by the humiliation of Serbia. Under
> these circumstances, we must urgently and impressively sug-
> gest to the consideration of the Vienna Cabinet the accept-
> ance of mediation on the above-mentioned honorable condi-
> tions. The responsibility for the consequences that would

otherwise follow would be an uncommonly heavy one, both for Austria and for us.[63]

The German Ambassador received this despatch while at lunch with the Austrian Prime Minister on July 30, and immediately read it to him.

"The Minister," he reported, "listened pale and silent while it was read twice and said . . . that he would make a report to the Emperor about it."

The only result, however, was that the Austrian Government, while informing the German Government that it had given instructions to its Ambassador at Petrograd to begin conversations with Sazonov on the basis suggested by Germany, in fact did nothing of the sort. On the contrary, the Austrian Cabinet decided not to stop hostilities against Serbia, although they had occupied Belgrade. This was on the thirty-first.

Meanwhile the Russian general staff at 11 A.M. on the thirtieth had once more urged upon the Czar the view that war was inevitable and general mobilization should be put in hand at once, because:

It was better to proceed with our preparations without fearing that by doing so we might precipitate events, rather than, from fear of provoking war, to be surprised by it.[64]

The Czar yielded after a long discussion, whereupon the chief of the Russian general staff issued a general mobilization order and then cut off his telephone and made himself scarce so as to block any attempt by the Czar to rescind the order.

The general mobilization orders were sent out and received between 6 and 7 P.M. on July 30.

At noon that day the German Ambassador had once more warned the Russian Foreign Minister of the dangers of mobilization.

In strong words I represented to the Minister how fearful would be this war, the scope of which it was impossible to foresee. No means should be omitted to stop the rolling stone. A compromise must be reached if possible. One could surely be found if there were good will on both sides.'

Sazonov suggested a formula and later accepted an amendment by Sir Edward Grey which made it run as follows:

If Austria consents to stay the march of her troops on Serbian territory, and if, recognising that the Austro-Serbian conflict has assumed the character of a question of European interest, she admits that the Great Powers may examine the satisfaction which Serbia can afford to the Austro-Hungarian Government, without injury to her sovereign rights as a State, and to her independence, Russia undertakes to preserve her waiting attitude.[65]

This proposal was rejected on the thirty-first by the Austrian Cabinet at the meeting already referred to, which had refused to stop the war against Serbia with the occupation of Belgrade.

The previous evening Von Moltke, the chief of the German general staff, had urged upon the Austrians a general mobilization. Upon receiving this communication the Austrian Prime Minister exclaimed: "Success! (*Das ist gelungen!*) Who rules? Moltke or Bethmann?"

At the same time the Kaiser once more urged the Austrian Emperor to accept the German plan of a halt in Belgrade. The Austrian Emperor returned a completely intransigent reply, and added that since receiving the despatch he had heard of the mobilization of Russia against Austria and had in consequence mobilized his whole army.

Before the Kaiser could reply to this communication, Berlin at 11:30 A.M. on the thirty-first had received the news of Russia's general mobilization. At 1:45 P.M. Germany was declared to be in danger of war (a condition preliminary to mobilization), Austria was informed of this fact, told that mobilization would follow and that war would then be inevitable, and: "We expect from Austria active participation in the war with Russia."

At 3:30 a twelve-hour ultimatum was sent to Russia to cease military preparations on pain of war, and shortly after, France was sent a sixteen-hour ultimatum demanding her neutrality and the handing over of the fortresses of Toul and Verdun as a pledge of neutrality.

During these days the French Government, while doing its best to second all British attempts at preserving peace, had also been vainly endeavouring to get the British Government to say where it stood in case of war.

As all efforts to draw Sir Edward Grey failed, the French President, in desperation, addressed a letter to the King on July 31, of which the following are extracts:

The military preparations that are being made by the Imperial Government, notably in the immediate neighborhood of the French frontier, are every day assuming additional intensity and acceleration. France, determined to do until the last all that she can for the maintenance of peace, has so far confined herself strictly to indispensable measures of precaution. It does not appear that her prudence and her moderation will abate the determination of Germany—far from it. We are therefore, perhaps, in spite of the discretion of the Government of the Republic and the calmness of public opinion, on the eve of the most formidable events.

From all the information that is reaching us, it is clear that if Germany were certain that the British Government would not intervene in a conflict in which France would be engaged, war would be inevitable; and that, on the other hand, if Germany were certain that in such case the Entente Cordiale would be operative, even to the battlefield, there would be the greatest chance that peace would not be broken. . . .

I believe that henceforth the last possibilities of peace depend on the language and the conduct of the British Government.

We have ourselves, since the beginning of the crisis, recommended to our allies a moderation to which they have adhered. In accord with the British Government and in conformity with the latest suggestions of Sir Edward Grey, we shall continue so to act. But if all the efforts at conciliation come from the same side, and if Germany and Austria are able to speculate on the abstention of Great Britain, the demands of Austria will remain inflexible and an agreement between Russia and her will become impossible.

I have the profound conviction that at the present mo-

ment the more Great Britain, France, and Russia present a
strong impression of unity in their diplomatic action, the
more we may still rely on the preservation of peace.[66]

The King returned a vague and ambiguous reply, in accordance with the wishes of the Government.

By that time it was too late to prevent war and, as we have
seen, Sir Edward Grey had managed to convey the impression to
the German Ambassador that England would probably come in,
but not in a manner sufficiently explicit to enable the German
Ambassador to convince his own Government until it was too
late.

On July 31 Sir Edward went through the solemn farce of
addressing a note to France and Germany asking whether they
would respect Belgian neutrality (for this was nothing but a
farce, in view of the fact that the war plans of Germany and the
Entente had for years been based on the assumption that in case
of war Germany would invade Belgium and that the Belgians,
British, and French would jointly resist that invasion).

The French said they would respect Belgium's neutrality. The
German Government was unable to reply, but asked whether
Great Britain would remain neutral if Germany agreeed not to
violate Belgium's neutrality. Sir Edward Grey declined to give
this assurance. The German Ambassador asked whether a guarantee of the integrity of France and her colonies would suffice to
secure British neutrality. He had previously asked whether Great
Britain would remain neutral if Germany did not use her navy
against the north coast of France.

To these questions Sir Edward Grey said:

> I felt obliged to refuse definitely any promise to remain
> neutral on similar terms, and I could only say that we must
> keep our hands free.

This was on August 1. In the same interview Sir Edward observed that

> he had also been wondering whether it would be possible
> for Germany and France to remain facing each other under

arms without attacking each other, in the event of a Russian war.[67]

The Kaiser's marginal comment on the despatch conveying this remark was "The rascal [*der Schelm*] is crazy or an idiot."

On August 2 a Cabinet meeting was held, after which Sir Edward Grey told the French Ambassador in writing:

> I am authorized to give an assurance that, if the German Fleet comes into the Channel or through the North Sea, to undertake hostile operations against the French coasts or shipping, the British Fleet will give all the protection in its power.[68]

This assurance of course meant that Great Britain intended to fulfil her naval agreement with France. The British position was stated publicly for the first time by Sir Edward Grey in the House of Commons in his famous eve-of-the-war speech of August 3, 1914. This is so important as to be worth considering carefully.

When that speech was delivered, Russia and Serbia were already at war with Germany and Austria-Hungary, and the German ultimatum to France had expired. The House knew that. Sir Edward Grey told them that "mobilisation of the Fleet has taken place; mobilisation of the Army is taking place." He told them, for the first time, of the naval and military agreements with France, and of how the French and British fleets had been disposed in pursuance of those agreements.

> The French Fleet is now in the Mediterranean, and the Northern and Western coasts of France are absolutely undefended. The French Fleet being concentrated in the Mediterranean, the situation is very different from what it used to be, because the friendship which has grown up between the two countries has given them a sense of security that there was nothing to be feared from us. The French coasts are absolutely undefended. The French fleet is in the Mediterranean, and has for some years been concentrated there because of the feeling of confidence and friendship which has existed between the two countries. My own feeling is that if a foreign fleet engaged in a war which France had

not sought, and in which she had not been the aggressor, came down the English Channel and bombarded and battered the undefended coasts of France, we could not stand aside and see this going on practically within sight of our eyes, with our arms folded, looking on dispassionately, doing nothing!

The day before, the Government, said Sir Edward Grey, had told France:

If the German Fleet comes into the Channel or through the North Sea to undertake hostile operations against the French coasts or shipping, the British Fleet will give all the protection in its power. This assurance is, of course, subject to the policy of His Majesty's Government receiving the support of Parliament, and must not be taken as binding His Majesty's Government to take any action until the above contingency of action by the German Fleet takes place.

I read that to the House, not as a declaration of war on our part, not as entailing immediate aggressive action on our part, but as binding us to take aggressive action should that contingency arise.

Sir Edward gave a full account of Anglo-Belgian relations and commitments. He cited the passage from Gladstone quoted above, including that in which he held that Great Britain should preserve the neutrality of Belgium, not because he subscribed to the doctrine that "the simple fact of the existence of a guarantee is binding on every party to it, irrespectively altogether of the particular position in which it may find itself at the time when the occasion for acting on the guarantee arises"—on the contrary, he dissented from that doctrine—but because of "the common interest against the unmeasured aggrandisement of any Power whatever."

Sir Edward argued that if Belgian

independence goes, the independence of Holland will follow. I ask the House, from the point of view of British interests, to consider what may be at stake. If France is beaten in a struggle of life and death, beaten to her knees, loses her position as a great Power, becomes subordinate to the will and power of one greater than herself—consequences which I do not anticipate, because I am sure that France has the power to defend herself with all the energy and ability and patriotism which she has shown so often—still if that were to happen, and if Belgium fell under the same dominating influence, and then Holland, and then Denmark, then would not Mr. Gladstone's words come true, that just opposite to us there would be a common interest against the unmeasured aggrandisement of any Power?

If Great Britain stood out, she would in any case suffer almost as much from the consequences of the war as she would by taking part.

I do not believe for a moment, that at the end of this war, even if we stood aside and remained aside, we should be in a position, a material position, to use our force decisively to undo what had happened in the course of the war, to prevent the whole of the West of Europe opposite to us—if that had been the result of the war—falling under the domination of a single Power, and I am quite sure that our moral position would be such as to have lost us all respect. . . .

There is but one way in which the Government could make certain at the present moment of keeping outside this war, and that would be that it should immediately issue a proclamation of unconditional neutrality. We cannot do that. We have made the commitment to France that I have read to the House which prevents us from doing that. We have got the consideration of Belgium which prevents us also from any unconditional neutrality, and, without those conditions absolutely satisfied and satisfactory, we are bound not to shrink from proceeding to the use of all the forces in our power. If we did take that line by saying, "We will have nothing whatever to do with this matter" under no conditions—the Belgian Treaty obligations, the possible position in the Mediterranean, with damage to British interests, and what may happen to France from our failure to support France—if we were to say that all those things mattered nothing, and to say we would stand aside, we should, I believe, sacrifice our respect and good name and reputation before the world, and should not escape the most serious and grave economic consequences.

[Events had moved so quickly that] the country . . . has not had time to realise the issue. It perhaps is still thinking of the quarrel between Austria and Servia, and not the complications of this matter which have grown out of the quarrel between Austria and Servia.

Germany was bound to support Austria, and Germany and Russia were already at war. France was involved "because of their obligation of honour under a definite alliance with Russia."

These were unanswerable arguments for the view that peace was indivisible, and that Great Britain could not keep out of the war if she wished to retain her empire and her reputation and to survive as a great power.

But these arguments were as true from the day the Austrian heir apparent was murdered on June 28 as they were on August 3. Why did not the Government take the country into its confidence and tell the world where it stood while there was still time to save peace? Why did Sir Edward Grey tell the House of Commons in his speech that "in this present crisis" the Government had "up till yesterday" given France "no promise of more than diplomatic support"?

Why did Sir Edward begin his speech with the assertion, so flatly contradicted by the rest of his statement that it would be ludicrous if the circumstances had been less tragic, that:

I have assured the House—and the Prime Minister has assured the House more than once—that if any crisis such as this arose, we should come before the House of Commons and be able to decide what the British attitude should be, that we would have no secret engagement which we should spring upon the House, and tell the House that, because we had entered into that engagement, there was an obligation of honour upon the country.

To the British people the reasons for Britain's going to war were summed up in the famous last talk of the British Ambassador, Sir Edward Goschen, with the German Chancellor:

I found the Chancellor very agitated. His Excellency at once began a harangue, which lasted for about twenty minutes. He said that the step taken by His Majesty's Government was terrible to a degree; just for a word—"neutrality," a word which in war-time had so often been disregarded— just for a scrap of paper, Great Britain was going to make war on a kindred nation who desired nothing better than to be friends with her. All his efforts in that direction had been rendered useless by this last terrible step, and the policy to which, as I knew, he had devoted himself since his accession to office had tumbled down like a house of cards. What we had done was unthinkable; it was like striking a man from behind, while he was fighting for his life against two assailants. He held Great Britain responsible for all the terrible events that might happen. I protested strongly against that statement, and said that, in the same way as he and Herr von Jagow wished me to understand that, for strategical reasons, it was a matter of life and death to Germany to advance through Belgium and violate the latter's neutrality, so I would wish him to understand that it was, so to speak, a matter of "life and death" for the honor of Great Britain that she should keep her solemn engagement to do her utmost to defend Belgium's neutrality if attacked. That solemn compact simply had to be kept, or what confidence could anyone have in engagements given by Great Britain in the future? The Chancellor said: "But at what price will that compact have been kept? Has the British Government thought of that?" I hinted to His Excellency as plainly as I could that fear of consequences could hardly be regarded as an excuse for breaking solemn engagements, but His Excellency was so excited, so evidently overcome by the news of our action, and so little disposed to hear reason that I refrained from adding fuel to the flame by further argument.[69]

"Remember Belgium," the desire to save small nations and to prove that treaties are not scraps of paper, became the very core of the British Government's war propaganda. This was the main reason why the great majority of the Labour party supported the war. Belief in the truth of this propaganda was the faith for which millions flocked to the colours.

136

WHY BRITAIN WENT TO WAR

It is not necessary at this date to labour the point that this propaganda was false in every particular, and that the governing class in Great Britain and every other belligerent country cared nothing at all for international law, or treaty obligations, or the rights of small nations. The *Times* was right when it wrote, on December 4, 1914, "We have always fought for the Balance of Power. We are fighting for it today." *

Sir Arnold Wilson put the same point when he said in the House of Commons on February 24, 1936, in the course of a glowing tribute to Sir Edward (then Lord) Grey, that he would "go down in history as a man who was the foremost in keeping the bond of this country when he thought that the interests of the country required it."

This does not imply any lack of personal sincerity on the part of the Liberal government and the Foreign Office. They were intensely sincere in identifying their view of "national interests" with "honour" and "right." Nor was it more wrong for the Asquith-Grey government to play power politics in defence of imperialism than for any other great power to do the same.

But it does mean that there was a vast gulf between what the rulers of Great Britain were really fighting for and what they persuaded themselves and the British people that they were fighting for. The same discrepancy existed in all the belligerent countries. Its nature is indicated in the conclusion of this chapter and made clearer in the next chapter.

At this stage in our analysis of events it is sufficient to point out that whereas all the belligerents believed they were fighting in

---

* The *Times* insisted on this point repeatedly—see *e.g.* its leader of March 8, 1915. See also the *Spectator* of December 19, 1914. The Conservative party, in Mr. Bonar Law's letter to Mr. Asquith of August 2, 1914, promising full support in case of war, said not one word of Belgium, but urged that "it would be fatal to the honour and security of the United Kingdom to hesitate in supporting France and Russia at the present juncture." Professor Gilbert Murray, in his semi-official Foreign Office propaganda pamphlet referred to above, argued that in no circumstances could Great Britain allow Germany to weaken France.

self-defence in a war that had been thrust upon them, each of them was in fact fighting a "preventive" war.

Austria-Hungary declared war on Serbia to prevent Pan-Serbian agitation from disrupting the Empire.

Russia mobilized against Austria to prevent Serbia from being crushed, for this would have meant Austro-German hegemony in the Balkans and Turkey and the end of Russian imperialist expansion in South-east Europe and Asia Minor.

Germany backed Austria to prevent her from being crushed and Russian hegemony established in the Balkans, as that would have meant the end of German imperialist expansion in South-east Europe and Asia Minor.

France supported Russia on the principle of "after Sadowa, Sudan"—i.e., if Germany won her war against Russia, she would become master of Central Europe from the Baltic to the Balkans, and would then be strong enough to help herself to French colonies.

Britain declared war on Germany because if Germany won her war against France and Russia she would become master of all Europe, and strong enough to help herself to British colonies.

Each side was defending its imperialist interests by preventing the balance of power from being tipped in favour of its opponents. These imperialist interests were in the last analysis the private interests of finance and monopoly capital, which, through the influence of the plutocracy on governments and public opinion, were identified in the minds of the rulers with "national honour and vital interests." There were, of course, other factors in the situation, and the psychological process by which promoting vested interests in imperialism and war preparations is transmuted in men's minds into loyalty to religious, philanthropic, and patriotic ideals is complex and largely unconscious.

But the more closely world affairs before World War I are studied, the clearer it becomes that the pursuit of profits by finance capital was the chief "social dynamic" behind the drive for imperialism, protectionism,* and armaments. It was these

* Tariff wars played a big part in the growing tension between Germany and Russia and between Austria and Serbia. They were started and maintained for the usual mixed motives—power politics and vested interests.

vested interests that put up most of the money for Navy and Air and Empire leagues, Colonial Societies, and similar patriotic poisoners of public opinion. It was the plutocracy that owned part of the press and influenced most of the press through the control of advertising. It was the plutocracy that financed the British capitalist parties, whose leaders and members of Parliament were almost exclusively drawn from the class that lives by rent, interest, and profit.

These people did not believe in the rightness of what they were doing as much as they were unconscious of the possibility of doing differently. Their framework of experience was to them coincident with the limits of reality. Anything beyond was idle dreams or pernicious rubbish. They accepted the economic foundations of society as part of the order of nature, and the private profit-seeking motive as almost divinely inspired. Therefore the social dynamic of the drift to war operated below the threshold of their consciousness, in a sphere that they regarded as not subject to political control. It followed that their attitude to war was fatalistic. The idea that war was a man-made thing and that its causes could be ascertained and eliminated belonged, in their view, to the category of "idle dreams" and "pernicious rubbish." For to tackle the problem seriously meant disturbing the vested interests by which they lived and which to them seemed part of the order of nature.

Nothing is more striking in the story of how civilization collapsed in World War I than the sense of helplessness, of the governments and diplomats being mere puppets in the grip of blind forces. Mr. G. M. Trevelyan, in his *Lord Grey of Falloden,* quotes the remark by Grey that "I used to hope that I was meant to keep the country out of war. But perhaps my real business was to bring her into it unitedly." It is not difficult to detect in this mystic resignation a refuge from the haunting sense of futility and failure.

As for the peoples, they were nothing at all, even in the most advanced democracies, except cannon fodder. No government ever dreamed of consulting them on matters of foreign policy, or hesitated to deceive them if they were presumptuous enough to question the ways of their rulers. All governments took it for granted that they would let themselves be butchered in unlimited quantities when the game of power politics made war necessary.

CONCLUSION

If even today public opinion learnt the lesson of our failure to preserve peace in 1914, it might understand why we failed again in 1939. In that case we should have a better chance to win the peace after World War II than we did after World War I. For that lesson goes to the roots of the present situation, and if we profit by it we still have time to apply our hardly won wisdom to the new peace settlement.

It will take all the chapters of this book to reveal the full lesson. But let us endeavour to indicate the conclusions that would appear to emerge from what has been said hitherto. In doing so it will make things clearer to go from the particular to the general, beginning with specific criticisms of British foreign policy before 1914.

Let us take first the criticism that it was wrong for Great Britain to conclude the military and naval agreements. This is an argument for isolation. "Splendid isolation" was abandoned, as shown in the early part of this chapter, because Great Britain had ceased to be strong enough to defend the whole British Empire against all comers. And the British ruling class believed, and had persuaded public opinion to believe, that colonies were worth acquiring and keeping.

A variant of this view is that France and Great Britain should have remained neutral, and let Germany and Austria-Hungary defeat Russia. But in that case Germany would have become the master of all Central and Eastern Europe from the Baltic to the Balkans, and would have compelled France and Great Britain to surrender their colonial empires.

A Russian defeat, or a British refusal to lend the Czar the money to put down the first (1905) Russian Revolution, might, it is true, have resulted in a successful revolution in Russia that would have led to the democratization of Germany. But that would have meant a double risk. In the first place, it would have weakened the Entente temporarily in comparison with the central powers, and the latter might have exploited the situation to acquire a colony or two, or to push on in the Balkans. In the second place, once a revolution begins, one never knows how far it will go.

The governing class in pre-1914 days had not begun to be seriously disturbed about the stability of the social order. But at the back of their minds there was a little uneasiness that was now and again expressed in words. One catches glimpses from time to time of a social motive in foreign affairs. The previous chapter quoted Cecil Rhodes's view of imperialism as an antidote to social unrest. Lord Salisbury in the '90's complained:

> Unfortunately we no longer live in the time of Pitt. Then the aristocracy was in power, and we could pursue an active policy which made England, after the Congress of Vienna, the richest and most respected of European Powers. Now the democracy rules, and has introduced a *régime* of persons and parties which has made every English Government dependent, unconditionally, on the *aura popularis.* . . . This generation can only be taught by events.

The first treaty of the Triple Alliance, concluded in 1882, began with a preamble stating that the contracting parties had made this agreement in order "to increase the guarantees of general peace, to fortify the monarchical principle, and thereby to assure the unimpaired maintenance of the social and political order in their respective States."

The Kaiser, in commenting on the idea of disarmament in connection with the First Hague Conference (1899), objected that it would mean "handing over his towns to anarchy and democracy."

Isvolski, at the Second Hague Conference (1907), dismissed disarmament as "a dream of Jews, Socialists, and hysterical women."

At an early stage (July 23) of the negotiations during the fateful twelve days that swept the world into Armageddon, Sir

Edward Grey warned the Austrian Ambassador that "if four great States, Austria-Hungary, Germany, Russia and France, should be involved in war," there would be economic bankruptcy and "the industrial centres in an uproar, so that in most countries, no matter who were victorious, many an existing institution would be swept away."

The Austrian Ambassador reports as follows his last talk with Sir Edward Grey, when all was lost and war was upon Britain:

Grey is in despair that his efforts to maintain the peace have gone to ruin. Again and again he said of the war, "I hate it, I hate it!" He recalled all the efforts we had made together, in the previous year, during the Balkan Conference. He had earnestly hoped that, once the present danger were passed, it might be possible to preserve the peace for years. "I was quite ready if ever Russia had been aggressive —in the case of France it was not likely that she should—to stand by Germany, and that we might come to some sort of understanding between the Powers. Now all that was shattered, and universal war, with all its horrible and revolting consequences, had broken out. . . . It was the greatest step towards Socialism that could possibly have been made. . . . We should have Labour Governments in every country after this."

This cry of the heart shows Sir Edward Grey's passionate sincerity about peace. But it also shows that the culminating horror of the world war to his mind was the danger of an advance towards socialism.

A Foreign Secretary who felt like that was not going to take any risk of encouraging revolution, either in Russia or anywhere else. He would prefer the certainty of power politics ultimately ending in a world war. And his feelings were not peculiar. They were typical of his Government, his diplomatic service, and his class.

A further criticism of British policy in those fatal three weeks was the failure to put pressure on Russia to postpone mobilization. But Lowes Dickinson, who is inclined to agree with this criticism, points out that Russia had the assurance of French support and

> would have risked war even without any certainty of British support. For consistently from the beginning she had made it clear that she would not stand by to see Serbia crushed by Austria. It is possible that Sir Edward was afraid that to stop Russia's preparations might encourage Germany to precipitate the war.[70]

The evidence adduced earlier in this chapter makes it clear that Russia, although the general staff finally forced the Czar's hand, did her best for some time to urge conciliation on Serbia and to secure a peaceful settlement, and that it was chiefly Germany and Austria that needed restraining—although the former did try to hold back Austria when she discovered—too late—that the British Government was going to stand by France. Bethmann-Hollweg says in his *Memoirs* that if he had only known earlier where Britain stood he could have restrained Austria and his own militarists and there would have been no war. In other words, if all concerned in Germany and Austria had known beforehand that they could not get away with a war, they might have kept the peace. Of the two, the Austrian Government, smarting under the assassination of the Archduke and really frightened of Pan-Serb propaganda, bore the chief, direct responsibility for turning the last diplomatic crisis into World War I.

There were occasions, notably during the Balkan Wars, when all the powers concerned had met in conference, when Sir Edward Grey helped to keep the peace by being careful, as Lowes Dickinson writes about the final crisis, "not to give the impression either that England would keep out of the war, under all circumstances, or that she would, necessarily, come in." But in 1914 this ambiguity, combined with the confusion and delays of diplomacy, played straight into the hands of those who pushed Europe over the edge.

On the other hand, there were two reasons why the British Government would not commit itself wholly to the Franco-Russian alliance. In the first place it was reluctant to give up the illusion of a free hand for the certainty of commitment, because it feared it would not get any corresponding measure of control over the foreign policies of the countries to which it was committed. Its members were genuine Liberals, in the sense of being reluctant and half-hearted about imperialism and power politics, and acquiescing in them only as the lesser evil (the greater evil being in their view the risks attaching to democracy in foreign politics).

In the second place, public opinion was isolationist and opposed to any commitments of any kind. Why, then, it may be asked, did not the Liberal government take the people into its confidence, and begin to educate them as to the necessity for an alliance to maintain the balance of power? Why did this course appear to it a greater evil than power politics and secret diplomacy?

The answer is that no one could tell where this process of democratizing foreign policy would stop. Many Liberals, and almost all Radicals and Labour men, were already displaying hostility to armaments and colonial imperialism. A certain Norman Angell had written an inconveniently plausible and popular book, in which he pointed out that the arguments of imperialists that colonies were necessary to the livelihood of the people were a "great illusion." Socialists had completed this demonstration by showing that the arms race and colonial buccaneering were inspired by the influence, of a more or less corrupt character, of big vested interests on governments and the press. It had not been altogether easy to keep public opinion from being too much interested in what was going on in Egypt, Morocco, Persia, and Tripoli. It would be optimistic to believe that the more the common people knew of these things, the readier they would be to pay in taxes, and finally in blood, for imperialism and power politics. For imperialism and power politics are the interest of plutocracy, but not of the common people. But the British Government saw no way of abandoning these things without shaking the foundations of the existing social order—that is, without incurring risks that were literally unthinkable.

To this day the British Foreign Office, unlike the rest of the civil service, is recruited by selection in addition to examination, and is the almost exclusive preserve of the upper middle class and the aristocracy.* Before World War I this was wholly the case, and the Foreign Office was in complete charge of British foreign policy. Sir Edward Grey was little more than a dignified mouthpiece for his permanent officials. He had no policy of his own. He acted only as a sort of emollient and brake on their conduct of foreign policy, and as an intermediary between them and the few members of the Cabinet who were adjudged worthy to be let into the secret.

Throughout the nineteenth century the rising tide of democracy submerged one aspect of public life after the other and engulfed more and more of the functions of government. The aristocracy and plutocracy were driven back step by step, convinced at every successive surrender that disaster would follow from the foolishness of the people, and yielding only because they had to. Finally they were left high and dry in diplomacy and foreign affairs, which they tenaciously defended against the encroachments of democracy. The development of finance capital, indeed, meant the beginning of a counter-offensive by the plutocracy against democracy, for it led to the development of a sort of economic feudalism whose political stronghold was imperialism and war preparations.

Gladstone once said that to understand the foreign policy of a country it is necessary to consider its internal affairs. It is significant that as finance capital developed in Great Britain and imperialism and the arms race gained momentum, the Liberal and Conservative parties agreed on "continuity in foreign policy." Mr. Lloyd George tells in his *War Memoirs* how as far back as 1910 there were negotiations that almost led to a "party truce" or "national government" on defence (*i.e.*, war preparations, including a form of conscription) and unemployment (*i.e.*, how to deal with working-class discontent).

These considerations explain why the idea of admitting democracy into the arcana of foreign affairs was literally unthinkable to

* The situation is not likely to be substantially changed by the much-heralded reform and fusion of the diplomatic and consular services.

the British rulers. The Asquith-Grey government was sincerely convinced that it knew better than the common people what was good for them in international matters, and that the people (including the rank and file of the Liberal party and their members of Parliament) had to be kept in ignorance and, if necessary, deceived to make them acquiesce in the Government's power politics.

In those days it was the governing class and the diplomats and military men who had a monopoly in the related domains of foreign affairs and defence. They were experts, who accepted unquestioningly the premises of imperialism and were skilful in playing the game of power politics that revolved about imperialism. They knew that public opinion was beginning to question the premises, and therefore tried to keep it ignorant of details, lest public opinion should learn too much and put an end to the whole game. In short, says Bertrand Russell, British policy was

> really dictated by the permanent officials of the Foreign Office. . . . Their secret power, especially in the time of Grey, was almost unbounded. Grey was a high-minded man, a sincere patriot, a perfectly honorable gentleman in his dealings with those whom he regarded as equals, and an enthusiast for fly-fishing. On these grounds Englishmen entrusted their lives and fortunes to his keeping, although he knew no foreign language, had hardly ever been out of England, and had too little industry to verify what his officials told him. Moreover his belief in honorable dealing did not extend to the house of Commons, since he held the aristocratic opinion that ordinary mortals could not understand foreign politics.[71]

The Foreign Office, by tradition, training, and class origin, saw "national interests" in terms of the interests of the plutocracy.

But let us not underestimate the difficulties of the Liberal government. It came into office in a world where international anarchy, power politics, and the arms race were the only known method of conducting international affairs, and where British imperialism was a going concern and faced by rival imperialisms. Liberals who might want to change these things knew they would have to fight the Foreign Office, the Colonial Office, and the fighting services, as well as the solidly imperialist and power-politics Conservative party.

Behind these hostile forces, and the press and propaganda they could command, were the plutocracy that subscribed most of the party funds to both the Liberal and Conservative parties. There was the difficulty that foreign powers would mistake concessions and conciliation for weakness, and merely ask for more. Although it was dangerous to educate public opinion out of its isolationism, it was difficult to innovate without the support of a militant and informed opinion. Liberals were impaled on the horns of an insoluble dilemma, and were borne along to World War I struggling vainly to free themselves.

The root of their difficulty and the fundamental fact that governed the situation were clearly stated as far back as 1903 by Mr. J. A. Hobson in his classic work, *Imperialism:*

> It is not too much to say that the modern foreign policy of Great Britain is primarily a struggle for profitable markets of investment. To a larger extent every year Great Britain is becoming a nation living upon a tribute from abroad, and the classes who enjoy this tribute have an ever-increasing incentive to employ the public policy, the public purse, and the public force to extend the field of their private investments, and to safeguard and improve their existing investments. This is, perhaps, the most important fact in modern politics, and the obscurity in which it is wrapped constitutes the gravest danger to our State.
>
> What is true of Great Britain is true likewise of France, Germany, the United States, and of all countries in which modern capitalism has placed large surplus savings in the hands of a plutocracy. . . . Thus we reach the conclusion that Imperialism is the endeavour of the great controllers of industry to broaden the channel for the flow of their surplus wealth by seeking foreign markets and foreign investments to take off the goods and capital they cannot sell or use at home.[72]

There could be no solution of that difficulty so long as economic life was based on the private profit-seeking motive, which, magnified and concentrated through finance capital, exercised a decisive political influence without accepting any public control.

One school of German socialists did indeed invent the comforting doctrine of "ultra-imperialism." They believed that finance capital would tend to coalesce more and more across frontiers, into international trusts and combines that would lay the economic foundations for some form of world government based on the international exploitation of colonial territories. There were certain developments in this direction. But the main current ran strongly in the direction of more and more economic nationalism,* imperialism, and war preparations.

The plutocracy, in short, showed no inclination to behave in the way German Social-Democrats had proved they must, and Norman Angellites argued they ought to, behave out of enlightened self-interest. They remained obstinately unenlightened, short-sighted, and selfish. Why this was, still is, and will probably remain the case until the plutocracy are literally put out of business need not be discussed at this juncture. It is enough to point out that this was so, and that the fact was of decisive importance in stultifying democracy and plunging the world into World War I.

Bertrand Russell, in a memorable passage of his pamphlet *The Policy of the Entente, 1904–14,* draws the moral, which remains as profoundly true and as vitally important today as when he first penned the words a quarter of a century ago and in the midst of World War I:

I wish only to make it clear that the guiding principles of European policy, in Asia as in Africa, are such as must bring

* In Great Britain, for the historical reasons touched on in the last chapter, free trade survived almost intact until the great slump. But absence of tariff discrimination, either in British or any other colonies, never meant effective equality of opportunity in investment, road, rail and engineering contracts, etc. With unimportant exceptions the bulk of the trade and almost all the loans and development projects in colonies have always been in the hands of nationals of the power having sovereignty over those colonies. This is a hard fact to which Norman Angellites are apt to pay too little attention.

horror and dismay to every man with a spark of humanity in his nature. . . .

How are we to prevent a repetition of this long history of deceit, cruelty, and preparation for war? The English people is, I believe, the most humane, generous, and peace-loving in the world: * consciously and of set purpose, it would never tolerate such a policy as its chosen rulers have carried on for the last eleven years. But public attention was engrossed by the struggle in home politics. . . . The first and most indispensable requisite, if this nation and others are not again to be led blindfold into crime and disaster, is that everywhere men should learn to be interested in foreign affairs, to follow them closely, and to bring the pressure of public opinion to bear upon diplomacy. The war, we may hope, will have taught the democracies this lesson, that they cannot safely permit themselves to ignore dealings with foreign countries, or blindly follow the lead of men who say they deserve their trust.

The next thing to be achieved is to destroy the evil tradition of "continuity" in foreign policy. This tradition, like much of what is worst in modern Liberalism, is due to Lord Rosebery. In the days of Gladstone and Disraeli, Palmerston and Lord Derby, Fox and Pitt, Chatham and Lord North, and right back to the times of the Stuarts, the parties were hotly divided on foreign policy. The absence of division dates from Gladstone's retirement, when Lord Rosebery dramatically dropped the agitation against the Armenian massacres. "Continuity" represents no real need of national safety, but merely a closing up of the ranks among the governing classes against their common enemy, the people. Ever since 1832, the upper classes in England have been faced with the problem of retaining as much as possible of the substance of power while abandoning forms to the clamour of democrats. They have gradually lost control over legislation, while retaining in the main their hold of the administrative and judicial sides of government. In foreign affairs, their ascendancy, threatened by the Manchester School and Gladstone, was completely recovered twenty years ago, and survived, as we have seen, even the collapse of 1906. Only by

* Except, perhaps, the people of America. (Russell's note)

reintroducing foreign affairs into the arena of party politics can this ascendancy be destroyed. . . . The interests of the British democracy do not conflict at any point with the interests of mankind. The interests of the British governing classes conflict at many points with the interests of mankind.

Bertrand Russell appears to attribute the "closing of the ranks" between the Liberal and Conservative wings of the upper classes chiefly to the personality of Liberal politicians. But he does point to class solidarity against the rising pressure from below as the underlying motive. We have carried this analysis one stage farther by drawing attention to the growth of finance capital, subsidizing and intermarrying with both the parties, as the prime cause of the Liberal-Conservative *rapprochement* and the consequent tradition of "continuity" in foreign policy.

If there is one lesson that stands out above all the others to be learned from the history of how World War I came, how the war ended, and what has happened since, it is the almost unbelievable blindness, tenacity, cruelty, and unscrupulousness with which the governing classes cling to their privileges and power at any cost to their suffering peoples and to the wider interests of peace and civilization. They are so expert and cunning on details, and so blind and foolish on fundamentals.

CHAPTER III

How the War Ended

THE WAR exaggerated all the evils that had made it impossible to preserve peace.

MILITARISM AND PLUTOCRACY

The belligerent nations were of course compelled to arm with all their might and to give immense power to their War Offices and Admiralties. In Germany the general staff was virtually in control of the country by the end of the war. Mr. Lloyd George tells us in his *War Memoirs* (p. 2786) of how in Great Britain a "military party" connected with certain generals in the War Office intrigued to overthrow the Government and to form one which would be their "nominee and menial." He also proves that these military men, in order to gain their end, published information about the strategical plans of the Allies of vital importance to the enemy. He roundly charges them with high treason —and gives chapter and verse for the charge.

The plutocracy acquired greatly enhanced influence. They had to submit to controls that were distasteful. But in return they entered into a kind of partnership with the state that gave them more political power than ever before and that did not prevent a vast amount of war profiteering. Their power was enhanced by the partial suspension of democracy in order to prosecute the war and by the way "national unity," as it invariably does, resulted in a Government dominated by the Right. In France this Government was that of Clemenceau and the national *bloc*. In Britain the Liberal government gave way to a National Coalition dominated by the Conservative party.

150

Imperialism and economic nationalism assumed extreme forms in the war aims of the belligerents. On each side, under the direct influence of the plutocracy, the government pledged themselves to a system of punitive and discriminatory tariffs intended to exclude the trade of the enemy after the war.

The German war aims were set forth in a manifesto by the six great industrial associations and a number of intellectuals.[1] Prince von Bülow's *Imperial Germany* and Friedrich Naumann's *Central Europe* also expressed the views of the men in control of the central powers. The Brest-Litovsk peace showed how far they would go if military conditions allowed. In general, these aims looked to an extension of territory in all directions and the acquiring of colonies so as to make Germany the mistress of a vast Central European *bloc* with an unchallengeable hegemony in Europe.

THE SECRET TREATIES

The Allies embodied their war aims in a number of secret treaties—namely, the Sazonov-Paléologue agreement, the Sykes-Picot treaty, and the Treaty of Saint-Jean de Maurienne, concluded in 1915, 1916, and 1917.

In these agreements the British and French approved the annexation by Russia of Constantinople, the west coast of the Bosporus, the Sea of Marmara and the Dardanelles, Southern Thrace up to the Enos-Midia line, the coasts of Asia Minor between the Bosporus, the River Sakaria, and a point to be determined later on the Gulf of Ismid, the islands of the Sea of Marmara and Imbros, and Tenedos. In return Russia agreed to the incorporation of the "neutral" or "intermediate" zone in Persia in the British sphere of influence.

In a second agreement between Great Britain, France, and Russia, those states partitioned the greater part of Persia and the Ottoman Empire, Russia obtaining the provinces of Erzerum, Trapezunt, Van, and Bitlis, together with parts of Southern Kurdistan; France, the coastal strip of Syria, the Vilayet of Adana, and the territory east and north of the new Russian frontier;

Great Britain, the southern part of Mesopotamia with Baghdad, and Palestine, with the ports of Akkad and Haifa.

Italy, after putting herself up to auction between the two sides, finally joined the Allies, as they could pay her so much more at the expense of Austria for coming in than the latter was prepared to give up in order to keep Italy neutral. The Italians were to receive Trentino, Southern Tyrol to the Brenner frontier, Trieste, Gorizia, and Gradisca, all Istria as far as Quarnero, the Istrian Islands, Dalmatia with most of the adjacent islands, and Valona as well as the Dodecanese Islands, and a small piece of Albania, the rest going to Montenegro, Serbia, and Greece; also a part of Southern Anatolia and, in addition, an unspecified adjustment of her African territory in her favour (the Italians always interpreted this as meaning a free hand in Abyssinia).

Rumania was to have Transylvania, Bukovina, and all Hungary up to the River Tisza.

Then France and Russia concluded a treaty which was kept secret even from Great Britain, by which the fate of Poland—that chief jewel in the crown of the Czar, as Premier Goremykin democratically put it—was recognized as an internal affair of Russia, in return for Russia's recognizing France's right not only to Alsace-Lorraine but also to the Saar and to cutting off the whole left bank of the Rhine, which was to form an "autonomous and neutral" state freed from "political and economic" dependence upon Germany, and to be under French military occupation until Germany had fulfilled all the terms of the treaty of peace.

These secret treaties all grew out of previous imperialist ambitions, and were inspired by capitalist vested interests and power-politics considerations.*

The governments had drifted into the war because they were

---

* Vol. VI of Temperley's *A History of the Peace Conference of Paris* (6 vols., London, 1920–24) begins with a chapter that describes the secret treaties and makes a temperate statement in their defence, which, however, amounts to little more than the plea that they should be judged in "the setting to which they inseparably belong—the gigantic struggle for national survival, which required of the nations involved in it the use of every expedient permissible in diplomacy and war."

helpless in the grip of social and economic forces that they would not understand, and so could not control. In the war they speedily found themselves slaves of even grimmer, blinder, and more elemental forces. Mr. Lloyd George observes in his *War Memoirs* that the war "was won not on the merits of the case, but on a balance of resources and blunders." [2] That is a striking way of saying that in war it is not justice but brute force that counts, for the object of war is to inflict so much suffering as to break the enemy's resistance and impose the will of the victor.

CONSCRIPTION

We have shown how in foreign affairs the views of the common people were never consulted. War, which is "policy continued by other means," carries this process much farther. Western civilization is based on the belief that the individual is an end in himself, and the state justified only in so far as it ministers to the welfare of the people. The greatest happiness of the greatest number is the basic idea of democracy. But in war the state becomes a Moloch, a totalitarian monster, demanding unlimited blood sacrifice. Men cease to be individuals, or even human beings, and become "man-power" and "cannon fodder." What this means is brought home vividly by Mr. Winston Churchill's account in *Great Contemporaries* of Earl Haig:

> He presents to me in those red years the same mental picture as a great surgeon before the days of anæsthetics, versed in every detail of such science as was known to him: sure of himself, steady of poise, knife in hand, intent upon the operation, entirely removed in his professional capacity from the agony of the patient . . . and if the patient died, he would not reproach himself. [3]

Mr. Lloyd George, who after all was Prime Minister at the time, accuses this great surgeon of having flung away thousands of young lives in the mud of Flanders out of incompetence aggravated by professional jealousy, and says that Earl Haig was a

man of limited vision who refused to face unpleasant facts * and
had, indeed, much in common with Marshal Joffre, who was the
"paragon type of those military idols . . . the great Generals who
never learnt anything from failure except how to stage an even
bloodier fiasco." (*War Memoirs*, pp. 1401-2, 1469.)

In war there is what may be described as an Asiatic relation-
ship between rulers and ruled.

MORALE AND PROPAGANDA

But modern war, precisely because it is totalitarian—that is,
demands the mobilization and concentration of all the national
energies and resources—and because it involves such frightful
suffering, demands national unity. Napoleon estimated the importance of morale to material factors as three to one, and in his
day war was still the "sport of kings."

In World War I whole peoples fought and had to be persuaded
that their cause was so just that they must endure. Moreover, the
resources mobilized were so gigantic and the defensive was so
much stronger than the offensive that material factors alone could
not end the war. That was why Von Hindenburg, the German
Commander-in-Chief, declared the war would be won by those
who had the strongest nerves, and why Lenin said the war would
be ended not at the front but in the rear.

The maintenance of morale was a capital factor. It was maintained by censorship of news and views and by propaganda. The
latter was of two kinds. There was a great deal of atrocity-
mongering—that is, playing on the primitive passions of fear and
hate. There was also an appeal to idealism.

* Captain Liddell Hart proves these charges to the hilt and adds many
horrifying details in *Through the Fog of War* (Random House, 1938). He
shows notably how Haig owed his promotion to influence, not ability, how
he conceived the idea of the Passchendaele massacre, in which hundreds of
thousands of the flower of our youth were mown down uselessly, and out of
sheer obstinate vanity secured the Cabinet's agreement by concealing the
adverse opinion of experts, misrepresenting the attitude of the French,
promising that he did not contemplate a large and costly offensive, and
then continuing with the horrible business even when its ghastly cost and
futility were patent.

At first the latter appeal was in the ascendant. On the Allied side the idea of a League of Nations was launched, accompanied by propaganda about the defence of democracy, the rights of small nations, and the sacredness of treaty obligations, against militarism and lawless force. Similar propaganda was indulged in by the other side.

That was why President Wilson, in his Note to the belligerents of December 18, 1916, took

the liberty of calling attention to the fact that the objects which the statesmen of the belligerents on both sides have in mind in this war are virtually the same, as stated in general terms to their own people and to the world. Each side desires to make the rights and privileges of weak peoples and small States as secure against aggression or denial in the future as the rights and privileges of the great and powerful States now at war. Each wishes itself to be made secure in the future, along with all other nations and peoples, against the recurrence of wars like this, and against aggression or selfish interference of any kind. Each would be jealous of the formation of any more rival leagues to preserve an uncertain balance of power amidst multiplying suspicions; but each is ready to consider the formation of a League of Nations to ensure peace and justice throughout the world. Before that final step can be taken, however, each deems it necessary first to settle the issues of the present war upon terms which will certainly safeguard the independence, the territorial integrity, and the political and commercial freedom of the nations involved.[4]

The Allies in their reply were virtuously indignant at being put on the same footing as the central powers. But needless to say they did not mention their secret treaties.

As the struggle dragged on and became a murderous deadlock, with growing privation and strain on both sides, the idealism grew weaker and the belligerents settled down doggedly and blindly to a war that seemed to become an end in itself, for they were dominated by the psychosis of military victory and the "knock-out blow." It became a heresy to suggest, as the small

groups of pacifists did, that there should be a negotiated peace
without victors or vanquished. Any talk of peace was taboo for
fear of sowing dissension and weakening the will to win.

LABOUR AND THE WAR

A further element in the situation was the importance attached
by all belligerent governments to the loyalty of organized labour.
It was quite impossible for any government to fight at all unless
it had the full and willing co-operation of its workers. And the
governments were at the outset somewhat nervous as to whether
they could rely on getting it.

At first, however, all went well. The Socialist parties, it is true,
had pledged themselves repeatedly:

> To use every effort to prevent war by all the means which
> seem to them most appropriate, having regard to the sharp-
> ness of the class war and to the general political situation.
> Should war none the less break out, their duty is to inter-
> vene to bring it promptly to an end and with all their
> energies to use the political and economic crisis created by
> the war to rouse the populace from its slumbers and to
> hasten the fall of capitalist domination.[5]

But when the 1914 crisis became acute, the International Socialist Bureau, which was supposed to co-ordinate working-class
action, limited itself to recommendations that the German and
French workers should bring pressure to bear on their governments, "in order that Germany may secure in Austria a moderating action, and in order that France may obtain from Russia an
undertaking that she will not engage in the conflict."

This was on July 28, the day Austria declared war on Serbia.
The French Socialist leader Jean Jaurès was murdered in Paris
on July 31 by a patriotic assassin. A German Socialist visited Paris
on August 1. The British Labour party issued a protest against
war on the same date, and on August 2 an anti-war meeting was
held in Trafalgar Square, at which a resolution was passed spe-
cially protesting against "any step being taken by the Govern-

ment of this country to support Russia either directly or in consequence of any understanding with France." *

But this was the extent of war resistance by the international
labour movement. In Russia the socialist leaders (except, of
course, Lenin, who was in exile) took the view that as Russia was
fighting on the side of the democratic Western powers against
semi-autocratic Germany and Austria-Hungary, they should support Czardom in the belief that victory would bring a democratic
revolution.

The socialists of the central powers argued that barbarous
Russia was the enemy and that they must support their governments as representing relative civilization and democracy against
the Czar.

The French and British socialist and trade-union leaders were
also convinced that they were defending democracy, the rights of
small nations, and the sanctity of treaty obligations against Prussian militarism.

WAR-WEARINESS, WILSON, AND THE RUSSIAN REVOLUTION

The situation was changed by three factors: war-weariness,
the Russian Revolution, and the entry of the United States into
the war. The two latter events broke the evil enchantment, the
taboo on talking about peace. They gave more reality to the
propaganda about the war as an ideological conflict between
democracy and militarism. They began the great debate on peace
terms and the awakening of the peoples.

Wilsonian idealism was important in encouraging the Allied
peoples and discouraging those of the central powers. But the
influence of the Russian Revolution was more far-reaching. It
had, indeed, a profounder influence on the ending of the war and
on the Peace Conference than has yet been realized. The rest of
this chapter will be devoted to analysis of how these three factors
—the Russian Revolution, the Allied governments, and President

---

* The Conservative party, on the other hand, urged the Government to
support France and Russia against Germany at any cost! This is an almost
exact inversion of the position of the two parties in the thirties.

Wilson—interacted on each other and on their peoples in the last twenty months of the war. The story is rich in lessons that are startlingly apposite today and cast a vivid light on the social dynamics of the Peace Conference and on subsequent history.

In order to follow a guiding thread through what may otherwise seem a confusingly complex narrative, the developments in Great Britain will be taken as the starting-point for the analysis of the situation. This is a logical approach, because the British Empire's war effort in men, material, money, and sea-power was far the greatest single factor on the Allied side, and Great Britain occupied politically and financially an intermediate position between the Continental Allies and the United States.

The central feature in organizing the British war effort was the necessity for securing the full co-operation of labour. Mr. Lloyd George, organizer-in-chief of victory, returns to this point again and again in his *War Memoirs*.

There was an advantage, he tells us, in having

a Liberal rather than a Tory Government in power when war was declared. There was a further advantage in having a Government at the head of affairs which had the support of Labour. This secured the adhesion of the great Labour organisations whose action and sympathetic aid were essential to its vigorous prosecution. Had Labour been hostile the war could not have been carried on effectively. Had Labour been lukewarm victory would have been secured with increased and increasing difficulty. The most prominent and influential leaders of trade unionism worked for victory throughout the war. Without their help it could not have been achieved.[6]

In his speech to the Labour Party Executive, urging them to be represented in the War Cabinet, Mr. Lloyd George said:

It is obvious that no Government can be carried on in this country, whether during war or peace, without, I won't say the support of Labour, but the co-operation of Labour. Upon its determination to help in winning this War, everything depends.[7]

In the subsequent discussion with the Executive, Mr. Lloyd George adds:

In reply to a question as to the position Labour would take in Peace Negotiations, when the time for such negotiations arrived, I said it seemed inconceivable that any Minister should make terms of Peace without consulting representatives of Labour.[8]

Mr. Lloyd George's *War Memoirs* recur again and again to the necessity for either coercing or conciliating organized labour into accepting progressively more drastic measures of industrial and military conscription and into surrendering one trade-union safeguard after another. Mr. Lloyd George shows sympathy with the reluctance of labour to make these concessions,* but is quite clear on the point that they had to be made in the superior interests of the war, and that the only criterion of whether force or persuasion should be used was the degree of resistance that might be expected.

In August 1915, he tells us:

I had to weigh carefully the alternatives of taking drastic action or trying conciliation. Had stern action proved successful without rousing wide antagonism, it would greatly have expedited the process of dilution. If it had failed against a massed opposition on the part of the skilled workers —for it would obviously have been impossible to punish them all—the campaign for dilution might have been permanently lost.

Conciliation was finally preferred to force as being a slower but

* He also understood the workers' point of view. Cf. the following: "As regards the control of our man-power, our difficulty throughout the War with the representatives of labour centred around the suspicion of profiteering by the proprietors of works engaged on Government contracts, so that the workers in them had not the same feeling of direct and wholehearted national service that they developed in the Army and Navy. To conscript men for industry seemed to the workers equivalent to forcing them by law to work for the benefit of private capitalists—a proceeding which they would quite rightly have resisted to the utmost." (Vol. III, pp. 1355-56.)

safer method. Or, to be more accurate, there was a mixture of coercion and conciliation, the proportions of the mixture varying according to the degree of militancy shown by the workers and their leaders. The stiffer the temper of labour, the more conciliation and the less coercion, and *vice versa*.

How the Russian Revolution impinged on this situation is made clear by the following quotation from the semi-official *History of the Peace Conference*, edited by Harold W. V. Temperley:

> . . . the whole situation was changed by the Russian Revolution and the unexpected length of the war. The success of the Russian workers in overthrowing the Czar's power gave confidence to the workers in other countries. Suggestions began to be popular in labour organizations that the Government was incapable of taking steps towards peace and there seemed to be no possibility of a conclusive victory.[9]

The Russian Revolution, the Allies, and Wilson

It is worth filling in the details of this picture. First of all it is necessary to understand just what happened in the Russian Revolution. In the account that follows it will be observed that the witnesses quoted are of unimpeachable authority, since they were themselves actors in the drama and, so far as Allied policy was concerned, were largely responsible for the decisions that were taken. None of them can be suspected of sympathy with socialist and left-wing views.

The first witness is Mr. Bruce Lockhart, who was British consul general in Moscow during the war and the first part of the Russian Revolution, and was afterwards British agent in Moscow accredited to the unrecognized Soviet Government until the rupture with the Bolsheviks and open intervention. Mr. Lockhart says:

> The revolution took place because the patience of the Russian people broke down under a system of unparalleled inefficiency and corruption. No other nation would have stood the privations which Russia stood, for anything like the same length of time. As instances of the inefficiency, I give the dis-

graceful mishandling of food-supplies, the complete break-down of transport, and the senseless mobilisation of millions of unwanted and unemployable troops. As an example of the corruption, I quote the shameless profiteering of nearly everyone engaged in the giving and taking of war contracts. . . .

What it is important to realise is that from the first the revolution was a revolution of the people. From the first moment neither the Duma nor the intelligentzia had any control of the situation. Secondly, the revolution was a revolution for land, bread and peace—but, above all, for peace. There was only one way to save Russia from going Bolshevik. That was to allow her to make peace. It was because he would not make peace that Kerensky went under.* [10]

The Duma was the consultative parliament set up after the 1905 revolution, but deprived of all its power, and given such a limited franchise in the 1906 counter-revolution that its deputies were almost all elected by landowners, the bureaucracy, and banking and business interests. After the first 1917 revolution the reactionary parties tended to coalesce with the "Cadets" (these were the initials of the Constitutional Democrats, a sort of Liberal party, which, however, after the revolution became mostly concerned with preventing political revolution from growing into a social revolution).

Side by side with the Duma a network of soviets (the Russian for councils) sprang up, composed of soldiers', workers', and

* Cf. also *The Intimate Papers of Colonel House*, letter from Mr. Arthur Bullard, of the American Red Cross Mission, dated Petrograd, December 12, 1917: "If the [Russian] soldier had been promised his land, if he had been made to believe that continued fighting meant the defense of the Revolution, if the real democratic idealism of the allied nations had not been hidden by the diplomatic rebuff to the Russian demand for a frank statement of war aims, the miracle might have been accomplished. But the Provisional Government and Kerenski were doomed because they refused to meet those two burning issues of the people—'land and peace.' The Bolsheviks got into power because they tried 'to meet the popular demands . . . because they had the men of sufficient daring to cut all the Gordian knots, to meet the real issues frankly, daringly, unscrupulously.' " (*Op. cit.*, 4 vols., Houghton Mifflin, 1926–28, Vol. III, pp. 387-88.)

peasants' deputies from farms, factories, and regiments. The local soviets elected representatives to a central All-Russian Soviet. From the outset the masses were behind the soviets, and did not support the middle-class and landowning elements represented in the Duma. The soviets, in their turn, were at first dominated by the Social Revolutionaries and the Mensheviks, who believed in the necessity for "national unity" with the bourgeoisie represented by the Cadets. They therefore supported the Provisional Government formed by the latter and afterwards joined them in a Coalition Government, of which the Prime Minister was Kerensky, a very Right-wing Social Revolutionary. Lockhart says:

> . . . the Allies greeted the revolution first with feigned enthusiasm and then with increasing alarm. They wanted—and on the part of the military advisers the wish was natural— things to be put back where they were before.[11]

In this connection it may be recalled that Lord Milner, returning from an official visit to Russia a fortnight before the revolution broke out, reported that there was no danger of revolution until after the war.

Mr. Lockhart complains frequently and bitterly of the complete lack of understanding for the Russian Revolution shown by the Government, of which he was the diplomatic representative on the spot:

> That British Ministers were unable to see any sign of order in the prevailing chaos was natural enough. Where they were to blame was in listening to too many counsellors, and in not realising the fundamental truth that in Russia the educated class represented only an infinitesimal minority, without organisation or political experience and without any contact with the masses. It was the crowning folly of Tsarism that outside its own bureaucracy it had sternly repressed every political outlet. When Tsarism collapsed, the bureaucracy collapsed with it, and there was nothing left but the masses. In Moscow, with one's finger on the pulse of events, everyone except the most obstinate traditionalist could realise that here was a cataclysm which had shattered all previous conceptions of Russia. London, however, continued

to regard it as a passing storm, after which the glass would
return to "set fair." The most dangerous of all historical ap-
horisms is the catch-phrase: *"plus ça change, plus c'est la
même chose."* During the spring and summer of 1918 it was
constantly on the lips of the British pro-interventionists.[12]

President Wilson was far more sympathetic to the revolution
than the Allies. During the spring of 1917, says the editor of *The
Intimate Papers of Colonel House,* it was clear that some sort of
restatement of war aims by the Entente was necessary if revolutionary Russia was to be kept in the alliance. Pressure was being
exerted by the soviets on the Kerensky Government to compel it

> . . . to disavow all imperialist war purposes. The new policy
> was summed up in the phrase, imported from German So-
> cialism, "Peace without annexations or indemnities on the
> basis of the right of nations to decide their own destiny."
> The response of the Entente Powers, as expressed in the
> speeches of their leading statesmen as well as in official notes
> sent to Petrograd, seemed evasive and did not satisfy the
> Russians. It was easier for President Wilson, whose hands
> were tied by no promises of territorial annexations, to meet
> the new Russian attitude.[13]

Wilson therefore began a policy of on the one hand trying to
induce the Allies to abandon the secret treaties and agree publicly to reasonable peace terms, and on the other of reassuring
the Russians and liberal and labour opinion by his own pronouncements on peace.

Kerensky's difficulties are vividly summed up as follows by Mr.
Bruce Lockhart:

> Kerensky was the victim of the bourgeois hopes which his
> short-lived success aroused. . . . From the start he was fight-
> ing a hopeless battle, trying to drive back into the trenches
> a nation which had already finished with the war. Caught
> between the cross-fires of the Bolshevik Left, which was
> screaming peace at every street-corner and in every trench,
> and of the Right and of the Allies, who were demanding the
> restoration of discipline by Tsarist methods, he had no

chance. And he fell, because whoever had tried to do what
he did was bound to fall.[14]

Now let us look at these events and at their repercussion on the
labour situation in Great Britain through the eyes of the British
Government at the time. Said Mr. Lloyd George:

As the year 1917 advanced we were faced, in addition to
our darkening war anxieties, with the necessity of handling
with a wise admixture of firmness and moderation the
domestic situation that arose from industrial and political unrest, aggravated to an acute degree by the forces released
through the Russian upheaval.[15]

"To maintain our national unity and pursue steadily our national purpose" in the circumstances labour had to be handled
"prudently as well as firmly. . . . In this part of the same struggle
Mr. Arthur Henderson became a war casualty."

By this Mr. Lloyd George means his dispute with Mr. Henderson over the Stockholm Conference, of which more is said below.
The social tension, anxiety, and war-weariness in all the belligerents on both sides were equally great, adds Mr. Lloyd George.

Sir George Buchanan, the British Ambassador in Petrograd,
was very much concerned at the growing power and pacifist in-
clinations of the Soviets. Sir George, says Mr. Lloyd George, was
so identified with the Cadets and the old régime that his position
since the revolution had become difficult. Moreover, he "never
concealed the fact that he had no sympathy whatever with Socialists." On being asked by M. Albert Thomas, the French
Socialist Minister of Munitions, who dined with him at Petrograd,
what he would have said five years ago if told that three Socialists would one day be guests at his table, Sir George replied:
"The very idea of such a thing would have appalled me." [16]

But Sir George Buchanan was prepared to do his duty, however distasteful. On March 15, 1917, he telegraphed:

"Open opposition is likely to develop very shortly between
the parties of the Social Revolution and the Duma. The
latter is for war, and should it prevail quickly, Russia will be
rendered stronger than in the past. Peace at any price is the

object of the former party, and military disaster would follow its advent to power. Could English Labour leaders be induced to send a telegram to Duma Labour leaders (Kerensky and Chkheidze) expressing their confidence that Kerensky and Chkheidze and their comrades will support the free peoples fighting German despotism. . . . The telegram might also refer to the unity of all classes in Britain, and especially to what the working classes are doing."

A telegram was accordingly drafted by Mr. Henderson, the representative of Labour in the British War Cabinet, and sent off to the Labour leaders in the Duma.[17]

This spontaneous gesture by the British workers does not seem to have produced the desired effect, for a further move was found necessary. It is described as follows by Lockhart:

As the dangers of the Russian revolution came home to the British ministers at home, strenuous efforts were made to bring the Russians to their senses and to recall them sternly to the obligations of their alliance. Some genius hit on the idea of sending out a Franco-British Socialist delegation to persuade the Russian comrades to continue fighting.[18]

The three Frenchmen were intellectuals. When they came home, they reported against the policy of the French Government and in favour of the Stockholm Conference and the peace terms desired by the Soviet. (Two later went Communist.) This started a movement in the French Socialist party that led to M. Albert Thomas's threat to resign from the Government in August owing to its Russian policy and opposition to the Stockholm Conference, and to the whole French Socialist party's joining with the British Labour party at the end of the year (1917) on a program for a negotiated peace (of which more is said below).

The British delegation were Messrs. Jim O'Grady (later Sir James O'Grady and a colonial governor), Will Thorne, and W. W. Sanders, who came "to preach wisdom and patriotism to the Soviets." Mr. Lockhart says of both delegations:

From the first the visit was a farce. The delegates fulfilled their task honourably. But, as anyone might have foreseen, they were completely lost in the wilderness of Russian revolutionary phraseology. They were bewildered by the endless discussions on peace terms. They understood the jargon of the Russian Socialists far less than I did. They were handicapped by their ignorance of the language. Worst of all, they never succeeded in winning the confidence even of the moderate Socialists, who from the first regarded them as lackeys of their respective governments.[19]

That the mission was indeed not very successful we gather from Sir George Buchanan's message of May 30, 1917:

> I do not think that the Council [i.e., Soviet] is likely to press for an early peace; but it will probably give us a good deal of trouble as to the terms on which the Allies ought to accept peace and as to the interpretation to be placed on the word "annexation."

The chief danger was that Germany would offer plausible conditions of peace, and the Russians would exert pressure on the Allies to open peace negotiations.

> They are now attacking our Labour Delegates as being the paid emissaries of the Government and not real representatives of British labour. It is very difficult to know what to do with people who stick to their preconceived ideas and will not listen to reason.[20]

The nature of the difficulty hinted at by Sir George Buchanan and the methods taken to overcome it are alike made clear by Mr. Lockhart. A few days after the Franco-British labour delegation, and almost simultaneously with the return to Russia of Lenin, M. Albert Thomas arrived in Petrograd to argue with the Soviet.

> One service, which seemed important at the time, he rendered to the Allies. The Soviets, at this moment, were engaged in abstract discussions about peace terms. They had invented the formula of "peace without annexations and contributions," and this phrase, adopted at thousands of meetings in the trenches and in the villages, had spread like wildfire throughout the country. It was a formula which caused considerable annoyance and even anxiety to the English and French Governments, which had already divided up the

spoils of a victory not yet won, in the form of both annexations and contributions. And both the French Ambassador
and Sir George Buchanan had been requested to circumvent
this new and highly dangerous form of pacifism. Their task
was delicate and difficult. There seemed no way out of the
impasse, and in despair they sought the advice of Thomas.
The genial Socialist laughed.

"I know my Socialists," he said. "They will shed their
blood for a formula. You must accept it and alter its interpretation."

So annexations became restitution and contributions reparations. It was, I imagine, the first time the word reparations was used officially, and Thomas certainly succeeded in
persuading the Soviets to accept a clause in their formula for
the restitution of Alsace-Lorraine. At the time it seemed an
important achievement. Actually, as the Mensheviks and
Social-Revolutionaries, who had yielded to the Thomas subtlety, were so soon to be swept away, it made no difference
whatsoever.[21]

Mr. Arthur Henderson too was sent to Russia. He, unlike his
British predecessors, ended by accepting the Soviets' formula for
a negotiated peace and became a partisan of the International
Socialist Conference at Stockholm, proposed by M. Branting, the
Swedish Socialist leader, and strongly supported by the Soviets
(except by the Bolsheviks, who were of the opinion that nothing
short of working-class revolutions could bring peace). Says Mr.
Lloyd George:

Fresh from the glow of that atmosphere of emotionalism
and exaltation which great Revolutions excite, Mr. Henderson was out of tune with the stern but frigid sense of responsibility and self-control which was dominant here. When he
came back from Russia the fine steel of his character was
magnetised by his experiences. He was in an abnormal frame
of mind. He had more than a touch of the revolutionary
malaria. His temperature was high and his mood refrac-
tory.[22]

How strong this peace atmosphere was in Russia and how well
Mr. Lloyd George understood it are made clear by the following:

The demand for peace was becoming more and more imperative. The speeches delivered at the endless meetings held at street corners in Russian cities were a prolonged keen for peace. Albert Thomas described them to me on his return. His account reminded me of the meetings I had witnessed in the Welsh Revival. The excitement was not violent, but deep. An eerie emotion, more religious than political, seemed to have possessed the Russian workers. With a nation in such a mood, anything was possible. But its temper did not conduce to an effective prosecution of the War.[23]

How different the atmosphere was in Britain is described by Lockhart, who records his impression of a visit to London that summer as follows:

> Hate of the revolution and fear of its consequences in England were the dominant reactions of Conservatives, who at that moment had an unnatural and to-day inexplicable dread of the machinations of Mr. Arthur Henderson. I found the same fears among the Labour patriots. At Cadogan Square I renewed my acquaintance with Jim O'Grady and Will Thorne. They, too, were critical of Mr. Henderson, who, they said, had gone over to the Snowdenites and was playing for revolution and the Labour Premiership.[24]

So far, it will be noted, whereas President Wilson thought that the Russian desire for peace required a revision of the Allied war aims so as to make them respectable enough for support by revolutionary Russia, the Allies had met the situation by trying to bamboozle the Russians into supporting annexations and indemnities under a different name. For this purpose they used what they believed were "safe" British and French labour leaders—with occasional boomerang effects. Their next step was to defeat the proposal for a Stockholm Conference.

THE STOCKHOLM CONFERENCE

The invitation to the latter was issued by the Dutch and Scandinavian labour organizations. The idea was that Austrian, Russian, German, British, French, Belgian, and Italian socialists should meet with the socialists of the neutral countries to hammer out a socialist basis for peace.

> . . . despair of any conclusion to the war was driving the people to look about for some new method of approach to a settlement. By the autumn of 1917 in all belligerent countries organized labour was inclined to feel that the Governments could do nothing and that labour itself must make the first move towards peace.[25]

The idea behind the Stockholm Conference, in other words, was that labour should take the job of peacemaking out of the hands of capitalist governments and do it themselves. That was precisely why the governments were opposed to the idea. Mr. Lloyd George gives two somewhat different explanations of his opposition. He says, first, that he objected to the Labour party's taking this action not because they were socialists, but because they were a party, and he would not have any political party dictating what should be the terms of peace. But in answer to questions by the British trade-union delegation in January, 1918, he stated his objection to the Stockholm Conference as follows:

> It is a fundamental misconception of democracy that any section, however powerful, really represents the whole of the people. Whoever goes there to speak and to negotiate must represent the whole of the country, and not merely a part of it. . . . I said that . . . it would be a very dangerous experiment. If you let the Socialist sections meet to confer on peace terms, you would have to let other sections do the same—the financiers of Britain and of Germany, the industrialists, merchants and so on. It would all end in confusion. The only effective way was for the people of each country to see that their Government represented their views, and then leave it to negotiate the peace.[26]

This explanation at least has the merit of recognizing that labour is not like any other party, because it represents the workers as an economic class. But it overlooks the fact that the British Government for all practical purposes represented the financiers, industrialists, and merchants, who had already expressed their views on peace terms in the secret treaties. Labour, on the other hand, although its co-operation was essential for the prosecution of the war, was not consulted on peace terms, in spite of Mr. Lloyd George's promises that it would be. In fact, labour was being deliberately deceived. For on the very occasion (January 18, 1918, at the Central Hall, Westminster) when Mr. Lloyd George had given his reply quoted above, he had told the assembled trade-union delegates that the Government's war aims were the same as those put forward by the Labour party and the Trade Union Congress (and by President Wilson in his Fourteen Points).

It was in exchange for these assurances as to what Great Britain was fighting for that the trade-unions agreed to more "combing out" of men for the front. The assurances were unfortunately false. The whole transaction is described in detail where it fits in chronologically after the events that now fall to be recorded.

THE RUSSIAN JULY OFFENSIVE

While they were defeating the attempts of the Russian soviets and of a large part of the working class in belligerent and neutral countries to bring about an explicit statement of war aims, the Allied governments were driving Kerensky into the July offensive. They also had a little trouble with President Wilson, who was still trying to induce France, Great Britain, and Italy to abandon their secret treaties.

The insistence on the July offensive had an obvious military motive. But it also had political and social motives. A British officer wrote from Cronstadt:

> I am inclined to think that the policy of the Government is to coax the people into a summer offensive in the hope that peace will then slip into the background. I am not hopeful. Everyone is clear that Russia is sick of the War.[27]

The social motive is revealed in a telegram from General (now Sir) Alfred Knox, an Ulsterman with an Indian Army background who was the British military attaché in St. Petersburg (Petrograd) before and during the war, after that interventionist-in-chief and Mr. Churchill's confidential agent in the unofficial war on the Russian Revolution (see next chapter), and later a die-hard member of Parliament. Mr. Lloyd George says he was "one of the shrewdest observers we sent to Russia" and was "at the head of Russian affairs at this time." He adds that General Knox's view of Russia was that "the heart of the people was sound, but that force was required, and force could have been assembled if the Government had contained a single man of will." The folly of that belief is commented upon repeatedly and bitterly by Mr. Lockhart.[28] Even Mr. Lloyd George is constrained to admit that President Wilson considered General Knox so reactionary that he not only refused to see him, but did not want him to cross the United States on his way to begin intervention in Siberia.[29] (General Knox had to go via Suez, India, China, and Japan.)

General Knox's telegram from Petrograd, dated August 4, 1917, says:

> The Socialists would prefer to run a class war rather than the national war, and to the mass of soldiers this appeals as being not so dangerous. . . . Tscretelli and others think they can run both wars simultaneously. We have to tell the Russian Government plainly that this is impossible. . . . Till discipline is established in the army, it is impossible to force the men in the railway repair shops and the mines to work.[30]

It is plain that in General Knox's mind running the national war was almost indistinguishable from conducting a class war in reverse. He was far from being alone in that view.

The results of the July offensive were graphically depicted by General Knox in a long wire on July 10. The army, he reported, did not want to fight, discipline had disappeared, there was a general collapse of morale, demoralization, and disintegration

> . . . the result of dissatisfaction with conditions which had prevailed since the beginning of the War, and before. . . .
> However, all the regular officers that have survived the War and the Revolution worked heroically to stem the tide of socialistic cowardice and to restore order out of chaos. . . .

The "delegate" is now looked upon as the universal panacea, but he is not half so effective as were the subaltern's boot and fist in former times. . . .

Korniloff told me that he considered the offensive the last chance, and that the economic condition of Russia and the breakdown of the railways will make the continuation of the War through a fourth winter impossible.

General Count Ignatiev, commanding the First Division of the Infantry of the Guard:

. . . considers that peace is essential for Russia, for if there is not peace soon there will be a general massacre. The prolongation of the War is driving the country to economic ruin. From the very beginning the peasants had hated the War, which was only at first popular with the educated classes.

General Knox adds the comment:

I believe this is true. The Revolution has been a revolt against the burden of the War, and not a protest, as the English Press at first tried to pretend, against the half-hearted way in which the late Government prosecuted the War.[31]

WILSON TRIES AGAIN

On top of the collapse of the July offensive and Russia's incontinent longing for peace came the Pope's peace proposals in August 1917, and President Wilson's embarrassing desire to utilize the occasion for a restatement of the Allies' war aims. Colonel House records with modest pride how he induced the President to amend his draft reply to the Pope. On August 24 he wrote the President:

England and France will not like some of it, notably where on p. three you say that "no peace can rest upon political or economic restrictions meant to benefit some nations and cripple others, upon vindictive action of any sort, or any kind of revenge or deliberate injury."

And again on p. four where you say "Punitive damages, the dismemberment of empires, the establishment of selfish and economic leagues, we deem childish," etc.

The next day he wrote again, suggesting that the President should substitute some other word for "childish," because:

This sentence may cause dissension and to apply the term "childish" to the group advocating these things would add fuel to the fire. Of course, what you say is true, but sometimes the truth hurts more than anything else.

Mr. Wilson obligingly changed "childish" to "inexpedient." Emboldened by this success, Colonel House suggested the Allies might agree to accept the President's note as their own anwer to the Pope and:

This would in itself go far towards a coördination of war aims and perhaps indicate a tendency towards the revision of the more extreme territorial aspirations of the Allies.
    [But] the President was conscious of such a difference between his point of view and that of the European Allies that he feared any attempt to reach an agreement. . . . It is likely that the French and Italians felt that such ratification would commit them too far in the direction of a revision of the aspirations that found expression in the secret treaties [unlike the British Government, which adopted the policy of endorsing President Wilson's statements in public, while hanging on to their share of the secret treaties in private].

Because of his "acute consciousness of the difference between his own war aims and those of the Allies," [32] President Wilson appointed a number of experts to formulate the American peace program. For he felt the "vital need" for:

. . . revision of what some termed the imperialist aspirations of the Entente. . . . The Allies must make it plain that they were waging their battle in behalf of permanent peace and not for the sake of territorial annexations. Only thus could the enthusiasm of liberal and labor elements be maintained.[33]

The Allies did not reply at all to the Pope, and did not associate themselves with Wilson's reply.*

The episode closed with "no change" as regards the secret treaties, but with some success in rekindling the enthusiasm of labour and liberal supporters of the war, who were, of course, blissfully ignorant of the existence of the secret treaties.

The War Cabinet and Kornilov

No sooner had the Pope and President Wilson's importunity been disposed of than there was more trouble from Russia. On September 7, 1917, General Knox, just back from that country, told the War Cabinet what he thought of the situation. According to the Cabinet minutes he explained:

> . . . there were three powerful forces tending to drive the Russians to make a separate peace [namely, first] The great mass of the soldiers did not want to fight. They had not wanted to fight before the Revolution, but had been forced on by their officers. There had been frequent cases of indiscipline before the Revolution; now they were quite general.
>
> In the second place, workmen were making huge economic demands on their employers, and British manufacturers were closing factories and moving away. It was expected that there would shortly be a general lock-out. The Government had repeatedly promised to organise a police force in Moscow and Petrograd, but nothing had been done.
>
> The third force was the confusion on the railways. . . .
>
> If Kerensky were to suggest a separate peace he would certainly have the great majority of the country with him.[34]

Did it occur to any member of the Cabinet at this point that perhaps, in view of the progressive collapse of Russia under the strain of war, and of President Wilson's wishes, and of the growing unrest of labour (of which more will be said shortly), there might be a case for abandoning the imperialist secret treaties and

* To illustrate the complexity of reality, we may add that one reason the Allies did not reply was Italy's quarrel with the Pope's claim to temporal power. But it was not the main reason.

trying the effect of a little common honesty? It did not. How the War Cabinet reacted to the situation is made clear by the minutes, which continue as follows:

In reply to questions as to the likelihood of a *coup d'état*, headed by General Korniloff [the Commander in Chief], General Knox said that he did not know what preparations were being made. When he left Russia, on the 18th August, Korniloff and Savinkoff were in agreement. Korniloff was a strong character, an honest patriot, the best man in sight. He had the support of the Cossacks. . . . He [General Knox] had no faith in Kerensky. . . . Kerensky was afraid of shedding blood and was letting things drift towards anarchy. A force of 10,000 loyalists would be enough to subdue Petrograd—the main source of disorder.*

In concluding his statement, General Knox strongly urged on the War Cabinet the importance of a joint representation from the Allied Governments, recommending to the Russian Government that in view of Russia's desperate situation and the peril of putting back democracy, General Korniloff should be fully supported in the measures which he wished to take to restore discipline at the front, on the railways, and in Petrograd.

Meanwhile, continues Mr. Lloyd George, Kornilov:

Roused to anger by Kerensky's procrastination in giving him full powers, including the reimposition of the death penalty for disobeying orders, had been persuaded to agree to an attempt to get himself proclaimed Military Dictator.

Did the fact that Kornilov had become a rebel against a government which was our Ally, and was aspiring to a dictatorship, shake the War Cabinet's belief that he should be supported for the sake of "democracy"? It did not. On September 12 the War Cabinet met again. The minutes state:

It was felt that, difficult though it was for the British Government to interfere in the present situation without appear-

* This is an interesting example of the discretion with which Cabinet minutes are edited. For there is no doubt that General Knox knew all about the Kornilov rebellion that broke out two days after his report to the Cabinet.

ing to take sides with General Korniloff, it was essential, in
the interests of the Allies and of democracy generally, to
make an effort to improve the situation . . . [Consequently]
It was suggested that [Kerensky] should be informed that
the British Government viewed with the greatest alarm the
probabilities of civil war, and urged him to come to terms
with General Korniloff not only in the interest of Russia herself, but in that of the Allies.

"Events, however," observes Mr. Lloyd George, "delivered us
from the dilemma of choosing between Kerensky and Korniloff,
for Korniloff was denounced as a traitor and arrested." * 35

Kerensky, it must be repeated, was the head of a recognized
government that was our ally in the war, and Kornilov was a
rebel against that government. Moreover, in pursuit of his rebellion, he abandoned Riga to the Germans and denuded the front
of his best troops in order to march on Petrograd. From start to
finish his rebellion was assisted by the Allied military attachés,
with the knowledge of the Allied governments.

THE BOLSHEVIK REVOLUTION, PEACE, AND THE WAR CABINET

The July offensive and the Kornilov rebellion between them
dealt a mortal blow to the Kerensky régime and made the October (or rather November) Revolution possible.

The Bolsheviks lost no time in carrying out their program of
"peace and land." They proclaimed that their first aim was a "just
and democratic peace." On November 20 and 29 Lenin proposed

* He adds: "Had he been successful in establishing a military dictatorship
it is more than doubtful, in view of the complete disintegration of the army,
whether it would have been helpful to the Allies. The stubborn qualities of
the Russian peasant soldier, which gave him that endurance which made
him formidable even in defeat, had now been converted into a sulky and
immutable resolve not to do any more fighting at anyone's bidding." This
view was based on General Knox's reports after the collapse of the July
offensive, and contained much truth. It also cast a curious light on the real
motives of the Cabinet's desire to support Kornilov's rebellion. (Vol. V,
p. 2563.)

to all belligerents that they should conclude an armistice and negotiate a general peace. On November 27, Trotsky, the War Commissar, informed the military attachés of the Allies that the Soviet Government was issuing an appeal for a general armistice, but would be obliged to negotiate a separate armistice if the Allies refused to come in, and would, if not recognized, appeal to the people over the heads of their governments.

On December 3 armistice negotiations began with the central powers, as the Allies had refused the Soviet invitation. On December 15 the armistice was signed, and on December 22 peace negotiations began at Brest-Litovsk. On that day the Soviet Government put forward terms for a general peace that Mr. Lloyd George describes as "plausible." They were as follows:

1. No forcible annexations of territory taken during the War.

2. Complete restoration of independence to the nationalities who had lost it during the War.

3. Nationalities not hitherto enjoying independence to have the right to decide by plebiscite whether they should be united to other States or acquire independence.

4. Safeguarding of the rights of minorities in territories inhabited by several nationalities.

5. No war indemnities, but war requisitions to be returned.

6. Colonial acquisitions to be decided on the same principles. Economic war was condemned by the Russians.[36]

At Brest-Litovsk the Bolsheviks

. . . were primarily concerned with setting forth their principles of peace settlement in such a manner as would react at once upon the proletariat of all the belligerents and would thus lead to the World Revolution, which would replace the Imperialist war by the Class War, which was the first essential of their political doctrines. They went to Brest-Litovsk "relying solely upon the revolutionary succour of the working classes of the other belligerent countries—above all, of Germany and Austria-Hungary." . . .

The Bolshevik insistence on "no secret diplomacy" gave the negotiations an entirely novel aspect from the start. They had begun the publication of the secret treaties in the last week of November, and they now began to issue a series of daily reports on the proceedings at Brest, supplemented by wireless invectives. . . .

The German Government were forced to follow suit and to issue their own account of the sittings.* [37]

The effect of these methods was to create dissension between the Germans and the Austrians, and between the German Government and its general staff. Above all, a deep and lasting impression was made on German and Austrian public opinion. The proceedings at Brest-Litovsk helped powerfully to open the eyes of the Austrian and German workers to the imperialism of their governments, and to create a revolutionary atmosphere in those countries.

What weakened the Bolshevik position was that the Allies, instead of helping them to resist German claims, had begun the policy of "drifting toward intervention." [38] The first-fruit of this policy was that the anti-Bolshevik government which the Allies were propping up in the Ukraine concluded a separate peace with Germany and Austria-Hungary, and then threw in its lot with those powers and welcomed a Germano-Austrian army of occupation.

If the Allies had replied to the Soviet Government's peace terms by an acceptance, coupled with a pronouncement upon the League, declared their readiness for conversations if German

* Temperley says, speaking of Brest-Litovsk and its consequences: "the Russian phrases 'self-determination,' 'no annexations,' and 'no punitive indemnities' were so attractive to many that even the German military *régime* seemed for a time to be finding a use for idealism. . . . German politicians feared the effect of revolutionary ideas and of President Wilson's principles and were anxious to disguise their designs by elaborate lip-service. . . . Their [the Bolsheviks'] revolutionary propaganda had penetrated far and wide— most notably in Germany." (Vol. I, pp. 212-222, 235.) General Smuts, on p. 14 of his Peace Conference pamphlet, *The League of Nations: A Practical Suggestion,* wrote: "The German battle-front collapsed the more readily before Foch because the scandalous Brest-Litovsk Treaty had thoroughly disillusioned and demoralised the German people."

troop movements to the West ceased,* and the proposed basis
for negotiations were also fully accepted by the central powers,
and helped the Bolsheviks to get ready to resist if the central
powers refused their terms, the Bolsheviks' bold bid for peace
might have succeeded, and the world been spared an infinitude
of suffering past, present, and to come. At the worst the Allies
should have still further disintegrated the German home front,
consolidated their own, and secured the Bolsheviks as Allies. But
that would have meant abandoning the secret treaties. What happened instead now falls to be related.

WILSON STILL TRYING

While the Soviet Government was struggling for peace, President Wilson was conducting a new offensive against the secret
treaties. In November 1917 he sent Colonel House across the
Atlantic in order to:

> . . . persuade the European Allies to issue a joint statement
> of war aims, which would weaken German propaganda and
> help the Allies to maintain friendly relations with Russia.
> Such a step, he maintained, was the more necessary because
> of the Bolshevik peace proposals and the increasing demand
> on the part of liberal and labor elements in Allied countries
> for an assurance that the war was not being continued for
> imperialistic ends.[39]

But the effort was abortive.

House found that Mr. Lloyd George was committed too
far to the British Conservatives to join enthusiastically in a
plan for a liberal restatement of war aims, and at Paris the
atmosphere was wholly unsympathetic.[40]

At an Inter-Allied Conference in Paris on November 30 House
tried to get agreement on the following resolution:

> The Allies and the United States declare that they are not
> waging war for the purpose of aggression or indemnity. The
> sacrifices they are making are in order that militarism shall

* Any military lull would have meant that time was on our side, because
of America's growing strength and the cumulative effect on the central
powers of the blockade.

not continue to cast its shadow over the world, and that nations shall have the right to lead their lives in the way that seems to them best for the development of their general welfare.[41]

The Allies would not hear of it.

Colonel House found it impossible . . . to persuade the Conference to agree upon even the mild resolution he had drafted. They were not ready to resign the hopes of territorial acquisitions.

The Italians in particular were almost frank in objecting to the resolution because it might be construed as denying them what they had been promised under the secret treaties.* [42]

Colonel House was so depressed at his failure that he wrote in his diary on November 30, 1917:

I feel a deep sympathy for the soldiers and sailors of the Allied nations who are dependent upon those of us here to give proper direction to the cause for which they are fighting. We are not doing all we could, and I realise it every time we meet in conference.[43]

THE ORIGIN OF THE FOURTEEN POINTS

But he soon found a way out. His diary on December 18 records how he had tried to persuade the Allies "to join in for-

* Mr. Lloyd George also mentions the Inter-Allied Conference of November 30. He says nothing, for obvious reasons, about House's offer and its reception. But he tells us (*op. cit.*, Vol. V, pp. 2570-71) he suggested that each Ally should inform the Russian Government that it was ready to discuss war aims, and pointed out that the Russian claims to Constantinople, the Bosporus, and Dardanelles, and the annexation of Bukowina, were no longer practical politics. "It was, therefore, not for us to refuse reconsideration of our avowed war aims." The suggestion does not appear to have found favour, presumably because the Allies were afraid the Bolsheviks might have been tactless enough to insist on discussing their *unavowed* war aims. For, unlike the Soviet Government, the Allies had not repudiated the secret treaties. Clemenceau turned down the British proposal that the Bolsheviks should be "released" from Russia's pledge not to make a separate peace.

mulating a broad declaration of war aims that would unite the
world against Germany, and would not only help to a solution
of the Russian problem but would knit together the best and
most unselfish opinions of the world. I could not persuade them
to do this and now it will be done by the President." [44]
This was indeed what happened.

From the inability of the Inter-Allied Conference to agree
upon a restatement of the war aims of the Entente in a liberal sense sprang the Fourteen Points. . . . Historians have
often wondered why Wilson chose to make the speech of the
Fourteen Points at the particular moment he selected. According to evidence in the House Papers, it was because the
American Mission failed to secure from the Inter-Allied
Conference a manifesto on war aims that might serve to hold
Russia in the war and result in an effective diplomatic offensive against the Central Powers. Complete diplomatic unity
between the Allies and the United States would have formed
the most useful weapon in such a policy. Because of the
failure to achieve this unity at Paris, President Wilson was
compelled to undertake the diplomatic offensive on his own
responsibility.[45]

Mr. Wilson took this step because he believed that "in default
of an inter-Allied manifesto, a comprehensive address by himself
might prove to be the moral turning-point of the war." His reasons for this belief were: (1) The Bolsheviks were already negotiating for a separate peace, and it was "impossible not to return
some sort of reply to their demand for a logical statement of why
the war should continue." (2) "Germany must not be allowed
to pose as the victim of Allied Imperialist aspirations." (3) On
December 13 the *Manchester Guardian* had published the texts
of the secret treaties released by the Bolsheviks. "Some correc-
tive was necessary." [46] (4) "It was important also to pledge, if
possible, the Allied Governments to the principles of a settlement which would justify the sacrifices of the war and maintain
the enthusiasm of the liberal and labor circles in Great Britain
and France. . . . President Wilson was the man best qualified by
position and ability to state the moral issues involved in the war

in such a way as to meet effectively the sentiment of protest that was rising in liberal and labor circles and was actively expressed in Russia." [47]

That was the origin of the Fourteen Points. "Their very vagueness . . . made of them an admirable tool of propaganda, but unfitted them for service as a peace programme.[48]

It is not surprising that the Fourteen Points speech had a great effect in reassuring labour and liberal opinion, but was coolly received by the Allied governments.

M. Clemenceau, "the Old Tiger," was indeed so irritated by it that he made a slighting reference in a speech in the Chamber to President Wilson's "noble candour." This was tactfully changed in the *Journal Officiel* to "noble grandeur" (*"candeur"* into *"grandeur"*).

How Labour Was Bamboozled

But the President's speech was a very present help in time of trouble to Mr. Lloyd George, who was just then in serious difficulties with organized labour.

The effect of the Russian Revolution on British labour has already been indicated. It weakened the agreement of official labour with the Government's war policy and broke the taboo on talking about peace. During 1917 the feeling grew that the governments were incapable of making peace and that labour must act independently. Mr. Henderson resigned from the War Cabinet in August.

. . . a new and definite labour policy in regard to war aims began to be formulated by various labour groups. A national conference of the Labour Party and the Trade Union Congress was held on the 28th December, 1917, at which a memorandum on war-aims was approved, and thus labour had a definitely expressed policy of its own in regard to the end of the war.[49]

The Labour movement's peace memorandum

accepts President Wilson's phrase "to make the world safe for Democracy" as the first reason for "supporting the continuance of the struggle." It sets out a scheme for a League of Nations, the reference of all disputes to arbitration, "the frank abandonment of every form of Imperialism," and it asserts, practically in Wilson's phrases, that "every territorial settlement involved in this war must be made in the interest and for the benefit of the populations concerned and not as a part of any adjustment or compromise of claims among rival States." In detail the memorandum proposes as war aims: (1) the restoration of Belgium and reparation by Germany for wrong done to Belgium; (2) a plebiscite for Alsace-Lorraine; (3) the evacuation of Serbia, Montenegro, Rumania, and Albania, and reorganization of the Balkan peoples under an International Commission; (4) an indefinite proposal with regard to Italian Adriatic problems; (5) the reconstitution of Poland; (6) a "free state under international guarantee" for the Jews in Palestine; (7) administration of Armenia, Mesopotamia, and Arabia by a Commission under the League of Nations, and "neutralization" of the Dardanelles; (8) not the dismemberment of Austria-Hungary but national independence, if demanded by the "Czecho-Slovaks and the Yugo-Slavs"; (9) in colonies and dependencies either "administrative autonomy" or "progressive participation in local government." Further, "the return of colonies to those who possessed them before the war or the exchanges or compensations which might be effected ought not to be an obstacle to the making of the peace," and it was proposed that a system of control under the League of Nations ought to be established for "the colonies of all belligerents in tropical Africa." The memorandum then proceeds to suggest freedom of trade, the open door, the international improvement of factory conditions, and the international control and allocation of exportable surpluses of foodstuffs and raw materials in order to prevent famine and unemployment.* [50]

The memorandum stipulated that there should be representation not only of governments but also direct representation of

* See the next chapter for further details of the nature and fate of this last proposal.

parliaments in the League, in some sort of international popular assembly.

Parallel with the development of political independence and opposition to the war in the labour movement there was growing industrial unrest.

Official trade unionism was unable to oppose the Government's industrial policy; but discontent was growing and the unofficial Shop Stewards' Committees, particularly in the engineering trade, became the exponents of the policy of "peace by negotiation." The difficulty was made still greater when it became necessary for the Government to seek for more men for the army in the early months of 1918. The "man-power controversy," as it was then called, brought out opposition in the industrial sphere.

An official ballot of the Amalgamated Society of Engineers gave a majority of 121,017 against and only 27,570 for the Government's proposals.

. . . at various conferences of Shop Stewards . . . the discussion turned upon the possibility of trade-union action to secure an early peace. Some district committees of trade unions proposed that the Government should adopt the war-aims of the Labour Party . . . before making any further call upon the man-power of the nation. Thus opposition, suspicion of the aims of the Government and an alternative policy were being developed. [Labour and trade-union organizations became more and more] eager to press upon public attention the statement of generous war-aims and the adoption of steps towards negotiation. It was now appreciated by the whole of organized labour that even domestic and industrial grievances, which were more easily understood by the rank and file, could not be redressed so long as the war continued. . . .

. . . despair of any conclusion to the war was driving the people to look about for some new method of approach to a settlement. By the autumn of 1917 in all belligerent countries organized labour was inclined to feel that the Governments could do nothing and that labour itself must make the first move towards peace.[51]

Mr. Lloyd George graphically describes how nervous the Government felt at this situation. Towards the end of 1917:

An answer was necessary to pacifist propaganda [because] There was a great deal of pacifist propaganda at home which, operating on a natural weariness, might develop into a dangerous anti-war sentiment that would undermine the morale of the nation at a time when events depended on the staying power of the nation.[52]

He had disquieting reports of large and enthusiastic peace meetings all over the country, and of the growing strength of the anti-war section in the Labour party. All the belligerent nations were confronted with a similar situation.*

It was essential to convince the nation that we were not continuing the War merely to gain a vindictive or looting triumph, but that we had definite peace aims and that these were both just and attainable.[53]

Against this background the labour situation was particularly disquieting.

Amongst the workmen there was an unrest that was disturbing and might at any moment become dangerous. The efforts we were making to comb out more men for the Army were meeting with resistance amongst the Trade Unions, whose loyalty and patriotism had been above reproach.[54]

In reckoning the limits of the combing-out process, he had, says Mr. Lloyd George, to

preserve peace on the home front. . . . The squeezing process in Germany of the last few months of the War was driving tens of thousands into desertion and ere many months passed it drove hundreds of thousands into rebellion which overthrew the throne. Some of the more powerful Trade Unions

* They were indeed. In France there was a widespread demand for peace and numerous mutinies in the army, involving no less than sixteen army corps. There were 21,000 desertions in 1917. In Germany there was a naval mutiny led by socialists and a series of strikes. Over a million workers took part in a general strike in January 1918.

were showing signs of becoming resistant to the pressure for combing out more of their men for the front.[55]

The men of military age were an often-sifted residue, all of them holding pledges of absolute or conditional exemption from military service; to call up a large, fresh batch of them * meant anxious diplomacy and frank consultation with the leaders of the Trade Unions.[56]

The difficulties with our man-power had almost produced a deadlock with the Trade-Unions. Without their goodwill and co-operation, we could not have secured further recruits from among the exempted—certainly not without a resistance which might have alienated organised labour throughout the land. . . . It therefore became necessary to open negotiations with them. . . . In order to ensure their co-operation it was necessary to place before them with complete frankness the purpose with which we were prosecuting the war.

The reader might be pardoned for believing that this meant the British Government had decided either to abandon the secret treaties or to confess their existence to the representatives of organized labour. But the reader would be wrong. What the Government meant by "complete frankness" is revealed by Mr. Lloyd George with startling candour. He explains that he studied labour's peace terms of December 1917 and then prepared a speech, discussed it with the Independent Liberal leaders (Asquith and Grey), and summoned the trade-union leaders to a meeting at the Caxton Hall on January 5, where he delivered an impassioned oration, asserting that the December 16 peace proposals of the Labour party and the Trade Union Congress did not differ materially "from those which we were putting forward. . . . I made it clear that our one object in the war was to defend the violated public law of Europe, to vindicate Treaty obligations and to secure the restoration of Belgium." [57]

After this, says Mr. Lloyd George, all opposition disappeared to releasing another 250,000 exempted men. The Labour party shortly afterwards issued a manifesto on the "War Aims of the

* To wit, a quarter of a million, namely 150,000 "A" men and 100,000 of other grades.

British People," with a special "Note on the Prime Minister's Statement" which read as follows:

> The great speech made by Mr. Lloyd George to a Congress of Trade Union delegates on January 5, 1918, is by far the most important which any statesman has made during the war.
>
> It makes plain the essential unity of purpose that now animates the British people.
>
> It reveals a Government and a people seeking no selfish or predatory aims of any kind, pursuing with one mind, one unchanging purpose: to obtain justice for others so that we thereby secure for ourselves a lasting peace. We desire neither to destroy Germany nor diminish her boundaries; we seek neither to exalt ourselves nor to enlarge our Empire.

That must have been pretty satisfactory to the Government.

But to make assurance doubly sure Mr. Lloyd George instructed his Foreign Secretary, Lord (then Mr.) Balfour, to ask President Wilson to "do his stuff" again about peace terms. This transaction is not mentioned by Mr. Lloyd George, for fairly obvious reasons. But it is described in detail in *The Intimate Papers of Colonel House*. The Balfour cable to Colonel House, dated January 5, 1918, puts the point clearly:

> Negotiations have been going on for some time between the Prime Minister and the Trades Unions. The main point was the desire of the Government to be released from certain pledges which were made to the labour leaders earlier in the war. This release is absolutely indispensable from the military point of view for the development of man-power on the Western Front. Finally the negotiations arrived at a point at which their successful issue depended mainly on the immediate publication by the British Government of a statement setting forth their war aims. This statement has now been made by the Prime Minister. It is the result of consultations with the labour leaders as well as the leaders of the Parliamentary Opposition.[58]

In the circumstances there had been no time to consult the Allies as to the terms of the statement. But:

It will be found on examination to be in accordance with the declarations hitherto made by the President on this subject.

The cable concluded with the hope that the President would likewise make a statement, in view of the Bolshevik appeal to the world.

. . . the Prime Minister is confident that such a statement would also be in general accordance with the lines of the President's previous speeches, which in England as well as in other countries have been so warmly received by public opinion.

Wilson needed no encouragement, for he had already decided to make his Fourteen Points speech in order to revive liberal and labour enthusiasm and to reassure the Russians (the Bolsheviks, however, took it badly—they hurt President Wilson's feelings by saying his speech was all humbug because the Allies were still fighting for the imperialistic secret treaties). He made the Fourteen Points speech on January 7, 1918.

Mr. Lloyd George then returned to the charge. At a meeting in the Central Hall, Westminster, on Januray 18, 1918, he told the assembled trade-union leaders in another impassioned harangue:

It was not a question of fighting on to gain some big imperialist aim. I had already indicated our peace terms to them a fortnight before, and President Wilson had almost at the same time put forward substantially the same demand. [The sole British purpose was to] realise those great aims which had been put forward alike by the Trade Unionists, the Government and President Wilson as the objects for which we were committed to fight.* [59]

* It is true Mr. Lloyd George also said in his harangue that "Mesopotamia and Palestine should not be handed back to Turkish tyranny." (*Op. cit.*, Vol. V, pp. 2659-60.) But his audience were not sophisticated enough to realize that this meant that the British Government had secretly contracted to annex those territories, in return for favouring similar annexations by the other Allies. He also gave reassuring replies when asked about the conscription of wealth, the ending of war profiteering, and the nationalization of the arms industry after the war. His audience could not know that twenty-five years later nothing would have been done to redeem any of these promises.

In spite of this statement, the Government neither abandoned the secret treaties nor accepted the Fourteen Points.

Refusing to be soothed by words that were not followed by deeds, the workers in all the belligerent countries grew more and more restive and suspicious of the governments throughout the last year of the war, until at last the Russian Revolution was followed and the war was ended by working-class revolutions in Germany and Austria-Hungary. But before treating of this subject it is necessary to consider further the dealings of the Allies with the Russian Revolution.

INTERVENTION

At the same time as they were successfully repelling the peace offensives of President Wilson, of their own workers, and of the Russian Revolution, the Allied governments were preparing a counter-offensive in the shape of intervention against what they regarded as the source of most of their difficulties on the home front.

On November 22, 1917, the British War Cabinet discussed

the difficulty that any overt official step taken against the Bolsheviks might only strengthen their determination to make peace, and might be used to inflame anti-Allied feeling in Russia, and so defeat the very object we were aiming at. Nor was anything known of the actual position which would justify us, at this juncture, in backing either Kaledin [a Cossak General] or any other leader of the party of law and order.* [60]

* Cf. the statement in House, *op. cit.*, Vol. III, pp. 330-31, that on November 30 Bakhmetiev, who had been appointed Russian Ambassador in Washington by Kerensky, told Colonel House that: "Although Lenin's Government, which seized control by force, cannot be regarded as representing the will of the Russian nation, the appeal which it addressed to the Allies in proposing an armistice cannot remain unanswered; for any evasion on the part of the Allies in the matter of peace will simply strengthen the Bolsheviks and help them to create an atmosphere in Russia hostile to the Allies. Any formal protest against Lenin's policy or any threats will have the same effect; they will simply aggravate the situation and aid the Bolsheviks to go to extremes."

Four days later, November 26, General Knox wired that, apart
from anything the Russian authorities might do, the Russian
troops were now insisting upon an armistice.

It appears quite clear that whatever happens politically
in Russia, the bulk of the Russian Army refuses to continue
the War.[61]

In spite of this information, however, the War Cabinet met
on November 29 and decided, on Sir George Buchanan's advice,
to reply to the Soviet Government's "insolent communication"
about an armistice by saying the Allies had determined to continue the war until permanent peace had been obtained, and
to suggest to the French that the Allies should release Russia
from her pledge not to make a separate peace in order to "make
it impossible for the Bolsheviks to reproach the Allies with driving Russian soldiers to slaughter for their Imperialistic aims." [62]
(Clemenceau, as mentioned above, refused to do this.)

At the same time the Cabinet was informed that the Foreign
Office Press Bureau had stopped a message from the Soviet
Government to the neutral countries Norway, Holland, Spain,
Sweden, Switzerland, and Denmark, asking that "pressure should
be brought to bear by the Socialist and working-class organisations
in these countries in favour of peace."

The Cabinet also had before it a telegram from General Bal-
lard, the British military attaché in Rumania, asking for a free
hand and £10,000,000 to support the Cossack General Kaledin.
Mr. Lloyd George explains:

The problem with which the British Government and indeed the Allies as a whole were faced, was a purely military
one. We were not concerned with the internal political troubles of Russia as such.

The Germans must be prevented from obtaining possession
of the vast stores of wheat and oil in the Ukraine and the Caucasus.

It was for this reason, and not for any anti-Communist

motives, that we decided to give support to the loyalist Russians who were in control of these fertile areas, and who were not prepared to desert the others. . . . The War Cabinet, therefore, discussed the need of organising the forces of resistance inside Russia. We examined the measures to be adopted to assist the anti-German formations which still existed in certain parts of Russia. The difficulty was to do so without appearing to wage war on the Bolshevik Government now established at Petrograd.[63]

This was the beginning of the British policy of intervention. It is necessary to examine the alleged motive for this policy, and to test that explanation by what actually happened. For a clear understanding of what was done then casts a flood of light upon much that has happened in World War II, in North Africa, Italy, the Balkans, and elsewhere.

First, as to the motive. There is a bewildering variety and richness in Mr. Lloyd George's explanations of the reasons for intervention. The only common feature is the denial that class-bias against the Bolsheviks had anything to do with it. The theme that the granaries and oil-fields of South Russia should be kept out of German hands recurs repeatedly.

But this is far from all. Mr. Lloyd George quotes a memorandum to the French in which the War Cabinet asserted (December 21, 1917) that the independence of Armenia and Georgia "is the only barrier against the development of a Turanian movement that will extend from Constantinople to China, and will provide Germany with a weapon of even greater danger than the Baghdad Railway." It is sad to relate that the French, who wanted to restore a united reactionary Russia, refused to be impressed by this argument and were base enough to harbour the suspicion that the British Government's desire to foster the independence of Georgia was not unconnected with the oil-fields around Baku. The French in their turn showed their hand in the agreements they concluded with Petliura (a White chieftain) in the Ukraine, as well as with General Wrangel in respect to the Caucasus. The agreement gave France control of Russian railways for fifty years and of financial, commercial, industrial, and

military policy for five years, as security for the payment of
Russian debts to France.

An even more horrific vision of things to come if there had been
no intervention is conjured up by Mr. Lloyd George to justify
intervention: . . . "it was imperative to prevent the Germans from
penetrating into Siberia and securing a hold upon it and its
great natural resources." [64] Germany might withdraw from Belgium and France, establish an impregnable front on the Rhine,
and carry out a "process of penetration and expansion in shattered
Russia and Siberia" that would leave her far bigger and stronger
than before. Worse still, Russia was in a state of anarchy, with
no government whatever, and there were millions of the best
fighting material in the world, which the Germans could enrol
in their armies, just as Napoleon recruited soldiers from all over
Europe to fight for him.[65]

The arguments that the Allies must succour the "loyal" Russians, defend democracy in Russia, and free the country from
foreign influence by intervention occur *ad nauseam* in the official
explanations of intervention.

Finally, Mr. Lloyd George says:

"And in any case, there were the Czechoslovaks." It is almost
as though he were half-defiantly addressing an invisible critic at
his elbow, and saying:-

"What, you remain sceptical about these lurid possibilities?
Well, anyway, you can't deny the Czechoslovaks were a fact." [66]

Yes, the presence of the Czechoslovak legionaries in Siberia
was certainly a fact. But Mr. Lloyd George forgets that on pages
3177-78 he explodes the fiction that intervention was started because they had to be "liberated," and on the contrary virtually
admits that the Allies kept the legionaries in Siberia because they
wanted to use them in conjunction with a Japanese invasion, as
part of their policy of "intervention."

The interesting part about Mr. Lloyd George's explanation as
to why the British Government embarked on intervention is that
they ignore patent facts which had been impressed on the Government again and again by its own agents on the spot.

To begin with, the idea that the "Eastern front" could be re-

stored by the Japanese invading East Siberia was as geograph-
ically ridiculous as suggesting that the Western front could be
reinforced by a Japanese invasion of California, supposing there
were land all the way from California to France, that the railways
had broken down, and there were no roads fit for mechanical
transport. The distances are about the same, and the feelings of
the Russians about the Japanese were, if anything, stronger than
those of the Americans.

The idea that Germany could occupy Russia and Siberia was
equally ridiculous for the same reasons, not to mention the war.

To go on, General Knox had impressed upon the British
Government again and again that the Russians were through
with fighting for anybody. He was partly wrong, for they showed
afterwards that they would fight to defend the revolution against
the Whites and the Allies. But at any rate he had in advance
shown up the absurdity of suggesting that Germany could make
Russians fight for her.

Further, the British Government knew that the Soviet régime
existed and that it was nonsense to talk of Russia's being in a
state of anarchy, with no government, for the British representative, Mr. Lockhart, was stationed at Moscow and giving it true
reports on the situation. Nothing is more interesting in Mr. Lockhart's *Memoirs of a British Agent* than his frequent insistence on
the fact that the Government and the Foreign Office simply refused to believe what he reported to them, although he was the
man on the spot. So much did they hate to admit the facts that
they threatened to cashier him because he persisted in reporting
them.

The German attitude towards the Bolsheviks and the Russian
Whites was the same as that of the Allies. Mr. Lloyd George
quotes General von Kuhl on Brest-Litovsk:

> The peace was in truth nothing but an armistice. The
> Soviet Government was our enemy for good and all.[67]

Ludendorff writes in his memoirs that the German Government had hoped that "we should at least obtain some assistance
from the sons of the land we had liberated from Bolshevik do-

minion." [68] Speaking of the Brest-Litovsk peace terms, Ludendorff observed that they were "aimed at the Bolsheviks, whose propaganda made a chronic state of warfare against them inevitable." [69]

It was the White Ukraine bolstered up by the Allies that welcomed German occupation. It was the Reds in the Ukraine that resisted the invaders by guerrilla warfare. There was official cooperation between the Allied forces in the Baltic and Black seas and the Germans in the Baltic Provinces and South Russia in helping the Russian Whites to fight the Bolsheviks.*

Both Mr. Lloyd George's *War Memoirs* and *The Intimate Papers of Colonel House* mention the frequent warnings of Lockhart and others in Russia that Allied intervention might throw the Bolsheviks into the arms of the Germans. Mr. Lockhart says the junior Allied representatives in Moscow, both diplomatic and military, were unanimously agreed that, from the point of view of fighting Germany, co-operation with the Bolsheviks was the best policy, and supporting the "White" Generals was disastrous folly.[70] The opposition to this view came from hysterical higherups who had fled to Vologda, where they fed their fears and hates on mare's-nests and refused to believe unwelcome facts.

Mr. Lockhart tells us also of the Soviet Government's requests for help to train the Red Army and resist German dictation at and after Brest-Litovsk. He gives a striking account of a conversation with Lenin, in which that far-seeing man summed up the whole situation with "amazing frankness." He said peace would be concluded with the Germans, but he did not know how long it would last.[71]

If the Germans forced their hands and tried to instal a bourgeois government, the Bolsheviks would fight even if they had to withdraw to the Volga and the Urals. But they would fight on their own conditions. They were not to be made a cat's-paw for the Allies.

If the Allies understood this, there was an excellent opportunity for co-operation. To the Bolsheviks Anglo-American capitalism was almost as hateful as German militarism, but

* For details, see below, page 276.

for the moment German militarism was the immediate
menace. . . .

But—he was sceptical about any possibility of co-operat-
ing with the Allies. "Our ways," he said, "are not your ways.
We can afford to compromise temporarily with capital. It is
even necessary, for, if capital were to unite, we should be
crushed at this stage of our development. Fortunately for us,
it is in the nature of capital that it cannot unite. So long,
therefore, as the German danger exists, I am prepared to risk
a co-operation with the Allies, which should be temporarily
advantageous to both of us. In the event of German aggression, I am willing to accept military support. At the same
time I am quite convinced that your Government will never
see things in this light. It is a reactionary Government. It
will co-operate with the Russian reactionaries." [72]

No wonder Mr. Lockhart remarks mournfully:

> The British Government was entitled to regard Bolshevism
> as a scourge and an evil. It might make war on it or ignore
> it severely. But it was sheer folly to continue to regard it as
> a movement fostered solely for the furtherance of German
> ends. [73]

Again and again he comments on the futility of his efforts to
"combat the firmly rooted conviction" in Whitehall and the
Cabinet "that Lenin and Trotsky were German staff officers in
disguise or at least servile agents of Germany policy." *

But in this comment Mr. Lockhart does less than justice to the
British Government's motives. If it was desired to add to the war
against Germany to make the world safe for democracy (and for
the secret treaties) a war against the Russian Revolution to restore
Czarism, it was necessary to connect the two in the public mind
by making out that the Bolsheviks were German agents. No
doubt there was no cold-blooded, clear-headed facing of this
necessity. The type of conservative who after November 1917
believed that all labour and colonial unrest was due to Moscow

* The double-edged irony of the remark about Trotsky, in the light of
subsequent events, will be appreciated.

gold was equally convinced then that the Bolshevik Revolution was due to German gold. There is more blind fear and hate than calculated deceit behind the fantasy life of the defenders of things-as-they-are. But the net result is the same as though they were consciously dishonest.

The following passage from Mr. Lockhart's *Memoirs*, relating to his return to Russia in January 1918, gives a candid view of what was really at the back of the minds of pro-interventionists:

In Christiania [now Oslo] . . . we met the first of the English refugees from Russia, members of our prosperous colonies in St. Petersburg and Moscow, who in a night had seen their comfortable existence swept away before their eyes in the maelstrom of revolution. One conversation, in particular, I noted in my diary. It was with Reynolds, a well-to-do timber-merchant, who had been very intimate with members of the Embassy staff. He had lost everything and was very nervous, and was obsessed with only one idea: that we should make peace as soon as possible, in order, in alliance with Germany, to restore order in Russia.

I recall this conversation because it was typical of the point of view we were to find among the Russian bourgeois in Moscow and St. Petersburg during 1918. Yet in the face of these facts, all through this period our military experts were writing memoranda about the loyal Russians and about the restoration of the Eastern front. As if there were any Russians who thought of any other interests than their own or of any other front than the civil war front, once the Bolshevik revolution had started. This is not anti-Russian prejudice. It is plain common sense. An Englishman or a German, situated in similar circumstances, would have had the same thoughts and the same mental reactions. If there were Russians who accepted the English formula of restoring the Eastern front and who talked of the sanctity of their oath to fight until victory was assured, they did so, consciously or sub-consciously, with their tongues in their cheeks. The one aim of every Russian bourgeois (and 99 per cent of the so-called "loyal" Russians were bourgeois) was to secure the intervention of British troops (and, failing British, German troops)

to re-establish order in Russia, suppress Bolshevism and restore to the bourgeois his property.* [74]

Mr. Lockhart's account suggests that class bias was not wholly
absent from the thought of those who favoured intervention.†
Was that true? Let us look at the facts.

The motives of intervention become progressively plainer as
the story unfolds of what actually happened. That story is set
forth in this chapter and the next.

On December 9, 1917, Lord (then Mr.) Balfour, the Secretary

* Cf. also p. 215: "More interesting was my dinner with Nobel—a member of the famous Swedish family [i.e., the family of the arms manufacturer
who founded the peace prize]. He had spent years of his life in St. Petersburg and had large interests all over Russia. He had formed a more accurate
estimate of the situation and was convinced that Bolshevism had not yet
reached its apogee. Like all foreigners who had property in Russia, he was
anxious for a general peace and for an Allied-cum-German intervention
against the Bolsheviks. He was one of the few people who at that time had
visualised Bolshevism as a world-danger. With other Swedes he had joined
a rifle club in order that he might take his place behind the bourgeois barri-
cades in the event of a proletarian rising in Sweden."

† In the case of some of the "loyal" Russians, however, the motives were
simpler. Cf. the report of the Captain of H.M.S. Suffolk, from Vladivostok
in February 1918, "that the Cossacks of Eastern Siberia had held a Conference at Iman, where they had condemned Bolshevik policy and all attempts
to make a separate peace, and had appealed to the Allies for financial and
material assistance." (Lloyd George, Vol. VI, p. 3173.) The Cossacks in question were the Transbaikal and Ussuri Cossacks. The leader of the former,
Ataman Semenov, and of the latter, Ataman Kalmykov, were highwaymen,
who lived chiefly by robbing passengers on the Chinese Eastern and Ussuri
Railways respectively. In addition they tortured and murdered all who they
thought were "Red." The following of each was only a handful of ruffians,
Russian, Chinese, and Mongol. They were first subsidized by the British
Government, through the British Consul-General in Harbin and one Captain
Steveni (himself half-Russian) of the M.I.S., and through the Consul-
General in Vladivostok, Mr. (later Sir Robert) Hodgson. The latter was at
the time the chief protagonist of intervention and Lockhart's bitter opponent.
Later, when these bandits became too unsavoury even for our interven-
tionists, and it became clear that they had no political standing whatever,
the British subsidy lapsed. Thereupon the Japanese took them over, and paid
them to be a thorn in the flesh of the Allied interventionists.

of State for Foreign Affairs, submitted to the British War Cabinet what Mr. Lloyd George calls one of his "most memorable State papers." It gave a comprehensive outline of the policy that should be adopted towards the Soviet Government. The following are extracts from the document:

> It was suggested at the Cabinet on Friday that, after their recent proclamations, the Bolsheviks could only be regarded as avowed enemies, and to treat them as anything else showed a lamentable incapacity to see facts as they are, and to handle them with decision.
>
> I entirely dissent from this view and believe it to be founded on a complete misconception. If, for a moment, the Bolsheviks show peculiar virulence in dealing with the British Empire, it is probably because they think that the British Empire is the great obstacle to immediate peace; but they are fanatics to whom the constitution of every State, whether monarchical or republican, is equally odious. Their appeal is to every revolutionary force, economic, social, racial or religious, which can be used to upset the existing political organisations of mankind. If they summon the Mohammedans of India to revolt, they are still more desirous of engineering a revolution in Germany. They are dangerous dreamers, whose power, be it great or small, transitory or permanent, depends partly on German gold, partly on the determination of the Russian Army to fight no more; but who would genuinely like to put into practice the wild theories which have so long been germinating in the shadow of the Russian autocracy.
>
> Now, contrary to the opinion of some of my colleagues, I am clearly of opinion that it is to our advantage to avoid, as long as possible, an open breach with this crazy system. If this be drifting then I am a drifter by deliberate policy.[75]

Mr. Lloyd George says he strongly supported this policy.

On December 21 the Cabinet discussed the situation again and approved a memorandum for despatch to the French Government, which explained how Mr. Balfour's "drifting" policy should be applied. The following are the two main proposals in the memorandum:

1. We should represent to the Bolsheviks that we have no desire to take part in any way in the internal politics of Russia, and that any idea that we favour a counter-revolution is a profound mistake. Such a policy might be attractive to the autocratic Governments of Germany and Austria, but not to the Western democracies or America. . . . But we should continually repeat our readiness to accept the principle of self-determination, and subject to that, of no annexations or indemnities.[76]

2. At the same time that they tried to make the Bolsheviks believe these assurances, the Allies were to supply

money to reorganise the Ukraine, to pay the Cossacks and the Caucasian forces, and to subsidise the Persians. . . . Besides finance, it is important to have agents and officers to advise and support the provincial Governments and their armies. It is essential that this should be done as quietly as possible so as to avoid the imputation—as far as we can— that we are preparing to make war on the Bolsheviks.[77]

This memorandum was accepted by the French on December 23 as the basis of Allied policy towards Russia. That policy might be described as one of deliberate duplicity and calculated drift towards intervention.

The British War Cabinet was divided into two sections: (1) A Right wing of Tories of the die-hard, high-living, and plain-thinking school, who wanted to make war on the Bolsheviks without further ado, because of hatred and fear of the Revolution. These were the straight interventionists. (2) A Left wing of moderate Conservatives and Liberals, with Balfour and Lloyd George at their head, who at bottom shared the feeling of their die-hard colleagues about the Bolsheviks, but were also troubled about the repercussions of intervention on the war with Germany, on public opinion, on labour, and on Wilson. These members of the Government were one-way drifters. They evolved a complicated and disingenuous policy, which consisted on the one hand in sending Lockhart to Moscow as a semi-official British representative and on the other in subsidizing various Cossack chieftains and Czarist generals and helping them to make war on the Bolsheviks.

The one-way drifters had greater intellectual and moral pretensions than their straight interventionist colleagues. They wanted to be led into temptation to intervene, but in such a way that it should be quite clear that it was not their fault if they subsequently fell. They were most careful to explain in public, and even sometimes in private (not always, as we shall see), that intervention had nothing whatever to do with a class war against social revolution, and was exclusively dictated by solicitude for democracy in Russia and by the desire to win the war against Germany. Mr. Lloyd George keeps on telling us this in his *War Memoirs,* apparently quite unconscious of the fact that the War Cabinet minutes he quotes contradict his story, and that he contradicted it himself in his secret memorandum to the Big Four at the Peace Conference (quoted in the next chapter). Mr. Lloyd George is equally careful to insist that the Government never wanted intervention, but that it was dragged into it against its own volition, because:

> Events were thus compelling us to take action on Russian soil, and in co-operation with organisations other than those who were associated with the Soviet authorities of Moscow and Petrograd, and without their concurrence. But it was not our business to determine whether the Bolshevik or the anti-Bolshevik sections of the Russian peoples would ultimately dominate the whole Empire.[78]

Outwardly, the Government were anxious to believe, and above all anxious that public opinion should believe, that theirs was a policy of drift and muddle, foolish perhaps, but inspired by worthy motives. Actually, the motives were worse and the head-work better—given the desire to destroy the Russian Revolution—than appeared on the surface. There was more method in their madness than the Government would admit.

In view of the strenuous efforts of part of the Cabinet to persuade themselves that class bias had nothing to do with their Russian policy, and to array the nakedness of their class war in a

sumptuous variety of publicly defensible motives, it is easy to
understand why they should have felt annoyed with Mr. Lockhart.

For he seems to have expressed himself about British policy in
Russia with a tactlessness only equalled by the famous child's
remark about the Emperor's clothes. So at least we gather from
a tart despatch by Balfour, approved by the whole Cabinet,
which told Mr. Lockhart:

> It is a mistake for you to suppose that we are "disinclined
> to take the line of a qualified recognition of the Bolsheviks,"
> and no less a mistake to fancy that our decision in this
> matter is influenced by "anxiety as to the injury that might
> be inflicted on the Bourgeois elements in Russia by such a
> course." I must state clearly and emphatically in regard to ﹀
> this second point that we are in no way concerned with the
> internal affairs of Russia as such; our sole interest in them is
> how they affect the War.[79]

Then followed a long dissertation on the Government's "drifting" policy, which contained nothing new except the statement
that there were of course two points on which there could be no
agreement with the Bolsheviks:

> We desire that they should refrain from Bolshevik propa-
> ganda in the territories of the Allies. And they wish us to
> refuse aid or encouragement to any military or political
> movement in Russia of which they disapprove.* [80]

Nevertheless there were matters on which agreement was possible, and:

> It is our earnest wish to postpone as long as we can a break
> with the Petrograd Government—even if in the end a break
> cannot be avoided—and to make our semi-official dealings
> with them in the meantime pleasant and businesslike. . . .

---

* This statement is almost frank, it will be observed, about the fact that
the military support of counter-revolution in Russia was due to the desire to
put a stop to propaganda for social revolution in the Allied working-class.
War was the Allied governments' answer to the spread of ideas.

As far as we can, we shall check Bolshevik propaganda
in this country.[81]

Mr. Lloyd George says his difficulties in getting the one-way-
drift policy accepted by the straight interventionist members of
the Cabinet were considerably enhanced by Trotsky's revolutionary appeal to all nations to rise against the rule of the "*Bourgeoisie.*" . . . There was a genuine fear that recognition would
involve admitting into Allied countries a swarm of Bolshevik
intriguers to foment revolution.[82]

Apart from this direct danger, "some members of the Government viewed with considerable misgivings any dealings with the
Bolshevik Government which could enhance its prestige and thus
increase its propagandist influence." [83]

Launched with this mixture of avowed and unavowed motives,
it was no wonder the Allies' Russian policy showed on the surface confusion, vacillation, and underneath a steady and deliberate drift to open though undeclared war on the revolution.
Mr. Lloyd George writes of the period immediately after the
October Revolution:

> Our own attitude towards the Bolshevik Government at
> this time was not easy of definition. On 17th January, 1918,
> Mr Balfour expressed to the War Cabinet the opinion that
> from a purely Foreign Office point of view there would be
> great advantages in cutting off all relations with the Bol-
> sheviks. The latter had broken their treaty with the Allies,
> had repudiated their debts to us, and were openly trying to
> raise revolutions in all countries. The Italian Government
> were anxious that this course should be taken. On the other
> hand, we still had great interests in Northern Russia, and a
> number of British subjects there whose position had to be
> considered.

Consequently, on January 22 Mr. Balfour, "in setting forth his
views on our Russian relations . . . made a statement which
showed that he, as well as the rest of us, was torn between con-
flicting considerations."

According to the War Cabinet minutes, this was what Balfour had to say:

> In view of recent events in Petrograd, it was necessary for the War Cabinet to consider very seriously what our relations were to be with the Bolshevik Government. . . . From the point of view of postponing a separate peace between Russia and Germany, and stopping the Germans getting supplies out of Russia, it would appear that the Bolsheviks were more likely to effect such a policy than any other party in Russia. The Bolsheviks, however, appeared determined to spread what he described as "passionate propaganda" in this country, and also in Germany.

He added that according to his information the danger of revolution in Germany was really serious.

The War Cabinet minutes continue:

> Sir George [Buchanan] said he would sooner see a rupture than allow Bolshevist propaganda on a large scale in this country, as such propaganda was dangerous, and attractive to those who had nothing to lose. He thought it was clear that the Germans would like to see a rupture between us and the Bolsheviks, and would like our representatives at Petrograd to be withdrawn, in order to give them a clear field. . . .
>
> Regarding the Social Revolutionaries, he thought that, although more correct in their methods, they were less of a nuisance to the Germans. The Social Revolutionaries had no backbone, and were, if anything, more anxious than the Bolsheviks to make a separate peace with Germany. Two things tended to cause him to modify his view that we should, if possible, avoid a rupture with the Bolsheviks, namely, the recent maltreatment of the Constituent Assembly by the Bolsheviks, and secondly, the possibility of the Japanese or Americans, or both, giving effective military assistance to those elements in Southern Russia who were inclined to resist the Bolsheviks.[84]

Both Balfour and Buchanan virtually admitted that from the

point of view of getting on with the war against Germany the best policy would be to support the Bolsheviks. And nevertheless both recommended a rupture—because of Bolshevik propaganda for social revolution. Here we have the British Foreign Secretary and the Cabinet's principal adviser on Russian affairs practically confessing, as recorded in the Cabinet minutes, that they shared the outlook of another diplomatic envoy, as described by Lockhart:

> In his political views he was an extreme Conservative, who would rather have lost the war than run the risk of social upheaval in England.[85]

The Cabinet seems, indeed, to have been divided into those who, like Mr. Lloyd George, did not much mind Bolshevik propaganda provided it were confined to our enemies,* and those who would have preferred to continue the war indefinitely rather than to win it through revolutions in the central powers. But all were agreed that, as stated in the Balfour despatch to Lockhart, the Government should make war on the Bolsheviks through supporting the Whites, who were fighting them, so long as the Bolsheviks persisted in revolutionary propaganda. Some, including, curiously enough, Sir George Buchanan, seemed to feel the need for combining this policy with the belief that they were not taking sides in Russian internal affairs, and that in backing Czarist generals and a Japanese invasion they were helping the Russians

---

* Cf. Lloyd George, Vol. V, p. 2591: At a Cabinet meeting on February 7, 1918, "I expressed the opinion that it was no concern of the British Government what Socialist experiment or what form of government the Bolsheviks were trying to establish in Russia. In regard to the particular questions before us [i.e., Russian policy, including the danger of Bolshevik propaganda], it was necessary to bear in mind that the Bolsheviks were a formidable menace to Austria and Germany, and that our information regarding the internal conditions in Austria was such as to encourage the view that the internal political conditions of that Empire were seriously embarrassed by the spread of Bolshevism."

A passage in the Balfour note to Lockhart mentioned above hints at willingness to do a deal with the Bolsheviks if they would be willing to confine their propaganda to the Central Powers. But Balfour was obviously too intelligent to believe in that possibility.

to become democratic and to free themselves from foreign influences. Others combined it with a policy of false assurances to and "pleasant and business-like" relations with the Bolsheviks, pending the break which they regarded as inevitable when the time was ripe to bring into the open their surreptitious support of the war waged by the Whites.

In March 1918 there was an instructive episode.

On March 2 Bakhmetiev told House that Japanese intervention would throw Russia into the arms of Germany.[86] Balfour "admitted that the advices which his Government had received from Russia were against intervention." Lockhart had reported that it would push Russia over to the Germans and that the Soviet Government "really wanted a working arrangement with the Allies." [87]

The Soviet Government asked what Allied help would be given if it did not ratify the Brest-Litovsk treaty, and whether "the U.S.A. and Great Britain would prevent a Japanese landing."

Wilson felt unable to give a definite reply, but on March 11 sent a goodwill message to the Congress of Soviets then meeting.[88] This did not satisfy the Bolsheviks, who had wind of the fact that the Allies were negotiating for a Japanese invasion. Nor did it please the British Government. For Mr. Lloyd George tells us that Lockhart's suggestion for similiar action was turned down by the Cabinet, on the ground that:

> The American public . . . had not the same cause for resentment against Russia as the European Allies, who had made great investments in Russia, and who had been deserted in the midst of the struggle.*

Wilson could not give a definite answer to the Soviet Government's request because he was trying to resist the Allies' demands for Japanese intervention.

The President and the American State Department had solid evidence for the belief

that the Japanese themselves were the instigators of the plan for an invasion; and they wished the expedition to be

* The first thing the Allies made the various White hopes they backed promise to do was to honour Russia's financial obligations to themselves.

exclusively and overwhelmingly Japanese in order to ensure
an occupation of the Maritime Province.[89]

That, of course, was precisely what did happen: The Japanese
sent 70,000 instead of the 7,000 men they were asked to send.
These forces occupied the Maritime and Amur provinces and
resisted all Allied demands that they should "re-form the Eastern
front." They were not dislodged until 1922, under strong American pressure at the Washington Conference.

The Allies must have known this would happen as well as
Wilson. Moreover, they knew all about Japan's record in general
and her treatment of China (who was our Ally) in World War I
in particular, as exemplified by the Twenty-one Demands in 1915
and the occupation of Shantung in 1917. Nevertheless on March
16, 1918, Balfour sent Wilson a despatch submitting the proposals on which the British, French, and Italian Prime Ministers
and Foreign Ministers had agreed the day before at a conference
in London. Russia, they said, should be helped by her friends,
who would ask the Japanese to do it. It is true that many observers "think that, if that assistance now took the form of a
Japanese Army operating on Russian soil, it would be regarded
with distrust, and even aversion." If so, this would be due to the
suspicion that Japan would rob Russia of territory. "No such suspicion can be entertained by those associated with Japan in the
present War." [90]

Mr. Balfour sent Colonel House an almost honest telegram. He
said the Japanese were preparing to take action in Siberia, and
"it seemed likely that considerable resentment would be raised
in Japan if, the Japanese Government being willing to act on behalf of the Allies, a mandate were refused." This might dangerously strengthen the "formidable pro-German party in Japan."
He had telegraphed suggesting that the Soviet Government
should invite Rumanian and Japanese co-operation to "organize
resistance to German aggression." He did not know the Rumanian
and Japanese attitude and did not believe the Soviet Government would accept. But "I have done this so we may put ourselves right with public opinion, if and when a statement is made

on the whole subject." This would enable the Allies to "justify completely" their invitation to Japan and show that they had "been actuated by no selfish or mean motives." [91]

Mr. Lloyd George confirms that as early as December 1917 Japan was "showing a very lively interest in the situation" in Siberia, and "it was difficult to refuse her proffered help." [92]

Naturally the seasoned power politicians and diplomats of the Allies knew very well why Japan was preparing to invade Russia. But instead of joining with the United States to make her desist, as they would have done if they had been really friends of Russia, or even if they had been thinking solely of winning the war, they exploited the situation to try to commit the United States to the war they were planning against the Russian Revolution.

Mr. Lloyd George, in a message endeavouring to disabuse President Wilson of the idea that General Knox was a reactionary, assured him that the British Government was far from sympathizing with reaction, and urged him to join in intervention so as to counterbalance the Japanese. The President himself was the real security against reaction in Russia. If he joined in intervention in Siberia "he could dominate its developments. . . . If, finally, Wilson was ready to send an important political mission to Siberia, I would certainly see that a Liberal or Labour representative from this country accompanied it." * [93]

Colonel House sums up as follows the stream of appeals and proposals for intervention that poured in on him and the President:

> The British Government considers that it is necessary for the Allies to unite in order to bring about a Russian national revival, and in order to adopt a policy of freeing Russia from foreign control by means of Allied intervention. The

* This probably accounted for the comic episode of the bloodless but, according to his own story, dramatic and decisive Siberian campaign of Colonel Ward and his Middlesex Labour Battalion from Hong Kong. Colonel Ward was an old trade-union official whose political views would not have disgraced Colonel Blimp. He had been retired to Parliament and was given a temporary commission during the war to look after a labour battalion.

Allies must, of course, avoid taking sides in Russian politics, and, if the Bolshevist Government will co-operate in resisting Germany, it seems necessary to act with them as the *de facto* Russian Government.[94]

' The Soviet Government had asked what help the Allies would give if Germany attacked them. The Allies would offer intervention. If it were accepted, the whole situation would be transformed. If it were refused "the position of the Bolshevik Government would at least be defined." The Japanese would furnish the main military force. But all the Allies would participate.[95]

As Wilson still hesitated, Lord Robert Cecil, the Blockade Minister and Under-Secretary for Foreign Affairs, sent House a personal telegram, in which he said: "I am convinced that there is growing up in this country a very strong feeling that Allied intervention in Siberia is being unduly delayed." If there were not action soon, public indignation might become "too strong to be repressed" and there might be a "dangerous explosion" and "international criticism and recrimination." [96]

This was on July 8, 1918, when the Allies were already on the offensive everywhere and the resistance of the central powers was ebbing fast. It is difficult to understand how public opinion, which was allowed to hear only what the Government thought was good for it, could become indignant at that moment because Japan failed to invade East Siberia. In the public mind Japan and Eastern Asia had only the remotest connection with the war, and things that did not happen in that part of the world could hardly arouse much indignation by their absence.*

As a result of this bombardment of proposals and appeals,

* A remark by Mr. Lockhart casts light on the mystery. He says he had a very difficult interview with Viscount (then Lord Robert) Cecil: "He was supremely sceptical of the usefulness of establishing any kind of relations with the Bolsheviks, and, as a sidelight on his subsequent development as an internationalist, it is worth putting on record that the man, who since the war has sat so often round the same table in Geneva as Litvinoff and Lunacharsky, was at that time the most convinced of all responsible English statesmen that Lenin and Trotsky were paid agents of Germany, working deliberately for German ends, with no policy and no ambitions of their own." (*Op. cit.*, p. 200.)

"House was convinced that it was no longer possible simply to return a blank negative to Allied demands for intervention, and he pondered methods by which an Allied force could be introduced into Russia without arousing suspicion of imperialistic motives." [97]

The unfortunate Colonel never did solve that conundrum. While he was brooding over it intervention gathered momentum and the Japanese invasion of Siberia began.

Mr. Lockhart prints an analysis by Lenin, in an interview on June 23, 1918, that shows up all the shams of Allied intervention with cold lucidity:

One of the weakest spots in Balfour's speech is the statement that the Japanese are going to help the Russians. Which Russians? In Russia to-day there is one power, which by its nature is destined to wage a life and death struggle against the attacks of international Imperialism—that is the Power of the Soviets. The first step, however, of those Russians, whom the Japanese intend to "help" as soon as they heard rumours of the advance of the latter, was to demand the abolition of the Soviet Power. Should the Japanese move into Siberia, these same "Russians" whom the Japanese are going to "help," will demand the abolition of the Soviets throughout the whole of Siberia. What can take the place of the Soviet Power? The only power that can take its place is a bourgeois government. But the bourgeoisie in Russia has proved clearly enough that it can only remain in power with foreign help. If a bourgeois government, supported by outside help, should establish itself in power in Siberia and Eastern Russia become lost to the Soviet, then in Western Russia the Soviet Power would become weakened to such an extent, that it could hardly hold out for long; it would be followed by a bourgeois government, which would also need foreign help. The Power to give this help would, of course, not be England. It is easy to understand what avenues are opened up by this possibility." [98]

Mr. Lockhart gives a biting account of how, under the pressure of Noulens, the French Ambassador, the Allied representatives at Vologda agreed to make a slight change in their proposals for "co-operation" with the Bolsheviks in "re-forming the Eastern front":

> M. Noulens was flatteringly congratulatory. He agreed
> with the report. He had only one amendment to make. If
> the Bolsheviks would not give their consent, we must inter-
> vene without their consent.[99]

And so the Allies did. How intervention developed after the Armistice and was brought to an end is described in the next chapter. Here it is enough to record Mr. Lockhart's summing up of the policy:

> The consequences of this ill-conceived venture were to be
> disastrous both to our prestige and to the fortunes of those
> Russians who supported us. It raised hopes which could not
> be fulfilled. It intensified the civil war and sent thousands of
> Russians to meet their death. Indirectly, it was responsible
> for the Terror. Its direct effect was to provide the Bolsheviks
> with a cheap victory, to give them a new confidence, and to
> galvanise them into a strong and ruthless organism. To have
> intervened at all was a mistake. To have intervened with
> hopelessly inadequate forces was an example of spineless
> half-measures which, in the circumstances, amounted to a
> crime. Apologists for this policy maintain that it served a
> useful purpose in preventing Russia from falling into the
> hands of Germany and detaching German troops from the
> Western Front. By June, 1918, there was no danger of Rus-
> sia being overrun by Germany. The effect of the interven-
> tion on the German situation in the West was insignificant.
> The fact remains that, whatever may have been the inten-
> tions of the Allied Governments, our intervention was re-
> garded by those Russians, who supported it, as an attempt
> to overthrow Bolshevism. It failed, and, with the failure, our
> prestige among every class of the Russian population
> suffered.[100]

LABOUR UNREST GROWS

By the summer of 1918 all the European belligerents were within measurable distance of famine, and labour unrest was becoming really serious. Allied mishandling of the Russian Revolution had powerfully contributed to the conclusion of the Brest-Litovsk peace and to the consequent release of German troops for the West. The result was Germany's March offensive, but also a growing revolutionary movement in Germany and Austria-Hungary. Then came the Allied offensive, and with it the growth of revolutionary sentiment in Great Britain and France.

The evolution of British labour has already been described. French labour had evolved on parallel lines, thanks "partly to the suffering of the working-classes in the war, but partly to suspicion of the motives of the various Governments which succeeded one another without perceptibly bringing nearer the possibility of peace." In the trade-union movement (the Confédération Générale du Travail) "a division between groups developed which at length turned the anti-war minority into an acknowledged majority at the Congress of July 1918. Food prices, the immense casualties, the length of the war and the stern repressions of any industrial movement all compelled the organized workers to distrust the Government." [101]

The trade-unions were in close contact with the French Socialist party. In the latter:

The division of opinion which first showed itself in the early part of 1917 was due very largely to the policy of the French Government in regard to Russia. Suspicions began to be aroused that the purposes of the Allies in the war were not what they had been or at least not what they were generally believed to have been at the beginning. . . . The Prime Minister, M. Ribot, was particularly opposed when he spoke in slighting terms in the Chamber of the League of Nations as programme for peace. . . . For some time the Party tried to affect French policy. . . .

[But] Labour organizations, both in the Chamber and outside, had become strongly critical of the Government. The Socialist Party was divided in regard to voting war credits and participating in the Government, as the October Conference at Bordeaux showed, the minority being more and more clearly opposed to the tendency of the Allied policy at this time. M. Clemenceau, who succeeded M.

Painlevé, made the Socialist opposition certain and unequiv-
ocal both by his action in the industrial sphere, and by his
open disregard of the aims publicly expressed by the representatives of organized labour.

A definite protest was made in January 1918 by the Socialist Party against the declaration of the Allied Governments at the Versailles Conference; and from the 18th
February the Socialist Party worked in close connexion with
the British Labour Party in its statement of war-aims. . . .

In the use of force for suppressing the great munition
strike, which occurred at St. Etienne, the Government did
not increase the friendship of Labour organizations; and in
July, at the first full congress of the C.G.T. held during the
war, the mood of the trade unionists was clearly shown to
be adverse to the Government's policy. In September, French
representatives were present at the Inter-Allied Labour
Conference in London, and in October those who had been
in the minority in the Socialist Party definitely gained control of the situation. Both sections, however, strongly supported the idea of the League of Nations; and the Left
Wing, now in control, was strongly internationalist. Thus
at the Armistice French Labour looked to President Wilson,
but was in open opposition to its own Government and thoroughly suspicious of the real aims of the Allies.

[As for Italy] . . . at the close of the war nearly the whole
of organized labour in Italy were not only in opposition to
their own Government but dissociated from the Socialist and
Labour parties of other Allied countries and looking to
Moscow and the third *Internationale*.[102]

In Germany there was the same division between an anti-war
minority and a pro-war majority in the Socialist party, with the
former gaining strength. The Austrian socialists were mostly anti-
war from the beginning. In January 1918 there were great strikes
in Austria and Germany.

. . . the actual position of the German labour organizations
at the Armistice was perhaps one of the chief causes of the
entire destruction of all German power. . . . The final overthrow of the military power was in great part due to the dis-

trust shown by German labour organizations. . . . The whole international situation was transformed by the complete collapse of the Empires of Germany and Austria. Republics, dominated by organized labour, were set up in Germany on the 9th November, 1918 and in Austria on the 12th November.[103]

On the invitation of the British Trade Union Congress an Inter-Allied Labour and Socialist Congress was held in London in February 1918, and approved the memorandum on peace terms adopted at the joint conference of the Labour party and the Trade Union Congress in December 1917.

The Conference also decided that it would be useful to call an International Conference of Labour and Socialist organizations in a neutral country, at which all the organizations represented should be those which declared their war-aims to be in conformity with the principles "No annexations or punitive indemnities and the right of all peoples to self-determination." It was plainly agreeed that representatives from the parties of the Central Powers should meet the Allied representatives. Further, it was resolved that a Labour representative should attend the Peace Conference.[104]

This memorandum was transmitted to the Socialist parties of the enemy countries. Favourable replies were received from the Austrian socialists and the German minority socialists. The German majority socialists replied demanding virtually the pre-war *status quo* for Germany and self-determination for Ireland, Egypt, India, Morocco, Finland, and Tripoli.

A fourth Inter-Allied Conference of Labour and Socialist groups met in London on the 17th September 1918, at which the American Federation of Labour was represented. The Conference resolved unanimously that the Allied Governments should issue a joint statement of their war-aims, thereby making it understood that, in the view of organized labour, the Governments had not yet definitely stated their terms. It had, indeed, been continually suggested that the aims of the Governments were not based upon any principles but changed with the military situation. The "Fourteen Points" of President Wilson were accepted in a resolution of the London Conference.[105]

It will be seen that the labour movement grew active and militant from the end of 1917, and that:

> ... throughout the closing stages of the war the influence of new schemes and policies of labour organizations in Russia ... affected the situation both in Central Europe and in the Allied nations.[106]

This change was accomplished only by bitter struggles of the rank and file and Left-wing minorities against the official leadership, under the pressure of tragic and tremendous events. In order not to complicate the narrative excessively, we have not attempted to describe this struggle, although it too contains lessons for today, nor to give an account of the abortive attempts at Zimmerwald in 1915 and Kienthal in 1916 (when Lenin was present) to bring together the anti-war minorities in both belligerent camps.

So far as the great Western democracies are concerned, it is fair to say:

> The British Labour movement took the lead in promoting the expression of an inter-ally labour policy for the conclusion of the war; and although the inevitable entanglements of war-time foreign negotiations were perhaps hardly appreciated by the majority of organized labour, suspicion was widespread that the European governments were not working towards the aims which labour had welcomed when President Wilson had given them expression. The terms of the Armistice, however, satisfied British labour and opposition to the Government died down.[107]

A PYRRHIC VICTORY

This last refers to the success at long last of those two good men, Wilson and House, in getting the Allies to endorse their Fourteen Points.

When Colonel House came to the Armistice Conferences:

The prime object of his mission he regarded as winning from the Allies an explicit acceptance of the principles of President Wilson, as expressed in the Fourteen Points and later speeches. . . . Whatever approval had been given to Wilson's speeches by Allied leaders had been entirely unofficial. Now that Germany seemed to be breaking up rapidly, it was vital to win an official agreement.[108]

Two days after arriving in Paris, Colonel House wrote in his diary:

It seems to me of the utmost importance to have the Allies accept the Fourteen Points and the subsequent terms of the President.[109]

After a severe struggle, in which threats of a public exposure of the Allies by the President in Congress had to be resorted to, the Allies finally consented to accept, with unimportant reservations, not only the Fourteen Points but a detailed commentary drawn up by Colonel House, as the basis of their peace terms. Germany accepted the Armistice on the basis of a solemn and written agreement that the Fourteen Points were to be the basis of the peace settlement.

No wonder House wired jubilantly to Wilson:

I consider that we have won a . . . diplomatic victory in getting the Allies to accept the principles laid down in your January 8 speech and in your subsequent addresses. This has been done in the face of a hostile and influential junta in the United States and the thoroughly unsympathetic personnel constituting the Entente Governments.[110]

Unfortunately it was a Pyrrhic victory. For the Allies had no serious intention of keeping their word. That they promptly took advantage of Germany's helplessness to break it is proved irrefutably by J. M. Keynes in *The Economic Consequences of the Peace*, and is touched upon in the next chapter.

In another direction Wilson's diplomatic victory had serious consequences, for it served once more to reassure labour and liberal opinion and to relax pressure from the left at a critical moment.

Peace seemed to be near, and in the minds of the majority foreign policy gave place to the re-settlement of domestic conditions. The interval between the Armistice and the opening of the Peace Conference at Paris on the 18th January 1919 was not used by labour organizations for the formulation or the advocacy of any definite programme of international policy, although preparations were made for the renewal of the Socialist *Internationale.* An International Labour and Socialist Conference was held at Berne from 26th January to 10th February 1919, at which resolutions in regard to the peace were proposed; but the separation between the Governments and the labour organizations of the various Allied countries was not bridged, and the attention paid by the workers to the problems of demobilization, unemployment, and the securing of their industrial position almost entirely absorbed the thought of organized labour, thus leaving labour organizations without direct power in international politics while the Peace Conference was being held.[111]

CONCLUSION

The entry of the United States into the war and the Russian Revolution gave more substance to the Allied propaganda about the war as an ideological conflict between democracy and militarism. But at the same time they made clearer the fact that the "vertical" international conflict between the two belligerent camps was merely a senseless orgy of mutual destruction and slaughter, except in so far as it affected the political struggle between Right and Left within each belligerent nation. The struggle between Right and Left in turn became more and more plainly the political expression of a "horizontal" social conflict between the workers and the plutocracy. The Right, representing the plutocracy, was in control of the governments, closely allied with militarism, and bent on war to the bitter end followed by an imperialist and punitive peace. The workers and their allies wanted to join hands with each other across the trenches and to make a peace of conciliation followed by some form of world government.

This, of course, simplifies an immensely complex situation. But it does summarize accurately the main tendencies and forces that determined events.

In the minds of the Allied, as of the German and Austrian, governments, the "honour and vital interests" of their nations had from the first been identified with the class interest of the plutocracy of which they were, through the capitalist parties to which they belonged, the political representatives. How that "lie in the soul," the unconscious identification of the interests of the plutocracy with those of the common people, although in fact the two are incompatible in important respects, was the chief cause of World War I has been shown in the previous chapter. In this chapter we have endeavoured to trace how through the operation of this belief, all the more dangerous because it is unconscious and so deep-seated as to underlie ideas of right and wrong, ideals, principles, and the sense of duty and honour, the Allied governments identified winning the war with frustrating their own working-class and attacking the Russian Revolution, as well as with defeating Germany. They must have a military victory and a dictated peace, because they were the only antidotes to revolution. The war against the Boche, wrote Sir Henry Wilson in his diary, is turning into a war against the Bolshie. Bolshevism, said Marshal Foch, is a disease that attacks only the defeated.

Nor were these fears idle. Even victory did not keep the social foundations in France, Great Britain, and Italy from rocking in the first two years of the peace. As it was, the war came uncomfortably close to ending in the way Lenin had predicted. He told Lockhart:

> "Like all your countrymen, you are thinking in concrete military terms. You ignore the psychological factor. This war will be settled in the rear and not in the trenches." [112]

An inconclusive war would almost certainly, in E. D. Morel's phrase, have meant a conclusive peace. But it would have been conclusive because the political representatives of the workers, through some such device as the Stockholm Conference, and if necessary through industrial as well as parliamentary action at home, would have taken the job of peacemaking out of the hands of the capitalist governments. An inconclusive war would have meant a negotiated peace, and as the Socialist parties were able to agree on peace terms, whereas the imperialist aims of the capitalist governments were irreconcilable, there was a real danger that the Socialists would have taken charge of the negotiations with the support of the masses.*

That prospect appeared to the Allied governments and to the plutocracy that ultimately controlled them as the road to ruin. It would have meant the fulfilmerit of what Grey prophesied as the culminating horror of the war—labour governments everywhere and a general advance towards socialism.

Rather than take the risks involved in that alternative, the Allied governments preferred to continue the world war for a year, start a war of intervention against Soviet Russia, and dictate the peace of Versailles.

The struggle, going from Right to Left, between the Allied governments, Wilson, the working-class, and the Russian Revolution against the background of the longing for peace, scarred and distorted by the dark passions released by the war, was continued in other forms at the Peace Conference. The next chapter will treat of that struggle, and of its relation to the birth of the League of Nations, the first faltering attempt to establish a system of world government.

* As pointed out in the preface, the situation was radically different in World War II, where a stalemate, negotiated peace would allow fascism to survive, whereas victory would smash the fascist and quisling régimes and open the path to power to the democratic revolutionary resistance movements.

CHAPTER IV

The Birth of the League

THERE WAS a tug of war at the Peace Conference between President Wilson and Clemenceau, with Mr. Lloyd George flitting distractedly from one to the other, torn between his personal sympathies for Wilson's conception of peace and his political commitments to imperialist war aims and his Conservative majority in the House of Commons.

But it is superficial to think of the Peace Conference in terms of the decisions of a handful of individuals, however exalted. They were not actors in the drama but puppets, controlled by the vast forces set in motion by the war. The exquisitely keen and subtle mind of Lord (then Mr.) Keynes sensed that fact.

One felt most strongly the impression described by Tolstoy in *War and Peace* or by Hardy in *The Dynasts*, of events marching on to their fated conclusion uninfluenced and unaffected by the celebrations of Statesmen in Council:

Spirit of the Pities.
Why prompts the Will so senseless-shaped a doing?

Spirit of the Years.
I have told thee that It works unwittingly,
As one possessed not judging.[1]

What were the forces that shaped events and possessed those who thought they were judging? Let us hear what those directly concerned with these events have to say on the matter.

Mr. Ray Stannard Baker, who was a member of the American delegation at Paris, tells us:

Critics after the event forget that peace had to be made in an atmosphere still reeking with the fumes of war and still more or less dominated by the military spirit. It could not have been otherwise. For four years the nations had been committed to the use of every agency in building up a war psychology; to giving men the martial spirit, instilling hatred as an antidote for fear, driving nations into an artificial unity of purpose by the force of sheer necessity. As a monument to this passion and bitterness there were 7,500,000 men lying dead in Europe and 20,000,000 had been wounded; there were devastated cities, ruined mines and factories, stupendous debts. Build up such a psychology for four years, inoculate the entire public opinion of the world with it, and then ask four men at Paris—or one man at Paris—to change it all in three months! It was not merely a world peace that had to be made but a world psychology that had to be changed.[2]

In *The Intimate Papers of Colonel House* we find the statement by the editor:

Even if the Allied leaders themselves agreed to the wisdom of American proposals, they were prevented from accepting them by the force of public opinion. By arousing popular emotion during the war, an orthodox belligerent measure, they had created a Frankenstein monster which now held them helpless.

This is the common explanation given after the event by liberals at the Peace Conference to explain why they failed to make the peace more like the Fourteen Points and less in the spirit of the secret treaties.

In so far as this explanation is true, it raises the question of what were the quarters from which came the agitation for harsh peace terms. The answer is that it came from the Right, from conservatism and plutocracy. Mr. Lloyd George's khaki election made him the prisoner of a majority of "hard-faced men who looked as though they had done very well out of the war," as they were described at the time. But Mr. Lloyd George was partly responsible for making his own prison. For when he saw his election campaign was hanging fire and that labour and the independent liberals were holding their own with propaganda for a moderate peace, he and his followers deliberately appealed to the basest jingoism and to the repulsive folly of slogans such as "Hang the Kaiser," "Make Germany pay for the war," "Squeeze the German orange till the pips squeak." [3]

THE FEAR OF REVOLUTION AND THE FOUNDING OF THE LEAGUE

But if we study contemporary utterances, it becomes doubtful whether it was the incurable jingoism of public opinion that forced the peacemakers against their wills to be vindictive. There are contemporary liberal complaints of pressure from the Right, but they are mild and few compared to the lively and constant fear exhibited by both liberals and conservatives at the Peace Conference of the danger of pressure from the Left, from the working-class and the Russian Revolution.

This subject has been surprisingly neglected in all subsequent accounts of the origin of the League. And yet a study of the records at the time suggests that this fear was the main influence that enabled liberals at the Peace Conference to wring from conservatism and plutocracy their assent to the establishment of the League, and that at the same time induced liberals to acquiesce in the Versailles Treaty rather than face the risk of a split with conservatism and plutocracy and of an alliance with the forces of working-class discontent. It was a common fear of the pressure from below that drove the Right wing of the governing class to make concessions to the Left wing, and both wings to compromise with each other rather than part company.

We get the first inkling of this frame of mind in a statement by President Wilson, as early as December 10, 1918, on board the S.S. *George Washington*, on his way to the Peace Conference.

The President remarked that we would be the only disinterested people at the Peace Conference, and that *the men whom we were about to deal with did not represent their own peoples.* . . . With great earnestness he re-emphasised the point that unless the Conference was prepared to follow

the opinions of mankind and to express the will of the
people rather than that of their leaders at the Conference,
we should soon be involved in *another break-up* of the
world, and when such a break-up came it would not be a
war but a cataclysm. [Italics in the original.]

The President said he could not see how a treaty of peace
could be drawn up or how both elasticity and security could be
obtained except under a League of Nations. The only alternative
was a return to the balance of power, and that had produced
only "aggression and selfishness and war." The peoples were
heartily sick of this and demanded a new order.

If it won't work, it must be made to work. . . . The poison
of Bolshevism was accepted readily by the world because
"it is a protest against the way in which the world has
worked." It was to be our business at the Peace Conference
to fight for a new order, "agreeably if we can, disagreeably
if necessary."

Colonel House wrote in his diary on March 22, 1919:

Rumblings of discontent every day. The people want
peace. Bolshevism is gaining ground everywhere. Hungary
has just succumbed. We are sitting upon an open powder
magazine and some day a spark may ignite it.

He too drew the conclusion that a moderately new order guaranteed by the League of Nations was the only way to avoid suc-
cumbing to the immoderately new order desired by the Bolsheviks.

Ray Stannard Baker is even more explicit:

. . . one remembers vividly how the councils at Paris were given
no rest, day or night, from hearing the woes of the world:
how they were constantly agitated by cries of hunger from
without . . . or alarmed by the voices of new wars . . . or
distracted by the fierce uprisings of peoples. . . . And at all
times, at every turn of the negotiations, there rose the
spectre of chaos, like a black cloud out of the East, threatening to overwhelm and swallow up the world. There was no
Russia knocking at the gates of Vienna! At Vienna, appar-

ently, the revolution was securely behind them; at Paris it was always with them. The new order was crowded always toward the old by a newer.[4]

The last sentence suggests that conservatism and plutocracy sometimes argued that the revolutionary danger was an additional reason for "firmness." But for the most part fear prompted the desire to seek safety by concessions and promises.

Thus in April 1919 an American officer stationed in Berlin wired the American Peace Commission that if the German socialist-bourgeois coalition government were "overthrown by a general strike or Spartacist *coup de main* . . . the Entente would be faced with a Germany without any constituted Government that could sign the Peace Treaty."

It was difficult, observes Temperley's *History of the Peace Conference,* to decide whether the Allies disposed of a weapon which could impel fulfilment of the reparation clauses if Germany became a group of independent states and communist republics, where the governments would indulge in fantastic experiments in the socialization of industry. "Military occupation might be worse than useless," because "the German troops had been contaminated with Bolshevist propaganda during the occupation of Russia. It might be equally dangerous for Entente troops to occupy revolutionary Germany."

The Allied governments' fear of revolution was again their chief motive in determining their policy on German disarmament. While making Germany incapable of aggression, they also desired, in the words of Temperley, "to leave Germany with a military force sufficient to maintain internal order." On March 17, 1919, the following conversation took place between Wilson, Foch, and Lloyd George:

President Wilson asked to be assured that the exterior dangers from the Bolsheviks and so forth, which the Germans might have to meet on their Eastern frontiers, had been considered by the Military experts in fixing the total number of effectives to be allowed to Germany.

Marshal Foch replied that the Commission considered

that the 100,000 men allowed, in addition to the Gendarmerie, would be quite sufficient for the maintenance of order within the territory of Germany and for the defence of her frontiers.

Mr. Lloyd George enquired, following up President Wilson's point, how many German troops had been engaged in suppressing the various Spartacist insurrections through Germany, including Bavaria.

Foch replied he did not know, but in any case less than 100,000. In pleading that food be sent to Germany, Mr. Lloyd George told the Allied Supreme Council that:

> British officers who had been in Germany said that Bolshevism was being created, and the determining factor was going to be food. As long as the people were starving they would listen to the arguments of the Spartacists, and the Allies by their action were simply encouraging elements of disruption and anarchy. It was like stirring up an influenza puddle next door. The condition of Russia was well known, and it might be possible to look on at a muddle which had there been created. But now, if Germany went, and perhaps Spain, who would feel safe? As long as order was maintained in Germany, a breakwater would exist between the countries of the Allies, and the waters of revolution beyond. But once that breakwater was swept away, he could not speak for France, and he trembled for his own country. . . . He begged the Council to reaffirm that decision [to abandon the blockade] in the most unequivocal terms for, unless this people were fed by the Allies, and the people of Germany were allowed to run riot, a state of revolution among the working classes of all countries would ensue with which it would be impossible to cope.

The clearest evidence of the connection between fear of revolution and the founding of the League is contained in Mr. Lloyd George's confidential memorandum to the Big Four, entitled "Some Considerations for the Peace Conference before They Finally Draft Their Terms." This document is of such poignant interest today, and casts such a vivid light on what Mr. Lloyd George really believed at the time as contrasted with his observations for public consumption, then and since, that we make no apology for quoting from it at length:

When nations are exhausted by wars in which they put forth all their strength and which leave them tired, bleeding and broken, it is not difficult to patch up a peace that may last until the generation which experienced the horrors of the war has passed away. Pictures of heroism and triumph only tempt those who know nothing of the sufferings and terrors of war. It is therefore comparatively easy to patch up a peace which will last for 30 years.

What is difficult, however, is to draw up a peace which will not provoke a fresh struggle when those who have had practical experience of what war means have passed away. History has proved that a peace which has been hailed by a victorious nation as a triumph of diplomatic skill and states-manship, even of moderation, in the long run has proved itself to be shortsighted and charged with danger to the victor. . . .

You may strip Germany of her colonies, reduce her armaments to a mere police force and her navy to that of a fifth-rate power; all the same in the end if she feels she has been unjustly treated in the peace of 1919 she will find means of exacting retribution from her conquerors. The impression, the deep impression, made upon the human heart by four years of unexampled slaughter will disappear with the hearts upon which it has been marked by the terrible sword of the great war. The maintenance of peace will then depend upon there being no causes of exasperation constantly stirring up the spirit of patriotism, of justice or of fair play to achieve redress.

As few Germans as possible must therefore be transferred from German sovereignty to that of other states.

But there is a consideration in favour of a long-sighted peace which influences me even more than the desire to leave no causes justifying a fresh outbreak 30 years hence. There is one element in the present condition of nations which differentiates it from the situation as it was in 1815.

In the Napoleonic war the countries were equally exhausted but the revolutionary spirit had spent its force in the country of its birth and Germany had satisfied the legitimate popular demands for the time being by a series of economic changes which were inspired by courage, foresight and high statesmanship. Even in Russia the Czar had effected great reforms which were probably at that time even too advanced for the half-savage population. The situation is very different now. The revolution is still in its infancy. The extreme figures of the Terror are still in command in Russia. The whole of Europe is filled with the spirit of revolution. There is a deep sense not only of discontent, but of danger and revolt amongst the workmen against pre-war conditions. The whole existing order in its political, social and economic aspects is questioned by the masses of the population, from one end of Europe to the other. In some countries, like Germany and Russia, the unrest takes the form of open rebellion, in others, like France, Great Britain and Italy, it takes the shape of strikes and of general disinclination to settle down to work, symptoms which are just as much concerned with the desire for political and social change as with wage demands.

Much of this unrest is healthy. We shall never make a lasting peace by attempting to restore the conditions of 1914. But there is a danger that we may throw the masses of the population throughout Europe into the arms of the extremists whose only idea for regenerating mankind is to destroy utterly the whole existing fabric of society. These men have triumphed in Russia. They have done so at a terrible price. Hundreds of thousands of the population have perished. The railways, the roads, the towns, the whole structural organization of Russia has been almost destroyed, but somehow or other they seem to have managed to keep their hold upon the masses of the Russian people, and what is much more significant, they have succeeded in creating a large army which is apparently well directed and well disciplined, and is, as to a great part of it, prepared to die for its ideals. In another year Russia, inspired by a new enthusiasm, may have recovered from her passion for peace and have at her command the only army eager to fight, because it is the only army that believes that it has any cause to fight for.

The greatest danger that I see in the present situation is that Germany may throw in her lot with Bolshevism and place her resources, her brains, her vast organizing power at the disposal of the revolutionary fanatics whose dream is to conquer the world for Bolshevism by force of arms. This danger is no mere chimera. The present government in Germany is weak; it has no prestige; its authority is challenged; it lingers merely because there is no alternative but the spartacists, and Germany is not ready for spartacism, as yet. But the argument which the spartacists are using with great effect at this very time is that they alone can save Germany from the intolerable conditions which have been bequeathed her by the war. They offer to free the German people from indebtedness to the Allies and indebtedness to their own richer classes. They offer them complete control of their own affairs and the prospect of a new heaven and earth. It is true that the price will be heavy. There will be two or three years of anarchy, perhaps of bloodshed, but at the end the land will remain, the people will remain, the greater part of the houses and the factories will remain, and the railways and the roads will remain, and Germany, having thrown off her burdens, will be able to make a fresh start.

If Germany goes over to the spartacists it is inevitable that she should throw in her lot with the Russian Bolshevists. Once that happens all Eastern Europe will be swept into the orbit of the Bolshevik revolution and within a year we may witness the spectacle of nearly three hundred million people organised into a vast red army under German instructors and German generals equipped with German cannon and German machine guns and prepared for a renewal of the attack on Western Europe. This is a prospect which no one can face with equanimity. Yet the news which came from Hungary yesterday shows only too clearly this danger is no fantasy. . . . If we are wise, we shall offer to Germany a peace which, while just, will be preferable for all sensible men to the alternative of Bolshevism. I would, therefore, put it in the forefront of the peace that once she accepts our terms, especially reparation, we will open to her the raw materials and markets of the world on equal terms with ourselves, and will do everything possible to enable the

German people to get upon their legs again. We cannot both cripple her and expect her to pay.

Finally, we must offer terms which a responsible Government in Germany can expect to be able to carry out. If we present terms to Germany which are unjust, or excessively onerous, no responsible Government will sign them; certainly the present weak administration will not. If it did, I am told that it would be swept away within 24 hours. Yet if we can find nobody in Germany who will put his hand to a peace treaty, what will be the position? *A large army of occupation for an indefinite period is out of the question. Germany would not mind it. A very large number of people in that country would welcome it, as it would be the only hope of preserving the existing order of things.* The objection would not come from Germany, but from our own countries. Neither the British Empire nor America would agree to occupy Germany. France by herself could not bear the burden of occupation. We should therefore be driven back on the policy of blockading the country. That would inevitably mean spartacism from the Urals to the Rhine, with its inevitable consequence of a huge Red Army attempting to cross the Rhine. As a matter of fact, I am doubtful whether public opinion would allow us deliberately to starve Germany. If the only difference between Germany and ourselves were between onerous terms and moderate terms, I very much doubt if public opinion would tolerate the deliberate condemnation of millions of women and children to death by starvation. If so the Allies would have incurred the moral defeat of having attempted to impose terms on Germany which Germany had successfully resisted.

From every point of view, therefore, it seems to me that we ought to endeavour to draw up a peace settlement as if we were impartial arbiters, forgetful of the passions of war. This settlement ought to have three ends in view. First of all it must do justice to the Allies, by taking into account Germany's responsibility for the origin of the war, and for the way in which it was fought. Secondly, it must be a settlement which a responsible German government can sign in the belief that it can fulfil the obligations it incurs. Thirdly,

* Italics ours.

it must be a settlement which will contain in itself no provocations for future wars, and which will constitute an alternative to Bolshevism, because it will commmend itself to all reasonable opinion as a fair settlement of the European problem.

II. It is not, however, enough to draw up a just and farsighted peace with Germany. If we are to offer Europe an alternative to Bolshevism we must make the League of Nations into something which will be both a safeguard to those nations who are prepared for fair dealing with their neighbours, and a menace to those who would trespass on the rights of their neighbours, whether they are imperialist empires or imperialist Bolshevists. An essential element, therefore, in the peace settlement is the constitution of the League of Nations as the effective guardian of international right and international liberty throughout the world. If this is to happen the first thing to do is that the leading members of the League of Nations should arrive at an understanding between themselves in regard to armaments. To my mind it is idle to endeavour to impose a permanent limitation of armaments upon Germany unless we are prepared similarly to impose limitations upon ourselves. I recognise that until Germany has settled down and given practical proof that she has abandoned her imperialist ambitions, and until Russia has also given proof that she does not intend to embark upon a military crusade against her neighbours, it is essential that the leading members of the League of Nations should maintain considerable forces both by land and sea in order to preserve liberty in the world. But if they are to present an united front to the forces both of reaction and revolution, they must arrive at such an agreement in regard to armaments among themselves as would make it impossible for suspicion to arise between the members of the League of Nations in regard to their intentions towards one another. If the League is to do its work for the world it will only be because the members of the League trust it themselves and because there are no rivalries and jealousies in the matter of armaments between them. The first condition of success for the League of Nations is, therefore, a firm understanding between the British Empire and the United States of Amer-

ica and France and Italy that there will be no competitive
building up of fleets or armies between them. Unless this is
arrived at before the Covenant is signed the League of Nations will be a sham and a mockery. It will be regarded, and
rightly regarded, as a proof that its principal promoters and
patrons repose no confidence in its efficiency. . . .

I should like to ask why Germany, if she accepts the terms
we consider just and fair, should not be admitted to the
League of Nations, at any rate as soon as she has established
a stable and democratic Government. Would it not be an in-
ducement to her both to sign the terms and to resist Bolshevism? Might it not be safer that she should be inside the
League than that she should be outside it?

The British Empire and the United States ought to give France
a guarantee against German aggression until such time as the
League was strong enough to preserve the peace and liberty of
the world.

III. If, however, the Peace Conference is really to secure
peace and offer to the world a complete plan of settlement
which all reasonable men will recognise as an alternative
preferable to anarchy, it must deal with the Russian situation. Bolshevik imperialism does not merely menace the
States on Russia's borders. It threatens the whole of Asia and
is as near to America as it is to France. It is idle to think that
the Peace Conference can separate, however sound a peace
it may have arranged with Germany, if it leaves Russia as
it is today. I do not propose, however, to complicate the
question of the peace with Germany by introducing a discussion of the Russian problem. I mention it simply in order
to remind ourselves of the importance of dealing with it as
soon as possible.[5]

This remarkable memorandum seems to have been more in the
nature of Mr. Lloyd George's moral alibi before history and his
own conscience than a political act. For he made no serious attempt to follow it up. Clemenceau acidly observed that after
taking most of Germany's colonies and merchant fleet and the
whole of her navy, and imposing a huge indemnity to boot, it

was too late for the British Government to urge moderation at the expense of France. After an "inspired" French press leakage, 370 of Mr. Lloyd George's Parliament of hard-faced members of Parliament—including, as Mr. Lloyd George has since pointed out, Sir Samuel Hoare, Lord Halifax, Mr. Neville Chamberlain, and other notorious appeasers of Hitler—sent him a wire protesting strongly against excessive mildness to the German Republic. Mr. Lloyd George collapsed at once.

The most striking feature of the memorandum (and of the previous quotation) is the extent to which the Prime Minister was obsessed by terror of "Bolshevism." It casts a curious light on the statement in his *War Memoirs:* "I do not fear Bolshevism" (inset heading on p. 2591, where we are told for the nth time that intervention in Russia had nothing to do with anti-Communist feeling). It shows, too, how intervention in Russia, which was still going on, and of which more will be said below, the use of the Allies' economic power to combat the social revolution in Germany and Hungary, and other forms of thwarting the demands of the working-class, filled the minds of the Paris peacemakers, not to the exclusion of everything else, but in such a way as to colour their thought on most other questions.

Another point is how weak the Allies' position vis-à-vis Germany really was, and how little courage it would have required for the German Social-Democrats to call the Allies' bluff, carry out a social revolution, and repudiate the Versailles Treaty. It is true the Allies threatened to renew the hunger blockade and to invade the country if the German people did either of these things. But Mr. Lloyd George admits frankly that they could not have made good their threat.

What Mr. Lloyd George said about the consequences of a harsh peace has come true, although he erred on the side of optimism in suggesting thirty years as the time limit for the Peace of Versailles. But that was because he was not reckoning with the economic breakdown of the great slump and the social forces it released, which were the chief cause of the drift into World War II.

Finally, Mr. Lloyd George's memorandum makes crystal-clear

how the fear of social revolution was used by the liberals at the Peace Conference as their main argument for establishing the League.

That, too, was evidently at the back of General Smuts's mind when he concluded his famous Peace Conference pamphlet *The League of Nations: A Practical Suggestion* with the statement that the League

> must be the wise regulator, the steadying influence in the forward movement now set going among the nations of the earth.
>
> For there is no doubt that mankind is once more on the move. The very foundations have been shaken and loosened, and things are again fluid. The terms have been struck, and the great caravan of humanity is once more on the march. Vast social and industrial changes are coming, perhaps upheavals which may, in their magnitude and effects, be comparable to war itself. A steadying, controlling, regulating influence will be required to give stability to progress, and to remove that wasteful friction which has dissipated so much social force in the past, and in this war more than ever before. These great functions could only be adequately fulfilled by the League of Nations. Responding to such vital needs and coming at such a unique opportunity in history, it may well be destined to mark a new era in the Government of Man, and become to the peoples the guarantee of Peace, to the workers of all races the great International, and to all the embodiment and living expression of the moral and spiritual unity of the human race.[6]

Here is clear recognition of the fact that great social changes were bound to come, and their international repercussions would be such that some form of world government was necessary to enable these changes to take place smoothly and progressively, instead of by upheavals "in their magnitude and effect comparable to the war itself."

This is what might be described as a genuine liberal view—the view of a statesman who recognizes the necessity of sweeping changes just as fully as the most extreme revolutionary, and is concerned not about how to thwart the forces of change, but about how to canalize them so that they flow smoothly and constructively, with the minimum of wasteful and destructive violence. This outlook may perhaps be called optimistic, but it was noble and intelligent, the outlook of a man who was the nearest approach at the Peace Conference to a philosopher-King.*

But the genuine liberal view passed over by imperceptible stages into the pseudo-liberal view to which Temperley's *History of the Peace Conference of Paris* draws attention in the following passage on the origin of the International Labour Organization.

> When at the first plenary session of the Peace Conference Clemenceau announced that one of the three first commissions to be appointed was to deal with International Labour Legislation, the general opinion seemed to be that this action was to be explained as a counter move to the labour conventions of the Socialists and Trade Unionists, which were at that moment threatening to throw the whole weight of the international labour movement in opposition to the work of the Paris Peace Conference. This interpretation, whatever its justification, implied a certain unreality in the work of the Labour Commission; for an attempt to meet the large industrial problems, which it would have to face, in the spirit of temporizing expediency, might easily discredit anything it should attempt to do. The taint of a suspicion that this was the case lingered all through the Peace Conference, and a certain indifference towards its work was noticeable upon

* Though, such are the inconsistencies of human nature and the complexities of reality that this was also the man responsible for the tissue of ingenious sophistries that finally persuaded President Wilson to accept the British demand that Germany should pay not only for the damage wrought in the devastated areas but for most of the general costs of the war to the Allies. This impossible demand was one of the greatest and most flagrant breaches of the Allies' Armistice promise to Germany, on the basis of which that country laid down its arms. It had more to do with bedevilling international relations and holding up reconstruction and reconciliation during the crucial post-war years than any other question. We may add that in his own country General Smuts is regarded as largely responsible for South Africa's authoritarian policy, based on segregation and imposed inferiority of status, towards the native population.

the part of those occupied with the more normal labours of
treaty-making, in the preparations of maps for new boundaries, and statistics for indemnities. It is possible, however,
that the Labour section of the Treaty, in spite of the relatively unfavourable circumstances under which it was prepared, may prove of as definite and lasting significance as
the political and economic sections. There was indeed a
grotesque side to the work of those exact scientists, the geog-
raphers, mapping the frontiers of a new Europe that was in
the midst of an eruption, with the molten currents of revolution sweeping away all old-time barriers in both the political
and the economic realm. Whatever could be done by the
Labour section to stem this international revolutionary current by way of positive promises for the future, if not through
achievement at the moment, was as effective a stabilising
action as the tracing of frontiers on the illusive blood-stained
map of Europe.[7]

The constitution of the International Labour Organization was
a direct response to the demands of organized labour. But it is
plain that it was far from being a sincere response. It was undertaken partly to forestall labour's intention of setting up a rival
workers' peace conference. This intention was mentioned in the
previous chapter, where it was explained that the idea was abandoned partly because of trust in the Allies' Armistice promise to
base the peace terms on the Fourten Points, and largely because
of labour's absorption with the problems of demobilization and
finding jobs for the demobilized. The brief post-war boom helped
this process. It accounts for the absence of any real labour pressure on the Paris peacemakers. But partly, too, a great deal of
labour opinion was as ready to believe assurances and promises
emanating from the Peace Conference as they had been to believe what President Wilson and Mr. Lloyd George told them
during the war, and as they subsequently were ready to trust
promises about "reconstruction" and "homes for heroes." The
case of the International Labour Office is only one example of
the concessions (real as well as apparent) made in those years
to avert the danger of revolution by "stabilizing action" intended
to induce the workers to content themselves with "positive

promises for the future" instead of "achievement at the moment."
The constitution of the I.L.O. begins by recognizing that:

the League of Nations has for its object the establishment of
universal peace, and such a peace can be established only if
it is based upon social justice; . . . conditions of labour exist
involving such injustice, hardship and privation to large
numbers of people as to produce unrest so great that the
peace and harmony of the world are imperilled.

The capitalist governments and parties who officially subscribed to this statement never took it seriously. So far as they
remembered its existence at all, they regarded it as a meaningless verbal concession to the demands of labour at the Peace
Conference.

The whole idea of a League of Nations was a revolutionary in-
novation forced on governments and Foreign Offices by a public
opinion that had been compelled to think about foreign affairs by
World War I. The idea was launched as a clean break with international anarchy as the "normal" and "inevitable" relation between "sovereign" states; with imperialism as a national interest
worth fighting for; and with the methods and morals of power
politics as a tolerable form of intercourse between civilized communities.

Apart from the personal views of a handful of exceptionally
enlightened individuals, the League throughout its lifetime never
outgrew its amateur status in the eyes of the "professionals" of
international and imperial affairs and defence—that is, the Foreign Offices, diplomatic and fighting services, and colonial Minis-
tries. The treaty obligations of the Covenant never acquired the
dignity, in the view of these professionals, nor of any conservative government or party, of a "national interest," still less of a
"matter of honour and vital interest," which it was worth taking
the risk of war to defend.

That is because the social and international content of the
phrase "national interest" continued to be what it was before
World War I and what for all practical purposes it remains today
—the power, privileges, and vested interests of property. Na-

tional self-preservation still meant and means primarily the social self-preservation of that class which has been described in these pages as the plutocracy.

Seen from this angle, the idea of world government (the League of Nations) was part of the demands for a new social and international order of the common people, stung to action by being plunged into four years of world war. That idea had to be "managed" somehow. If it could not be turned down outright, at least let it be watered till it became an adjunct of, rather than an alternative to, the old diplomacy, so that the world, instead of becoming safe for democracy (as that, unfortunately, meant unsafe for capitalism), once more became safe for the old order by reverting to international anarchy, power politics, and an arms race within the fading framework of the League.

THE PEACE TREATIES

We now realize what were the social dynamics of the Peace Conference. They explain the nature, outcome, and inter-connections of the four principal conflicts at the conference—over the peace treaties, economic reconstruction, the League, and Russia respectively.

The Allied governments wanted a peace of power politics based on the secret treaties. But their rival egotisms and imperialisms did not always agree. They were opposed by President Wilson, who wanted a peace based on the Fourteen Points. The Russian Revolution made it impossible to carry out important parts of the secret treaties, and the absence of Russian support weakened the most reactionary elements in the Allied governments. Moreover:

> The Russian catchword of "peace without annexations or indemnities," which the Bolsheviks had taken over and amplified, had made a deep, if indefinite, impression. The demand for no economic boycotts figures among the war-aims of many anti-Bolshevik bodies of opinion, and the precedent of the attempt to realise "no secret diplomacy" was not forgotten. The effect of these ideas was conflicting and to a large extent impalpable, and they had become, in the main,

divested of any specifically Bolshevik setting, but, in conjunction with President Wilson's enunciation of principles, they coloured the minds and imaginations of such numbers that they exercised an immediate and profound influence upon the Peace Conference.

In short:

The effect of the Russian problem on the Paris Conference was profound: Paris cannot be understood without Moscow. Without ever being represented at Paris at all, the Bolsheviki and Bolshevism were powerful elements at every turn. Russia played a more vital part at Paris than Prussia.[8]

The final result was that the Versailles and other peace treaties were a compromise in which power politics had the lion's share. But the worst parts of the treaties were temporary, and it was made possible to revise them through the League.

The peace treaties were such a disappointment to the labour movement that the French Socialist party voted against the Versailles Treaty when it was submitted to the Chamber. The British Labour party was also strongly critical. However, as the German Social-Democrats accepted the Versailles Treaty as a lesser evil than the dangers of resistance, it was impossible for the Allied Socialist parties to be more royalist than the king.

THE LEAGUE OF NATIONS

It is impossible to understand the significance of the struggle out of which the League was born without knowing something of how the League was conceived.

The idea of a League of Nations was not new, but had not entered public life before World War I. The necessity for a European League of Nations if peace was to be preserved had, it is true, been mentioned at the International Socialist Congress of 1912. But the proposal had never been publicly pressed by any statesman, party, society, group, or individual during the era of modern imperialism.

This is the more curious because, as explained in a previous chapter, the conception of a League of Nations was rooted in the older tradition of the unity of civilized mankind. Numerous attempts had been made to revive that tradition. The growing interdependence of nations and the increasing destructiveness of war facilitated the formation of a League and supplied an ever stronger incentive. Such institutions as public international unions, the Hague Tribunal, and the concert of Europe meant, in Woolf's words:

A vague protoplasmic International Authority had made its appearance in the nineteenth century; a primitive organism with two rudimentary organs, one consisting of judicial tribunals and the other of Conferences of representatives.[9]

Bertrand Russell has stated that he found in the papers of his grandfather Lord Amberley a complete scheme for a League of Nations with economic and military sanctions, arbitration, and political conferences. Similar schemes were put forward in the United States in the first two-thirds of last century. T. H. Green, in his *Principles of Political Obligation,* predicted sixty-five years ago that some form of world law and world government must come if civilization is to survive. The idea is, indeed, implicit in the liberal philosophy of the state and in the liberal view of what constitutes civilization. The development of plutocracy and imperialism meant regression for liberalism in this as in other respects.

In the feverish twelve days' negotiations that ended with World War I Grey mentioned to the German Ambassador that he hoped that if the crisis were tided over, it might be possible in the resulting relief and relaxation to bring the two rival camps of great powers together in such a way as to convert the balance of power into a League of Nations. From the first the British Liberal government lent a ready ear to proposals for a League.

But the pioneer work was done on what was then the extreme Left, in the writing and propaganda of socialists and radicals, such as E. D. Morel, Norman Angell, G. Lowes Dickinson, Leonard Woolf, H. N. Brailsford, Bertrand Russell, working through organizations such as the Union of Democratic Control, the Fabian Society, and the League of Nations Society (which was later changed to the "League of Free Nations Society," when more "respectable" people joined it, and its Left-wing founders resigned as a protest against the idea that Germany should to begin with be excluded from the League).

The bulk of the political support for the idea of a League of Nations came from labour and liberal opinion. In the governments it was taken up and pushed by progressive statesmen such as Wilson, Smuts, Cecil, and Léon Bourgeois. But essentially the governments and Foreign Offices yielded without believing, as a concession to the pressure of a public opinion they despised as mawkishly sentimental, impracticably idealistic, and dangerously ignorant of the realities of foreign affairs. For the most part, Foreign Offices and conservative politicians still think the same.

Viscount (then Lord Robert) Cecil brought a paper on the subject of the League before the British Cabinet in 1916. This was presented to the Imperial War Cabinet in 1917 and afterwards considered by a committee presided over by Lord Phillimore. Their report was communicated to President Wilson and subsequently General Smuts, and formed the basis of the Anglo-American drafts that in their turn became the basis of the Covenant.

Temperley suggests that:

> The League of Nations as constituted at Paris probably owed less than is generally supposed to its intellectual forerunners, though it owed much to general popular aspirations and idealism. The creative force behind it was the passionate hatred of war, but the practical problem how war could best be avoided or diminished, having in view the inveteracy of nationalist feeling, was presented for solution to men who for four and a half years had been absorbed in crushing administrative tasks. Such men learn mainly, not from books, but from experience. During these years experience had forced three main ideas upon Western statesmanship, and these became the foundation of the Covenant.

The three practical causes for desiring a League, he says, were as follows:

In the first place, the course of negotiations in the twelve days immediately preceding the outbreak of war drew attention to the need for some settled Council of the Nations responsible for the maintenance of peace. This lesson was later reinforced by recurrent disputes between the Allies on matters political, military, and economic. The Balkan failure, directly due to continuous disagreement between London, Paris, Petrograd and Rome, discredited ordinary diplomatic machinery. Successive military disasters brought up the problem of unity of command. Bitter controversies in regard to equality of economic sacrifice, arising first out of the operation of the blockade and later out of the general shortage of supplies, indicated the need for a common economic policy. Hence, the Supreme War Council, the Allied Military Committee at Versailles, and the Allied Maritime Transport Council.

In the second place, the violation of Belgium demonstrated the need for a more comprehensive guarantee of the safety of small nations than could be furnished by incidental treaties between a group of Powers. This truth was, however, hardly realized until the diplomatic conflict between the Allies and neutral nations, arising mainly out of the blockade, drew attention to anomalies of the doctrine of neutrality in a world war.

Finally, the increasing exhaustion of Allied resources during the later stages of the War forced upon the Allies a co-operation not merely in the formulation of broad policies but in the detailed administrative execution of such policies. National resources, instead of being made the subject of general agreements between statesmen, were actually, in a measure, pooled under the joint management of international bodies. From the experience thus gained, it began to be realized how great were the possibilities of such co-operation, how meaningless had been many of the economic rivalries which had divided nations in the past and how beneficial in a practical way, apart from any question of conciliation or the settlement of problems of high policy, might be an organized system of international administration in affairs of common interest to all nations. Moreover, experience during 1917 and 1918 showed that Inter-Allied bodies tended to succeed or fail in proportion as they were provided with efficient secretaries capable of carrying out the detailed administrative work entailed by the policy laid down at periodical meetings.[10]

This account would seem to underestimate the degree to which the foundation of the League was in fact due to pressure upon the governments by public opinion, and in particular from labour and liberal quarters. Governments absorbed in the crushing administrative tasks and political problems of conducting a great war are even less ready than governments in normal times to consider any new idea, except under very considerable pressure. As we have seen from the previous chapter, their acceptance of the idea of a League was due to the absolute necessity of convincing labour and liberal opinion that they were undergoing the horrors of a world war for something worth while.

The Phillimore Committee's report begins by stating that their attention had been, says Baker,

directed mainly to the various proposals for a League of Nations which were formulated in the 16th and 17th centuries, and to those which have been put forward since the recent revival of the movement.

They add:

The earlier projects which aimed at setting up a kind of European Confederation with supernational authority we have after consideration rejected, feeling that international opinion is not ripe for so drastic a pooling of sovereignty, and that the only feasible method of securing the object is by way of co-operation or possibly treaty of alliance on the lines of the more recent schemes.

We have accordingly carefully considered those schemes, all of which substitute, in place of the earlier idea of confederation, a system working by means of a permanent conference and an arbitral tribunal. None of them, however, in their entirety appear to your Committee to be practicable or likely to meet with acceptance. We have therefore drafted a Convention in which, while embodying their leading ideas, we have endeavored to avoid their more obvious stumbling blocks.[11]

Liberal and labour opinion had gone very far by the end of the war in working out the implications of this new idea of a League of Nations. How far unofficial opinion had gone is shown by the following quotation from an article by Mr. H. G. Wells, who at that time was working for the Ministry of Propaganda:

The League of Free Nations must, in fact, if it is to be a working reality, have power to define and limit the military and naval and aerial equipment of every country in the world. This means something more than a restriction of state forces. It must have power and freedom to investigate the military and naval and aerial establishments of all its constituent powers. It must also have effective control over every armament industry. And armament industries are not always easy to define. Are aeroplanes, for example, armament? Its powers, I suggest, must extend even to restraint upon the belligerent propaganda which is the natural advertisement campaign of every armament industry. It must have the right, for example, to raise the question of the proprietorship of newspapers by armament interests. Disarmament is, in fact, a necessary factor of any League of Free Nations, and you cannot have disarmament unless you are prepared to see the powers of the Council of the League extend thus far. The very existence of the League presupposes that it and it alone is to have and to exercise military force. Any other belligerency or preparation or incitement to belligerency becomes rebellion, and any other arming a threat of rebellion, in a world League of Free Nations.

But here, again, has the general mind yet thought out all that is involved in this proposition? In all the great belligerent countries the armament industries are now huge interests with enormous powers. Krupp's business alone is as powerful a thing in Germany as the Crown. In every country a heavily subsidized "patriotic" press will fight desperately against giving powers so extensive and thorough as those here suggested to an international body. So long, of course, as the League of Free Nations remains a project in the air, without body or parts, such a press will sneer at it gently as "Utopian" and even patronize it kindly. But so soon as the League takes on the shape its general proposition makes logically necessary, the armament interest will take fright. Then it is we shall hear the drum patriotic loud in defence of the human blood trade. . . .

I am suggesting here that the League of Free Nations shall practically control the army, navy, air forces, and armament industry of every nation in the world. What is the alternative to that? To do as we please? No, the alternative is that any malignant country will be free to force upon all the rest just the maximum amount of armament it chooses to adopt. . . .

So long as patriotic cant can keep the common man jealous of international controls over his belligerent possibilities, so long will he be the helpless slave of the foreign threat, and "Peace" remain a mere name for the resting-phase between wars. . . .

The plain truth is that the League of Free Nations, if it is to be a reality, if it is to effect a real pacification of the world, must do no less than supersede Empire; it must end not only this new German imperialism, which is struggling so savagely and powerfully to possess the earth, but it must also wind up British imperialism and French imperialism, which do now so largely and inaggressively possess it. And, moreover, this idea queries the adjective of Belgian, Portuguese, French and British Central Africa alike, just as emphatically as it queries "German." Still more effectually does the League forbid those creations of the futurist imagination, the imperialism of Italy and Greece, which make such threatening gestures at the world of our children. Are these incompatibilities understood? Until people have faced the clear antagonism which exists between imperialism and internationalism, they have not begun to suspect the real significance of this project of the League of Free Nations. They have not begun to realise that peace also has its price.[12]

How far official liberal opinion went is shown by General Smuts's remarkable pamphlet *The League of Nations: A Practical Suggestion*, which was used extensively by Wilson and the

more progressive members of the British delegation to the Peace
Conference. His leading ideas were as follows:

The League was to be nothing more nor less than a world
government occupying the place left vacant by the disappearance
of the defeated empires.

The greatest opportunity in history would be met by the
greatest step forward in the government of man. On the
debris of the old dead world would be built at once the en-
during Temple of future world-government. The new creative peace world would come to us, not as a fleeting visitant
from some other clime, but out of the very ruins of our own
dead past. In that way the most exalted position and the
most responsible and beneficent functions would be entrusted
to the new organ of world-government.

In view of the novelty and gigantic scale of this enterprise, too
much store must not be set on past precedents, although the
British Commonwealth was in many ways a working model.
They must make a constitution that was elastic and capable of
growth, expansion, and adaptation to future needs, and avoid
cut-and-dried schemes.

And from this point of view let us proceed at once to discard the idea of a super-State which is in the minds of some
people. No new super-sovereign is wanted in the new world
now arising. States will here be controlled not by compulsion
from above but by consent from below. Government by consent of the governed is our formula.

All ideas of federation or confederation, let alone the old imperial systems of centralization and absorption, were inapplicable,
and would not be agreed to by any of the existing sovereign
states. Therefore the conference system of the British Commonwealth with very considerable modifications was the only hope-
ful line of advance.

But while we avoid the super-sovereign at the one end,
we must be equally careful to avoid the mere ineffective de-
bating society at the other end. The new situation does not
call for a new talking shop. We want an instrument of govern-

ment which, however much talk is put into it at the one end, will grind out decisions at the other end. We want a League which will be real, practical, effective as a system of world-government. . . .

In endeavouring to find a workable constitution for the League let us, even at the risk of appearing pedantic, begin at the beginning. Government, like thought or mathematics or physical science, rests on certain fundamental unalterable forms, categories, or laws, which any successful schemes must conform to. The division of government into legislation, administration and justice is fundamental in this sense, and should be adhered to by us in devising this new system of world-government.[13]

General Smuts then made proposals concerning the organization of the League, which are very similar to what the League subsequently became as described in the next chapter.

But General Smuts was insistent that the League should be made

not only a possible means for preventing future wars, but much more a great organ of the ordinary peaceful life of civilisation, as the foundation of the international system which will be erected on the ruins of this war. . . .

It is not sufficient for the League merely to be a sort of *deus ex machina,* called in in very grave emergencies when the spectre of war appears; if it is to last, it must be much more. It must become part and parcel of the common international life of States, it must be an ever visible, living, working organ of the polity of civilisation. It must function so strongly in the ordinary peaceful intercourse of States that it becomes irresistible in their disputes; its peaceful activity must be the foundation and guarantee of its war power.[14]

Now it seems to me that some people expect too much from the new machinery of international Arbitration and Conciliation which emerges as the chief proposal for preventing future wars. War is a symptom of deep-seated evils: it is a disease or growth out of social and political conditions. While these conditions remain unaltered, it is vain to expect any good from new institutions superimposed on those conditions. Hence it is that I have argued all through this discussion for an inner transformation of international conditions and institutions. If the League of Nations merely meant some new wheel to the coach, I do not think the addition worth making, nor do I think the vehicle would carry us any farther. The League must be such as to mean much more than new Councils to provide for Arbitration and Conciliation in future troubles. The new institution of peace must not be something additional, something external, superimposed on the pre-existing structure. It must be an organic change; it must be woven into the very texture of our political system. The new *motif* of peace must in future operate internally, constantly, inevitably from the very heart of our political organisation, and must, so to speak, flow from the nature of things political. Then, and not till then, will the impulse to war atrophy and shrivel up, and war itself stand stripped in all its horrible nakedness, and lose all the association of romance, all the atmosphere of honour, which has proved so intoxicating and irresistible in the past. That is why I am pleading for a more fundamental conception of the League, for a League whose task will not be to stem the on-coming tide with a broom, but for one which will prevent the tide from flowing at all.[15]

General Smuts makes a series of sweeping proposals as to the functions that should be assumed by the new world government:

Quite recently the practice of the Allies in controlling and rationing food, shipping, coal, munitions, etc., for common purposes through the machinery of Inter-Allied Councils has led to the idea that in future a League of Nations might be similarly used for the common economic needs of the nations belonging to the League—at any rate for the control of articles of food or raw materials or transport in respect of which there will be a shortage. In other words the economic functions of the League would not be confined to the prevention of wars or the punishment of an unauthorised belligerent, but would be extended to the domain of ordinary peaceful intercourse between the members of the League.[16]

The League should be charged with establishing equality of

trade conditions by removing economic barriers between members of the League and assuring free transit by land, water, and air.

Questions of industry, trade, finance, labour, transit and communications, and many others, are bursting through the national bounds and are clamouring for international solution. Water-tight compartments and partition walls between the nations and the continents have been knocked through, and the new situation calls for world-government. If the League of Nations refuses to function, some other machinery will have to be created to deal with the new problems which transcend all national limits. The task is there; all that is required is a carefully thought out form of government by which that task could be undertaken. It is a unique problem, both in its magnitude and in the benefits for the world which a successful solution will secure.[17]

General Smuts's most interesting and ambitious suggestion concerned the functions the League should assume in Central Europe. He pointed out that the great multi-national empires of Germany, Russia, and Austria had, as a result of their defeat, broken down and left a welter of new states between the Baltic and the Balkans.

In a rudimentary way all such composite empires of the past were leagues of nations, keeping the peace among the constituent nations, but unfortunately doing so not on the basis of freedom but of repression. Usually one dominant nation in the group overcame, coerced, and kept the rest under. The principle of nationality became over-strained and over-developed, and nourished itself by exploiting other weaker nationalities. Nationality over-grown became Imperialism, and the Empire led a troubled existence on the ruins of the freedom of its constituent nations. That was the evil of the system; but with however much friction and oppression the peace was usually kept among the nations falling within the Empire . . .

In the place of the great Empires we find the map of Europe now dotted with small nations, embryo states, derelict territories. Europe has been reduced to its original

atoms. For the moment its political structure, the costly result of so many centuries of effort, has disappeared. But that
state of affairs must be looked upon as temporary. The creative process in the political movement of humanity cannot
be paralysed; the materials lie ready for a new reconstruc-
tive task, to which, let us hope, the courage and genius of
Western civilisation will prove equal. . . .

The question is, what new political form shall be given to
these elements of our European civilisation? On the answer
to that question depends the future of Europe and of the
world. My broad contention is that the smaller, embryonic,
unsuccessful leagues of nations have been swept away, not
to leave an empty house for national individualism or
anarchy, but for a larger and better League of Nations.
Europe is being liquidated, and the League of Nations must
be the heir to this great estate.[18]

The only statesmanlike course was to make the League "the
reversionary in the broadest sense of these Empires."

The pamphlet does not go into details on just what should be
the relation of the League to the new states. But what was apparently intended was a considerable development with regard
to them of the extensive functions in the domain of economic and
social co-operation, which the League was to discharge towards
all its members, as well as League control over their tariff
policies, transport, and military establishments.

As regards armaments and arms industries, the pamphlet proposes the abolition of conscription and its replacement by some
form of militia system; limitation of armaments by the Council's
determining what categories and numbers of war weapons should
be allowed for forces of a certain size; and the nationalization of
armament factories on the ground that:

. . . as long as the production of munitions of war remains a
private commercial undertaking, huge vested interests grow
up around it which influence public opinion through the
Press and otherwise in the direction of war. There is no
doubt that the influence of Krupps has been harmful to the
great peace interests of the world, and, in a less degree, the
same could probably be said of most other similar under-

takings. The very success of that sort of business depends on the stimulation of the war atmosphere among the peoples. The Press, influenced by the large profits and advertising enterprise of the armament firms, whips up public opinion on every imaginable occasion; small foreign incidents are written up and magnified into grave international situations affecting the pacific relations of States; and the war temperature is artificially raised and kept up.[19]

General Smuts's proposals for preventing and stopping war are equally drastic. The essential principle, he says, should be a compulsory "moratorium," or delay, during which states would have to submit their disputes to some form of pacific settlement and would be forbidden in any circumstances to resort to war. A state which accepted a peaceful award should also be protected against resort to war by the other party.

In order to be sure that the "moratorium on war" and the protection of a law-abiding state were a reality, the moratorium "must be guaranteed with all the force which is behind the League."

The breaker of the moratorium, or a state resorting to war against a member that complied with the League's award

. . . should therefore become *ipso facto* at war with all the other members of the League, great and small alike, which will sever all relations of trade and finance with the law-breaker, and prohibit all intercourse with its subjects, and also prevent as far as possible all commercial and financial intercourse between the subjects of the law-breaker and those of any other State, whether a member of the League or not. No declaration of war should be necessary, as the state of war arises automatically on the law-breaker proceeding to hostilities, and the boycott follows automatically from the obligation of the League without further resolutions or formalities on the part of the League.

The effect of such a complete automatic trade and financial boycott would necessarily be enormous.

It is because of this power of the economic and financial weapons that many writers are of opinion that the obliga-

tions for action by members of the League should not go beyond the use of these weapons. My view, however, is that
they will not be enough if unsupported by military and naval
action. A powerful military State may think that a sudden
military blow will achieve its object in spite of boycotts, provided that no greater military reaction from the rest of the
League need be feared. This fear may under certain circumstances be a more effective deterrent than even the boycott;
and I do not think the League is likely to prove a success
unless in the last resort the maintenance of the *moratorium*
is guaranteed by force. The obligation on the members of the
League to use force for this purpose should therefore be absolute, but the amount of the force and the contribution from
the members should be left to recommendation of the Council to the respective Governments in each case. . . .

In order to secure world-peace I would pile up the dangers
and risks in front of an intending breaker of the *moratorium.*
Should the rigours of maritime warfare be mitigated at the
peace and a measure of freedom be restored to the seas in
the direction contended for by President Wilson, I would advocate the power of full revival of all these rigours as against
such a law-breaker. Not only the right of visit and search, but
also complete naval blackade should be exercisable against
such a State. And the question requires careful consideration
whether such a State should be accorded the status of legalised
war, and whether it should not be outlawed and treated as
the common criminal that it is.[20]

British labour opinion went event farther than the liberals in
demanding economic co-operation, control of raw materials, etc.,
and in pressing for some form of international parliamentary representation. The Fabian Society issued a study, edited by Leonard
Woolf, entitled *International Government.* A book by H. N.
Brailsford on *A League of Nations* put the socialist conception of
the League. Pamphlets by E. D. Morel and others made detailed
proposals for a far-reaching system of international trusteeship
and the open door in all African colonies.

The idea of some form of international assembly, composed of
delegations elected direct by proportional representation from

the parliaments of members of the League, got as far as the League of Nations Commission of the Peace Conference, where, however, it was coolly received and finally defeated by American objections.*

RECONSTRUCTION AND THE ABOLITION OF WAR-TIME CONTROLS

The second defeat suffered by labour's proposals was in the economic field. This defeat is such a good illustration of the forces behind the statesmen at the Peace Conference and has such an important bearing on present controversies that it is worth describing in detail: On August 25, 1917, the *New Statesman* published an article entitled· "A World Famine," which was the work of Mr. Sidney Webb. The article argued that there was grave risk of the war's being followed by unemployment, famine, and revolution. To avert this risk the extensive controls over importing and exporting, manufacture and distribution, raw materials and food, that had been established by the Allies in the course of the war and linked up internationally through the various Inter-Allied Transport and Economic boards should be

* As put forward by the British Government the idea was watered down and given an anti-socialist twist: the Foreign Office, in its "Memorandum Prepared for the Consideration of the British Government in Connexion with the Forthcoming Peace Settlement," early in November 1918 proposed a League of Nations with a Council and Assembly. In a section entitled "Arrangements for Popular Discussion" it observed that "President Wilson laid stress in his Mount Vernon speech on the formation 'of an organised opinion of mankind.' It would seem desirable to establish some body which would serve as a medium for the formation and expression of such a body of opinion. If this is not done, the Socialist International, which has, as it were, a vested interest in international opinion, will cover the same ground with unsatisfactory results. The best expedient would seem to be the institution of a periodical congress of delegates of the Parliaments of the members of the League. . . . The delegations of this Congress might be chosen on a proportional system from amongst the various parties in the national Parliaments." The Cecil plan, one of the earliest drafts of what became the Covenant, is virtually an abstract of this Foreign Office memorandum and makes the same proposal for "a periodical congress of delegates of the Parliaments of the States belonging to the League, as a development out of the existing inter-Parliamentary Union" to cover "the ground claimed by the Socialist International."

enlarged at the Peace Conference by the inclusion of both ex-neutrals and ex-enemies, put under the future League of Nations, and used for the purpose of reconstruction after the war. This policy was adopted by the Allied Socialist and Labour parties and trade-unions and formed part of their program for the League of Nations.

The British labour movement successfully pressed the matter on the Government, and a detailed plan was prepared by the Foreign Office. It aimed at tiding the world over the transition from war to peace and creating firm economic foundations for the League of Nations.

It was, in fact, in the words of the Foreign Office document, "the inevitable corollary of the whole idea of a League of Nations as it is beginning to take form both in the United States and in this country." It would have set before the peoples, from the moment of the firing of the last gun in the war, an example of international co-operation for a peaceful and beneficial purpose, touching them closely in their daily lives and activities. In such an atmosphere, with such a working model before their eyes, the elaboration of the political machinery and functions of the League of Nations would no longer have seemed a visionary enterprise provoking doubt and scepticism in practical minds. Indeed, it is tempting to speculate on what might have followed from the successful working of such a scheme. Certain it is that the new states, such as Germany, would have started on their careers under very different economic and psychological conditions from those which they had actually to face, and that this would have had a powerful influence on the whole subsequent development. One affirmation at any rate can be made without fear of contradiction. If the peace, as is so often said, was lost, its first great defeat, perhaps its greatest defeat of all, was suffered not in the Peace Conference itself but during the days and weeks immediately following the Armistice, when the economic forces were allowed to slip out of the control of statesmanship.[21]

The truth is that the statesmen were all along in the control of the economic forces. The nature of those forces is made clear by the fate of these proposals.

Mr. Herbert Hoover, American big business man and a fanatical believer in the sacred rights of private enterprise, was United States Secretary of State for Commerce and primarily responsible for the rejection of the plan. His representative in Paris was Mr. Bernard M. Baruch, also a leading American business man and a strong believer in untrammelled capitalism. The latter's letter of April 12, 1919, to Lord Robert Cecil, refusing the appointment of a commission to consider the matter, contains as its key sentence "The salvation of the world must rest upon the initiative of individuals."

Lord Robert Cecil's reply contains the following:

> You think that without question the economic situation can be solved by individual initiative. It may be so, though my own opinion is to the contrary, and it is for that reason that I pressed for the summoning of a small expert Committee to which Colonel House agreed. It may be that the result of the enquiry will show that without American assistance on a large scale, nothing can be. done, and it may also be that America will decline to give that assistance. If she intends to take that attitude, forgive me for saying that she ought to take it quite openly and before the face of the world. Then we in Europe shall know the extent of the problem that faces us.
>
> I am afraid if I write more plainly, I shall offend even your partiality.[22]

Mr. Lloyd George wrote a letter to President Wilson enclosing a financial scheme drawn up by Mr. Keynes for American co-operation in post-war reconstruction. This letter contains the following passage:

> In some quarters the hope is entertained that with the early removal of obstacles in the form of the blockade and similar measures to free international intercourse, private enterprise may be safely entrusted with the task of finding the solution. I am in accord with the view that an early removal of such obstacles is an essential measure, and that in

the long run we must mainly look for our salvation to the
renewed life of private enterprise and of private initiative.
Indeed, so far as trading and manufacture is concerned, as
distinct from finance, no other measures should be necessary
from the outset. Nevertheless, in the financial sphere, the
problem of restoring Europe is almost certainly too great for
private enterprise alone and every delay puts this solution
further out of court. There are two main obstacles: (a) the
risks are too great; (b) the amounts are too big and the
credit required too long. The more prostrate a country is and
the nearer to Bolshevism the more presumably it requires
assistance. But the less likely is private enterprise to do it.
To a small extent and with a great margin some trade will be
done and some barter. But not enough to meet the situation.[23]

The scheme outlined a comprehensive plan for rehabilitating
European credit and for financing relief and reconstruction by
large international loans linked up with reparation payment
bonds to be issued by the central powers.

In his reply rejecting the scheme President Wilson makes the
following points:

(a) Germany requires working capital. Without that, she
will be unable to start her industrial life again, and therefore unable to make any substantial progress in the way of
reparation, but

(b) The provisions of the reparation clauses of the proposed treaty demand that Germany shall deliver over at once
all her working capital, that is, practically the whole of her
liquid assets.

(c) Simultaneously the suggestion is in effect made that
America should in a large measure make good this deficiency,
providing in one form or another credit, and thus working
capital, to Germany.

Throughout the reparation discussion the American delegation has steadily pointed out to the other delegations that
the plans proposed would surely deprive Germany of the
means of making any appreciable reparation payments. I
myself, as you know, have frequently made the same obser-

vation. But whenever any of us was urgent on this point, he was accused of being Pro-German. Our delegation finally gave assent to the reparation clauses as drawn, only because the reparation problem was one that chiefly concerned France, Great Britain, Belgium, and the other European countries, and not America.

The United States had incurred enormous expenditure, and the American investing public had pretty well reached saturation point.

You have suggested that we all address ourselves to the problem of helping to put Germany on her feet. But how can your experts or ours be expected to work at a *new* plan to furnish working capital to Germany, when we deliberately start out by taking away all Germany's *present* capital? How can any one expect America to turn over to Germany in any considerable measure new working capital to take the place of that which the European nations have determined to take from her? Such questions would appear to answer themselves, but I cannot refrain from stating them, because they so essentially belong to a candid consideration of the whole difficult problem to which we are addressing ourselves, with as sincere a desire as that of our colleagues to reach a serviceable conclusion.[24]

It is pretty clear that the fanatical belief of American big business in unfettered private enterprise and the insensate greed and vindictiveness of the Allied governments, under the pressure of their respective plutocracies, were jointly responsible for the Peace Conference failing to adopt a labour proposal which might have changed the whole future of the world. Behind all this was the pressure of the Allied and American business worlds to get rid of war-time controls at the earliest possible moment, with the object of removing all restrictions on profits, and with small regard for social and political consequences.

What these consequences were is analyzed in *Europe's Overseas Needs 1919–20 and How They Were Met*, a monograph published in 1943 by the Economic Financial and Transit Department of the League of Nations Secretariat:

In the last two years of the War the Allies had worked out
a system for the joint purchase, distribution and transport of
raw materials and foodstuffs. . . . At the end of the war some
endeavour was made both to preserve these organisations at
least for the reconstruction period and to extend their operation to cover the whole of Europe.[25]

These attempts were frustrated by the abrupt withdrawal of
economic control in the United States before the end of 1918.
There was some international relief work, mostly conducted by
the A.R.A. (American Relief Administration), but no international co-operation in reconstruction. As a result, by the spring
of 1919 prices on the world market started to rise.

With wartime controls, especially in the United States, almost instantaneously abolished, pent-up demand exercised a
potent influence on prices. The very rise in prices stimulated
further demand for speculative purposes. Borrowing expanded rapidly.

This meant a boom in some countries and in others acute difficulty in securing the raw materials necessary to restart production.

In the absence of international action, and indeed of any
concerted plan for international action during almost two
years after the Armistice, the countries of Central and
Eastern Europe took such domestic measures as they could.

These measures included subsidizing exports, severely restrict-
ing imports, and inflation. But this was only a beginning.

The acquisition of raw materials was left almost entirely
to the quite inadequate buying, bargaining and borrowing
power of the individual countries. The absence of an effective international scheme for furnishing raw materials to
those countries that were in need of them, and were not in a
position to buy them themselves, had two main effects. The
first effect, which was dominant in 1919, was that these countries simply did not obtain as much raw materials as their
industries were able to work up, that their factories were
idle, and that unemployment continued at a high level.

The continuation of large-scale unemployment for a year or more after the armistice was particularly unfortunate both from the narrower point of view of financial and from the wider point of view of social and political stability. Government expenditure, already at a high level owing to the continuation of military expenditure and other factors, thus continued to be inflated by unemployment benefits, and the attainment of some sort of balance in the budget was shifted still further into the future both on this account and because the taxable income of the community remained low owing to lack of raw materials and the consequential unemployment. More serious still was the continued presence of millions of workers for whom the miseries of the war were succeeded by the frustration of forced idleness.

The second effect was of a different nature. Inadequate provision of credits to finance the countries' requirements of raw materials did not always prevent their acquisition, especially after 1920. But it did result in a tragic cost having to be paid for that acquisition, not only by the countries in question, but by the whole world.

Under the pressure of the demand for foreign exchange to pay for raw materials and other essential imports currency values depreciated and many in the end finally collapsed. The depreciation continued in many countries for a number of years, during which it was impossible to re-establish stable business conditions. . . .

Exchange depreciation stimulated exports. It did so because it enabled the countries with a depreciating currency to practise "exchange dumping." This "exchange dumping," the intensity of which varied almost from week to week with the erratic fluctuations in depreciating exchanges, induced other countries to restrict imports either by special measures or by a general increase in their tariff rates, and commercial policy was thus forced down the wrong road at the outset.

Serious as these effects on other countries and on international trade were, they were far over-shadowed by the consequence of depreciation and inflation in the countries subject to these currency disorders.

The price paid by them for the stimulus to export and greater opportunity for employment was the disintegration of their whole economic, social and political fabric. Exports were stimulated because the real income of the workers, the "rentier" and all those who received a fixed or more or less fixed money income was reduced as prices rose. Employment improved because labour had become cheap. The full force of the disturbances caused by the war was thus felt by these countries; their standard of living was reduced, and for a time their competitive power increased.

Those who lived on the yield of bonds, the interest on savings, or old-age and war pensions or on salaries not subject to monthly or weekly adjustment to the cost-of-living index suffered the most. These classes which as a whole constituted a stable and industrious section of the population were reduced to destitution while the speculator acquired the wealth which others had earned. Confidence in saving was undermined and took long to revive, if it was ever fully revived. In subsequent years, those who owned capital were often more anxious to hoard it in safety than to use it for promoting production. A section of those who had lost their savings in the maelstrom of inflation became the nucleus of revolution later.

In point of fact, the middle classes who had lost their savings through inflation became the raw material out of which the fascist movements were fashioned.

The League analysis sums up as follows:

The acquisition of raw materials and other essential goods from abroad by countries with inadequate means of effecting foreign purchases at their immediate disposition was rendered still more difficult by the price boom that resulted from the removal of all wartime restrictions in the financially stronger countries and the indiscriminate rush to return to business as usual.

Governments in many parts of Europe, in which peace was only gradually restored, frequently uncertain of the boundaries of the states they governed, in possession of inadequate fiscal machinery, uncertainly controlling an unstable political situation, were unable to meet their budgetary expenditures without recourse to the printing press. The failure of national production and therefore of income to revive owing to lack of raw materials and other essential goods kept their power to collect receipts either from taxation or from borrowing at a low ebb, and this contributed directly to currency inflation. Simultaneously the pressure on the exchanges resulting from the desperate attempts to acquire such goods at any cost, depreciated the external value of the currencies of these countries and thus contributed indirectly to further inflation.

Action was only taken when inflation and the threat of social upheaval rendered it an unavoidable political necessity. But the effects of inflation, still less of hyperinflation, cannot be eradicated. They influence not only, indeed not so much, the current volume of production, but the whole organisation of society and its psychological equilibrium.

When action was taken after the collapse of currencies, it inevitably assumed the form rather of curing one festering spot after another than of attempting to restore health and vitality to the whole economic body of the continent.

The schemes that were applied were too superficial, as they inclined to confuse financial reform with economic reconstruction.

But their real weakness was due to the fact that they came too late and only after irreparable harm had been done by the failure to formulate any general plan for reviving European industry and furnishing promptly the raw materials and other goods necessary for that revival.

It is impossible to compare the monetary cost of the reconstruction loans with what it would have cost to furnish Europe with a fair proportion of the raw materials and other goods that were available in the two first post-war years. It is more useful to recall the magnitude of the disaster that resulted from the absence of any general plan, the failure of production and trade to revive, the social and political effects of inflation and the extent to which these social and political effects were accentuated by the depression at the end of the first peace decade, and that depression accentuated by the burden of debt that Europe had assumed.

The depression of 1921 passed like a ripple over the inflating countries—but, when the more serious depression of the thirties occurred, the weight of their external debt coupled with the dread of a recurrence of inflation undermined their powers, both of resistance and of recuperation.

The effects of the failure to face the problem of Europe's post-war requirements of raw materials and essential manufactured goods with any imagination or courage comparable to that shown in furnishing food relief, were no more local than transitory. The penury of European countries induced them to husband their resources by quantitative restrictions on exports and on imports, and the fear of their lowered standard of living induced others to refuse to accept their products. Commercial policy was driven from the very outset down the wrong road and never found another.

It is probable that the only alternative road—namely, that of international planning and action based on the maintenance of war-time controls for reconstruction purposes, would have set capitalism on the path that leads to socialism. But at any rate this analysis makes crystal-clear what were the social and economic consequences of the road which was actually taken by the leaders of the banking and business world after the 1918 Armistice,* and which most of them seem to be bent on taking again at the end of World War II, because it still seems the only way to save their own position, power, and profits.

The struggle between planners and economic anarchists was a decisive part of the long battle between the international anarchists and the believers in the necessity for some form of world government. But that battle between Right and Left was also waged in other fields.

THE STRUGGLE FOR THE LEAGUE

The first attempt of the forces of conservatism and plutocracy, led by Clemenceau and supported by the strongest elements in the British Government, was to postpone consideration of the League until after the Peace Conference. It is almost certain that this would have meant the League's never coming into existence

* For an account of the political consequences as well, see the quotation below, pages 351-53, from Sir Arthur Salter.

at all. President Wilson's reply was to insist upon the Covenant of the League, as an integral part of the Peace treaties. In this way he was successful in ensuring that the League should not be side-tracked, although he was not able to make it the centre and foundation of the peace settlement.

The second general engagement was between the Anglo-American and the Franco-Continental view respectively on the nature and attributes of the League. The British and Americans had some serious differences, notably on the economic issue and on the question of the freedom of the seas. The latter showed a curious inability on the part of both sides to appreciate that the sanctions obligations of the Covenant would render irrelevant the whole question of neutral rights *versus* the British view of sea-law. Finally, however, a growing realization of this fact ended the controversy.

But on the whole, the delegates of the two powers agreed and worked together intimately in framing the Covenant. The original Phillimore Report was the basis for various drafts by House, Wilson, Cecil, and Smuts, which were in turn exchanged and ultimately combined in the Hurst-Miller draft (Sir Cecil Hurst and Mr. David Hunter Miller were the legal advisers respectively of the British and American delegations), which became the basis for the proceedings of the League of Nations Commission of the conference.

The Anglo-American view was in favour of the immediate inclusion of the central powers in the League and of immediate measures of disarmament, but wished to keep the sanctions and other obligations of the Covenant as vague and self-interpreted as possible.

The French, on the other hand, were the chief representatives of the view that the central powers should, to begin with, be excluded from the League, and that disarmament should be postponed until security had been satisfactorily organized. On the other hand, the obligations concerning sanctions and arms manufacture should be as comprehensive and precise as possible and put under international supervision.

France throughout took the lead in attempting to strengthen the provisions of the Covenant dealing with the enforcement of peace. This was indeed the central point of difference in the proceedings of the Commission. The French representatives made repeated attempts, not only to increase the scope of the obligations assumed by members of the League under Article 16, but to provide for international machinery to supervise national armaments, with power to pass upon their adequacy from the point of view of an international police force as well as upon their compliance with any limitations that might be imposed upon them as the result of the procedure foreshadowed in Article 8.[26]

The French also wanted an international general staff.

If the British and Americans had agreed to accept the French demands as regards security and international control of armaments and arms manufacture, in return for the French agreeing to the immediate admission of the central powers, more moderate peace terms, and immediate reduction and limitation of armaments, the League would have begun far stronger than was the case. But, as so often happens in diplomacy, a compromise was reached on the basis of each side dropping the good points in its demands and both sides agreeing upon their respective bad points, because they were the ones the negotiators cared about most. The central powers were excluded, disarmament was postponed, the peace treaties were harsh, the obligations of the Covenant were left vague, and the French did not get their alliance with the United States and Great Britain.

The next chapter explains in detail just what the League was like that emerged from this battle of contending forces. What is important to realize at this point is that the League was in a triple sense inseparably connected with taking sides in an ideological conflict. It was, first, the result of the Allies winning in what they considered was an ideological conflict between democracy and militarism. It was, second, the result of a partial victory for the liberals at the Peace Conference over the conservatives (using "liberal" and "conservative" in a broad non-party sense), with the liberals using as their principal argument the danger of working-class revolutions. The nearest analogy in history, perhaps, is the way the middle class in Britain, with the help of the threat of working-class revolutionary action, compelled the landowning aristocracy to acquiesce in the Reform Bill of 1832, which laid the foundations of modern democracy. In the third place, the League was intended as the spearhead of a policy for making the world safe for democracy and for guaranteeing it against a return to power politics.

INTERVENTION AGAIN

We have seen how the Russian Revolution haunted the Versailles peacemakers like a nightmare, and how Mr. Lloyd George ended his remarkable memorandum to the Big Four at the conference by urging that the Russian situation must be dealt with. Russia was almost the first subject discussed when the conference met in the middle of January 1919. Intervention went on before, during, and after the Peace Conference. So did futile attempts to substitute some other policy.

The Council of Ten—*i.e.*, the body including not only the Big Four but also the heads of minor Allied delegations—met on January 16, 1919, two days before the conference. According to the minutes, Mr. Lloyd George said Denikin was occupying only a back-yard on the Black Sea, and that "to support Kolchak and Denikin would involve the restoration of the old *régime*, since Kolchak has been collecting members of the old *régime* about him, and they seem to be a party of Monarchists."

On January 22 the Big Four approved of Wilson's proposal that the Soviet Government and the various "White" governments should be invited to a peace conference on the island of Prinkipo. The Whites, who were represented at Paris, refused the invitation, and protested bitterly against its ever being issued. The Soviet Government, which was not allowed by Clemenceau to send any representative to Paris, either permanently or temporarily, received the invitation only after some delay. It accepted the proposal, but not the part referring to an armistice. As the Whites had already said they intended to go on fighting, observes Temperley, it was difficult to see what else the Bolsheviks could do, since it takes two to make an armistice. "Mr. Lloyd George was," he adds, "severely economical of fact when he told the House of Commons in the following April that the Soviet Government 'would not accede to the request that they should cease fighting.'"

The statement referred to, it will be observed, was not technically a falsehood. All it did was to economize truth to the point where the impression was created that the failure of the Prinkipo proposal was the fault of the Bolsheviks, whereas in fact it had been turned down by the other side. And that, of course, was precisely the impression the statement was intended to convey, and the reason why fact was economized. The history of those years is strewn with examples of the more or less successful and subtle use of this technique.

In February 1919, the Soviet Government offered to renounce propaganda and to pay the debts due to Allied subjects if the Allies ended intervention. The Allies did not even reply to this offer.

The next attempt to make peace was the mission of Mr. William C. Bullitt, then a member of the American delegation and later United States Ambassador in Paris. He was sent to Moscow by Mr. Lansing, Wilson's Secretary of State, to ascertain on what terms the Soviet Government was ready to conclude peace. According to his testimony before the Senate Commission in September, 1919, Mr. Bullitt said that before his departure he had a conversation with Mr. Lloyd George's private secretary, Mr. Philip Kerr (the late Lord Lothian), who said he had discussed the matter with Lord Balfour and Mr. Lloyd George. An outline of possible peace conditions was prepared.

President Wilson refused either to deny or to confirm the accuracy of this testimony. Mr. Lansing said, "It was impossible to make an absolute denial." Mr. Lloyd George declared that Mr. Bullitt's testimony was "a tissue of lies."

On reaching Helsingfors on his return from Moscow, Mr. Bullitt telegraphed the American delegation in Paris a seven-point armistice and peace offer from the Soviet Government providing for (1) cessation of hostilities; (2) the *status quo* for all the *de facto* governments of Russia; (3) the end of the Allied blockade of Russia; (4) Soviet Russian access to all Russia's former ports; (5) a general amnesty and resumption of diplomatic relations; (6) complete cessation of all forms òf Allied intervention; (7) the Soviet and other governments to recognize foreign financial obligations. Copies of these telegrams were communicated by the American delegation to Mr. Lloyd George. Thirty-six hours after rejoining his delegation at Paris, Mr. Bullitt breakfasted with Mr. Lloyd George and General Smuts. Mr. Lloyd George attached importance to the proposals brought from Russia, but "spoke of British public opinion as a fatal obstacle to the action he per-sonally would desire to take."

The time limit fixed for the acceptance of these proposals by the Russians—namely, April 10—passed without any action being taken. On April 16, a fortnight after the talk with Mr. Bullitt, Mr. Lloyd George answered a question by Mr. Clynes in the House of Commons and denied knowledge of approaches or peace proposals of any kind from the Soviet Government.

We have had no approaches at all. Of course there are constantly men of all nationalities coming from and going to Russia, always coming back with their own tales from Russia. But we have had nothing authentic. We have no approaches of any sort or kind. I have only heard of reports that others have got proposals, which they assume to have come from authentic quarters, but these have never been put before the Conference by any member of the Conference at all. There was some suggestion that there was some young American who had come back. All I can say about that is that it is not for me to judge the value of these communications. But if the President of the United States had attached any value to them he would have brought them before the Conference, and he certainly did not.

Temperley relates this incident and comments as follows:

That declaration—the ethics of which may, perhaps (in words employed by Mr. Lloyd George later in another connection), be left to the unprejudiced judgment of posterity—

ended any possibility that might have attached to the Bullitt Mission, and advocates of peace with Russia were left to discover some new method of approach.[27]

The next attempt to make peace came from Dr. Nansen, the famous Norwegian polar explorer. He drew attention to the widespread and severe suffering from hunger and disease in Russia, and took the lead in organizing humanitarian aid in the hope that this, if given on a sufficiently big scale, would automatically necessitate an armistice, and so open the road to peace. But the Allied governments defeated this attempt as well.

In the summer of 1919 Admiral Kolchak succeeded for a few weeks in advancing from Western Siberia into East Russia. The Allied governments rushed through a recognition of his government based on his promises to respect the independence of Poland and Finland, to pay Russian debts, and to summon a constituent assembly after victory had been won. He had hardly been recognized when his offensive collapsed and he began a retreat which turned into a rout and ended with the complete collapse of the White régime in Siberia and the shooting of Admiral Kolchak by the Bolsheviks.

On July 6, 1920, the *Daily Herald* published a summary of the war diary of the British Military Mission in Siberia (*i.e.*, General Knox's mission) which casts a curious light on the way in which the Allies were induced to give their premature recognition:

At the end of June, 1919, General Knox telegraphed to Mr. Churchill that Kolchak's failure at the front necessitated a reconsideration of the whole position. He laid it down that there was no longer any hope of a military success that summer; and declared that either

(*a*) a force of 100,000 men should be thrown in to take Petrograd and Moscow and "so finish" the war, or

(*b*) an immediate armistice and peace should be made. This telegram reached London just at the time the Supreme Council was preparing to recognise Kolchak.

It provoked an agitated reply from Sir Henry Wilson at the Hotel Astoria in Paris.

The reply is remarkable. Wilson said flatly that he could

not believe the situation to be as Knox described it. He required Knox to answer clearly whether or not there was any chance of a military success. Everything, he said, depended on that answer, because it was only by promising a military success that summer (1919) that he (Sir Henry Wilson) and Mr. Churchill had been able to persuade the War Cabinet to agree to Kolchak's practical recognition.

After this it is not to be wondered at that General Knox decided that a success was, after all, possible! *

The thwarting of attempts to seek peace was the negative side of the efforts of the Allied governments to continue and intensify their intervention and of their growing unscrupulousness in pursuit of their object. At first glance it might be supposed that the ending of the World War 1 would have deprived intervention of even the pretence of any military justification, and that the universal horror of bloodshed which filled a desolate and ruined world would have made it morally impossible to continue the promotion of slaughter in our fallen ally, Russia. It is instructive to study by what means the interventionists triumphantly surmounted these two obstacles.

In the first place, they dropped even the pretence that intervention was anything but a policy of class war. Mr. Bonar Law, in the British House of Commons on July 5, 1920, stated:

> The policy which the Government pursued throughout last year of aiding the anti-Bolshevik forces is well known and has often been debated in Parliament.

In the second place, in proportion as the British Government grew frank about the meaning of intervention, those in the Government who wished to cherish illusions about what they were doing were elbowed aside by more ruthless and clear-sighted colleagues. Mr. Churchill, the War Minister, practically took charge of intervention over the head of his own Prime Minister, Mr. Lloyd George, whose heart never seems to have been in that policy.

* Sir Henry Wilson appears to have "suppressed" General Knox's telegram, so that the vital information it contained was not known to Mr. Lloyd George when he assented to the recognition of the Kolchak government.

It is useful to recall how far this process went. Colonel Wedgwood by skilful questioning in the House extracted from the Government, after some preliminary attempts at denial, a virtual admission of the fact that:

In October 1919, Mr. O'Reilly, acting British High Commissioner in Siberia, complained that General Knox was dealing with political questions with Admiral Kolchak on a direct wire with the Secretary of State for War, and without reference to the Foreign Office or the High Commissioner. . . . General Knox wired to the Secretary of State for War commenting strongly on this telegram. . . . Mr. O'Reilly was told to hand over his duties to the Consul-General and return home.[28]

The *Daily Herald* of July 6, 1920, in the article already referred to, adds the detail that Mr. O'Reilly complained in his telegram that General Knox was posing as the highest British representative in Siberia and that if it were:

H.M. Government's desire that General Knox should handle political questions directly, without reference to the Foreign Office or to the High Commissioner, H.M. Government had better make General Knox High Commissioner or instruct the General to mind his own affairs.

The best short comment on this episode is the statement in Mr. Lloyd George's telegram to Wilson, who had refused to see General Knox or even to let him cross the United States on his way to Siberia, on the ground that he was reactionary, that General Knox "was not a politician," and was wholly concerned with "the military aspects of the Siberian question." [29]

On November 5, 1919, Mr. Churchill defended the policy of intervention in a speech in the House of Commons which he began by saying, "If we are unable to present an absolutely clearcut policy it is no good blaming the War Office or the British Government." [30]

On the same occasion Sir Samuel Hoare, who was a fanatical advocate of intervention, made a speech expressing his strong support for the "definite and consistent policy" which the Secretary of State for War had applied "throughout the whole of this period" when the Allied Governments were "weak and vacillating." [31]

These are practically official admissions that the War Office was the prime mover in intervention, and that the straight class-war element in the Government had triumphed over the one-way drifters.

Mr. Churchill made it equally plain for what object the Allies were waging war on Russia. In expounding the War Office's policy on November 5, 1919, he told the House that the Bolsheviks'

> ideal is a world-wide proletarian revolution. . . . Therefore I cannot believe that the title-deeds of national Russia will ever rest durably or recognisedly in those hands. . . .
>
> There is, however, a Russia somewhere, and not far away if it could only be evoked, which represents and embodies all that treasury of the centuries which the nation has built up from the days of Peter the Great. . . . There is that decent civilised Russia that existed in the world sometimes as a force for evil and sometimes as a force for good. Well did we know it in the early days of this war.

The best short comment is Mr. Lloyd George's statement, in one of his numerous explanations of just why the War Cabinet intervened in Russia: "None of us had the least wish to restore Czarism." [32]

The best summary of what Allied intervention would have accomplished if successful is contained in Balfour's Cabinet memorandum of July 16, 1918:

> The fact is that an autocratic system is not only repulsive to Englishmen of all shades of opinion, but that the re-establishment of Russian autocracy would, so far as I can judge, be a misfortune for the British Empire. Autocracy and militarism naturally go together; and it is almost inconceivable that, if the Czar could be re-established, Russia would not again become a purely military Empire. If so, she would inevitably be a danger to her neighbours; and to none of her neighbours so much as ourselves. . . .

In my opinion, moreover, a restored Czardom would be more dangerous to British interests than the Czardom which has just vanished; for it would almost certainly be dependent upon Germany. . . . If I am right, Russian autocracy, always in danger at home, would have to look for support to its autocratic neighbour in Germany. If the German autocracy survives both the war and the political agitation which will succeed the war, it is very difficult to believe that it will not thus control the policy of the Russian Empire.[33]

How did the British Secretary of State for War succeed in getting virtually a free hand after the Armistice and £100,-000,000 for a private war that would if successful have had the disastrous results to British imperial interests which the Secretary of State for Foreign Affairs so ably described? Chiefly because the Right wing of the Conservative party were wholeheartedly for class war as their nearest and dearest interest, and entirely reckless of anything else, whereas the Lloyd George-Balfour wing were half-hearted and confused because they were divided between their fear of the Bolsheviks, which was just as great as that of their colleagues, and their sense of other interests to be safeguarded and of some decencies to be preserved. The die-hard wing of the Government were strong because they were honest with themselves and had the plutocracy solidly behind them, whereas the Lloyd Georgians and Balfourians were weak because they deceived themselves and were not really trusted by the vested interests. Both groups were, of course, in agreement in the necessity for deceiving public opinion and Wilson as much as was necessary for their ends.

Even on this last point there was a difference—and this was the third development in the policy of intervention. Whereas Messrs. Lloyd George and Balfour preferred a minimum of veracity that would keep them somewhere in the no man's land between a half-truth and a total falsehood, the die-hard standard of mendacity had no upper limit in matters political—or, if the reader prefers, their standard of political truthfulness had no lower limit. The War Office even practised its arts on the Prime

Minister. In July 1920 Colonel Wedgwood compelled Mr. Bonar Law (answering for the Prime Minister) to admit:

> The Secretary of State for War, in May or June 1919, cabled to General Knox, in Siberia, instructing him to tell Admiral Kolchak that the Prime Minister, who is all-powerful, is a convinced democrat, and particularly devoted to advanced views on the land question, and suggesting, consequently, that Admiral Kolchak should issue a "broad and stirring appeal," promising the land to the peasants and a Constituent Assembly, in order to strengthen his hands in urging the Prime Minister and Cabinet to recognise Admiral Kolchak's Government.* [34]

The telegram explained that Mr. Lloyd George was getting doubtful about the merits of intervention and the democratic *bona fides* of Czarist admirals and generals such as Kolchak and Denikin, and that the proposed "broad and stirring appeal" could be used to re-kindle the Prime Minister's faith.

Admiral Kolchak refused, as the *Daily Herald* somewhat unkindly put it, to "make a noise like a democrat" in order to help the Secretary of State for War to hoodwink the Prime Minister and public opinion. The White general staff in Siberia was, in fact, full of ex-landowners, who flogged and murdered the peasants that had divided up their estates so soon as the summer offensive into Russia proper enabled them to recover possession. Admiral Kolchak was therefore unable to oblige the British War Office, even with a helpful form of words.

On June 6, 1919, the Secretary of State for War told the House of Commons that "we are not at all involved in these operations of Admiral Kolchak in any military sense, except in the sense that if these operations continue to prosper it will facilitate our withdrawal from North Russia."

* Bonar Law, who lacked skill in these matters, first gave a somewhat amateurish display of the arts of evasion, *suppressio veri et suggestio falsi*, but capitulated after a deadly series of supplementaries from Colonel Wedgwood. The interchange of questions and answers is instructive as an example of how misleading a Minister can be when answering questions, and how effective ruthless and skilful cross-questioning may be in dragging out a virtual admission of the truth.

This referred to Kolchak's short-lived advance into Russia from Siberia. A few days previously (June 1) General Ironside, the commander of the British force at Archangel, had given an interview to a local paper, which he tried too late to keep from reaching England, saying that there was to be an advance south and east in order to effect a junction at Kotlas with Kolchak's forces, who were moving westward along the railway line from Perm in the Urals towards Viatka. Mr. Churchill's declaration was only one of the attempts of the British Government to make public opinion believe that there was no question of plunging deeper into intervention, but, on the contrary, only of withdrawing British troops as rapidly as possible.

Mr. Negley Farson, in *The Way of a Transgressor*, tells how in the summer of 1919 he was recruited by one Colonel Maund, in charge of the Air Force attached to the Denikin Expedition.

Nearly every day we officers sat in Bolo House before a map of South Russia, and held conferences about the supplies we should take out.

There were four of us who were to be pilot instructors, later command squadrons, and seven technical officers, with a complement of mechanics and R.E.8 planes. Winston Churchill was over in Paris off and on making contacts and arrangements with the White Russian officer *émigrés* over there. We were told not to talk too much about the Denikin show in London; and one day I understood full well why. For walking out of one of our conferences in Bolo House I bought a copy of the evening *Star* in the Strand, and read Lloyd George's statement in the House:

"ALL BRITISH TROOPS BEING WITHDRAWN FROM RUSSIA."

One of my first contacts with that official mendacity that was to give me such an ironic relish in exposing when I was a foreign newspaper correspondent.[35]

In this case the official mendacity was not exposed in the House of Commons till a year later. General Golovin, an emissary of Denikin's returned from London, was captured by the Bolsheviks some time later with the despatches he was carrying to Admiral

Kolchak. These despatches described his conversations with Mr. Churchill, and were published by the Bolsheviks. In due course translations reached London. According to these despatches, Mr. Churchill had told General Golovin in the summer of 1919 that he was sending reinforcements to Russia on the pretext of facilitating withdrawal, but that what was really being planned was a big offensive. He added that he was doing all he could to help the Russian Whites, and that it was the hostility of organized labour and the fear of labour proceeding from words to deeds if he acted too openly that prevented him giving help on a larger scale.

On July 5, 1920, the matter was raised in the House, and Mr. Bonar Law had to submit to some searching questions. He admitted the interview had taken place, but said Mr. Churchill told him he had been misunderstood by General Golovin and that the report of the conversation was inaccurate, especially as regarded the actual words and expressions employed. Colonel Wedgwood then took a hand and asked:

> Was it not admitted by the Secretary of State for War himself that these troops [i.e., those sent to Archangel in May and June 1919] were used not for withdrawal but to hold out a left hand to Kolchak coming from Siberia?
> Mr. Bonar Law: Where is the mystery and where is the secrecy? That statement was made in the House of Commons itself.[36]

This virtually admitted what had been charged in connection with the Golovin conversations and General Ironside's interview. The next day the *Daily Herald* brought confirmation from a third source—the war diary of the British Military Mission in Siberia:

> Mr. Churchill is proved by the Diary to be making plans with Kolchak as late as June, 1919, to throw his right wing forward to meet the Archangel force at Kotlas and sweep on to Petrograd.

In the speech already referred to of November 5, 1919, Sir Samuel Hoare tried to make war against the Bolsheviks less odious to public opinion by the following argument:

I believe that a policy of no intervention is in principle a negation of everything that the League of Nations stands for. I believe that if the League of Nations is to develop and be a force in the world it will have to take sides between what it believes to be good and what it believes to be bad; and I believe that if . . . it stood aside and allowed it to be thought that there was no difference between one faction and another faction in Russia, it would be doomed . . . to sterility. . . . I do not believe that a policy of no intervention is possible.[37]

He concluded that the whole Russian problem should be handed over to the League.

Now in those days the League had not yet been officially born (for the Versailles Treaty had not yet been ratified by Germany and the Allies), Russia was not a member of the League, and the *de facto* Red and White governments were both not recognized. There would therefore have been a strong case for genuine non-intervention and for "not taking sides in the ideological conflict." There was a still stronger case for not putting the vast problem of Russia into the hands of the unborn League.

But France, Great Britain, Japan, and the United States were all at that time helping the Whites, and also in complete control of the League. Therefore "handing over to the League" would have simply meant these powers deciding through the Council of the League to continue their policy of helping the Whites to make war on the Reds.

Whereas in the case of Spain in 1936 the lawful and recognized Spanish Government was a member of the League, and the victim of a war of aggression waged by the fascist powers behind their puppet Franco in defiance of Article X of the Covenant. This fact would inevitably have become the basis of any policy for dealing with the situation if it had been "handed over to the League." France of the Popular Front, together with the U.S.S.R., would have supported the Spanish Government in the League Council by insisting on the treaty obligation to help Spain against external aggression. Therefore it was necessary for the British Government to go in for "non-intervention," and "not taking sides in the ideological conflict," and to oppose the Spanish attempts to get the matter dealt with through the League. Sir Samuel Hoare as Foreign Secretary was prominent in this policy and made a notorious statement about the British Government's neutrality and indifference as between one faction and another in Spain (i.e., as between the lawful government of the Spanish Republic, which was a fellow member of the League with Britain and the then unrecognized fascist rebel General Franco, who had broken his oath to the Republic and was paid and armed by Hitler and Mussolini).

Anyone who believes that Sir Samuel Hoare's glaring inconsistency on these two occasions was just a sign of muddleheadedness may, in Bertrand Russell's phrase, be congratulated on his charitable disposition. Those who look farther may observe that the seeming inconsistency conceals a perfectly definite and consistent policy—that of deceiving public opinion into acquiescing in a policy of backing reaction and counter-revolution in a class war against the working-class.*

In the case of Russia this policy consisted of proposing that the war should be conducted under cover of the nascent League, whose moral authority was great with liberal and labour opinion —i.e., among those opposed to intervention. In the case of Spain the war of intervention was labelled "non-intervention" and was conducted by starving the Spanish Government of arms, depriving it of its rights under international law, disregarding our obligations to Spain under the Covenant, conniving at Franco's air piracy against our shipping, ignoring the despatch of German and Italian troops, planes, and arms to fascist rebels, and bargaining with Mussolini on the basis of a free hand for his war of aggression against the Spanish people. The pretexts varied to fit the circumstances, but the underlying policy was one and the same.

* Another example of the same seeming inconsistency concealing identity of purpose was Sir Samuel Hoare's great speech in the League Assembly on September 11, 1935, promising sanctions against Italy—the day after Sir Samuel had privately assured Laval (who passed it on to Mussolini) that the British Government would never apply any sanctions involving any risk of war, and a few weeks before the Hoare-Laval deal.

CO-OPERATION BETWEEN THE ALLIES AND THE GERMAN GENERAL STAFF *

An interesting aspect of intervention is the relations that grew up during the Armistice period between the Allied Governments and the German commanders in the field in Eastern Europe. When the Armistice was signed, the Baltic provinces, Poland, and the Ukraine were occupied by German troops. In all these areas the German army of occupation had set up puppet governments, who were mercilessly exploiting the population and governing by the most harsh and tyrannical methods.

Nevertheless, whereas the Armistice agreement provided for the "immediate evacuation of the invaded countries of the Western front," and similarly stipulated the "immediate withdrawal of all German troops from the occupied areas of Turkey, Austria-Hungary and Rumania," it went on to state that the German troops in occupation of Russian territory (*i.e.*, the Baltic States, Eastern Poland, and the Ukraine) "were only to withdraw as soon as the Allies shall think the moment suitable having regard to the internal situation of these territories."

The motive is quite frankly stated as follows in Temperley's *History of the Peace Conference:*

> When the victory of the Allies was achieved, these small nationalities [Baltic States, Ukraine, etc.] overwhelmed them with protestations and appeals for assistance and recognition. Yet in the case of the Baltic States, the menace of the Bolshevik irruption was so pressing that the armistice allowed the continuation of German occupation.

An American official mission sent to investigate the situation of the Baltic States at the time reported:

> The Germans were present in the Baltic provinces with the full consent of the Allies, and indeed by their implied command. The framers of the armistice agreement recognized that the Red tide could not be held by any bulwark

* This section is based on a MS. containing a full account of these events shown me by Mr. Peter Floud, to whom I herewith make my grateful acknowledgements.—K. Z.

which any of these native races could maintain. Esthonia and Latvia were themselves permeated with the Bolshevistic poison.[38]

A Polish Socialist leader in London, M. Ciolkosz, has revealed how the Allies attempted to keep the German army of occupation in Eastern Poland for fear of Bolshevism, and were seriously troubled when most of the army proceeded to go red, elect soldiers' councils, etc., and the whole of it was disarmed and sent home by the Poles.[39]

As regards the Ukraine, the Allies worked out a sort of Box-and-Cox arrangement with the German troops on the spot, by which the latter were ordered to remain in occupation until the former could go in and take over. On October 27, 1918—that is, *before* the Armistice—Clemenceau sent a telegram to General Franchet d'Esperey, in charge of the Balkan command, ordering him to halt the pursuit of the German and Austrian armies retreating across the Danube and instead to divert his troops eastward towards Russia, so that they could be used to fight the Bolsheviks. This is a concrete illustration of Sir Henry Wilson's, chief of the imperial general staff, remark in his diary: "The war against the Boche is turning into a war against the Bolshie."

On November 18, 1918, Marshal Foch sent a strongly worded telegram (No. 5956/3) ordering the Germans to remain in the Ukraine until further notice, while Allied troops were being hastily assembled to replace them. Meanwhile the German army of occupation was going from pink to red. Accordingly, towards the end of November the supreme Eastern command of the German general staff telegraphed urgently to Marshal Foch imploring him to hurry up, and to send Allied warships and landing parties to the Baltic and Black sea ports without delay.

In the Ukraine the Allies were not content to be anti-Bolshevik. They also supported the dictatorship of the German puppet and extreme reactionary Czarist Cossack chieftain, Hetman Skoropadski, against the republican (although anti-Bolshevik) peasant nationalist Petliura. M. Hainnot, the French consul-general in Odessa, arrived in Kiev about a week after the Armistice, and found that the German garrison had elected a soldiers' council, which had taken over the effective power from their commanders, and were negotiating to transfer their support from Skoropadski to Petliura. To this M. Hainnot was violently hostile. According to the official German account, he stated that

> the Allies could not possibly allow the German troops to adopt a sympathetic attitude towards the Ukrainian Republicans [that is, Petliura], nor in particular to sign an agreement with them. . . . He threatened reprisals against the Germans if they delivered any of their munitions to the Ukrainians, or if they dared to abandon Kiev to Petliura.[40]

Hainnot published a proclamation in support of Skoropadski, got into touch with the latter's Commander-in-Chief, and promised him that French troops would soon be arriving.

The Allies ordered the German garrison in Odessa to take over the policing of the city and to make themselves responsible for the maintenance of law and order, and as the situation got more critical, and it became clear that only a handful of officers could be collected from the local Russian population, "incredible though it may seem, incorporated the German troops into the Allied forces under the command of General d'Anselme." [41]

In general, both in the Ukraine and the Baltic States, the Allied commanders on the spot co-operated closely with the old imperial Prussian command against not only the Bolsheviks, but nationalist and democratic movements in the local populations. There were even cases of Allied help being asked by and given to German officers to "restore discipline" among revolutionary German soldiers.

How Labour Stopped Intervention in Russia

Labour misgivings about intervention had begun during the war. But for a long time the British Labour party was deluded by the plea that intervention was for the purpose of restoring democracy in Russia and was part of World War I. It was impressed by the assertion that these were questions solely of military expediency and the conduct of military operations against Germany, on which the Government alone possessed the information necessary to judge, and it would be unpatriotic for the public to be too curious. The Labour party could not question the Government's statements without challenging their good faith. It took a long time before labour leaders realized that that was necessary, and still longer before they mustered up courage to do anything so ungentlemanly.

In December 1918—that is, just after the Armistice—the Labour Party Executive asked the Government to define its intentions with regard to Russia. They received no reply.

In the spring of 1919, at a special joint conference of both the political and industrial wings of the labour movement that was called to discuss the Draft Covenant, the Miners' Federation tabled a resolution demanding the end of intervention and the summoning of a special conference to organize resistance to intervention.

At the Labour Party Conference in June there was a discussion of the need for direct action to stop the war on Russia. This was described by Mr. William Brace, who shortly afterwards accepted a government post, as "a slippery slope." Mr. Clynes observed that the conference was "threatening a blow at democracy," and Sir James Sexton said he did not believe in letting mad dogs loose.

This drew the following retort from Bob Smillie:

> It was rather strange that the Executive Committee of the Labour Party should have taken up exactly the position of every exploiter and capitalist and politician in this country at the present time. They feared more than anything else what had come to be called direct action. But he wanted to put it that direct action might be constitutional action. . . . They were told their action was unconstitutional. He would like to follow Mr. Williams' statement as to whether the action of the Government of this country was constitutional. Had they not deceived the people? Were they not returning to power under false pretences? Did not every member of their Committee believe that the present Government was sitting in its place through fraud? If they believed that the Government deceived and lied to the people in order to get

returned, if that was true, was the great Labour Movement not to take any action to get rid of a Government that was sitting there through fraud and deceit?

Mr. Herbert Morrison had the following pungent comments to make:

He wanted to know what the Party had done in the matter of the war on the Socialist Republic of Russia. . . . They had got to realise that the present war against Russia on the part of this country, France and other Imperialist Powers, was not war against Bolshevism or against Lenin, but against the international organism of Socialism. It was a war against the organisation of the Trade Union movement itself, and as such should be resisted with the full political and industrial power of the whole Trade Union Movement. But what ·had the Parliamentary Party done? They had done so much that the matter was not worth a single reference in the report which was under discussion. This report was an insult to the energy, the intelligence and the vigor of the whole Labour Movement of the country.

By 1,893,000 votes to 935,000 the conference passed a resolution demanding an immediate end to intervention, and prescribing Labour party and trade-union co-operation "with the view to effective action being taken to enforce these demands by the unreserved use of their political and industrial power."

By the autumn of 1919 the awakening of the movement had gone still further. The Glasgow Trade Council proposed a twenty-four-hour general strike, and there were big street demonstrations in London.

On May 10, 1920, at the height of the Polish offensive, the dockers engaged in loading the London freighter *Jolly George* with munitions for Poland struck work with the support of their union. The coal-trimmers refused to coal the vessel, and the owners were compelled to unload the munitions again.

A week later the Dockers' Union decided to put a general ban on the loading of munitions for use against Russia.

In June, when the Labour Party Conference met at Scarborough, a resolution was moved requesting an immediate summoning of the National Conference, "having for its object the organisation of a General Strike that shall put an end once and for all to the open and covert participation of the British Government in attacks on the Soviet Republic," and further recommending "that Unions should support their members in refusing to do work which directly or indirectly assists hostilities against Russia."

This was rejected by the Executive, not on principle, but on the ground that the time was not ripe for drastic action.

Then came the defeat of the Polish Army and the advance of the Red Army on Warsaw. In the House of Commons on July 21 Mr. Lloyd George plainly hinted at war, and orders to stand by were given to the British fleet in the Baltic. British troops broke a strike of dockers at Danzig against the landing of munitions for the Poles. On August 7, Lord Curzon, the Foreign Secretary, sent a note threatening the Soviet Government with war if the advance of the Red Army were not stayed.

The next day Labour-party headquarters telegraphed all local parties and trade-union councils urging demonstrations against war on Russia. The result was nation-wide demonstrations on an impressive scale.

The following day, August 9, the Parliamentary Committee of the Trade Union Congress, the Labour Party Executive, and the Parliamentary party met in the House of Commons and unanimously decided to warn the Government that "the whole industrial power of the organised workers will be used to defeat this war," notified the executives of all affiliated organizations "to hold themselves ready to proceed immediately to London for a National Conference," advised them "to instruct their members to down tools on instructions from that National Conference," and constituted a representative Council of Action with full powers to implement these decisions.

The conference met in the Central Hall, Westminster, four days later, and fully endorsed these decisions. It "pledged itself to resist any and every form of military and naval intervention against the Soviet Government of Russia," mandated the Council of Action to remain in being until it had secured recognition of the Soviet Government and the establishment of normal trading relations, and authorized the council "to call for any and every form of withdrawal of labour which circumstances may require to give effect to the foregoing policy."

Mr. Ernest Bevin told the delegates at the conference that "this question you are called upon to decide today—the willingness to take any action to win world peace—transcends any claim in connection with wages or hours of labour." Mr. J. R. Clynes said that "no Parliamentary or political measures, we felt, could be effective in themselves to save the country from being committed to war against its will." "No Parliamentary effort could do what we are asking you to do," urged Mr. J. H. Thomas, adding bluntly, "When you vote for this resolution do not do so on the assumption that you are merely voting for a simple down-tools policy. It is nothing of the kind. If this resolution is to be given effect to, it means a challenge to the whole Constitution of the country" (Cheers). Mr. Thomas was that year's president of the Trade Union Congress.

Mr. A. G. Cameron of the Wood-workers, chairman of the Labour Party Executive, was even more outspoken. Declaring that "Constitutionalism can only exist as long as it does not outrage the conscience of the community." Mr. Cameron said that power was needed "for a united Council to declare action at a given moment." "If the day should come when we do take this action," he concluded, "and if the powers that be endeavour to interfere too much, we may be compelled to do things that will cause them to abdicate, and to tell them that if they cannot run the country in a peaceful and humane manner without interfering with the lives of other nations, we will be compelled, even against all Constitutions, to chance whether we cannot do something to take the country into our own hands for our own people."

The moment the Government realized that the labour movement meant business, it promptly backed down. There was no war and intervention was ended. But not until then.

CONCLUSION

We now know how reaction, reform, and revolution interacted at the Peace Conference. If it is borne in mind that the statesmen at the Peace Conference were little more than puppets, the mouthpieces and symbols of great social forces, Mr. Keynes's analysis of them becomes extraordinarily illuminating. He sums up Wilson and Lloyd George as follows:

> . . . the President . . . had not much of that culture of the world which marks M. Clemenceau and Mr. Balfour as exquisitely cultivated gentlemen of their class and generation. But more serious than this, he was not only insensitive to his surroundings in the external sense, he was not sensitive to his environment at all. What chance could such a man have against Mr. Lloyd George's unerring, almost medium-like, sensibility to every one immediately round him? To see the British Prime Minister watching the company, with six or seven senses not available to ordinary men . . . perceiving what each was thinking and even what each was going to say next, and compounding with telepathic instinct the argument or appeal best suited to the vanity, weakness, or self-interest of his immediate auditor, was to realise that the poor President would be playing blind man's buff in that party. Never could a man have stepped into the parlour a more perfect and predestined victim to the finished accomplishments of the Prime Minister. The Old World was tough in wickedness anyhow; the Old World's heart of stone might blunt the sharpest blade of the bravest knight-errant. But this blind and deaf Don Quixote was entering a cavern where the swift glittering blade was in the hands of the adversary.

> But if the President was not the philosopher-king, what was he? After all he was a man who had spent much of his life at a University. He was by no means a business man or an ordinary party politician, but a man of force, personality, and importance. What, then, was his temperament?

> The clue once found was illuminating. The President was like a Nonconformist minister, perhaps a Presbyterian. His thought and his temperament were essentially theological not intellectual, with all the strength and the weakness of

that manner of thought, feeling, and expression. It is a type of which there are not now in England and Scotland such magnificent specimens as formerly; but this description, nevertheless, will give the ordinary Englishman the distinctest impression of the President.[42]

To complete the picture of Mr. Lloyd George we might add Trotsky's remark, quoted by Mr. Lockhart, "Your Mr. Lloyd George is like a roulette player who scatters his chips on every number."

Mr. Keynes psychoanalyzes Wilson's failure as follows: The President found he could not induce the Allies to abandon war aims incompatible with the Fourteen Points, and so he had to compromise.

Now it was that what I have called his theological or Presbyterian temperament became dangerous. Having decided that some concessions were unavoidable, he might have sought by firmness and address and the use of the financial power of the United States to secure as much as he could of the substance, even at some sacrifice of the letter. But the President was not capable of so clear an understanding with himself as this implied. He was too conscientious. Although compromises were now necessary, he remained a man of principle and the Fourteen Points a contract absolutely binding upon him. He would do nothing that was not honorable; he would do nothing that was not just and right; he would do nothing that was contrary to his great profession of faith. Thus, without any abatement of the verbal inspiration of the Fourteen Points, they became a document for gloss and interpretation and for all the intellectual apparatus of self-deception, by which, I daresay, the President's forefathers had persuaded themelves that the course they thought it necessary to take was consistent with every syllable of the Pentateuch.

The President's attitude to his colleagues had now become: I want to meet you so far as I can; I see your difficulties and I should like to be able to agree to what you propose; but I can do nothing that is not just and right, and you must first of all show me that what you want does really fall within the words of the pronouncements which are binding on me. Then began the weaving of that web of sophistry and Jesuitical exegesis that was finally to clothe with insincerity the language and substance of the whole Treaty. The word was issued to the witches of all Paris:

> Fair is foul, and foul is fair,
> Hover through the fog and filthy air.

The subtlest sophisters and most hypocritical draftsmen were set to work, and produced many ingenious exercises which might have deceived for more than an hour a cleverer man than the President.[43]

The German delegation naturally contended that the treaty violated the Armistice agreement to base the peace on the Fourteen Points.

But this was exactly what the President could not admit; in the sweat of solitary contemplation and with prayers to God he had done *nothing* that was not just and right; for the President to admit that the German reply had force in it was to destroy his self-respect and to disrupt the inner equipoise of his soul; and every instinct of his stubborn nature rose in self-protection. In the language of medical psychology, to suggest to the President that the Treaty was an abandonment of his professions was to touch on the raw a Freudian complex. It was a subject intolerable to discuss, and every subconscious instinct plotted to defeat its further exploration.

Thus it was that Clemenceau brought to success, what had seemed to be, a few months before, the extraordinary and impossible proposal that the Germans should not be heard. ... To his horror, Mr. Lloyd George, desiring at the last moment all the moderation he dared, discovered that he could not in five days persuade the President of error in what it had taken five months to prove to him to be just and right. After all, it was harder to de-bamboozle this old Presbyterian than it had been to bamboozle him; for the former involved his belief in and respect for himself.[44]

In point of fact the hypocritical exegesis of the peace treaties
was for the benefit of liberal and labour opinion, and not only
because of Wilson. Mr. Lloyd George abandoned his last-minute
attempt to undo the evil he had wrought because he had no support in his own Government and hard-faced parliamentary majority.

On these as on other points Mr. Keynes is unfair to Wilson and
underrates what he contributed to the Peace Conference and to
world history. This is partly the typical reaction of a disappointed
idealist *—Mr. Keynes is as extravagant in his eulogy of Wilson
the philosopher-king who gave the world the bright promise of
the Fourteen Points as he is unmeasured in his denunciation of
him as part-author of the Versailles Treaty. According to Mr.
Keynes, President Wilson was an unmitigated success until he
reached Paris and an unqualified failure from that moment.

Not the least value of Mr. Keynes's book lies in the fact that it
was written by one who took part in the events it describes, and
accurately reflects the mood of the progressives who had been so
magnificently taken in by Wilsonian propaganda because they
shared Wilson's illusions, and now vented their disappointment
on him because they persisted in the most dangerous illusion of
all—that which regards great events exclusively in terms of the
personal shortcomings or merits of individuals. For although Mr.
Keynes seems dimly to have apprehended that there were great
forces looming in the background that were the real masters of
events, he makes no serious attempt to analyze those forces and
describes what happened in terms of the personal actions and
reactions of the Big Four and their advisers. To do anything else
was difficult for one who wrote before the ink on the Versailles
Treaty was dry.

We know now that Wilson's failure did not begin at the Peace
Conference. In a sense he had been a failure ever since the
United States entered the war. Or, to put the same point differ-
ently, he had never succeeded, although he tried repeatedly, in

* Partly also Mr. Wilson's cavalier rejection of Mr. Lloyd George's letter
enclosing the Keynes plan of financial reconstruction rankled, it may be
conjectured, in the mind of the author of that plan.

inducing the Allies to abandon their imperialist war aims. And each time he failed he consoled himself by making a statement of his own and hoping that somehow it would eventually represent the views of the Allies as well as his own. It never did. But he went on trying. With President Wilson it was a case of "Hope deferred maketh the heart grow fonder."

Colonel House, in an extraordinarily interesting passage in his diary for March 3, 1919, puts his finger on the chief reason for Wilson's failure:

> It is now evident that the peace will not be such a peace as I had hoped, or one which this terrible upheaval should have brought about.

The United States Congressional and the British and French general elections had weakened Wilson's position. Nevertheless House reports:

> If the President should exert his influence among the liberals and labouring classes, he might possibly overthrow the Governments in Great Britain, France and Italy; but if he did, he would still have to reckon with our own people,* and he might bring the whole world into chaos. The overthrow of governments might not end there, and it would be a grave responsibility for any man to take at this time.[45]

Wilson was a democrat, none better. But he did not believe in the people enough to trust them with the truth, for he was afraid of what they might do if they learned it. The point at issue is not whether Wilson might have failed if he had tried appealing to the peoples over the heads of their governments. Mr. Keynes gives reasons why that risk was considerable. But the point is that, as House clearly shows, Wilson would not even try, *because he was afraid not of failure, but of success.* It was not fear lest "the liberals and labouring classes" would not listen to him that held him back. On the contrary, it was the danger that they might take him at his word and overthrow the governments that had betrayed them.

Rather than face the risk of keeping faith with the common

* There was a big "Red" scare in the United States at the time.

people whom he now knew he had unwittingly misled because the Allied governments had used the popular trust placed in him to betray both Wilson and their peoples, he preferred the responsibility of acquiescing in the Versailles Treaty and in the continuation of intervention in Russia, just as he had previously acquiesced in the Allies' refusal to abandon their secret treaties, their mishandling of the Russian Revolution, and their prolongation of the war in order to avoid the necessity of a negotiated peace and to be able to impose a dictated peace.

And yet, on his way to the Peace Conference the President had told the American delegation that "unless the Conference was prepared to follow the opinions of mankind and to express the will of the people rather than that of their leaders at the Conference, we should soon be involved in another break-up of the world, and when such a break-up came it would not be a war but a cataclysm." But his chief motive even in making that statement (quoted in full above, p. 221) was fear of revolution.

Wilson's proceedings at the Peace Conference were simply a continuation of his war-time tactics. At Paris he was driven to put all his hope in the League as the future undoer of the wrongs in which he had unwillingly acquiesced, because he saw no alternative. Or if he saw it, he did not dare to try it. He threatened to break with the Allied governments, and actually got his special train ready and ordered the S.S. *George Washington* to have steam up for his return to the United States. But he shrank from carrying out his threat. Therefore there was nothing left for him to do but to make a virtue of the "necessity" of accepting the Versailles Treaty, and to console himself with more deferred hopes—this time centring on the League.

In all this Wilson was merely summing up and typifying in his own person the inner weakness and tragic dilemma of liberal and orthodox labour opinion in those terrible years. Because hindsight is easier than foresight, it would be wrong to pass any moral judgments. For the same reason there is no excuse for failing to understand a quarter of a century later that Wilson and the whole vast, confused "progressive" and "middle-of-the-road" opinion he represented were defeated chiefly because they persisted in treating the Bolsheviks and the revolutionary unrest in the working class as though they were just as much their enemies as plutocracy and conservatism. Whereas in point of fact the Bolsheviks and the extreme left at bottom wanted the same kind of peace as liberals and orthodox labour, and were wiser than they in refusing to trust the Allied governments and the forces of big business behind them.

This does not, of course, mean that the Bolsheviks and the extreme Left would have been easy to work with, nor that they did not make serious mistakes and give legitimate grounds for apprehension. Nor does it mean that we should underrate the magnitude of Wilson's achievement, or the difficulties with which he and those he represented had to contend. But it does mean that the history of those years contains a lesson that has not yet been learned by this generation, and that must be learned if liberalism and labour are not to suffer a new and immeasurably greater defeat now that World War II has ended.

Mr. Lloyd George was as typical of the forces behind him as Mr. Wilson. He summed up in his inconsistencies, the contrast between his frequently good intentions and almost invariably evil actions, his daring disingenuousness and his weak vacillations, the mixed motives, confused policy, and fundamental servitude to reaction and imperialism of capitalist coalition governments in Great Britain. He was the incarnation of what happens to liberalism when liberals put class solidarity with plutocracy before political co-operation with all who are in earnest about peace and social justice.

It is impossible to separate Mr. Lloyd George's record at the Peace Conference from what he did in the war. He was the great organizer of victory. But in order to win the war he lost the peace. He became the head of a Coalition government dominated by plutocracy and conservatism. He clung to power at the price of becoming the tool of imperialism and reaction. The British Government thought of the war in terms of "dog-fights" and "knock-out blows," and of peace as imposing as much as possible of the secret treaties on the vanquished.

During the war the Federation of British Industries was

founded, and grew from some 53 firms in 1916 to 18,000 firms and combines in 1919. War profiteering flourished apace with the strengthening of plutocracy. The sale of titles assumed the dimensions of a major scandal. Mr. Lloyd George's wing of the Liberal party accumulated a fund from this source of £2,000,000, and Cardiff became "the City of Dreadful Knights."

A new race of great press magnates sprang up, closely connected with the plutocracy. One of them—Lord Northcliffe, who later went mad—became director of the Propaganda Ministry. These were the forces that controlled the Government and its parliamentary majority of "hard-faced men who looked as though they had done well out of the war."

The Left wing of the British Government and their supporters —particularly Lord Cecil, and among Dominion statesmen General Smuts—were the allies of Wilson and the representatives of liberal and labour opinion rather than the willing instruments of conservatism and plutocracy. But they were given only intermittent and half-hearted support by Mr. Lloyd George.

There is small doubt, in the light of the facts related above, that Mr. Lloyd George threw in his lot with conservatism and plutocracy largely because he was obsessed by fear and hatred of the Russian Revolution. As late as 1933 and 1934 he was begging the "National" government to do nothing that might imperil the Nazi régime, for it was the bulwark against Bolshevism in Europe.

M. Clemenceau was the almost ideal incarnation of the forces of conservatism and plutocracy. He is unforgettably portrayed by Mr. Keynes as he sat

> throned . . . on the brocade chair . . . (with an impassive face of parchment, his gray gloved hands clasped in front of him) . . . dry in soul and empty of hope, very old and tired, but surveying the scene with a cynical and almost impish air. . . .

He felt about France what Pericles felt of Athens—unique value in her, nothing else mattering; but his theory of politics was Bismarck's. He had one illusion—France; and one disillusion—mankind, including Frenchmen, and his colleagues not least. His principles for the Peace can be expressed simply. In the first place, he was a foremost believer in the view of German psychology that the German understands and can understand nothing but intimidation, that he is without generosity or remorse in negotiation, that there is no advantage he will not take of you, and no extent to which he will not demean himself for profit, that he is without honour, pride, or mercy. Therefore you must never negotiate with a German or conciliate him; you must dictate to him. On no other terms will he respect you, or will you prevent him from cheating you. But it is doubtful how far he thought these characteristics peculiar to Germany, or whether his candid view of some other nations was fundamentally different.

His philosophy had, therefore, no place for "sentimentality" in international relations. Nations are real things, of whom you love one and feel for the rest indifference—or hatred. The glory of the nation you love is a desirable end—but generally to be obtained at your neighbor's expense. The politics of power are inevitable, and there is nothing very new to learn about this war or the end it was fought for; England had destroyed, as in each preceding century, a trade rival; a mighty chapter had been closed in the secular struggle between the glories of Germany and of France. Prudence required some measure of lip service to the "ideals" of foolish Americans and hypocritical Englishmen; but it would be stupid to believe that there is much room in the world, as it really is, for such affairs as the League of Nations, or any sense in the principle of self-determination except as an ingenious formula for rearranging the balance of power in one's own interests.[46]

The Old Tiger was genially frank about his beliefs. He complained humorously that whereas the good God had been content with Ten Commandments, Wilson had brought over Fourteen. He used to tell Lord Cecil, "I like your League, I like it very much—but I don't believe in it."

M. Clemenceau's belief in power politics and imperialism was shared by a strong section of conservative and big-business opinion in the United States, as well as by most of the members of the Allied governments, including the British Government. But in the case of Britain it was complicated, rather than weakened, by various forms of scruple and self-deception among certain members of the Government. Just as French logic often consists, in the words of Cavour, in "turning obstinate when circumstances change," so British contempt for logic often results in cherishing two incompatible ideas simultaneously, one as a moral alibi and basis for speech and emotion, the other as a working belief and basis for action. It is this "double-mindedness" which the Continental unduly simplifies when he calls it British hypocrisy.* But it must be admitted that its practical consequences are often indistinguishable from those produced by hypocrisy, and that the transition from unconscious self-deception to deliberate duplicity is all too easy.

What the Allied governments actually did is plain enough. They prolonged World War I unnecessarily and waged a war against the Russian Revolution for exactly the same reason that they inflicted a punitive peace on Germany and threatened the German people with dire penalties if they dared to carry out a social revolution. They exploited Wilson's idealism skilfully to secure liberal and labour support for their power politics and imperialism. They never dreamed of keeping faith with Wilson, let alone with the masses they were using as cannon fodder. They adopted Wilson's policy of "no negotiations with imperial Germany, but only with a democratic Germany" as an ideal excuse for insisting on a military victory and a dictated peace. But it never entered their heads to treat a democratic Germany in any way differently from imperial Germany, for they believed only in power politics.

When all allowances have been made for the exasperation, short views, and mistakes due to the frailties of human nature under the awful strain of war, there remains a factor of capital importance without which the gulf between what the peoples thought they were fighting for and what their governments did in the war and at the Peace Conference cannot be fully understood. That factor was the fear and hatred of the plutocracy and

* "Humbug" is a word that exists in no other language.

of the capitalist political parties for the revolutionary unrest in the working-class.

In the last analysis the events of 1917–21 represent successive stages in a long, confused, and complicated struggle to defend and reconsolidate the existing social order shaken by the war and the Russian Revolution. The governments began World War I under the pressure of their respective plutocracies, believing it was going to be like previous wars. They soon found it was turning into a world revolution. Towards the end the latter became in their eyes the chief enemy. They identified winning the war with defending the power and privileges of the plutocracy against the social danger arising out of the war. That was why a military victory became in their eyes an absolute necessity—it was the only antidote to revolution. A negotiated peace without victors or vanquished would have been fatal to the old order.*

The actors in the drama were far from realizing that this social motive was at the bottom of their minds. They were, of course, also swayed by other motives. But in the light of the knowledge we now possess it seems difficult to doubt that fear of their own working-class and the desire to defend the existing social order against the menace of the Russian Revolution was the largely unconscious "driving force behind the driving force" of most of their sincerely held views on right and wrong, of their care for the "honour and vital interests" of their countries, of their conception of victory, and of their ideas about peace and the future.

It was the Russian, Austrian, and German working-class revolutions that ended World War I. It was the Russian Red Army and working-class resistance in the West that prevented the Allied governments from creating a fascist Russia † which would have helped them to defeat Wilson utterly, to postpone the establishment of the League to the Greek kalends, to carry out the

* That is the capital difference between World War I and World War II. For in the latter war a negotiated peace "without victor or vanquished" would have meant a victory for the Axis, for fascism, and for appeasement.

† The propaganda and program of General Kornilov and his supporters foreshadowed the ideology and methods of fascism with extraordinary faithfulness.

secret treaties to the full, and to support reaction in the defeated central powers. If the Allied governments had had their way in Russia, fascism would have swept the world in the first post-war slump instead of breaking out only in Italy, and having to reckon with the obstacle of the Soviet Union and the survival of democracy in the Western powers when in the great slump plutocracy in Japan and Germany also turned to fascism.

The British Coalition government took a crucial part in the struggle against the working-class and the Russian Revolution. It is fascinating to study in the light of the abundant information now available how British policy worked out in terms of the psychology of the statesmen concerned. For thanks to the publication of secret documents, memoirs, etc., we are now able to study our governing class in World War I "with the lid off," and to see how they react when faced with a challenge to the social order. There seem to have been three main stages (and of course innumerable variations and mixtures of these stages) in the spiritual evolution of our rulers:

The first stage, what might be called their natural or normal condition, was characterized by Plato's "lie in the soul." By this we mean the unconscious identification of the class interests of the plutocracy with the vital interests of the nation, a class egotism so extreme as to be criminal. For great criminals are generally such egotists that they are genuinely incapable of realizing that other people can have rights which conflict with their own interests, and believe that the only criterion of what is permissible is what they can "get away with." That has always been the attitude of all governing classes and privileged minorities to the rest of the community. Power corrupts. Human nature being what it is, no body of men can be entrusted with uncontrolled power over their fellow men, for they always abuse and exploit their privilege. Modern plutocracy is no exception to that rule, and its attitude to the working-class is no different from what all history shows to be the typical attitude of ruling classes to any challenge from below.*

* Cf. Thomas Hill Green, *Principles of Political Obligation* (Longmans, Green, 1941): "Patriotism, in that special military sense in which it is dis-

Under the stress of such extraordinary events as World War I and the Russian Revolution, and the resulting challenge to the social order, "the lie in the soul" of the propertied classes rose up into their consciousness in the form of the "lie in the mind"—that is, of the double-mindedness to which we have referred. This leads to blindness to obvious facts, credulity in swallowing fiction, wishful thinking, sophistries, evasions, quibbles, half- and quarter-truths, every form of self-deception, humbug, and variation on the gentle art of *suppressio veri et suggestio falsi*, saying one thing and doing another. Those who have reached this stage cannot fairly be accused of deliberate untruthfulness. But they do not let the left lobe of their brain know what the right doeth. Their Freudian censors have become class-conscious and abnormally active in the interests of property, with the result that obvious facts are literally "unthinkable" and the void is filled with fantasies, self-righteousness, and wish fulfilments.

The third stage, when the situation becomes critical and the forces of labour are too vigorous to be coerced (for at every stage the readiness to resort to coercion is a constant factor, held in check only by prudence), is "the lie in the throat"—that is, the lie direct, frigid and calculated, plain perjury, clear-eyed betrayal. It is only when there is really no other way of defeating the enemy, either class or national, that a British statesman or diplomat will resort to this extreme measure. But few statesmen or diplomats hesitate to "prefer honour to truth," as did Lord Salisbury, in the words of his biographer, when a real emergency arrives and no other means will serve.* If they ever stopped to think about it, they might echo Cavour's reflection, "What scoundrels we should be if we did for ourselves what we do for our

---

tinguished from public spirit, is not the temper of the citizen dealing with fellow-citizens, or with men who are themselves citizens in their several States, but that of the follower of the feudal chief, or of the member of a privileged class conscious of a power, resting ultimately on force, over an inferior population, or of a nation holding empire over other nations."

* Diplomats, according to the classic definition, are "men who lie abroad for their country." A Foreign Office official is only a diplomat at home.

country." * And of course the "honour and vital interest" of their country are indistinguishable in their minds from the interests of their class. But for the most part they do not stop to think. They cannot in their own estimation be liars, because they take a pragmatic view of truth, and they cannot be wrong, for their criterion of right is what they can get away with. If they fail, they are unfortunate, not immoral. They will always play the game—but when they are in danger of losing they will change the rules.

Politicians who identify the capitalist social order with civilization are just as much power politicians in the defence of their class interests against the workers of their own country as they are in defence of national interests against other countries. For in their minds class interests and national interests are one, and workers who threaten the former are as much "traitors" and outside the pale of the nation as foreigners who threaten the latter. In power politics there is neither honour, justice, mercy, nor truth, but only force and fraud. The only thing that counts is resistance.

With all this it must be realized that our capitalist statesmen are mostly honourable gentlemen in private life, who act in public life from a sincere sense of duty and devotion to their conception of the highest interests of the state. This is true, and an important truth. But it does not alter the fact that as power politicians defending their class interests against the threat of social revolution they will go to almost unbelievable lengths of cruelty and fraud, and display an almost incredible tenacity of purpose. As abundantly proved in this and the preceding chapter, it was in this cause that they shed torrents of blood, showed bewildering ingenuity and unscrupulousness in deceiving Wilson and the workers, prolonged the war, jeopardized the victory of the Allies, and inflicted an infinitude of suffering on their own peoples and on the peoples of Russia.

The chief differences between the situation during the years of appeasement that ushered in World War II and the situation at

* Or, as the Reform Bill Lord Grey wrote to Princess Lieven, "I am a great lover of morality, public and private, but the intercourse of nations cannot be strictly regulated by that rule."

the end of World War I was that conservatism and plutocracy in 1917–21 were fighting a rearguard action against the revolutionary and progressive forces emanating from World War I and the Russian Revolution. At home it was necessary to make at least verbal concessions and sweeping promises to labour—"homes for heroes," "reconstruction," nationalization of mines and railways, an end to profiteering from the manufacture of arms, and much else. The Labour party grew rapidly. Abroad the chief concessions wrung from conservatism and plutocracy by the fear of revolution were the establishment of the League and the abandonment of the attempt to crush the Russian Revolution.

In the years of appeasement plutocracy and conservatism were on the offensive, under the impulse of the reactionary forces coming from the great slump and the fascist counter-revolutions. The first casualties were the League and the lengthening list of victims of aggression. In Great Britain the National government was pressing the workers to accept worsening hours and conditions of labour, and ultimately industrial and military conscription. Abroad its policy was directed to agreements with the fascist powers giving the latter a free hand against the working-class, democracy, anti-fascist and anti-colonial peoples in Europe, Asia, and Africa, and particularly against the U.S.S.R.

After World War I the British Coalition government, although not so reactionary as the French, was a far more potent influence on the side of imperialism and intervention in Russia. During the years of appeasement the policy of the National government, although the latter was far less extreme than the fascist régimes, was a greater factor than their own efforts in enabling them to become a menace to world peace, and so in promoting the drift to world war.

The concessions wrung from conservatism and plutocracy at the end of World War I were the first steps to peace. The offensive of conservatism and plutocracy during the years of appeasement and the British National government impelled the world along the road to World War II.

CHAPTER V

The Assumptions of the Covenant

THE ORGANIZATION AND FUNCTIONS OF THE LEAGUE

THE LEAGUE OF NATIONS in its final form was a loose association of states. Any fully self-governing state, Dominion, or colony could become a member if admitted by a two-thirds majority of the Assembly. All the Allies and the neutrals were invited to be original members,* mentioned as such in the annex to the Covenant.

All decisions, with few and unimportant exceptions, such as matters of procedure, had to be taken unanimously. Except in counting the votes for a report of the Council under Article XV of the Covenant, this unanimity included the parties to a dispute.

The basic organizations in the League were the Assembly and Council. Both were conferences of government delegates. In the Assembly all the members of the League were represented on an equal footing, each with one vote. In the Council the great powers were permanently represented, and the Assembly elected a contingent of other members of the League from time to time. These two political conferences were given identical powers under the Covenant to concern themselves with any matter within the competence of the League or affecting the peace of the world. In addition the Assembly was responsible for the League's budget, and for admitting new members, whereas the chief function of the Council was to settle disputes and deal with disturbances to the peace. The great powers at first wanted none but

* Except Mexico, which was ignored because President Wilson, under the pressure of American big business, was half-intervening there at the time.

themselves represented in the Council, and accepted a contingent of elected small powers only when the latter's representatives in the League of Nations Commission bluntly said they would refuse to become members of the League unless they too were represented on the Council. The Assembly was regarded as a somewhat shadowy body, which was not expected to meet often or to do much. A Foreign Office memorandum quoted by Professor Zimmern in his book on the League mentioned above shows that it was clearly realized by the authors of the Covenant that the Assembly and Council were a development of what had existed in embryonic form in the concert of Europe.

One Article in the Covenant provided in brief and vague terms for co-operation in matters of common concern, such as economic and financial questions, transport and communications, public health, control of the traffic in narcotics, in social and labour questions. This and the I.L.O. were all that was left of the proposals of some liberals and of the labour movement to give the League wide powers in connection with organizing the economic and social life of the world. The technical organizations that sprang from this Article were originally intended to absorb the public international unions that existed before the war, just as the International Labour Office did in fact absorb the old International Association for Labour Legislation.

All these bodies were served by a Secretariat, or international civil service. This was partly the result of the experience of the war and partly modelled on the practice of the pre-war public international unions.

Article XIV of the Covenant pledged the members of the League to establish a Permanent Court of International Justice (usually called the World Court). This, which was done largely at the instigation of the neutrals, was intended to complete the work which had been begun at the Second Hague Conference (1907).

The League was given certain special functions in the peace treaties in connection with settling disputes arising out of the peace settlement, questions of railway and waterway transit, the duty of supervising the relations between Poland and Germany in the Free City of Danzig, and a measure of responsibility for the treatment of ethnic, racial, and religious minorities in the new states formed as a result of the war. For these states were induced to accept treaties by which they recognized an international obligation to give their minorities equality of treatment with all other citizens, and the right of such minorities to appeal to members of the Council, as well as the right of the Council to concern itself with such issues and to refer them to the World Court for a decision on whether or not the provisions of the minorities treaties were being observed. These limited functions were all that was left of General Smuts's sweeping proposals for the League to take the place left vacant in Central Europe by the destruction of the great empires that held in bondage the nations that had now become independent states. The temporary function of governing the Saar Basin until the population should settle their future fifteen years later was also given to the League. Lastly, the colonies taken from Germany and the territories of the Turkish Empire, divided up so far as possible in accordance with the secret treaties, were put under the so-called mandate system, by which the Allies that had entered into possession of these territories undertook to govern them according to certain principles and to report on their administration to an Advisory Committee of the League Council. Dominion objections based on the desire for straightforward annexation nearly defeated the mandate system at the outset.

The general obligations of the Covenant provided that the members of the League should all meet from time to time in the Assembly and should co-operate on matters of common concern. The Council also was to meet regularly. In Article VIII the members of the League undertook to reduce their armaments, on the advice of the Council, to the lowest limits consistent with national safety and the execution of international obligations, as well as to put an end to the evils of private manufacture of armaments. This and Clemenceau's letter to the German delegation promising that the disarmament of the central powers would in due course be followed by that of the Allies were all that was left of the far-reaching demands of the liberals at the Peace Conference for all-round disarmament and the nationalization of the arms industry.

The Covenant bound the members of the League not to resort to war and to submit all their disputes to some form of pacific settlement. Either party might summon the other before the Council, or both parties might agree to arbitration. If a state resorted to war against a member of the League while the matter at issue was being considered by the Council or an arbitral tribunal, or against a state which had accepted the unanimous (excluding the parties) report of the Council or an arbitral award, all the members of the League were bound immediately to sever all economic and personal relations with the aggressor, and might if they saw fit take military or naval action on the advice of the Council. They also bound themselves under Article X of the Covenant to respect and to preserve against external aggression the territorial integrity and political independence of any member of the League.

Under Article XI any member of the League might call the Council's attention to a circumstance affecting the good relations between states, and it was the duty of the League to take any action that it deemed wise and effectual to safeguard the peace of nations.

Under Article XIX the Assembly was to advise

the reconsideration by Members of the League of treaties which have become inapplicable and the consideration of international conditions whose continuance might endanger the peace of the world.

The Looseness of the Covenant

This was a comprehensive but vague system for consultation, co-operation, and preserving the peace. It was so loose that it could hardly be called a form of world government, although, as we have seen, it was intended to be precisely that.

How loose the Covenant was is made clear by the following quotation from Temperley:

The decision (see Article XVI), whether any of the engagements under Articles XII, XIII or XV had in fact been
broken, was not entrusted to the Council under the Covenant, but was left to the individual judgment of members,
each of whom undertook thereupon to break off relations
with the Covenant-breaker. . . . The less important right of
declaring a defaulting State to be no longer a Member of the
League is entrusted to the Council by the last paragraph of
Article XVI. Except for this last case, the Council and Assembly have no right of deciding whether Members of the
League have or have not fulfilled their obligations, as President Wilson was at great pains to explain to the Senate. . . .
No more has been put in the Covenant than what appeared the necessary minimum to give the League a fair
start; its future lines of development are left to itself.

The view that the Covenant contains no more than the bare
minimum of obligations necessary to form a collective system at
all was stressed by no less an authority than the Secretary-General of the League so late as January 1, 1938, when in a broadcast address he repeated the statement he made in a speech to a
group of members of Parliament at the British House of Commons on December 11, 1933:

If I lay stress on the Covenant, it is not only because the
Council and the Assembly have put upon my shoulders a
heavy responsibility respecting it, but because I am profoundly convinced that in its general structure it represents
the minimum number of obligations without which no League
and no effective international co-operation could exist.

This "necessary minimum," it may be observed, was arrived at
not by reference to any principle or standard, but simply as the
outcome of the struggle between Right and Left at the Peace
Conference. The obligations of the Covenant merely registered
the point beyond which plutocracy and conservatism refused to
make any more concessions to the liberals at the Peace Conference, and the liberals acquiesced rather than take the risk of a
break that would align them with the revolutionaries.

It is easy today to see that the framers of the Covenant were more successful in avoiding the Scylla of a "superstate" than the Charybdis of a mere talking-shop where nothing could be done because all decisions had to be unanimous and all obligations were self-interpreted, and because there were no obligations and machinery to weave a network of common social and economic interests binding nations into an "organic" international community that they felt they had a vital stake in preserving. It was a fact (given the unwillingness of the liberals to join forces with the revolutionary left) that the Covenant was all that could be got at the Peace Conference. But it was a complete *non sequitur* to deduce from this fact that the Covenant was good enough to constitute the basis for what General Smuts called "a League of Nations that will be real, practical, effective as a system of world-government." If it had been, that would have been a purely fortuitous piece of good fortune. Events have proved that in fact it was not.*

But it is important to realize that the League was the first step from international anarchy and power politics towards world government. As the Secretary-General of the League put it in his December 1933 speech already quoted:

> Whatever may be the details of the constitution of the League or of the tasks which it has to perform, the really essential thing about it is that it represents the first and only practical measure which has been taken by the human race as a step towards establishing the rule of law in the relations between countries. It has long been realised that such a step is the necessary and logical development of advancing civilisation, but the difficulties are such that it

* But die-hards of the Covenant, like Lord Cecil and Mr. P. J. Noel Baker, M.P., were still stoutly telling the faithful at the League of Nations Union General Council in December 1943 that the Covenant was an "inspired document," that there was nothing wrong or inadequate in its provisions, and that the League "almost succeeded" in preserving peace. The reason the League just fell short of complete success, they explained, was merely that governments were unwilling to carry out their treaty obligations. Their attitude is interesting as a fossil survival of a long-extinct species, a ghostly caricature, defying time and reality, of the Peace Conference liberals of all parties.

needed the huge pressure of the war to induce the nations
of the world to accept a written instrument governing the
more important aspects of their relations with one another. . . .
It is true that the United Kingdom, and to some extent the
British Empire, have a constitutional existence without a
written constitution. But this is a unique phenomenon which
could not possibly be repeated anywhere else, least of all in
the relations between the sixty or so sovereign States which
make up the international world.

The historic importance of founding the League was that it
represented the well-nigh unanimous recognition by civilized
states that international anarchy and power politics had become
too murderously inefficient to be any longer tolerable, and that the
adventure of world government must be attempted. The fact that
the League was intended as an attempt at world government is
far more important than its relative success or failure in that
capacity. For it is the first time in the history of the world that
the attempt had been made, and the fact that it was made marks
a new stage in the evolution of humanity.

General Smuts, in a broadcast address from the League of
Nations wireless station on New Year's Eve of 1938, said:

> The Covenant marks the furthest point yet reached in our
> progress towards a co-operative peaceful human society.
> That is its greatness, that is also its weakness. But there is no
> going back. The light once seen should never sink below our
> human horizon again. That would be a betrayal of those
> who died in the great war, a sacrifice of the generations yet
> unborn. That should be an unthinkable surrender.

Bearing in mind the general character and fundamental purpose of the League, let us now examine the assumptions on which
the framers of the Covenant built mankind's first attempt at
world government. These assumptions were as follows:

THE FOUR ASSUMPTIONS

First, that those parts of the peace settlement which were too
bad to be workable would gradually disappear because they were

either temporary in character or could be revised and ultimately abolished through the use of the machinery provided for that purpose, in particular Article XIX of the Covenant.

Secondly, they assumed that the League would shortly include every important country in the world.

Neither of these assumptions was unreasonable in the circumstances of 1919. Nor was the third assumption unreasonable, that the victory of the democratic powers in what they regarded as their ideological conflict with militarism meant, as General Smuts so strikingly put it in his pamphlet, that:

> The old institutions on which imperialism and autocracy flourished lie crumbled in the dust; a great wave of advanced Democracy is sweeping blindly over Europe.[1]

President Wilson voiced the same thought when he said that the purpose of the Allies and of the League they had founded was to "make the world safe for democracy." As a logical corollary of this view he wished to make democracy a condition for membership of the League.

The more the records are studied, the clearer it becomes that the belief in the intimate and inseparable relation between democracy and the structure and purpose of the League was a fundamental part of the assumptions of the authors of the Covenant. They knew quite well that the Covenant made only small formal encroachments on sovereignty. What they relied on to make the future of the world different from its grim past was that in the Covenant the states members of the League had pledged themselves to a code of conduct which was the very opposite of power politics. They thought that the war had caused a moral revolution and that in Wilson's phrase:

> Nations must in the future be governed by the same high code of honour that we demand of individuals.

Or, as Colonel House put it:

> The agreement or promise of a power shall be inviolate.[2]

As late as 1933 Lord Cecil admitted that the League could succeed in preventing war

... if, but only if its powerful Members have a sincere will to make it operate.[3]

This was undoubtedly the view on which the Covenant was founded, as the contemporary records show. For instance, Temperley says that the object of the League is

> to secure agreement, not to enforce decisions; to help what is good in the nations to assert itself, not to compel the nations to be good. It is a league of nations, not a world-state. In other words, it depends on public opinion in the several countries. . . .
> There is no body entitled to interpret the Covenant, or to pronounce as to what is, or is not, consistent with it. This omission would be indefensible if the Covenant were a body of legal obligations, like a national constitution; it is intelligible if we look on it as a statement of principles by which the signatories express their intention of being guided. The agreement of to-day must be repeated and consummated in the future. That is the spirit of the League. It is to be a league of free, not of fettered nations.[4]

Mr. P. J. Noel Baker, M.P., who was a member of the British delegation throughout the proceedings of the League of Nations Commission of the Peace Conference, and is recognized as an authority on everything connected with the League, has this to say on the subject:

> The Covenant which was made at Paris was founded, as has just been said, on the basis of the national sovereignty of its Members. Its purpose was the creation of a system of political institutions in which those Members could co-operate freely in the conduct of their common affairs. In the constitution which the Covenant lays down for these institutions, the principle of freedom and elasticity, urged from first to last by the Anglo-Saxon delegates, prevailed against the stricter legal and constitutional conceptions of some continental Members of the Commission. The result is that the Covenant, having created the institutions, leaves to the statesmen who have to use them the fullest liberty to

work out, untrammelled by detailed constitutional rules, the development of the machinery they use.

It would not be true to say that there are no rules laid down for the guidance of the statesmen of the League. There are some; but they were reduced to the very minimum which the Paris Commission thought essential to enable the institutions of the League to function. Within these rules, the purpose of the Covenant is to eliminate from international affairs the factor of physical force and the consequences to which a reliance on physical force inevitably leads. It leaves free, within the political institutions which it created, a field for the operation in the affairs of nations of those political forces—public opinion, the consciousness of the supreme interest of the community as a whole, the desire for organised justice—which dominate in the domestic affairs of civilised peoples.[5]

When the final text of the Covenant was published in Great Britain it was accompanied by a semi-official commentary, from which the following is an extract:

The document that has emerged from these discussions is not the Constitution of a super-State, but, as its title explains, a solemn agreement between sovereign States, which consent to limit their complete freedom of action on certain points for the greater good of themselves and the world at large. Recognising that one generation cannot hope to bind its successors by written words, the Commission has worked throughout on the assumption that the League must continue to depend on the free consent, in the last resort, of its component States; this assumption is evident in nearly every article of the Covenant, of which the ultimate and most effective sanction must be the public opinion of the civilised world. If the nations of the future are in the main selfish, grasping and warlike, no instrument or machinery will restrain them. It is only possible to establish an organisation which may make peaceful co-operation easy and hence customary, and to trust in the influence of custom to mould opinion.

But while acceptance of the political facts of the present has been one of the principles on which the Commission has

worked, it has sought to create a framework which should
make possible and encourage an indefinite development in
accordance with the ideas of the future. If it has been chary
of prescribing what the League shall do, it has been no less
chary of prescribing what it shall not do. A number of
amendments laying down the methods by which the League
should work, or the action it should take in certain events,
and tending to greater precision generally, have been deliberately rejected, not because the Commission was not in
sympathy with the proposals, but because it was thought
better to leave the hands of the statesmen of the future as
free as possible, and to allow the League, as a living organism, to discover its own best lines of development.[6]

In the light of these eyewitness quotations it is perfectly clear
on what principles and assumptions the Covenant was framed
and how fundamental was the belief that political democracy
would continue to flourish. For reliance on the working of a free
public opinion and emphasis on persuasion, discussion, agreement, postulate the existence of democracy.

But this third assumption in its turn took it for granted that
political democracy would continue to prevail in the world *on the
economic and social basis of a smoothly working capitalism.* This
last belief, the belief in the stability of the social order, although
in fact it constitutes the fourth and fundamental assumption on
which the League was founded, was so deeply rooted in the
minds of the authors of the Covenant as to be unconscious. It
was the mental conditioning on which all their other assumptions,
and indeed their whole outlook, rested rather than a distinct and
consciously realized assumption.

CONCLUSION

It is important to understand both the strength and the weakness of the liberal view. Its strength lay in the fact that it was
not unreasonable to suppose in 1919 that democracy would become the prevailing system of government in the world, that the
advance begun in the nineteenth century and accelerated by the
war would be completed in the years to come. Democracy meant

a free public opinion. The war had engendered a passionate longing for peace and a great volume of opinion that believed that the new code of international conduct to which the governments had pledged themselves in the Covenant was the only way to prevent the recurrence of a more terrible world war. That feeling would last long enough and be strong enough to bend governments and diplomatic services to its will, to clothe with the flesh and blood of institutions, and to breathe life into the new obligations that had been born on paper.

In this way, gradually but quickly enough to retain and increase the Peace Conference lead over the forces that make for war, a new tradition would grow, a world loyalty operating through the free public opinions of the democracies, to make a reality of man's first attempt at world government. At every emergency, or at least in a sufficient number of emergencies to make the League's successes outweigh its failures, there would be an effective majority of states in the world in which an effective majority of public opinion would feel it a matter of national honour and vital interests to make the League work—and would feel it strongly enough to compel the governments to live up to their treaty obligations. Thus the League would slowly become universal, revise the peace treaties, achieve disarmament, and organize world peace.

That was the theory. It was, it will be seen, part and parcel of the liberal faith in democracy, in good will and reason. That was a noble, intelligent, and in its essentials a true faith. Its weakness in 1919 was that it over-estimated the extent to which democracy already existed, or could exist in our present economic system. Liberals could not see that capitalism as an economic system made democracy as a political system largely a sham, because it weighted the political scales heavily in favour of the rich. They would not admit that the plutocracy used its economic power to pull political strings that ultimately controlled governments, and made them act in its class interest against the interests of the great majority of the community. They did not see that the political stronghold of the plutocracy was defence and foreign and imperial affairs, where democracy had scarcely begun to make

itself felt. Nor did they realize how dependent for survival plutocracy had become on war preparations, power politics, and imperialism and on the political atmosphere they generate.

Because in the eyes of liberals the social and economic foundations of society were part of the order of nature and impossible
to change by the act of man, they met the Russian Revolution and
the social unrest in the working-class with incomprehension and
fear. This, as we have seen, was in the last analysis the chief
reason for their being so readily gulled by conservatism and
plutocracy, and for their acquiescing in the unnecessary prolongation of the war, Russian intervention, the harshness of the peace
treaties, and the weakness of the League. The liberals could not
play the trump-card of a break with the forces of conservatism
and plutocracy, because that would have obliged them to take
the side of the forces emanating from the Russian Revolution.
Therefore, as they would not break, they felt they had to yield—
and consoled themselves by making an objective virtue of their
subjective necessity.

The Peace Conference liberals, therefore, in deference to the
obduracy of conservatism and plutocracy, agreed to a very low
minimum of obligations in the Covenant. By way of "compensation" they constructed out of this shadowy document a theory
about the virtues of "elasticity," which was, to say the least, optimistic, and read into the Covenant powers to revise the peace
settlement and to reshape the life of the world which were an
overestimate. They took comfort in believing in a brilliant future
for the moral forces that they were uneasily aware had been
badly defeated at the Peace Conference.

The exaggeratedly optimistic and friendly view taken by 1919
liberals of the peace settlement and the potentialities of the
League was the psychological compensation for their exaggerated pessimism and hostility towards the Russian Revolution
and the extreme Left. The latter, it must be added, was for the
most part in those days politically inexperienced, morally arro-
gant, narrow-minded, dogmatic, and fierce, and regarded liberals
and moderate labour with bitter hostility. But viewed historically,
as we can now afford to do, the extremists were mostly right in

trusting all that the Russian Revolution stood for internationally and in wholly distrusting conservatives and plutocracy. Whereas liberals and moderate labour were far too trustful towards the latter and mistrustful towards the former. They believed they were on the side of the masses against the classes, but they were in fact more afraid of the many poor than of the few rich—and so in the last analysis they came down on the side of "national unity" with the latter against the former.

What is the conclusion to be drawn? That, it may be suggested, drawn by General Smuts on January 1, 1938, in the broadcast already quoted:

> It is true that the Covenant is a vision but not that it is visionary. It is the truest, most realist vision yet seen in the affairs of the world, and simply carries into world affairs that outlook of a liberal democratic society which is one of the great achievements of our human advance. Perhaps that is the real reason why the new dictators object to it. Surely the concept of a world society settling its affairs, not by force of war, but by common consultation and in co-operation, is essentially sound. The Covenant simply carries a step further the process by which the State has already succeeded in suppressing private feuds and public violence and has substituted peaceful parliamentary action for both.

The fate of what the League stood for—that is, world government—and the fate of democracy are ultimately inseparable, and the fate of both is inseparable from the future of social justice and world peace. These things were recognized at the Peace Conference, and they remain true today. To act on this truth has once again become tragically urgent. But this time we should learn the lesson of the failure of the last attempt.

The League was founded by liberals with the help of labour in order to make the world safe for democracy, because they understood, after the awful lesson of World War I, that power politics and international anarchy breed war, and that if civilization does not end war, war will end civilization. Today we can see that they were not bold enough in laying the economic foundations of world government, by paying heed to their own maxim that peace could endure only if based on social justice. We know now too the main reason for this failure—the resistance of conservatism and plutocracy. But it would be worse than useless to employ this knowledge in order to blame the shortcomings of the pioneers of world government, who, whatever their failures, did have the historic courage to take the first step.

It is for our generation to learn from the faults of our predecessors how to take the next step, how to make a new start with the idea of world government. In doing so we must not underestimate the magnitude of what was actually achieved at the Paris Peace Conference, nor overlook how valuable the experience of the League can be as the starting-point for a new attempt to build up a world government capable of maintaining peace and of making the world safe for democracy. But we must learn the lesson that was not learned by most progressives at the Peace Conference, and which has still not been adequately learned, the lesson to which the late Arthur Henderson, one of the most successful British Foreign Secretaries and winner of the Nobel Peace Prize, drew attention in the following memorable words:

> Many years of work in the cause of peace, culminating in two and a quarter years as Foreign Secretary and three years as President of the Disarmament Conference, have convinced me that . . . the roots of war lie deep in the private profit-making system of production. A Government that is to make peace must be strong enough to grasp and hold the keys to economic power. It must have the whip-hand over the arms industry and the banks, and must control the whole economic life of the country and base it on the common good instead of private profit as the dominant motive. Those who do not face the necessity for breaking the vested interests that blindly push Governments into war in their scramble for profits are only playing with the problem of peace.[7]

Light is cast on the strength and weakness of the liberal view in 1919 of the world's future, and on much of what has since happened, by Mr. A. G. Tansley's *The New Psychology and Its Relation to Life*. In this book, which first appeared in 1920, the author

says he is endeavouring to present the educated lay reader with
"an attempted synthesis, necessarily crude and incomplete in the
present state of knowledge, of the biological and psychoanalytic
views of the human mind, and to indicate the position of the
higher human interests and efforts in such a synthesis." [8]

Discussing the League of Nations, Mr. Tansley points out that
it cannot become a reality until there is a living sense of international solidarity, of human brotherhood. This is the essential
psychological basis without which a world federation is not possible. But:

Before there can exist an international life which has any
reality, and particularly before it can correspond with a sense
of world solidarity in the minds of the common people, and
thus create a complex of the world herd which alone can
give solid support to international organization, a very long
road will have to be traversed. When disappointment is expressed because an effective League of Nations cannot be
brought into existence in the course of a few months, it is
forgotten that we are dealing with the whole of the last
stage of social evolution—a tremendous affair which, even
with the increased rate of development we may fairly expect,
cannot possibly be consummated in a few months or in a few
years. . . .

The notion that a living, effective world federation can be
manufactured to order is a good example of that unprac-
tical idealism which imagines that a scheme of such magnitude can be realized at once, because it is an admirable
ideal scheme. The cognitive faculty and the faculty of forming ideals are constantly envisaging solutions of practical
problems which are not ripe for solution, and thus running
far ahead of reality. There is confusion between what can
be brought about by unimpeachable logical schemes, and
what can only be done by the slow and laborious process of
detailed evolution and integration in the human mind. In
this case what must be attained is a harmony between the
organization of herd instinct in the national and partial herd
form with a new organization of universal herd instinct, the
process of which has hardly more than begun, even though

the desire for its consummation may exist in the hearts of millions.* [9]

Turning to a discussion of "partial herds and the universal herd," Mr. Tansley points out that hitherto the nation is the nearest to a "universal herd," since there is no sense of human brotherhood strong enough to warrant talking of a "world herd." But within the nations there are many partial herds, in particular,

. . . the stratified *classes* of society within the old and complex nations like those of Western Europe . . . some of these show the characteristics of the partial herd in a marked degree. An old aristocracy forms one such well-marked partial herd. . . . In modern times the old aristocracy has more and more begun to feel the threat not only to its power, but to its very existence, involved in the rising strength of the proletariat. The passing of political power to the middle classes scarcely threatened seriously the prestige and influence of the aristocracy. The middle classes had some interests in common with the aristocracy, and in any case were too comfortable, too loosely knit and too snobbish to aspire to usurp their power. But with the further transference of power to the proletariat, which is now complete, the aristocrats are actually threatened with a deadly menace. The process of modern social evolution has been too much for them, and they are, in fact, a decadent herd with no adequate weapons of self-defence. Another partial herd in the upper range of the social scale is formed by the plutocrats, primarily the successful merchants, business men, financiers and speculators. Diverse as are the qualities of this heterogeneous class, they are held together by the possession of money and the power which money brings. With the progress of industrialism the limits between this class and the old aristocracy have become more and more blurred. The creation of peers from among the ranks of men who have become rich, intermarriage, and the turning of some of the old aristocrats to commerce or speculation has tended to weld the two classes together and to make one class only, charac-

* Cf. Graham Wallas: "The consciousness of a common purpose in mankind, or even the acknowledgement that such a common purpose is possible, would alter the face of world-politics at once."

terized by the possession of wealth. This process, though not quite complete, has advanced a long way, and the class thus created is very far from decadent. Its interests also are very seriously threatened by the rise in the power and organization of the proletariat. What the result of the inevitable conflict may be, remains to be seen; the next few years, of course, are critical for the development of social organization.

The middle classes form, as has been said, too loosely knit a herd to have any great significance. It is doubtful, indeed, if they can properly be called a herd at all. It is possible that a very serious direct threat to their interests also may weld them together into an effective organization. Attempts in this direction are already being made, but it is doubtful if they will meet with any considerable measure of success, because the factors making for class consciousness (partial herd consciousness) are relatively weak. Their circumstances and tastes are too diverse. They are too unimaginative as a whole, and they cannot, like the proletariat, enlist in their cause the unselfish devotion of men and women who are stung by an abiding sense of injustice, inequality, and miserable conditions of life, and are inspired by the ideal of a fair and rational social organization. Still, many members of the middle classes have suffered a great deal during the war, and if they continue to suffer they may show an unexpected power of consolidation in defence of their interests—they may become really integrated as a partial herd.*

Finally, we have the great partial herd of the proletariat itself, whose "class consciousness" has increased so enormously, and is still increasing with every step in the direction of better education, improved means of inter-communication and more clearly realized demands upon society at large. Trade unionism, of course, has been the most potent instrument in this development, which took place at first on occupational lines, creating a number of highly and deliberately organized partial herds. Lately these have reached

* The great slump—in Italy the first post-war slump—and other alarming social developments after this was written gave the necessary impulse to middle-class herd instinct. In its militant state this herd instinct expresses itself in the organizational form of fascist movements.

out in different ways so as to embrace the whole, or nearly the whole, of the wage-earners of the country; and although this universal proletarian organization is not yet complete, it is rapidly becoming so. And at the present time the proletariat is certainly the most intensely class conscious of all the social classes; and this, apart from its preponderating numbers, means that it is much the most powerful and important of all existing partial herds—potentially at least, for it has, of course, by no means reached the zenith of its political power.

So powerful, indeed, had become the class consciousness of the proletariats of the different nations of Western and Central Europe, even before the war, that it threatened, or was thought to threaten, the primary division of mankind into national herds, by cutting across the boundaries of nations and welding together the proletariats of that part of the world. It used to be said, for instance, that if the Governments of France and Germany declared a state of war between those nations, the proletariats of each would throw down their arms and refuse to fight against their brothers. This, as we know, did not in fact happen. The national herd proved stronger than the international proletariat. The ties of common race, common language, and common tradition, the love of fatherland—in a word, all the bonds of the national herd, prevailed against the newer and, as yet at any rate, weaker ties of common economic interests. But the circumstances of the test were all in favour of the national herd. . . .

Whether this intense heightening of national feeling will last, or whether the "Internationale" will arise rejuvenated and stronger than ever, we cannot yet tell. The issue will largely depend, no doubt, on economic factors, on the rate of recovery of Western and Central Europe, on the success of the efforts that will be made to bring about a more equal distribution of wealth, or rather of the amenities of life, among the different classes of society, on the measure in which the peoples can obtain relief from the burden of armaments. If these things can be successfully accomplished, there can be little doubt that the evolution of the world will take place more smoothly and harmoniously on national lines than it will on the lines of the programme of the "Internationale." [10]

Up to the great slump the steady growth of the League's activities and membership, and the success of post-war reconstruction, gave reason to hope that the liberal belief in progress to human brotherhood through national unity embracing all classes, and international co-operation between all states, might be justified. But the collapse of the League and the increasing acuteness of social conflicts after 1931; the fascist aggressions and conservative appeasements that were at bottom a defensive-offensive by the propertied classes to meet the gathering challenge to the social order; the growing ambitions, appetites, and power of the business and banking world, working within the wartime controls in the Western democracies; the welding together of these social elements with the fascist and quisling regimes in the Axis-controlled countries; the semi-socialist programs and revolutionary character of the underground resistance movements in enemy-occupied Europe; the Anglo-American official support of Continental monarchy, clericalism, and reaction, mostly in the shape of phantom *émigré* governments—all these things and others too suggest that whatever else may happen, Mr. Tansley's belief at least, so closely akin to that of the Peace Conference liberals, must be abandoned. Drastic social change is visibly becoming the only possible foundation for any effective system of world government. It seems equally clear that that change will be resisted to the uttermost by the propertied classes, and will have to be accomplished principally through the agency of the workers and their allies in the different countries. The conclusion seems inevitable that one of the corner-stones of the edifice of peace will have to be a bigger and better workers' International.

CHAPTER VI

The First Decade of the League

THE LEAGUE OF NATIONS that was born of the long and bloody travail of four years of world war was a puny infant. It saw the light of day in a forbidding world—large parts of Europe a desert, almost all Europe in rags and starving, 10,000,000 dead and 20,000,000 wounded, the fires of revolution and war still smouldering everywhere and burning brightly in Russia and the Near East.

Nevertheless during the first ten years of the League's existence the four assumptions on which the Covenant had been framed broadly held good and the League slowly but steadily gained in membership and influence. It looked as though the liberal faith in the virtues of elasticity and freedom for development were going to be justified, and as though the League were to outgrow its original disabilities and weaknesses.

WORKING OUT OF THE FOUR ASSUMPTIONS

It was true that the peace settlement was harsh, unjust, and one-sided. But the frontiers that had been drawn were far better from the point of view of the distribution of nationalities than what had existed before the war, and the minorities treaties held out the hope that the treatment of national minorities would improve to the point where there would be no serious irredentist grievances. A number of minor, boundary and transit questions had been dealt with through the League and had ceased from troubling. The Rhineland was evacuated five years before the period fixed by the treaty. The Dawes and Young plans promised

318

a settlement at long last of the vexed question of reparations. A plebiscite would in due course return the Saar to Germany. Poland and Germany looked like reaching a *modus vivendi* over Danzig. The Upper Silesian minority and economic arrangements on the basis of reciprocity were working satisfactorily. A Disarmament Conference was being prepared and would settle the big question of Germany's equality of rights and the demand of France and other states for a better organization of collective security.

It was true that the United States withdrew from the League at its inception and that the Soviet Union had never become a member of the League. But co-operation with both these states was growing, and the ex-enemy powers had become members of the League, Germany in addition taking her place as a permanent member of the Council. The membership of the League had increased almost year by year, until it did not seem unreasonable to expect it to become truly universal in the near future.

It was true that in the first post-war slump Italy had gone Fascist and that it was difficult to reconcile the principles of this régime with either democracy or international co-operation. But the Italian Government, after the first collision with the League over Corfu, seemed to realize that it could best serve its national interests by taking an active part in the work and development of the League. Japan was not a democratic state either. But she was rather on the fringe of world politics, and through her acceptance of the Washington treaties in 1922 and the Kellogg-Briand (Paris) Pact in 1928 appeared to be accepting the international outlook of the great democracies, which had retained the leadership in world affairs.

It was true that although the League had taken up the question of disarmament from its first Assembly, progress had been disappointingly slow. But no state was rearming intensively, nor apprehended war. The political and technical preparations for disarmament had resulted in a considerable number of decisions. Resolution 14 of the Third Assembly fixed the connection between disarmament on the one hand and strengthening the system of collective guarantees of security against aggression on the other, which became the basis of the League's work on this subject. At the Fourth Assembly in 1923, the Draft Treaty of Mutual Assistance was drawn up, which attempted to give effect to this principle. That failed, but only to be replaced by the even more ambitious Geneva Protocol of 1924, which added the third idea of arbitration to those of disarmament and security. The Geneva Protocol in its turn failed. But a partial and local application survived in the Locarno treaties, which also resulted in Germany's entry into the League.

After that political and technical preparations for disarmament followed three main lines: A growing number of states concluded arbitration and/or conciliation treaties. Through the League the General Act of Arbitration was drawn up and opened to signature. The Optional Clause, conferring compulsory jurisdiction on the Permanent Court of International Justice, was adopted by a large number of states. On the second line of advance—in the realm of security—there was the Treaty for Strengthening the Means to Prevent War and the Treaty of Financial Assistance, which were both opened to signature but made dependent on the coming into force of a disarmament convention. A good deal of work was done on interpreting Articles X, XI, and XVI of the Covenant, and on methods of making the sanctions system work and the Council of the League meet rapidly and function effectively in an emergency.[1] The non-aggression treaties concluded by the Soviet Union with many of her neighbours were the forerunners of the Kellogg-Briand (Paris) Pact for the Renunciation of War, which was adopted by a large number of states. The Assembly took up the question of revising the Covenant so as to include in it the complete renunciation of war contained in the Paris Pact. As regards the third line of advance— disarmament proper—the Preparatory Committee of the Disarmament Conference at last evolved a Draft Convention. The date of the Disarmament Conference was fixed and its president was chosen.

It was true that at the Peace Conference the attempt to underpin the political structure of the League by maintaining and internationalizing under League auspices the whole inter-Allied war-time organization of economic, transport, and raw-material controls had suffered defeat. It was also true that reparations and war debts, which dominated most of the economic problems of the day, were kept out of the purview of the League. Nevertheless the first act of the League was to hold the Brussels Financial Conference, which drew up the principles of financial recovery and stabilization, according to the tenets of capitalist statesmanship of those days (balancing budgets by retrenchment, return to the gold standard, independent banks of issue, etc.). These principles subsequently guided the financial policies of many countries and were the basis of a number of League loans and plans of reconstruction in Central and South-eastern Europe, which appeared eminently successful until the great slump.

The brief references in the Covenant to co operation on matters of common concern had proved the starting-point for building big technical organizations and embarking on important enterprises. The Transit and Health organizations, the Committees on Social Questions and on the Control of Opium and Narcotic Drugs, promoted the conclusion of a number of world-wide agreements and accomplished solid and useful work. The International Labour Organization was forging ahead.

THE 1927 ECONOMIC CONFERENCE

In the economic field a somewhat gingerly beginning was made by tackling the question of customs nomenclature. After that the League was allowed to take up customs formalities. The ice being thus broken, governments agreed to the whole question of the lowering and simplification of tariffs being taken up at the Geneva Economic Conference of 1927. This was to be a replica in the economic field of the Brussels Financial Conference. The delegations represented not governments, but cross-sections of the economic life of their respective countries. There were Treasury and Board of Trade officials, but without instructions; distinguished economists; representatives of banks, employers' associations, trade-unions, co-operatives, chambers of commerce, etc. The International Chamber of Commerce, the

International Labour Organization, the International Institute of Agriculture in Rome, the Trade Union International (I.F.T.U.), the World Co-operative Alliance, were also represented. The purpose of the conference was to elicit a body of opinion so authoritative and so well-nigh unanimous on certain broad principles of economic policy as to give an agreed program and an impetus to those in all countries who were working for a freeing of the channels of trade from the obstructions that had grown up during and since World War I.

The fundamental idea was that there was no real cleavage of interests between economic classes, or at least that their common interests transcended their differences, that our post-war economic troubles were due chiefly to the dislocation and political and administrative difficulties caused by war conditions. It followed that it was merely a matter of removing these government-created obstacles in order to allow economic life to pick up the threads where they had been dropped before the war. Capitalism, it was believed, could continue to develop indefinitely and international trade and investment would be resumed on the old lines, if only the governments would cease the forms of interference they had begun to practise during and since the war. This was a typically liberal or progressive capitalist approach to the problem.

Those who held this view were quite conscious of the connection between the obstacles to international trade and investment they were attempting to remove and the question of peace. Thus M. Theunis, the former Belgian Prime Minister and eminent industrialist and financier, who presided at the Economic Conference, said in his presidential address that:

> Economic conflicts and divergence of economic interests are perhaps the most serious and the most permanent of all the dangers which are likely to threaten the peace of the world. No machinery for the settlement of international disputes can be relied upon to maintain peace if the economic policies of the world so develop as to create not only deep divergencies of economic interest between different masses of the world's population, but a sense of intolerable injury

and injustice. No task is more urgent or more vital than that of securing agreement on certain principles of policy which are necessary in the interests of future peace. And there is perhaps no question which, in comparison with its intrinsic importance, has had so little careful collective deliberation.

Sir Arthur Salter, who was the secretary-general of the conference, quoted this opinion with approval a year later, and added:

In a word, if we want peace we must not merely rely upon a machinery for the settlement of disputes when they arise; we must so lay the foundations of peace that the disputes which do arise will be relatively unenvenomed by previous dissensions, and will not be deeply rooted in a long-standing sense of divergent interest and injustice. . . . If we, comfortably believing that there is a machinery for stopping war, are content to allow the economic forces of the world to move along lines which lead and guide to war, even the machinery of the League will not, at the last moment, save us from the consequences.

These remarks, it will be seen, proved only too prophetic—they were made without prevision of the great slump, but the slump proved their truth with a vengeance.

During the year 1928 there were some signs of a movement of opinion and even of government policy along the lines laid down by the resolutions of the Geneva Economic Conference, which was emphatic and unanimous in stating that tariffs were too high and too variable and should be lowered and stabilized. But as from 1929, with the onset of the great slump, post-war tendencies towards economic nationalism set in again with redoubled intensity. Government experts, bankers, and business men met in conference after conference and committee after committee at Geneva, Basle (the International Bank of Settlements), Paris (the International Chamber of Commerce), and elsewhere to deplore the policies of economic nationalism and to demand in the strongest terms that these suicidal policies should be reversed. After which they went home and each in his respective country proceeded to carry further the very policies they had been jointly condemning in solemn international conclave. Nor was this just hypocrisy. Economic (like military) rearmament seemed to them an evil necessity, in whose grip they were helpless. In fact the governments and experts in these matters were nothing but tools in the hands of vested interests bent on surviving the partial breakdown of the economic system in the great slump by resorting to economic nationalism and war preparations.

ANGLO-FRENCH LEADERSHIP

But before passing on to this subject it is necessary to consider what it was that made the League·work in the first ten years of its existence. For because of the looseness of the Covenant and the degree to which states preserved their sovereignty after becoming members of the League, there was no central authority, no "League policy." The League did not have any unity, or motive force, or political responsibility of its own. Everything the League did or did not do was the result of the foreign policies of the nations in the League. The League was simply machinery that was put in motion—or left standing idle—by the governments, according to the way they interpreted their treaty obligations under the Covenant.

During the first ten years of the League, France and Great Britain still had a position of almost unchallenged supremacy in Europe. Everything that was done at Geneva was the outcome of the joint decisions of these two powers. When they disagreed, as they not infrequently did, the League was paralyzed until their views had been adjusted by a compromise. These differences gave the other members of the League the chance to make their views felt.

The supremacy of France and Great Britain was not absolute. It did not exclude consultation with other states and taking account of their views. But the joint Anglo-French power to decide all issues in the last analysis was the driving force behind the League in the first ten years. Behind Great Britain were the Dominions and India and generally the Scandinavians and the Dutch. Behind the French were the Poles, the Little Entente, and generally the Baltic States. Germany, Italy, the South Americans, the Asiatic States, Austria, Hungary, Bulgaria, and Greece were "intermediate" and generally not active. Belgium and Czechoslovakia were the mediators *par excellence* between the British and French points of view.

Generally Great Britain had more influence but a vaguer policy in the League than the French. Compromise, and adjournment until a compromise was achieved, were the means by which the League functioned under Anglo-French direction.

The following account will describe in particular Great Britain's contribution to the first ten years of the League.

In general French conservatism wanted to develop the League into a machine for holding down Germany and assuring French hegemony in Europe, whereas British conservatism wanted to prevent it from developing into anything that would interfere with Britain's free hand in the pursuit of imperial power politics. Therefore the two could not agree except on lines that did nothing to develop the League towards world government. The Left wings in the two countries, on the other hand, though amateurish and far from seeing eye to eye, were at one in genuinely desiring to make a reality of the collective peace system outlined in the Covenant. Therefore on the one occasion when they were in office simultaneously, they were able to take a big step forward at Geneva (the Protocol).

In the first few years after World War I Great Britain was under the Coalition government that had issued from the khaki election, while France was ruled by Poincaré and the National bloc resulting from the "horizon-blue" election. Peace-treaty issues were still dealt with by dictation through the Ambassadors' Conference, which was a continuation of the Allied Supreme Council.

CORFU AND THE RUHR

Italy during this period went Fascist in the first post-war slump and fell foul of the League over Corfu. The French invaded the Ruhr in an attempt to extract reparations payments with the bayonet. The Italians induced Poincaré to refrain from supporting the British proposals (somewhat half-hearted in any case) to take a strong line through the League against the Italian bombardment of Corfu, on the ground that if the League succeeded on this question, it would become so strong as to tackle France in the Ruhr next.

No Compulsory Arbitration

At the first Assembly in November 1920 Mr. Balfour explained at length why Great Britain could not accept the proposals of the Jurists' Conference that the World Court should be endowed with compulsory jurisdiction—that is, that states should recognize the right of either party to a dispute on questions of law, fact, or treaty interpretation, to summon the other before the Court and the obligation of both parties to accept the Court's judgment. He argued that the powers conferred upon the Court "should not go beyond what I take to have been the intention of the statesmen who framed the Covenant," and that the latter

> never intended that one party to a dispute should compel another party to go before a Tribunal; and this omission cannot have been a matter of choice, since the subject of compulsory arbitration has been before the legal authorities of the whole world now for many years. It has more than once been brought up for practical decision, and has always been rejected.

The leading jurists of the world who had framed the constitution of the World Court had argued that since the idea of pledging states to go to law instead of leaving them free to resort to force had been seriously discussed at the Hague Conference in 1907, and that since there had been four years of world war in the ensuing eleven years, it did not seem too much to suggest that the civilized nations in the light of that awful experience might pledge themselves to recognize the compulsory jurisdiction of the Court on all disputes concerning:

(a) The interpretation of a treaty;
(b) Any question of International Law;

(c) The existence of any fact which, if established, would constitute a breach of an international obligation;

(d) The nature or extent of the reparation to be made for the breach of an international obligation.

Mr. Balfour's speech was a further example of the extraordinary tenacity shown by the representatives of conservatism and plutocracy in sticking to international anarchy and power politics in the midst of a world still prostrate and bleeding after a world war. Under strong pressure from the small powers, the Assembly finally carried the compromise of the Optional Clause by which signatories to the Statute of the World Court could, if they wished, pledge themselves also to recognize its compulsory jurisdiction for the classes of disputes enumerated above. But all the great powers opposed compulsory jurisdiction.

No Help to Soviet Russia

At the second and third Assemblies in September 1921 and 1922 the fearful conditions in Russia that were the aftermath of war, civil war, intervention, disease, and famine were discussed. The governments unanimously showed their determination not to pay a penny to save human lives, in the hope that they could by helping to starve tens of millions destroy the Communist régime that they had failed to overthrow by waging war on Russia. The Yugoslav delegate was the only one uncivilized enough to state frankly that that was his Government's political motive in refusing any humanitarian assistance. The other governments expressed their profound sympathy with more or less eloquence, but by some curious coincidence unanimously found themselves unhappily unable to render any assistance. In the upshot something was done by raising money from private charity, and the United States contributed a large amount of wheat that had become unsalable in the first post-war slump.

Break-up of the Anglo-French War Governments

The invasion of the Ruhr was a failure as regards extracting reparation payments. It gave a great fillip to German reaction, broke the franc, and caused such indignation in French public opinion that it proved the decisive factor in the formation of the first Radical and Socialist electoral combination, the so-called Cartel, that won the 1924 general election and brought in the Radical government of Herriot with Socialist support. This coincided with the advent of the first Labour government in Great Britain.

THE GENEVA PROTOCOL

At the Fifth Assembly in September 1924 the British Labour government made a big push for disarmament and found the French Radical government ready to meet it half-way. The result was the Geneva Protocol, which may be described as a brilliant improvisation. Its League background was Resolution 14 of the Third Assembly, which laid down the principle that reduction and limitation of armaments by international agreement must be accompanied by organizing collective security on the basis of the Covenant. The next year, at the Fourth Assembly in 1923, a Draft Treaty of Mutual Assistance was reported to the Assembly by its "Temporary Mixed Commission for Disarmament." (This quaint name was invented because of the presence of both civilians and military men on the Committee.) This draft was circulated to the governments for their comments and rejected by the British Labour government, on the ground that it left the door open to regional agreements that might degenerate into alliances and did not provide a satisfactory criterion of what constituted aggression.

The result of the Anglo-French discussion at the Fifth Assembly was to produce an agreement that provided for the pacific settlement of all disputes, including the compulsory jurisdiction of the World Court; invent the ingenious "presumption of aggression," by which in case hostilities broke out between two states one of which had accepted and the other rejected arbitration the latter should be presumed to be the aggressor unless it were unanimously disculpated by the Council; lay down the principle that economic sanctions only were obligatory, whereas military sanctions were optional, and provide measures for organizing the former and for voluntary declarations by states to the Council as to what they were prepared to do as regards military sanctions for certain areas; and provide that the Protocol should come into force only when a disarmament convention had not only been ratified but was actually being carried out as decided by the Council. At that time the armaments of the victorious great powers were at a low level, and the central powers were disarmed.

In the speeches at the conclusion of this Assembly several delegates declared that the success of the Disarmament Conference and the coming into force of the Protocol would be the starting-point for far-reaching policies of economic and financial co-operation.

One of the reasons why the British and French delegations were able to agree so rapidly was that the British and French socialists had for a couple of years previously hammered out these questions of arbitration, collective security, and disarmament in various committees and conferences of the reconstituted Labour and Socialist International. Mr. Henderson, the chief author of the Protocol on the British side, had in this way acquired a fund of experience and knowledge which he put to good use.

The fate of the Protocol showed how little public opinion in Britain had learned from the war and the framing of the Covenant. Well-nigh all Conservative, a large part of Liberal, and a considerable section of Labour opinion were opposed to the Protocol on grounds that applied equally to the fundamental obligations of the Covenant, and showed complete inability to realize what were Great Britain's commitments since she had become a member of the League. The Conservatives were anarchists on power-politics and imperialist grounds, whereas Liberal and dissident Labour opinion were still in the state of sentimental, semi-pacifist isolationism and hankering for a free hand and no commitments that had characterized them in the years that had ended in World War I.

Early in 1925 a Conservative government replaced the brief period of Labour rule. It rejected the Protocol. Its reasons were its unalterable objection to compulsory arbitration and to restrictions on movements of armed forces during the discussion of a dispute, and its desire to localize sanctions obligations (*i.e.*, the obligation to oppose aggression). The economic sanctions of Article XVI were not formally repudiated. But the argument was used that the withdrawal of the United States from the League made their application prohibitively difficult and doubtful. These arguments were not demonstrably wrong. They were merely based on preferring the risks of international anarchy and power politics to the risks of attempting to make a reality of the collective peace system embodied in the Covenant.

LOCARNO

Nevertheless, having rejected the Geneva Protocol, the governments found it necessary to produce a positive alternative. This was the regional treaty system of Locarno. In these treaties France, Belgium, and Germany undertook to respect the demilitarization of the Rhineland and to accept the compulsory jurisdiction of the World Court in disputes as to their rights. They also agreed to conciliation over other disputes. Germany made similar agreements as to the settlement of disputes with Czechoslovakia and Poland. Any violation of the agreement to keep the Rhineland· demilitarized should be regarded as flagrant aggression and as justifying immediate measures of self-defence by France. Great Britain and Italy acted as the guarantors of this arrangement. Great Britain did not accept any obligations to refer disputes to the World Court. Nor were the sanctions obligations of Locarno reciprocal—*i.e.*, Britain gave a guarantee without obtaining any guarantee in return.

Germany agreed to apply for admission to the League the moment she became a party to these treaties, and the other signatories undertook to support her admission with a permanent seat on the Council.

The good points of Locarno vastly outweigh the bad. It was a great achievement to bring Germany into the League and to inaugurate the policy of reconciliation with that country, which Briand and Stresemann subsequently pursued for some years. Nevertheless Locarno was something like a declaration of want of confidence in the general obligations and machinery of the League. It was based on the idea that whereas preserving peace in Western Europe was important, it mattered less in other parts of Europe. It was said at the time that whereas Briand looked upon Locarno as a means of obtaining an Anglo-French alliance and Stresemann thought of it as the first step to equality of rights for Germany, the chief value of Locarno in Austen Chamberlain's eyes was that it restored the concert of the great powers and enabled Great Britain to resume her traditional *rôle* of holding the balance of power.

It was true, as Mr. Amery said many years later in the House of Commons, on October 23, 1935, in the course of a plea for giving Fascist Italy a free hand to make war against Abyssinia, that the government of which he was then a member had unhesitatingly rejected the Geneva Protocol, which attempted to make effective the system for preserving peace laid down in the Covenant.

The arguments which they used were not arguments merely against the Protocol, but arguments against the whole conception of a League based on economic and military sanctions. But His Majesty's Government were not content with that. They were prepared with their alternative, and the alternative was, admitting the impossibility and undesirability of sanctions imposed universally in any and every case, to substitute the co-operation of particular nations for a definite purpose, for particular tasks of peace. That was the policy of Locarno, and the policy of Locarno, if I may venture to say so to my right hon. friend, was not merely an alternative to the Protocol, but an alternative to Article XVI. After all, unless it was that, it was meaningless. The obligations under Locarno are the same in essence as the obligations under Article XVI. If Article XVI was still in full and literal effect—and no one has suggested enforcing it literally today—Locarno was purely superfluous.

A few months later—March 26, 1936—the Foreign Secretary, Mr. Eden, told the House of Commons:

> We have never been able in all our history to dissociate ourselves from events in the Low Countries, neither in the time of Elizabeth, nor in the time of Marlborough, nor in the time of Napoleon, and still less at the present day, when modern developments of science have brought striking force so much nearer to our shores. It is a vital interest of this country that the integrity of France and Belgium should be maintained and that no hostile force should cross their frontiers. The truth is, and I say it with apologies to my right hon. friend the Member for West Birmingham [Sir A. Chamberlain], there was nothing very new in Locarno.
>
> Sir Austen Chamberlain: Hear, hear!
>
> Mr. Eden: It was a new label, but it was an old fact, and that fact has been the underlying purpose of British foreign policy throughout history.

It is quite clear, therefore, that in the eyes of the Conservative government, Locarno was not so much a means of applying the principles of the Covenant as a way of reviving traditional balance-of-power policy within the framework of the League and in spite of the Covenant.

It is important to realize this fact. But it is equally important to understand that this did not imply any unfriendliness towards the League by the government of that day. On the contrary, it was genuinely convinced that this was the best possible use that could be made of the League, and it really wished the League well. Nor is there any doubt that Locarno did mark an important step forward in the policy of appeasement and reconstruction in post-war Europe. This is broadly true, although as Mr. Palme Dutt conclusively shows in *World Politics*, the idea of combining the other great powers against the U.S.S.R. lurked in the background of the Locarno policy.

In the economic domain the Briand-Stresemann policy translated itself into an attempt to bring about agreement between French and German big business. On the French side the chief negotiator was M. Loucheur and on the German side a certain

Herr Rechberger. The result of this attempt was to supply striking practical proof of the impossibility of the plutocracy's sacrificing selfish claims enough to come to an agreement across frontiers with competitiors. As a foot-note to history it may be added that M. Loucher's chief liaison man in Berlin for the purpose of these negotiations was one Pierre Viénot, the son of a rich French industrialist. The effect on him of his inside view of the workings of plutocracy was such that he became a Socialist and was subsequently the Under-Secretary for Foreign Affairs in M. Blum's first government.*

GREAT BRITAIN, ITALY, AND ABYSSINIA

The next noteworthy event was an Anglo-Italian exchange of notes over Abyssinia. The dealings of the great powers with Abyssinia, or rather with each other about Abyssinia, go far back in the nineteenth century. The only thing that prevented the Abyssinians' being carved up and reduced to a colony was their nasty habit of defending themselves when attacked. This led to the defeat of Italy at Adowa.

In 1906 France, Great Britain, and Italy concluded a treaty which began by declaring that it was to the common interest of the three Powers:

> . . . to maintain intact the integrity of Ethiopia, to provide for every kind of disturbance in the political conditions of the Ethiopian Empire, to come to a mutual understanding in regard to their attitude in the event of any change in the situation arising in Ethiopia, and to prevent the action of the three States in protecting their respective interests, both in the British, French and Italian possessions bordering on Ethiopia itself, from resulting in injury to the interests of any of them.

The tripartite agreement then enumerates nine other agreements and protocols between the contracting parties as to the claims they had pegged out for themselves in Abyssinia.

* And later was the Ambassador in London of the Fighting French Committee of National Liberation.

Article 2 binds the three powers when demanding agricultural, commercial, and industrial concessions in Abyssinia:

. . . to act in such a way that concessions which may be accorded in the interest of one of the three States may not be injurious to the interests of the other two.

By Article 3 they pledge themselves to non-intervention in Abyssinian internal affairs, and by Articles 6 and 7 to prolong the Jibuti railway to Addis Ababa and to arrange that an Englishman and an Italian, as well as a representative of the Emperor of Abyssinia, shall be appointed members of the French Railway Company, and that the British and Italian governments shall put a Frenchman on any boards they may form to build railways in Abyssinia.

Article 4 says that:

In the event of the *status quo* laid down in Article 1 being disturbed, France, Great Britain and Italy shall make every effort to preserve the integrity of Ethiopia. In any case they shall act together, on the basis of the Agreements enumerated in the above-mentioned Article, in order to safeguard:

(*a*) The interests of Great Britain and Egypt in the Nile Basin, more especially as regards the regulation of the waters of that river and its tributaries (due consideration being paid to local interests), without prejudice to Italian interests mentioned in 8 (*b*);

(*b*) The interests of Italy in Ethiopia as regards Eritrea and Somaliland (including the Benadir), more especially with reference to the *hinterland* of her possessions and the territorial connection between them to the west of Addis Ababa;

(*c*) The interests of France in Ethiopia as regards the French Protectorate on the Somali Coast, the *hinterland* of their protectorate and the zone necessary for the construction and working of the railway from Jibuti to Addis Ababa.

Abyssinia protested against this treaty at the time, saying that as she was not a party to it, it had no binding force, and that the great powers had no right to dispose of the future of Abyssinia. Naturally no notice was taken of these observations from the intended victim. There is small doubt that the treaty would have been the prelude to a policy of increasing pressure leading to the partition of Abyssinia, according to the usual methods employed in such cases, if World War I had not supervened.

In the 1915 secret treaty with Italy she was promised facilities for territorial adjustments in Africa which the Italian Government interpreted as a free hand to conquer Abyssinia.

In 1919, at the time of the Peace Conference, the Italian Government pressed for an agreement implementing this undertaking.

In 1923 Abyssinia was admitted as a member of the League.

In 1925 there was an exchange of notes between the Baldwin government and Signor Mussolini as to what they proposed to do in and with their fellow member of the League, Abyssinia.

The first note, dated December 14, 1925, from the British Ambassador in Rome to Signor Mussolini, read as follows:

Your Excellency is well aware of the vital importance to Egypt and the Sudan of maintaining and, if possible, increasing the volume of water for irrigation purposes available in those countries from the Blue and White Niles and their tributary streams. Various schemes for the purpose have been carried out or are projected, and you are informed of the negotiations undertaken at Addis Ababa by His Majesty's Government, acting in a fiduciary capacity for the Sudan Government and mindful of Egyptian interests in the matter, in order to obtain a concession from the Government of Abyssinia for the construction of a barrage at Lake Tsana with a view to storing its waters for use in the Blue Nile. So far these negotiations have led to no practical result.

In November 1919 the delegates of the Italian Government then in London were good enough to offer Italian co-operation in this question in the following terms: "In view of the predominating interests of Great Britain in respect of the control of the waters of Lake Tsana, Italy offers Great Britain her support, in order that she may obtain from Ethiopia the concessions to carry out works of barrage in the lake itself, within the Italian sphere of influence, pending the delimitation of the extent of the territorial zone to be recog-

nised as pertaining to Great Britain in respect of the latter's
predominant hydraulic interests, and pending a just consideration of the reservation on behalf of Italy by the Tripartite
Agreement likewise in respect of her hydraulic interests.
Italy further offers her support to Great Britain in order that
the latter may obtain from Ethiopia the right to construct
and maintain a motor road between Lake Tsana and the
Sudan.

"Italy requests the support of Great Britain in order that
she may obtain from the Ethiopian Government the concession to construct and to run a railway from the frontier of
Italian Somaliland; which railway according to the Tripartite
Agreement must pass to the west of Addis Ababa. It is understood that this railway, together with all the necessary works
for its construction and its running, must have an entirely
free passage across the above-mentioned motor road.

"Italy requests from Great Britain, as she also reserves to
herself the right to request from France, an exclusive economic influence in the west of Ethiopia and in the whole of
the territory to be crossed by the above-mentioned railway,
and the promise to support with the Ethiopian Government
all requests for economic concessions regarding the Italian
zone."

The above offer was not entertained at the time chiefly
owing to the strong objection felt to the idea of allowing a
foreign Power to establish any sort of control over the head
waters of rivers so vital to the prosperity and even the
existence of Egypt and the Sudan. But in view of the relations of mutual confidence so happily existing between our
two Governments, H.M. Government desire to extend to this
question the principle of friendly co-operation which has
proved so valuable in other fields. His Britannic Majesty's
Government have accordingly further examined the question
and recognise that the Italian proposal is not in contradiction
with the stipulations of the London Agreement of the 13th
December, 1906, since the object of that Agreement is to
maintain the *status quo* in Ethiopia on the basis of the international instruments indicated in Article 1 thereof and the
co-ordination of the action of signatory States to protect their
respective interests so that they should not suffer prejudice.

They would therefore welcome the Italian support offered provided that it can be accepted without prejudice to those paramount hydraulic interests of Egypt and the Sudan which the Italian Government have not failed to recognise.

I have therefore the honour, under instructions from H.H. Principal Secretary of State for Foreign Affairs, to request Your Excellency's support and assistance at Addis Ababa with the Abyssinian Government in order to obtain from them a concession for H.M. Government to construct a barrage at Lake Tsana, together with the right to construct and maintain a motor road for the passage of stores, personnel, etc., from the frontier of the Sudan to the barrage.

H.M. Government in return are prepared to support the Italian Government in obtaining from the Abyssinian Government a concession to construct and run a railway from the frontier of Eritrea to the frontier of Italian Somaliland. It would be understood that this railway, together with all the necessary works for its construction and its running, would have entirely free passage across the motor road mentioned above.

With this object in view, the necessary identical instructions should be sent to the British and Italian representatives in Ethiopia to concert for common action with the Abyssinian Government in order to obtain that the concessions, desired by the Governments of Great Britain and Italy regarding Lake Tsana and the construction of a railway to join up Eritrea with Italian Somaliland, should be granted contemporaneously. It remains understood that, in the event of one of the two Governments securing the concession sought for while the other Government failed to do so, the Government which had obtained satisfaction would not relax their wholehearted efforts to secure a corresponding satisfaction for the other Government concerned.

In the event of H.M. Government, with the valued assistance of the Italian Government, obtaining from the Abyssinian Government the desired concession on Lake Tsana, they are also prepared to recognise an exclusive Italian economic influence in the west of Abyssinia and in the whole territory to be crossed by the above-mentioned railway. They would further promise to support with the Abyssinian

Government all Italian requests for economic concessions in the above zone.

In his reply accepting the various proposals Signor Mussolini observed that when first discussed in London in November 1919, they "had formed part of a wider negotiation of a colonial character arising out of the Treaty of London of 1915." *

Years later, in an interview in the *Petit Journal* of September 29, 1935, Signor Mussolini gave his view of the 1925 transaction in the following words:

> Until very recently Great Britain was the first to consider that Abyssinia's independence constituted a sort of usurpation.† Remember the Treaty that Great Britain and France signed with us in 1906. In 1925, I signed, with Sir Ronald Graham, the British Ambassador, an act that divided—please note this—that practically carved up Abyssinia.

The British and Italian governments kept their correspondence secret, in spite of the obligation in Article 18 of the Covenant to register with the League and publish any "international engagement." But the Abyssinian Emperor (then Regent) took the same view as Signor Mussolini about the real meaning of the 1925 exchange of notes. He therefore in June 1926 brought the matter to the attention of the world by addressing a letter to the British and Italian governments and to the Secretary-General of the League, saying that:

> Our Government has recently received from the British and Italian Governments identical notes informing us that these Governments have arrived at an agreement to support

* This was the war-time secret treaty promising Italy opportunities for unspecified extensions of her colonial territories in Africa—a promise that the Italian Government interpreted to mean a free hand in Abyssinia. In the light of the terms of the 1906 treaty and the respective records of the two powers in and around Abyssinia the interpretation was not wholly unreasonable.

† Cf. above (page 84), Signor Giolitti's remark in justifying Italy's attack on Tripoli in 1911, that Tripoli was the only part of the Ottoman Empire on the African littoral not occupied by a great power and was, therefore, an "anachronism."

each other with a view to obtaining a concession for the British Government to undertake the conservancy of the waters of our Lake Tsana, and for the Italian Government to construct a railway through our Empire.

We have been profoundly moved by the conclusion of this agreement, concluded without our being consulted or informed, and by the action of the two Governments in sending a joint notification. . . .

On our admission to the League of Nations we were told that all nations were to be on a footing of equality within the League, and that their independence was to be universally respected, since the purpose of the League is to establish and maintain peace among men in accordance with the will of God.

We were not told that certain members of the League might make a separate agreement to impose their views on another member, even if the latter considered those views incompatible with its national interests. . . .

We cannot help thinking therefore that, in agreeing to support each other in these matters, and in giving us a joint notification of that agreement, the two Governments are endeavouring to exert pressure on us in order to induce us to comply with their demands prematurely without leaving any time for reflection or consideration for our people's needs.

The people of Abyssinia are anxious to do right, and we have every intention of guiding them along the path of improvement and progress; but throughout their history they have seldom met with foreigners who did not desire to possess themselves of Abyssinian territory and to destroy their independence. With God's help, and thanks to the courage of our soldiers, we have always, come what might, stood proud and free upon our native mountains.

For this reason prudence is needed when we have to convince our people that foreigners who wish to establish themselves for economic reasons in our country, or on the frontiers between it and their possessions, are genuinely innocent of concealed political aims; and we doubt whether agreements and joint representations such as those now in question are the best means of instilling that conviction. . . .

We should like to hear from the members of the League

whether they think it right that means of pressure should be exerted upon us which they themselves would doubtless never accept.

We have the honour to bring to the notice of all the States Members of the League of Nations the correspondence which we have received in order that they may decide whether that correspondence is compatible with the independence of our country, inasmuch as it includes the stipulation that part of our Empire is to be allotted to the economic influence of a given Power. We cannot but realise that economic influence and political influence are very closely bound up together; and it is our duty to protest most strongly against an agreement which, in our view, conflicts with the essential principles of the League of Nations.

In this case publicity justified the hopes placed by liberals in the League. There was considerable adverse comment in the world press and in the British Parliament on the nature of the transaction to which the Abyssinian Government had called attention. The British and Italian governments entered hasty disclaimers. The British Government in particular adopted an attitude of pained innocence and regretted in a note to the Secretary-General of the League that the purport of the Anglo-Italian notes should have been so misconstrued by the Abyssinian Government and:

. . . intentions attributed to the British and Italian Governments which they have never entertained. The Abyssinian protest is so worded as to imply that the British and Italian Governments have entered into an agreement to impose their wishes on a fellow-member of the League, even against the latter's interests. Members of the League are asked to state whether it is right that pressure should thus be exerted on Abyssinia which they would doubtless repudiate if applied to them.

There is nothing in the Anglo-Italian notes to suggest coercion or the exercise of pressure on the Abyssinian Government. Sir Austen Chamberlain has stated in Parliament that the agreement was certainly not to be used and could not be used for the purpose of coercing the Abyssinian Government.

The note concluded by stating that Sir Austen Chamberlain would be happy to repeat these explanations and assurances to Abyssinia in the presence of the League Council, if so desired. The Italian Fascist government was not quite so fulsome, but on the whole more honest than its British Conservative colleagues, for it stated:

Neither in the letter nor in the spirit of these notes can anything be found which would justify the apprehension on the part of the Abyssinian Government that the Italian and British Governments intended to exert precipitate and forcible pressure on Abyssinia.

This disclaimer, it will be noted, is careful not to deny that the Italian and British governments did in fact propose to exert pressure on Abyssinia. In their view this pressure would not be "precipitate and forcible." But it would of course include the right of self-defence if Abyssinia should be so ill-advised as to injure British or Italian interests by resisting their unforcible and unprecipitate pressure.

If the reader thinks this is an unduly harsh judgment, let him read again the account of the record of the great powers before World War I given at the beginning of this book, including the 1906 treaty, the 1915 arrangement, and the 1919 offer about Abyssinia, and recall the subsequent proceedings in 1935 of Great Britain, France, and Italy with regard to that country.

The important point to note is how, barely seven years after the great war, the British Conservative government was acting with complete disregard of every principle and obligation of the Covenant and attempting to do an imperialist deal on the classic pre-war model. For Abyssinia after all had just been made a member of the League, and according to Article X of the Covenant the members of the League are pledged to respect and to preserve against external aggression each other's territorial integrity and existing political independence. So far as the Anglo-Italian exchange of notes was concerned this article and the whole Covenant, indeed everything that had happened during and since World War I (except the secret treaties), might have been so much thin air.

Once again we have the spectacle of the extraordinary tenacity with which conservatism and plutocracy cling to power politics and imperialism, as well as an object lesson in what these things mean in terms of common honesty or regard for human life and happiness.

ARBITRATION

In the succeeding years the British Conservative government maintained its stubborn opposition to any attempts at organizing collective security and gaining wider acceptance for the Optional Clause conferring compulsory jurisdiction on the World Court. In this connection the following extracts from the Baldwin government's note to the League (C. 165, M. 50, 1928), commenting on the program of work of the Committee on Arbitration and Security of the Preparatory Commission for the Disarmament Conference, are interesting:

> An arbitration treaty which goes beyond what the public opinion of a country can be counted on to support when the interests of that country are in question and when a decision unfavourable to those interests is pronounced is a treaty which is useless. It is merely concluded to deceive the public. . . . It is because it is so generally felt that there are some questions—justiciable in their nature—which no country could safely submit to arbitration, that it has been usual to make reservations limiting the extent of the obligation to arbitration. These limitations may vary in form, but their existence indicates the consciousness on the part of Governments that there is a point beyond which they cannot count on their peoples giving effect to the obligations of the treaty.

The note then quotes the 1903 Arbitration Treaty between France and Great Britain, which expressly exempted from its operation all questions affecting the "vital interests, the independence or the honour" of the contracting parties.

"It may well be," observes the note, "that this formula . . .

first adopted a quarter of a century ago, requires re-examination."

Nevertheless there must be some limitations on the obligation to submit justiciable disputes to arbitration. Moreover, there are advantages in bilateral over general arbitral obligations.

In contracting an international obligation towards another State a country must take into account the nature of its relations with that State. Obligations which it may be willing to accept towards one State it may not be willing to accept towards another.

This argument is interesting because it shows once more the tenacious clinging to power politics and international anarchy. Putting the blame on the alleged unwillingness of public opinion to abide by the verdict of a court on questions of fact, treaty interpretation, and international law is an example of a very common technique. A government for some reason does not want to do a thing, but finds it less invidious to say that it cannot do it because public opinion would not let it. Incidentally, it is surely strange that the British people should be traduced by their own Government before the nations of the world by the charge that they had learned so little from the awful experience of world war that they would be willing to risk war rather than to abide by an impartial verdict which they had sworn to accept.

THE PARIS (KELLOGG-BRIAND) PACT

The next development was the proposal of the United States for a pact renouncing war as an instrument of national policy. This proposal was the outcome of a movement in the United States for the so-called "outlawry of war." The movement was extraordinarily confused, for it renounced war without abandoning the right of self-defence and without even attempting to suggest how "self-defence" could be distinguished from "the use of war as an instrument of national policy." As we have seen, the two things are one and the same in the conditions of international anarchy.

But for the states bound by the Covenant the Paris Pact could be incorporated in the collective peace system by providing that the Council should interpret whether or not it had been violated. And acceptance of the proposal could form a useful political bridge between the United States and the League.

The British and French governments accordingly welcomed the American proposal. They were particularly cordial about Secretary of State Kellogg's own interpretation of his proposal, when he declared that of course the pact did not affect the right of self-defence, and each state would continue in the future as it had done in the past to be the sole judge of what action it must take in self-defence. This made nonsense of the pact so far as the United States was concerned. Whereas under the Covenant all the members of the League were in the last analysis pledged to decide whether or not a state had acted in self-defence or resorted to war, and to act on that judgment by applying sanctions to the aggressor.

But the Baldwin government in its proceedings over the Paris Pact did not betray any consciousness of the fact that the Covenant had made any difference to pre-war international anarchy. Thus Sir Austen Chamberlain, in the House of Commons, announced his government's acceptance of the pact in a speech in which he asserted that Great Britain "has never treated war as an instrument of national policy." In other words, he took the view that Great Britain was as free to "defend national interests" under the Paris Pact as she had been throughout her history— in which she had managed to acquire one quarter of the world as an empire in sheer self-defence, without ever using war as an instrument of national policy.

Nevertheless, the government did not feel it wise to leave any ambiguity in this important matter. It therefore replied to the Kellogg proposal renouncing war in a note which contained the following passage:

> There are certain regions of the world, the welfare and integrity of which constitute a special and vital interest for our peace and safety. His Majesty's Government have been at pains to make it clear in the past that interference with these regions cannot be suffered. Their protection against attack is to the British Empire a measure of self-defence. It

must be clearly understood that His Majesty's Government in Great Britain accept the new treaty upon the distinct understanding that it does not prejudice their freedom of action in this respect.

There is, it will be noted, no definition of where these regions of the world are situated. The only thing clear is that they are not within the British Empire. In other words, this reservation constitutes the clearest possible assertion of the British Government's intention to use war as an instrument of national policy for defending its view of British interests in any part of the world outside the British Empire where it considers such action necessary.

At that time the world outside the British Empire, except for the United States and the U.S.S.R., was in the League, so that this reservation really amounted to reserving the right to commit aggression against fellow members of the League.* That, of course, was not the intention—the Covenant as usual never entered the consciousness of those responsible for drafting this reservation. Once again their attitude was based on clinging to power politics, international anarchy, and imperialism.

THE OPTIONAL CLAUSE

In 1929 the second Labour government took office. Ever since the fall of the first Labour government the Labour party had conducted a campaign for Great Britain accepting the compulsory jurisdiction of the World Court. The Labour party, the Liberal party, the League of Nations Union, and the peace movement in general were also active in this sense. In the general election the Labour party put forward a statement of its foreign policy which included signing the Optional Clause, renewing diplomatic relations with the U.S.S.R. (the first Labour government had restored diplomatic relations with that country; they had been broken off again by the Baldwin government after the

---

* In their controversy with the League and the United States over the overrunning of Manchuria and Jehol the Japanese quoted the British note on the Paris Pact in support of their argument that they were acting in self-defence and doing nothing contrary to either the Paris Pact or the Covenant of the League.

famous Arcos raid); the bringing into force of the Treaty for
Financial Assistance to victims of aggression or states threatened
by aggression, and of the Treaty for Strengthening the Means to
Prevent War; the revision of the Covenant so as to incorporate
in it the renunciation of war as an instrument of national policy
contained in the Paris Pact; the evacuation of the Rhineland; the
summoning of the Disarmament Conference.

Every one of these promises was implemented by the Labour
government. But it had a stiff fight with the Foreign Office and
the Admiralty before it was able to sign the Optional Clause
and the General Act of Arbitration. The objections, particularly
of the Admiralty, were based on the doctrine that Great Britain
should keep her hands free to threaten force against—e.g., Persia,
and could not therefore afford to bind herself to submit disputes
to the World Court in her dealings with that country. The Admiralty were annoyed but gravelled for an answer when it was
pointed out to them in reply that under the Covenant Great
Britain had already renounced the right to behave in this way
and rendered herself liable, if she did, to be summoned before
the Council by Persia and denounced as an aggressor. Persia
was particularly mentioned as an example. This lends an ironic
relish to the fact that some years later a dispute over the oil-
fields did arise and a British gunboat was despatched. On the
Persians' then making clear that they were prepared to resist
force by force and would refer the matter to the World Court,
the British Government dropped its gunboat policy and hastily
brought the whole matter before the Council, where it was
speedily settled to the satisfaction of both parties.*

---

* The late Arthur Henderson was fond of telling the story of how he was
waked up at one o'clock in the morning on the night after he had completed
the Protocol negotiations by a representative of the Admiralty, who arrived
post-haste from London to urge the Foreign Secretary on no account to accept any restrictions on the right to mobilize the British Navy during a dispute with another power. This would have wrecked the whole project, for
the obligation on parties to a dispute not to aggravate it by warlike measures was an essential part of this attempt to organize the collective peace
system. Mr. Henderson refused to entertain the Admiralty's proposal for a
return to power politics.

After a long struggle the Labour government was able to sign the Optional Clause and the General Act—but only with reservations that in the view, for instance, of such a good jurist as Professor Lauterpacht, stultified the purpose of the Optional Clause by giving either party the right to bring the question before the Council and keep it there indefinitely as an alternative to the compulsory jurisdiction of the World Court. Professor Lauterpacht is perhaps too severe in his criticism. But the whole episode is a further illustration of the tenacity and ingenuity with which the Foreign Office and the fighting services cling, like the Conservative party and the plutocracy behind them, to power politics.

There has not, it will be observed, been any continuity of foreign policy between the British Labour and Conservative parties. That is because the differences between these two parties reflect a real cleavage of interest and outlook between the working-class and the plutocracy. This cleavage runs through home as well as foreign policy, for, as Mr. Gladstone once remarked, there is an intimate connection between the two, and in order to understand a country's foreign policy it is necessary to study its domestic affairs.

CONSERVATIVE GOVERNMENTS AND THE LEAGUE

As from 1931 British conservatism and plutocracy have been frightened and militant in defence of the old order at home and abroad. The "National" governments through which they acted became consciously and increasingly hostile to all that Geneva stood for, and more and more anxious to go back to pre-last war power politics.* But it would be quite unfair to say that the Conservative governments between the war and the great slump were in any way hostile to the League. On the contrary, they were generally friendly. They were conservative and not reactionary governments. They did not consciously want to diminish the League in any way or to undo what had been done at the

* How and why they did this is set forth in some detail in the "Vigilantes" books: *Inquest on Peace; The Road to War; Why the League Failed; Why We Are Losing the Peace; Between Two Wars?* See also *Guilty Men* and *The Trial of Mussolini.*

Peace Conference and by their predecessors in office. They wished
the League well. Locarno, the entry of Germany and the inauguration of the practice of Foreign Ministers' attending Council
meetings—all due to Sir Austen Chamberlain—strengthened the
League, although at the same time it made it more like the prewar concert of the great powers. But what the Conservative governments did want was to keep the League from going ahead
too fast. They were really afraid that peace might be organized
too quickly. Above all, they felt it their duty to prevent the
League developing on lines inimical to their conception of British
interests. That was the crucial point.

Gradually a "friendly" Conservative view of the League
evolved, according to which it had a field of modest usefulness
as a sort of bigger and better concert of Europe where nations
could meet, discuss their differences, and co-operate on technical
and humanitarian questions. At Geneva the great powers, in addition to discussing their own affairs, could settle how they
wanted to adjust their interests with regard to weaker states and
how to keep the latter in order if they were tempted to disturb
the peace. But the League could not and should not be used for
trying to settle questions of "honour and vital interests" between
great powers.*

In this view almost everything that distinguished the League
from the pre-war rudiments of international organization was
ignored. There was no recognition of any obligation to stop
aggression by collective action except in areas where "national
interests" made it expedient to do so. Stopping aggression was
not in itself a "national interest." There was no reference to disarmament and no trace of the original conception of a world
government. In other words, the British Conservative party never
either during the war or since dreamed that the League could
or should develop into something capable of interfering with
power politics and imperialism. Some individual Conservatives
did. In that case they generally ended by severing their connection with the Conservative party, as did Viscount Cecil and the

* See the exposition of this point of view by Sir Austen Chamberlain in
the House of Commons on March 11, 1935.

Duchess of Atholl. (Mr. Eden is an intermediate case; for years he talked of resigning as League Minister and finally had to resign as Foreign Secretary. But he remained a good Conservative.)

This was not due to original sin in the Conservative party, but to the fact that they are the political representatives of vested interests in the social and imperial *status quo*. These vested interests would suffer if the League were to develop into a real world government, if internationalism and the reign of law were to replace power politics and imperialism, if the adventure of organizing peace were so successful as to put an end to preparations for war and the fear of war.

Moralists are wont to condemn those who are too prompt in being "off with the old love and on with the new." But in politics, it may be suggested, it is a far more common and dangerous failing to be on with the new love without being off with the old. The way in which British Conservative governments have combined friendliness towards the League with devotion to pre-war power politics and imperialism is an example of this kind of "double-mindedness."

There were, in fact, three groups in the British Conservative party during the pre-slump years, with of course various "transitional" and "intermediate" states of mind. First, those who felt that the League was incompatible with imperialism and power politics and therefore wanted to scrap the League as a menace to British interests. This was an insignificant minority of diehards. Second, there were those who believed the League might if, so to speak, taken in moderation, be modestly useful in promoting certain British power-politics interests and was not without value for philanthropic purposes and securing the approval of public opinion for whatever policy the Government might feel itself obliged to pursue. The first group, in other words, wanted to keep their pre-war vintage power politics in the old bottles, whereas the second saw advantages in pouring the old wine of imperialism into the new bottles with the Geneva and Kellogg labels.

The second school was in control and far the largest. But on its Left wing a third school began to develop of young Conservatives of the war and post-war generation. In their personal views this third school were almost as much in earnest about the League as liberal opinion and almost as unorthodox in their attitude to the sacred rights of private property as moderate labour opinion. But their political influence was negligible and their party and class loyalties very strong.

CONCLUSION

Nevertheless during the first ten years after World War I there was a slow process at work of educating public opinion to take more interest in foreign affairs and to a dawning realization of what the collective peace system meant. All this began to have an effect on party programs and electoral slogans which there was reason to hope might in due course develop into influencing the policies of governments. If the economic system had continued to function as smoothly as it did before 1914, the laborious work of building up a world government capable of canalizing the forces of change and withstanding the shocks of conflict might in another couple of generations have been completed. Each time a "Left" government came we should have advanced a little, while the intervening conservative governments at least consolidated the gains made.

But the Left governments were few and far between and conservatism reigned almost uninterruptedly. Progress was therefore so slow as to be almost imperceptible. Meanwhile other forces were at work, and their cumulative effect became evident in the great slump. The slump took the world by surprise. It showed that the march of events had once more outstripped the slow movement of human ideas and institutions. The differences between the interests of the plutocracy and the interests of the common people became acute. The plutocracy started a tremendous world-wide reactionary offensive-defensive to preserve their class power and privileges against the gathering demand for social change. In international relations this offensive-defensive took the form of an aggressive return to power politics and imperialism. In domestic affairs it took the form in some countries of fascist, in others of "national" governments, whose prime —and common—purpose it was to defend the social order.

The slump produced these consequences because, if it really was desired to thwart the forces of social and colonial change in order to preserve the class privileges of the plutocracy, it was necessary to revert to international anarchy, imperialism, power politics, and an arms race. In the concrete that meant the necessity to appease fascist aggressors and not to aid their victims.

The conclusion that emerges from this chapter is contained in the following quotation from Sir Arthur Salter. Sir Arthur has a unique experience which gives his survey of world events unrivalled authority. Endowed with a first-rate mind, his training as a high civil servant developed to its highest pitch his capacity for lucid analysis. During the war years he was secretary of the Inter-Allied Maritime Transport Board. After that a brief period as director of the Economic and Financial Section of the League Secretariat, then one year as secretary-general of the Reparations Commission (when it was hoped that body might be transformed into an organ of international financial reconstruction), and then a decade as again the director of the League Economic and Financial Section. Here is how Sir Arthur, out of his rich experience, sums up the lesson of the League's first ten years:

It is only too easy as we look back over nearly twenty years, with the troubles of the last six years vividly in our minds, to look upon all the efforts of post-war coöperation or negotiation as a long succession of follies and failures. Such an impression would be a profound mistake. The success of the first ten years' effort of recovery was as striking as its later collapse. It realized its objective, which was to rebuild the pre-war system. Failure came because that system was in several vital respects inappropriate to the new conditions and because it was too weak to resist and control the new and greater forces that had developed within our economic and political system.

This I believe to be the essential significance of the post-war period.

It is not surprising that in 1919 we should have failed to realize that we needed not only to rebuild on the old foundations, but to enlarge and strengthen the foundations themselves. The war itself was so shattering and stupendous an event that it seemed a sufficient explanation of all the distresses from which the world was suffering when it ended. Its obvious direct effects in material destruction, the diversion of the channels of trade, and the depreciation of currencies, were so great in themselves that they obscured more profound changes in the economic system and in society itself.

By comparison with 1919 the world of 1913 seemed to most of us a paradise from which we had for some years been excluded by the flaming sword of destruction. It seemed a sufficient goal for our efforts to regain the paradise we had lost. It was natural therefore that the first effort of the war should have been directed in nearly all countries, not to changing the foundations or the main structure of our society, but to repairing and rebuilding upon the old foundations and upon the familiar design. This basic conception underlay the policy pursued in every sphere of action. . . .

After the first needs of urgent relief . . . the vast reconstruction effort of the post-war world was directed to the reëstablishment of the pre-war system with the one notable addition of the League of Nations. The removal of State control and the establishment of conditions favourable to private enterprise; the balancing of national budgets, and the restoration of currencies and of the gold standard; the resumption of greater freedom of international trade by the reduction and stabilization of tariffs; the relief of social distress by the development of social services, on a larger scale but on familiar lines; the restoration of the system of foreign investment by the settlement of reparations and war debts; the reconstruction by combined action of the weaker countries; and lastly the creation of a new international organization, which would supplement, but would not necessarily change fundamentally, national sovereignty and the traditional social and economic system: these were the objectives—and they seemed for the time the sufficient objectives—of the efforts of the first decade after the war.

In spite of all that has happened since, those who took part in these efforts need not be ashamed of their achievement, and they can scarcely be blamed for failing to see the latent weaknesses in the foundations on which they were building. Never had the constructive intelligence of mankind been faced with so stupendous a task; never did it show such resources or achieve such results. For a time the success seemed almost complete, and likely to be permanent. Consider the position ten years after the cessation of hostilities—in 1928. Everywhere throughout the western world pre-war standards of prosperity had been surpassed, and the pre-war system reëstablished. . . .

. . . in spite of local distresses, some political menaces, and many difficult problems, prosperity seemed to have been regained; parliamentary government to have been justified and reinforced; peace to be reasonably assured. A little further progress along the lines on which such success had already been achieved; steady work in each country upon its domestic and social problems—and the future seemed to promise a civilization, perhaps not less stable and certainly much richer, than anything known in the last century.

Then came the sudden and devastating collapse in the economic life of the world, in its financial system, in parliamentary government, in the new structure of peaceful international relations. The world depression of 1929; the financial chaos of 1931; the new dictatorship in Germany of 1933 and its profound repercussions elsewhere; the diminished membership and reduced authority of the League as disputes and menaces alienated Japan, Germany, and Italy, came in rapid succession; and a new race in armaments, at once a reflection and a cause of political tension, was inaugurated with the breakdown of the Disarmament Conference.

The tale of collapse, extending over the whole range of man's collective constructive efforts of the first decade after the war, cannot now be retold. But it is necessary to emphasize the central feature to be observed in every sphere of disintegration. It was the old system that had been rebuilt; and this system proved in some respects unsuitable to the new conditions, and not strong enough to control the new forces.[2]

The fatal mistake of those who tackled the job of reconstruction after World War I was that they attempted to restore the pre-war world. They treated as enemies the Soviet Union and those who wanted to change the social order.

They said that social justice was the foundation of world peace. They declared that they wanted a real, practical, and effective system of world government.

But when it became clear that to pursue these declared aims meant interfering with private enterprise and colonial imperialism, and curtailing national sovereignty, they abandoned the attempt in all but words and reverted to international anarchy and power politics. The result was a new arms race and the devil's minuet of fascist aggression and Tory appeasement ending in World War II.

Notes

CHAPTER I

1 Henry Wheaton, *Elements of International Law*. 2 William Edward Hall, *op. cit.*, 8th ed., Oxford, 1924, pp. 65, 322. 3 Alphonse Pierre Rivier, *op. cit.*, 2 vols., Paris, 1896. 4 Johannes Haller, *Die Aera Bülow*, Stuttgart and Berlin, 1922, p. 18. 5 *Ibid.*, p. 101. 6 Frederick Edwin Smith, Earl of Birkenhead, *International Law*, 6th ed., Dent, 1927, p. 283. 7 Charles Ghequiere Fenwick, *International Law*, Century, 1924, p. 143. 8 Birkenhead, *op. cit.*, pp. 11-12. 9 James Bryce, Viscount Bryce, *International Relations*, Macmillan, 1922, p. 3. 10 *Op. cit.*, Longmans, Green, 1930, pp. 95-96. 11 Roscoe Pound, in *Bibliotheca Visseriana*, Vol. 1, 1923, p. 75. 12 Bertrand Russell, Earl Russell, *Freedom versus Organization, 1874–1894*, Norton, 1934, p. 142. 13 *Op. cit.*, London, 1920, p. 15. 14 *Op. cit.*, Macmillan, 1929, p. 1. 15 *Op. cit.*, University of Pennsylvania Press, 1936, p. 77. 16 *Op. cit.*, pp. 319-20. 17 *Property and Improperty*, London, 1937, pp. 105-06. 18 *Op. cit.*, Longmans, Green, 1930, p. 107. 19 *Ibid.*, p. 25. 20 *Ibid.*, p. 98. 21 *Ibid.*, pp. 98-99. 22 *Ibid.*, pp. 19-20. 23 *Ibid.*, p. 22. 24 *Ibid.*, p. 52. 25 *Ibid.*, p. 51. 26 *Ibid.*, p. 22. 27 *Ibid.*, pp. 22-23, 27. 28 *International Government*, London, 1916, p. 75. 29 Goldworthy Lowes Dickinson, *The International Anarchy, 1904–1914*, Century, 1926, pp. 357-58. Hereafter referred to as Dickinson.

CHAPTER II

1 *Hansard's Parliamentary Debates*, August 3, 1914, col. 1822. 2 Dickinson, pp. 101-02. 3 *Op. cit.*, Manchester and London, 1916? pp. 144-46. 4 Dickinson, p. 123. 5 *Ibid.*, p. 126. 6 *Ibid.*, pp. 133-34. 7 See the sections on "The Naval and Military Conversations" and "The Final Crisis." 8 *Times*, London, Feb. 1, 1906. 9 *Op. cit.*, pp. 177-78. 10 Dickinson, p. 259. 11 *Idem.* 12 Russell, *op. cit.*, p. 52. 13 Dickinson, p. 271. 14 *Ibid.*, p. 272. 15 *Ibid.*, p. 273. 16 *Op. cit.*, 4 vols. in 5, Scribner, 1923–29, Vol. I, p. 36.

17 Dickinson, p. 204. 18 *Ibid.*, p. 205. 19 *Ibid.*, p. 198. 20 *Ibid.*, p. 209. 21 *Op. cit.*, 6 vols., Little, Brown, 1933–37, Vol. I, p. 51. Hereafter referred to as Lloyd George. 22 *Ibid.*, Vol. I., p. 41. 23 Dickinson, pp. 241-42. 24 *Ibid.*, p. 211. 25 *Ibid.*, p. 212n. 26 *Ibid.*, p. 221. 27 *Ibid.*, pp. 317-18. 28 *Ibid.*, pp. 331-32. 29 *Ibid.*, p. 319. 30 *Ibid.*, p. 336. 31 *Ibid.*, p. 335. 32 *Ibid.*, p. 338. 33 *Ibid.*, p. 337. 34 Hansard, August 3, 1914, col. 1812. 35 *Ibid.*, col. 1813. 36 *Op. cit.*, Cassell, 1923, p. 83. 37 Lloyd George, Vol. I, pp. 49-50. 38 Dickinson, p. 367. 39 *Op. cit.*, Funk & Wagnalls, 1920, p. 32. 40 *Journal and Letters of Reginald, Viscount Esher*, 4 vols., London, 1934–38, Vol. III, p. 61. 41 Dickinson, pp. 387-88. 42 *Ibid.*, p. 395. 43 Hansard, 1915, Vol. I, cols. 42-43. 44 Dickinson, p. 397. 45 Philip Noel Baker, *op. cit.*, 2 vols. in 1, London, 1936, p. 434. 46 *Ibid.* 47 *Ibid.*, p. 435. 48 *Ibid.*, p. 440. 49 Esmé Cecil Wingfield-Stratford, *The Victorian Aftermath*, London, 1933, p. 310. 50 Lloyd George, Vol. I, p. 64. 51 *Op. Cit.*, 2 vols., Stokes, 1925, Vol. I, pp. 89-90. 52 Dickinson, p. 401. 53 *Ibid.*, p. 406n. 54 *Ibid.*, p. 402. 55 *Ibid.*, pp. 402-03. 56 *Ibid.*, p. 346. 57 Quoted by Lord Rankeillour in the House of Lords on Nov. 19, 1936. 58 Dickinson, p. 431. 59 *Ibid.*, pp. 433-34. 60 *Ibid.*, p. 435. 61 *Ibid.*, p. 438. 62 *Ibid.*, p. 440. 63 *Ibid.*, p. 441. 64 *Ibid.*, p. 444. 65 *Ibid.*, p. 445. 66 *Ibid.*, pp. 454-55. 67 *Ibid.*, p. 456. 68 *Ibid.*, p. 457. 69 *Ibid.*, p. 461. 70 *Ibid.*, p. 458. 71 *Freedom versus Organization*, p. 444. 72 *Op. cit.*, London, 1902, pp. 53-54.

CHAPTER III

1 Published in *The Issue* by J. W. Headlam Morley. 2 Lloyd George, Vol. VI, Introduction, p. xiii. 3 *Op. cit.*, London, 1937, p. 227. 4 *Documents and Statements Relating to Peace Proposals and War Aims, December 1916-November 1918,* ed. by Lowes Dickinson, London, 1919, p. 5. 5 Resolution of the International Socialist Congress, 1907. 6 Lloyd George, Vol. I, p. 220. 7 *Ibid.*, Vol. II, p. 1051. 8 *Ibid.*, Vol. II, p. 1058. 9 Royal Institute of International Affairs, *op. cit.*, 6 vols., London, 1920–24, Vol. I, p. 207. Hereafter referred to as Temperley. 10 R. H. Bruce Lockhart, *Memoirs of a British Agent*, Putnam, 1932, pp. 171-72. Hereafter referred to as Lockhart. 11 *Ibid.*, p. 173. 12 *Ibid.*, p. 264. 13 *The Intimate Papers of Colonel House*, 4 vols., Houghton Mifflin, 1926–28, Vol. III, p. 130. Hereafter referred to as House. 14 Lockhart, pp. 177-78. 15 Lloyd George, Vol. IV, p. 1882. 16 *Ibid.*, Vol. IV, p. 1893. 17 *Ibid.*, Vol. IV, pp. 1883–84. 18 Lockhart, p. 183. 19 *Ibid.*, p. 183. 20 Lloyd George, Vol. V, p. 2533. 21 Lockhart, p. 185. 22 Lloyd George, Vol. IV, p. 1900. 23 *Ibid.*, Vol. IV, pp. 1892–93. 24 Lockhart, p. 197. 25 Temperley, Vol. I, p. 216. 26 Lloyd George, Vol. V, p. 2661. 27 *Ibid.*, Vol. V, p. 2537. 28 Lockhart, pp. 172, 261-62. 29 Lloyd George, Vol. VI, pp. 3191-92. 30 *Ibid.*, Vol. IV, p. 1909; Vol. V, p. 2358. He quotes two different versions of the text on these pages. 31 *Ibid.*, Vol. V, pp. 2541-42, 2548. 32 House, Vol. III, pp. 164-68. 33 *Ibid.*, Vol. III, pp. 172-73. 34 Lloyd George, Vol. V, pp. 2561-62. 35 *Ibid..*

Vol. V, pp. 2362-64. **36** *Ibid.,* Vol. V, p. 2581. **37** Temperley, Vol. I, pp. 222-23. **38** See *Ibid.,* pp. 166-67. **39** House, Vol. III, p. 278. **40** *Ibid.,* Vol. III, p. 280. **41** *Ibid.,* Vol. III, pp. 282-83. **42** *Ibid.,* Vol. III, p. 268. **43** House, Vol. III, p. 283. **44** *Ibid.,* Vol. III, p. 317. **45** *Ibid.,* Vol. III, pp. 285-86, 316. **46** Cf. Temperley, Vol. I, p. 212: "The publication of hitherto secret treaties shook the confidence of some labour groups in Allied countries" (only of some, be it noted). **47** House, Vol. III, pp. 317-18. **48** *Ibid.,* Vol. III, p. 152. **49** Temperley, Vol. I, pp. 207-08. **50** *Ibid.,* Vol. I, pp. 217-18. **51** *Ibid.,* Vol. I, pp. 208-09, 216. **52** Lloyd George, Vol. V, p. 2483. **53** *Ibid.,* Vol. V, p. 2484. **54** *Ibid.,* Vol. V, pp. 2483-84. **55** *Ibid.,* Vol. V, pp. 2648-49. **56** *Ibid.,* Vol. V, p. 2657. **57** *Ibid.,* Vol. V, p. 2486. **58** House, Vol. III, p. 340. **59** Lloyd George, Vol. V, p. 2659. **60** *Ibid.,* Vol. V, pp. 2565-66. **61** *Ibid.,* Vol. V, p. 2566. **62** *Ibid.,* Vol. V, p. 2568. **63** *Ibid.,* Vol. V, pp. 2572-73. **64** *Ibid.,* Vol. VI, p. 3172-74. **65** *Ibid.,* on pp. 3156-64 of Vol VI there is a sort of symposium of all these reasons. **66** *Ibid.,* Vol. V, p. 3178. **67** *Ibid.,* Vol. VI, p. 3162. **68** *My War Memoirs,* Vol. II, p. 566. **69** Temperley, Vol. I, p. 232. **70** Lockhart, pp. 247-48. **71** *Ibid.,* pp. 248-50. **72** *Ibid.,* p. 239. **73** *Ibid.,* p. 231. **74** *Ibid.,* pp. 212-13. **75** Lloyd George, Vol. V, pp. 2574-75. **76** *Ibid.,* Vol. V, pp. 2582-83. **77** *Ibid.,* Vol. V, pp. 2584-85. **78** *Ibid.,* Vol. VI, p. 3185. **79** *Ibid.,* Vol. V, p. 2592. **80** *Ibid.,* Vol. V, p. 2593. **81** *Ibid.,* Vol. V, p. 2594. **82** *Ibid.,* Vol. V, p. 2567. **83** *Ibid.,* Vol. V, pp. 2591-92. **84** *Ibid.,* Vol. V, pp. 2585-89. **85** Lockhart, p. 212. **86** House, Vol. III, p. 405. **87** *Ibid.,* Vol. III, p. 412. **88** *Ibid.,* Vol. III, p. 411. **89** *Ibid.,* Vol. III, pp. 403-04. **90** Lloyd George, Vol. VI, p. 3176. **91** House, Vol. III, pp. 397-98. **92** Lloyd George, Vol. VI, p. 3172. **93** *Ibid.,* Vol. VI, pp. 3191-92. **94** House, Vol. III, p. 404. **95** *Ibid.,* Vol. III, p. 416. **96** *Ibid.,* Vol. III, p. 414. **97** *Ibid.,* Vol. III, p. 408. **98** Lockhart, p. 230. **99** *Ibid.,* p. 283. **100** *Ibid.,* pp. 311-12. **101** Temperley, Vol. I, p. 209. **102** *Ibid.,* Vol. I, pp. 210-12. **103** *Ibid.,* Vol. I, pp. 213, 219. **104** *Ibid.,* Vol. I, p. 218. **105** *Idem.* **106** *Ibid.,* Vol. I, p. 212. **107** *Ibid.,* Vol. I, p. 209. **108** House, Vol. IV, p. 150. **109** *Ibid.,* Vol. IV, p. 155. **110** *Ibid.,* Vol. IV, p. 188. **111** Temperley, Vol. I, p. 219. **112** Lockhart, p. 240.

CHAPTER IV

1 John Maynard Keynes, *The Economic Consequences of the Peace,* Harcourt, Brace, 1920, pp. 6-7. **2** *Woodrow Wilson and the World Settlement,* 3 vols., Doubleday, Page, 1922, Vol. I, pp. 165-66. **3** See Mr. Keynes's devastating analysis of Mr. Lloyd George's rake's progress in the election, *op. cit.,* pp. 138-45. **4** *Op. cit.,* Vol. I, p. 102. Major Tasker Bliss's memorandum to Wilson. **5** *Ibid.,* Vol. III, pp. 451-56. **6** *Op. cit.,* p. 71. **7** Temperley, Vol. II, pp. 32-33. **8** *Ibid.,* Vol. I, p. 235. **9** *International Government,* p. 98. **10** Temperley, Vol. II, pp. 21-22. **11** *Woodrow Wilson,* Vol. III, p. 68. **12** Quoted by H. G. Wells, *Experiment in Autobiography,* 2 vols., London, 1934, Vol. II, pp. 697-99. **13** *Op. cit.,* pp. 30-33. **14** *Ibid.,* p. 8. **15** *Ibid.,*

pp. 46-47. **16** *Ibid.*, pp. 7-8. **17** *Ibid.*, p. 43. **18** *Ibid.*, pp. 9-11. **19** *Ibid.*,
pp. 54-55. **20** *Ibid.*, pp. 60-63. **21** See Sir Alfred Zimmern, *The League of
Nations and the Rule of Law*, Macmillan, 1936, pp. 154-55, 208. **22** Baker,
op. cit., Vol. III, pp. 334-35. The texts of this and other letters mentioned
are on pp. 332-46. **23** *Ibid.*, Vol. III, p. 338. **24** *Ibid.*, Vol. III, pp. 345-46.
25 Described in detail in *Relief Deliveries and Relief Loans, 1919–23*, also
a League of Nations Secretariat monograph. **26** Temperley, Vol. II, p. 30.
27 *Ibid.*, Vol. VI, pp. 315-16. **28** Hansard, July 12-13, 1920, cols. 1949,
2167-68. **29** Lloyd George, Vol. VI, pp. 3191-92. **30** Hansard, Vol. 120, col.
1628. **31** *Ibid.*, Vol. 120, col. 1581. **32** Lloyd George, Vol. VI, p. 3183. **33**
Ibid., Vol. VI, p. 3190. **34** Hansard, Vol. 131, cols. 1947–48. **35** *Op. cit.*,
Harcourt, Brace, 1936, p. 352. **36** Hansard, Vol. 131, col. 1008. **37** *Ibid.*,
Vol. 120, cols. 1582-83. **38** Report of the Mission to Finland, Latvia and
Lithuania by Robert Hale, 66th Congress, Senate Document 105, 1919.
39 *Rabotnik Polski*, Mar. 15, 1943. **40** *Darstellungen aus dem Nachkriegs-
kämpfen deutscher Truppen und Freikorps*, Reichsministerium, Vol. I,
"Die Rückführung des Ostheeren." **41** F. J. Deygas, *L'Armée d'Orient dans
la guerre mondiale, 1915–19.* **42** Keynes, *op. cit.*, pp. 41-42. **43** *Ibid.*, pp.
50-51. **44** *Ibid.*, pp. 53-54. **45** House, Vol. IV, p. 372. **46** Keynes, *op. cit.*,
pp. 30, 32, 33.

CHAPTER V

1 Smuts, *The League of Nations*, p. 49. **2** Both quotations in H. R. G.
Greaves, *Reactionary England*, London, 1936, pp. 79-80. **3** Leonard Woolf,
ed., *The Intelligent Man's Way to Prevent War*, London, 1933, p. 305. **4**
See Temperley, Vol. VI, pp. 459-60. **5** *Les Origines et l'œuvre de la Société
des Nations*, 2 vols., Rask-orsted Fundet, Copenhagen, 1923–24, Vol. II,
p. 67. **6** *The League of Nations Starts*, Macmillan, 1920, pp. 226-27. **7**
Labour's Way to Peace, London, 1935, pp. 108-09. **8** *Op. cit.*, 6th imp.,
rev. and enl., 1922, p. 6. **9** *Ibid.*, pp. 215-16. **10** *Ibid.*, pp. 211-14.

CHAPTER VI

1 *Fifth Assembly Report*, A. 14, 1927. **2** *World Trade and Its Future*,
pp. 30-36.

Index

359